Maternal Bodies

# Maternal Bodies

Redefining Motherhood in Early America

. . . . . . . . . . . . . . . . . . . . . . . . . . . . . . . . . . . . . . . . . . . . . . . . . . . . .

NORA DOYLE

The University of North Carolina Press  Chapel Hill

*This book was published with the assistance of the Greensboro Women's Fund of the University of North Carolina Press.*
Founding Contributors: Linda Arnold Carlisle, Sally Schindel Cone, Anne Faircloth, Bonnie McElveen Hunter, Linda Bullard Jennings, Janice J. Kerley (in honor of Margaret Supplee Smith), Nancy Rouzer May, and Betty Hughes Nichols.

Set in Charis and Lato by Westchester Publishing Services
Manufactured in the United States of America

The University of North Carolina Press has been a member of the Green Press Initiative since 2003.

Library of Congress Cataloging-in-Publication Data
Names: Doyle, Nora, author.
Title: Maternal bodies : redefining motherhood in early
   America / Nora Doyle.
Description: Chapel Hill : University of North Carolina Press, [2018] |
   Includes bibliographical references and index.
Identifiers: LCCN 2017026941 | ISBN 9781469637181 (cloth : alk. paper) |
   ISBN 9781469637198 (pbk : alk. paper) | ISBN 9781469637204 (ebook)
Subjects: LCSH: Motherhood—Social aspects—United States—History. |
   Women—United States—History. | Human body—Social aspects—
   United States.
Classification: LCC HQ759 .D69 2018 | DDC 306.874/3—dc23
   LC record available at https://lccn.loc.gov/2017026941

Cover illustration: *Portrait of unidentified woman breastfeeding a baby* (ca. 1848). Courtesy of the Schlesinger Library, Radcliffe Institute, Harvard University.

Portions of chapters 3 and 4 were previously published as "'The Highest Pleasure of Which Woman's Nature Is Capable': Breast-Feeding and the Sentimental Maternal Ideal in America, 1750–1860," *Journal of American History* 97:4 (2011): 958–973. Used here with permission.

*For my grandparents*

*Ruth Peterson Doyle (1918–2012)*

*John Doyle (1918–2015)*

# Contents

Acknowledgments, xi

Introduction, 1
*In Search of the Maternal Body*

1 The Tyrannical Womb and the Disappearing Mother, 14
*The Maternal Body in Medical Literature*

2 Writing the Body, 52
*The Work of the Body in Women's Childbearing Narratives*

3 The Highest Pleasure of Which Woman's Nature Is Capable, 86
*Breastfeeding and the Emergence of the Sentimental Mother*

4 Good Mothers and Wet Nurses, 115
*Breastfeeding and the Fracturing of Sentimental Motherhood*

5 The Fantasy of the Transcendent Mother, 146
*The Disembodiment of the Mother in Popular Feminine Print Culture*

6 Imagining the Slave Mother, 175
*Sentimentalism and Embodiment in Antislavery Print Culture*

Conclusion, 203
*In Search of the Maternal Body Past and Present*

Notes, 211
Bibliography, 241
Index, 267

# Figures

1.1 From Jane Sharp, *The Compleat Midwife's Companion* (1724), 27

1.2 From William Hunter, *The Anatomy of the Human Gravid Uterus* (1774), 30

4.1 *Portrait of Unidentified Woman Breastfeeding a Baby* (ca. 1848), 126

4.2 *Portrait of Unidentified Woman Breastfeeding a Baby* (ca. 1850), 127

4.3 "Wanted—A *Dry* Nurse," *Turner's 1839 Comic Almanack*, 139

5.1 *The Empty Cradle*, in *Godey's Lady's Book* (1847), 154

5.2 *Maternal Affection*, in *The American Juvenile Keepsake* (1834), 155

5.3 *Maternal Instruction*, in *Godey's Magazine and Lady's Book* (1845), 158

5.4 *The Unlooked for Return*, in *The Keepsake* (1833), 159

6.1 *Views of Slavery*, New York (ca. 1836), 195

6.2 "Selling a Mother from Her Child," in *American Anti-slavery Almanac for 1840*, 197

# Acknowledgments

However solitary it may feel at times, the process of research and writing is in truth a collective endeavor, and my intellectual debts are numerous. I treasure the knowledge that every page of this book has been shaped by the collective insight and creativity of a group of extraordinary people. I am especially grateful to Jacquelyn Hall and Kathleen DuVal for their unwavering support and enthusiasm and for their unerring ability to tell me what it was I was really trying to say. Kathleen Brown, Crystal Feimster, John Kasson, Joy Kasson, and Heather Williams were generous with their time and knowledge, and their comments pushed me to clarify and expand my ideas. I am also grateful to the readers and editors at the University of North Carolina Press who helped push me through the final stages of this project.

This book would surely never have been completed without the insights of many friends and fellow historians who read chapter drafts, debated the intricacies of historical methodology, and in some cases picked apart my prose word by word. I am especially grateful to Rike Brühöfener, Mary Beth Chopas, Jennifer Donnally, Joey Fink, Aaron Hale-Dorrell, Jonathan Hancock, Rachel Hynson, Anna Krome-Lukens, Kim Kutz, Liz Lundeen, Zsolt Nagy, Rebecca Rosen, Jessie Wilkerson, and David Williard. I also gained invaluable feedback on numerous occasions from the members of the Triangle Working Group in Feminism and History and the Triangle Early American History Seminar.

I have been fortunate to receive support from many institutions that allowed me to expand the scope of my research. I am especially grateful to the American Association of University Women, the Historical Society of Pennsylvania, the Library Company of Philadelphia, and the Massachusetts Historical Society for the generous funding that made it possible for me to pursue this research.

As it turns out, it takes a village to raise a historian. I owe a great deal to the historians of Grinnell College for first setting me on this path. Until I took their courses as an undergraduate, it never occurred to me that I could be a historian. I am particularly grateful to Sarah Purcell, Victoria Brown,

George Drake, and Dan Kaiser, who amazed and inspired me with their teaching and scholarship, who taught me to think and to write, and who have been unstinting in their support and encouragement.

Too many friends and family to name—both near and far—have fed and housed me so that I could complete my research, given me their love and support, and patiently endured my elation and despair throughout the various stages of research and writing. In particular, I owe special thanks to Hannah Fuhr for the many laughs we have shared and for inadvertently starting me on this project many years ago with an offhand comment about breastfeeding.

In this as in everything, my deepest gratitude goes to my family. My parents, Mary Doyle and Steve Ostrem, have encouraged me in every endeavor, and their home has always been a place for me to recharge and return to the work of research and writing with renewed enthusiasm. My sister, Eve Doyle, inspires me to laugh and take myself less seriously. I am fortunate to have such a friend. My grandparents, John and Ruth Doyle and Fred and Helen Ostrem, instilled in me a love of books and history as a child and have always inspired me with their example of lives well lived.

My special love and gratitude go to David Winski, a true friend and companion who graciously tolerates my many historical tangents and reminds me of the things that are most important in life.

Maternal Bodies

# Introduction

## In Search of the Maternal Body

. . . . . . . . . . . . . . . . . . . . . . . . . . . . . . . . . . . . . . . . . . . . . . . . . . . . . . .

In 1798 Gertrude Meredith reported to her husband that she was "better than I have been this summer, but extremely thin notwithstanding. Mama tells me this is owing to my suckling my Child—she is very anxious that I should wean her, but this I cannot think of doing."[1] Meredith's brief update highlighted the toll that childrearing could take on a mother's health, but also emphasized her dedication to what she saw as her duty to nourish her daughter from her own body. A year later, an American women's magazine printed an article on breastfeeding in which the author argued that by nursing her child, a "woman undergoes a kind of happy metamorphosis, which almost renders her difficult to be known. Her skin becomes fine, soft, and fair; her features are refined into an uncommon degrees of sweetness, under the influence of this new regimen. The too-ardent carnation of her cheeks, tempered by the milky revolution, assumes a milder teint."[2] This portrait of the refined and beautiful nursing mother exposed a gulf between the lived experiences of women such as Gertrude Meredith and the cultural representations of motherhood that increasingly permeated American society. Although these two perspectives exposed a disconnect between the maternal body as it was lived and as it was imagined, perceptions of the body were integral to each writer's vision of motherhood. In this respect both writers were representative of their time, for ideas about the body became central to defining motherhood both as a lived identity and as a cultural symbol in late eighteenth- and early nineteenth-century America.

This study begins in the 1750s, a time when childbearing and childrearing occupied the physical and emotional energies of most American women, who could expect to be pregnant or breastfeeding and tending young children almost constantly between their early twenties and early forties. Women gave birth in their homes attended by other women—midwives, friends, kinswomen—who had lived through the same cycles of pregnancy, childbirth, and nursing, and who understood the physical rigors of motherhood. Those women who enjoyed a comfortable home and the ability to take time away from their duties spent an additional period recuperating in bed, supported by female companions. Those who lacked that luxury still depended on the women around them to boost their spirits and provide practical assistance in negotiating work and motherhood. The shared experiences of motherhood bound female friends and family members together as they tended one another or wrote letters sharing reproductive news and advice and commiserating over the anxieties and discomforts wrought by motherhood. Women were also the primary caretakers of their children, particularly of young ones, and they spent their days balancing the demands of domestic work and other labor, depending on their socioeconomic status, with the demands of mothering. Women clothed, fed, healed, and educated their children, all tasks that involved tiring physical and intellectual labor. Sarah Hale, for one, complained in 1822 amid the squabbling of her young children, "My cares are never ceasing."[3]

This study concludes in the 1850s, encompassing roughly a century of both change and continuity in women's lives as mothers. By this time the average number of children in an American family had decreased from more than seven to just over five children, a fertility revolution that particularly affected white middle-class women in the North, who now spent less of their adult lives pregnant, recovering from childbirth, and breastfeeding.[4] Yet even with this decline in fertility, the rhythms of childbearing and childrearing continued to define most women's lives, prompting both anxiety and satisfaction as women watched their families grow. At the same time, while growing numbers of women gave birth under the supervision of physicians, the majority continued to deliver their babies much as their mothers and grandmothers had, with the assistance of other women. Other changes were also slow in coming. It was not until the second half of the nineteenth century, for instance, that anesthetized childbirth became an option for some women, while it was even longer before the development of infant formula offered women a safe means of raising their children without breast milk. Moreover, women continued to do most of the work of childrearing, so that the rhythms of daily life were still defined by the work of mothering. Thus the period between the 1750s and the 1850s encompassed significant continuities in the lives of American mothers.

More visible changes emerged in the realm of feminine ideology in this period. Although women's lives were profoundly marked by the experiences of motherhood, in 1750 the figure of the mother was not yet imbued with the cultural importance she would gain by the turn of the nineteenth century. Print culture—sermons, prescriptive texts, and popular literature—taught that the dutiful woman's primary function was as a "help-meet" to her husband, a position that implicated many different roles, including that of motherhood.[5] Print culture put more emphasis on women's ability to produce offspring than on their efforts in childrearing. A mother was first and foremost a reproductive body, and she was celebrated more for her fecundity than for her ability to shape the minds, morals, and bodies of her children.[6] Many early parenting advice manuals, in fact, were addressed to fathers rather than mothers in the belief that it was the father's responsibility to direct how his children would be raised and educated.[7] The popular literature of the time similarly put less emphasis on women as mothers than as virtuous virgins, loyal daughters, and obedient wives.

The second half of the eighteenth century, however, marked a transitional period in ideas of womanhood as British and American writers articulated a new emphasis on motherhood as women's most important role.[8] This new cultural vision stemmed from Enlightenment ideas that circulated among England, Scotland, France, and America in the eighteenth century as well as from the growing evangelical Protestant impulse in both England and America. Although different in many ways, both Enlightenment thought and evangelical religion constructed a popular and enduring vision of women's superior virtue and natural tenderness that combined to foster the ideal of what Ruth Bloch has called the "moral mother."[9] Enlightenment thinkers extolled women's superior virtue and tenderness, while religious writers commended women's natural piety. Both strains of thought contributed to a growing emphasis on the affective ties of motherhood and on women's ability to transmit virtue to their children.[10] Women themselves echoed this new emphasis on motherhood, expressing a greater sense of responsibility in the lives of their children.[11]

The rise of republican ideology during the era of the American Revolution also contributed to this shift in cultural depictions of motherhood. The need for order in a society newly bereft of class-based social distinctions and anxious about the production of a virtuous citizenry made the role of the mother ideologically and practically central to the new republic. The new figure of the "republican mother," as Linda Kerber has called her, was responsible for creating a domestic space in which to endow her children with moral sensibility and civic responsibility, thus ensuring the enduring success of the republican project.[12]

By the beginning of the nineteenth century, then, an array of influences had converged to place motherhood at the center of American notions of virtuous womanhood. At a time when American society was becoming more diverse, urban, industrial, and market-driven than ever before, the figure of the good mother counterbalanced these rough and unpredictable forces by becoming a symbol of morality and stability, particularly for the middle classes that were at the center of many of these social, cultural, and economic changes. During the first half of the nineteenth century, cultural depictions of motherhood developed a vision of what Nancy Theriot has called "imperial motherhood."[13] As mothers, women not only bore children but were expected to be wholly child-centered, nourishing their children's bodies and guiding their moral and intellectual development. In return for their dedication as mothers, women gained—ideologically, at least—a significant degree of power and influence in society. As one nineteenth-century author earnestly explained, "The *mistress* and *mother* of a family occupies one of the most important stations in the community."[14] Thus by the early decades of the nineteenth century the mother had become one of the most potent symbols of virtue and order in American society. I will refer to this vision of women's role as the ideal of *sentimental motherhood*, a term that encompasses the traits of the moral mother, republican motherhood, and imperial motherhood, while also recognizing the ways in which sentimental expression and the power of feeling became central to the definition of the good mother.

Ideas about the body were deeply implicated in the construction of the sentimental mother. By the late eighteenth century the body had long been subordinated in Western intellectual traditions to the mind or soul, allegedly superior sites of reason, truth, and virtue. As Susan Bordo has written, "The body as animal, as appetite, as deceiver, as prison of the soul and confounder of its projects: these are common images within Western philosophy."[15] Plato, for instance, linked concepts such as knowledge, truth, beauty, and love to the soul, while he understood the body to be the site of vulgar and dangerous appetites. He also drew a clear link between women and the body, arguing that one of the defining characteristics of women was their preoccupation with materiality. To focus on the body and its senses was to behave like a woman. To be embodied was to be tethered to the particularities of one's time and place, to lack objectivity and autonomy.[16] The legacy of Plato and subsequent thinkers was a vision of the body, particularly the female body, as debased and disorderly. Thus, by creating new images of the mother—defined not by her sheer reproductive capacity and the messiness of her body, but by her ability to nurture the morals of her children—the sentimental maternal ideal marked a significant departure from long-standing notions of female corporeality. By emphasizing women's emotional and moral qualities, cultural representations of sentimental motherhood contested the ways in which women had been defined as inferior and corrupted by their bodies.

· · · · · ·

At the heart of this study is an examination of the role the body played in defining motherhood. Putting the body at the center of the history of motherhood reveals that perceptions and representations of corporeality were crucial to defining motherhood, both as it was lived by childbearing women and as it was configured into a potent cultural symbol. Making the body the central category of analysis brings together two different narratives. On the one hand, this book explores women's own descriptions of their bodies during repeated cycles of childbearing to understand how the work of their bodies shaped women's attitudes toward motherhood. On the other hand, it examines the vast realm of print culture, which included medical texts, prescriptive literature, visual culture, and popular literature, to reveal the increasingly elaborate cultural prescriptions for how the maternal body was supposed to look, act, and feel. This work is structured around the tension between perceptions of the lived maternal body, as articulated by childbearing women themselves, and the imagined maternal body that was created in the realm of print and visual culture.

In exploring this tension, I argue that the lived experience of the maternal body was the foundation of women's perceptions of childbearing and childrearing and prompted feelings of ambivalence toward motherhood. When I write of women's experience, I borrow from Nancy Theriot's concept of experience not as an event that happens (a pregnancy, a birth) but as the meaning that women created for themselves around that event.[17] Women loved their children and derived emotional and intellectual satisfaction from mothering, but the pain, fatigue, and unwieldiness of their bodies during cycles of childbearing and childrearing also made them regard motherhood with trepidation. In contrast, I argue that beginning in the mid-eighteenth century, cultural representations of motherhood increasingly sought to refine the maternal body, and even make it disappear entirely, in order to project a vision of motherhood that was defined by women's spiritual and emotional work rather than by their physical labor. In other words, while childbearing women acknowledged the messy physical work that gave a range of meanings to motherhood, the emerging ideal of sentimental motherhood effaced the body and privileged women's abstract moral and emotional qualities.

Several important issues emerge from these distinct narratives of the maternal body, first among them the question of historical continuity. While print culture revealed an uneven but definite change over time toward a disembodied vision of the sentimental mother, women's personal depictions of the maternal body were predominantly defined by continuity. This continuity is somewhat dismaying to the historian, who typically seeks to identify and explain change over time.[18] Yet tracing some of the consistencies in the lives of American mothers in the eighteenth and early nineteenth centuries may alleviate some discomfort. For instance, we might expect that the changing childbirth practices wrought by the professionalization of midwifery as part of the male medical profession would dramatically impact women's perceptions of the physical experiences of childbearing. But the material changes surrounding childbirth were gradual and uneven, and the use of male physicians did not dramatically change the outcomes for birthing women. In fact, Judith Walzer Leavitt has shown that women's perceptions of the pain and danger of childbirth did not change significantly until the twentieth century, when deliveries moved from the home to the hospital.[19] Moreover, we might expect that declining fertility rates would change the way that women regarded the physical rigors of childbearing. But although some women in this period bore fewer children than their mothers and grandmothers, most still spent a significant period of their adult lives pregnant, recovering from childbirth, breastfeeding, and tending young children. Finally, women's perceptions of motherhood were shaped by preceding generations. Older women shared advice and the wisdom gleaned from their own experiences, and women often created explicit links between their own childbearing experiences and those of their mothers. In 1793 Maria Flagg, for instance, drew a connection between her future suffering in childbirth and the past suffering of her mother: "I always thought & think now, that if I am ever married, what she suffer'd for me, I shall for *another*, believe me in such a case it will comfort me to think I am paying the debt I owe."[20] Thus we cannot assume that a woman's vision of the corporeal work of motherhood in the 1850s was radically different from that of her mother or even grandmother.

A second issue relates to the ways in which changing cultural depictions of motherhood paralleled ongoing developments in the ways that Americans thought about women's work. Jeanne Boydston has shown that in the late eighteenth and early nineteenth centuries women's productive activities began to be dissociated from notions of real (that is, breadwinning) labor. By the mid-nineteenth century women's work was no longer viewed in middle-class culture as economically productive; instead, women's responsibilities were understood to revolve around motherhood and the creation of an ideal home. Even these homemaking responsibilities came to be described "less as purposeful activities" than as "emanations of an abstract but shared Womanhood."[21] Although Boydston's argument does not focus specifically on depictions of motherhood, I would argue that this shift away from acknowledging women's productive work was an essential part of the evolution of the sentimental maternal ideal. As the maternal body began to vanish from cultural representations of motherhood, so too did the impression that motherhood involved (re)productive labor. Instead, motherhood came to be presented as an effortless and joyful experience, and the work that women did was imagined as solely emotional and spiritual.

Finally, as the concept of physical labor vanished from cultural depictions of motherhood, it also became clear that sentimental motherhood was profoundly defined by notions of class and race. Physical labor was associated in American society with the lower classes and the enslaved. Wet nurses, for instance, were often lower-class immigrant women, and by the nineteenth century they came to be regarded as laboring bodies that disrupted the values of sentimental motherhood. Enslaved women were defined even more profoundly by the productive and reproductive labor of their bodies. At the same time, white middle-class Americans became increasingly preoccupied with the presentation and management of the body, creating a culture that sought to restrain the body in order to privilege the mind and soul and to project an appearance of gentility. Bodily restraint became the hallmark of the white middle class.[22] Disorderly bodies—often defined in terms of unrestrained sexuality or intemperance—came to be associated exclusively with the poor, with immigrants, and with nonwhite Americans. Because the sentimental mother came to be envisioned as a noncorporeal figure who did not work but simply emanated virtue and love, women who were socially and culturally defined by their laboring or disorderly bodies simply could not be sentimental mothers. Thus the disembodied sentimental mother of print culture became clearly defined as white and socioeconomically privileged, precluding many women from claiming the moral and emotional authority and privilege of the good mother.

This study endeavors to capture a broad range of ways in which Americans living between the 1750s and the 1850s thought about the maternal body. I have drawn on women's letters and diaries as well as slave narratives and interviews to uncover the diverse meanings created around the lived experience of the maternal body. Middle-class and elite white women left a more substantial archive of first-person accounts of childbearing than did lower-class women and women of color, but the less abundant testimonies left by enslaved women offer powerful insights into the importance of the body and provide a needed counterpoint to the experiences of socioeconomically privileged women. Putting the insights of enslaved women and privileged white women side by side illuminates critical commonalities and differences in the role that corporeality played in defining motherhood. The majority of the women I write about came from the more populous Eastern Seaboard, though some lived as far west as Missouri, Texas, or even Oregon. Although the West is underrepresented in this study, the sources I have examined suggest that region was less important in differentiating women's perceptions of embodiment than other factors such as enslavement, age, number of children, and the particularities of individual experiences.

In order to uncover the cultural perceptions of the maternal body that shaped the mind-set of an increasingly literate American public, I have focused on a seemingly disparate selection of print sources. Although medical literature, prescriptive literature, popular literature and visual culture, and antislavery print culture may at first glance appear to have little in common, by focusing on depictions of the body I show that all of these print sources worked together to generate the cultural icon of the noncorporeal sentimental mother. To a large extent the cultural history of the maternal body is a transnational one. Much of the print culture that was consumed by eighteenth-century Americans was originally published in Britain before making its way to America. An indigenous American print culture emerged more fully at the beginning of the nineteenth century, though it too was heavily influenced by trends across the Atlantic. American print culture largely emerged in cities in the Northeast such as Philadelphia, New York, and Boston, but in spite of this northeastern bias these texts were widely consumed and constituted an influential national culture.[23]

This book is organized thematically to consider different issues and types of sources while also mirroring the cycles of motherhood that structured women's lives. The chapters function in pairs, moving from the processes of pregnancy, childbirth, and breastfeeding through which motherhood was imagined in medical and prescriptive literature and by which women entered the realm of motherhood, to broader visions of the mother as an imagined figure in popular print culture. The chapter organization also re-flects the broader tension between change over time and continuity that structured the history of the maternal body in this period. The chapters that focus on print culture depict the gradual emergence of the disembodied sen-timental mother, and these are interwoven with chapters depicting the underlying continuity in women's descriptions of the physical experiences of motherhood. Each chapter alone provides only one facet of the varied perceptions of the maternal body that coexisted in American society, but taken together they re-create the complex and often contradictory culture within which women lived as mothers.

This book begins by exploring the first stages of motherhood—pregnancy and childbirth—from the perspective of the male medical profession and the perspective of childbearing women. Chapter 1 looks back to the sixteenth and seventeenth centuries to locate some of the earliest print culture depictions of the maternal body and to explore how the develop-ment of midwifery as part of the male medical profession in the eighteenth century reshaped medical representations of the maternal body. I argue that in the mid-eighteenth century medical writers began to shift their focus away from the elite white mother as an active corporeal figure and toward the uterus as the primary agent in childbearing, thus replacing her labor with the work of the physician and the uterus. The dissociation of the mother from the labor of her body opened the way for an emerging cultural vision of the mother as a refined, moral, and spiritual figure.

Chapter 2 approaches the experiences of pregnancy and childbirth from a very different angle by examining the ways in which women discussed the experiences of childbearing. Middle-class and elite white women left frequent references to pregnancy and childbirth in their letters and diaries. These brief textual moments reveal that women viewed the experience of motherhood as profoundly rooted in the work of their bodies. Moreover, their writings show that the physical challenges of childbearing made them deeply ambivalent toward motherhood. Enslaved women also left behind references to childbearing in published narratives and interviews and re-vealed that the maternal body signified different things in bondage than in freedom. While white middle-class and elite women emphasized the day-to-day physicality of pregnancy and childbirth, enslaved women's testimo-nies show that their experience of childbearing was most profoundly shaped by the commodification of their bodies as mothers. Childbearing women, both free and enslaved, placed the work of their bodies at the heart of their understanding of motherhood, but for vastly different reasons.

Next, the focus shifts from childbearing to the early stages of childrearing by exploring breastfeeding as it was depicted in maternal advice literature and women's personal writings. Chapter 3 explores how debates about the importance of maternal breastfeeding underwent a rhetorical shift beginning in the late eighteenth century. Maternal advice manual authors moved from a focus on women's divine duty and the practical benefits of nursing for infant and maternal health to a new sentimental rhetoric that emphasized maternal pleasure in the act of breastfeeding. In doing so, they effaced the real labor involved in mothering and presented a newly idealized vision of motherhood as natural, effortless, and delightful.

Women's discussions of breastfeeding both echoed and contradicted the ideals set out in prescriptive literature. Chapter 4 examines white middle-class and elite women's letters and diaries to show that frequent discomfort tempered the pleasure they derived from nursing their children, resulting in ambivalence toward the physical act. In spite of their ambivalence, women agreed with prescriptive authors that breastfeeding was practically and symbolically crucial to the identity of the good mother. Because the act of breastfeeding was so important to the idealization of motherhood, by the beginning of the nineteenth century it became a central issue around which the very definition of the mother became fractured. Middle-class and elite white women's attitudes toward their hired wet nurses reveal that the issue of breastfeeding helped widen race- and class-based fissures in the definition of the good mother. Middle-class and elite mothers viewed themselves as good mothers, while they came to see nonwhite and lower-class mothers merely as useful or troublesome reproductive bodies.

Finally, I move from the more concrete experiences of childbearing and childrearing to the imaginary realm of literary and visual culture. Chapter 5 examines representations of the mother in the popular sentimental poetry and visual culture that were widely produced and voraciously consumed by Americans in the first half of the nineteenth century. By the 1830s this sentimental print culture consistently portrayed the ideal mother in terms of her moral and emotional influence, disguising the work of her body in favor of the more intangible qualities of maternal love and piety. These texts took the image of the sentimental mother a step further by defining her as a transcendent figure whose ethereal influence was infinite and everlasting, granting her a unique kind of power over her children and, by extension, society as a whole.

The figure of the mother was also central to antislavery print culture, and chapter 6 explores the ways in which the enslaved maternal body was depicted in antislavery poems and visual culture. Like mainstream print culture, antislavery poems and pictures used sentimental language and imagery to create a common bond between mothers, enslaved and free, but they did not invoke the fantasy of the transcendent mother in their representations of enslaved women. Unlike the white mother in the sentimental poetry of popular middle-class culture, the enslaved mother was bound to her corporeality by the physical torments of slavery. By emphasizing the disorderly corporeality of the enslaved mother, antislavery poems and images exposed and perpetuated a culturally entrenched race-based division between white transcendent mothers and black embodied mothers. Ultimately, these sources show that the maternal body came to be used to symbolize the forces of order and disorder in American society.

· · · · · ·

The study of the history of the body is a relatively recent project that has added new depth to our understanding of the human experience.[24] Although the material body does imply a certain biological constant—after all, physiological processes such as conception, pregnancy, or lactation have not changed markedly over time—scholars have shown that the body is always defined, regulated, and reinvented by its social and cultural context.[25] The very same living human body may be burdened with different meanings in different contexts, while the imagined bodies that appear in print, visual, and material culture vary according to the beliefs of the overall culture whose values they articulate and shape. Different notions of power and social worth, as well as a host of identities based on categories such as gender, sexuality, race, class, nationality, ethnicity, religion, and age, are inscribed on the body. Thus scholars have explored the body as individual and collective, coerced and contestatory, and as a site of inscription and performance. Historians in particular have been interested in the ways in which oppression and agency have been located in the body and how notions of class, gender, and race have been inscribed on and contested by the body at different times and in different places.[26] Historical analyses of the body have revealed that representations of embodiment helped to define social and cultural belonging, and this was certainly true in the context of motherhood.

The pioneering work of Michel Foucault has provided the foundation for much of the scholarship on the body across disciplines. He has argued that power acts on the body in society and in doing so creates the body as a recognizable signifier of identity and status. In Foucault's formulation, the body must be understood as a discursive product; there is no original or natural nondiscursive material body.[27] I do not wish to deny the existence of an original material body, yet following Foucault and other scholars I do work from the understanding that everything we know about the body is mediated through language and other forms of representation. As Judith Butler has written, "To claim that discourse is formative is not to claim that it originates, causes, or exhaustively composes that which it concedes; rather, it is to claim that there is no reference to a pure body which is not at the same time a further formation of that body."[28] Although many of our experiences in life may be rooted in the materiality of the body—touch, sounds, smells, pain, pleasure—we can never know or understand those moments outside of language, and language is what gives meaning to our bodily actions and encounters. Thus historians can approach the body as a purely discursive construction, as I do in my analyses of the imagined maternal body in popular print culture, or as a site of experience, which is always given meaning by language.

The study of the body has been particularly fraught for feminist scholars whose work seeks to challenge the biological essentialism that has historically constrained women's opportunities, while simultaneously striving to understand the fullness of women's lived experiences. There is no doubt that women's place in American society, and elsewhere, has been historically defined by their biological capacity to bear children. Feminist scholars are right to contest the enduring tendency to define women in terms of their sexual and reproductive bodies. Yet in writing about the women of the past, it is also important to recognize the ways in which the biological capacities of their bodies truly did shape their lives. Women *did* lactate, not men, and this seemingly simple fact shaped the rhythms of their lives and the meanings they drew from their roles as women and mothers, as well as influencing the ways in which women were imagined in American culture. Elizabeth Grosz has challenged feminist scholars to consider the body in explorations of subjectivity and identity instead of privileging the mind, and this book seeks to respond to her call.[29] In writing the history of the maternal body, my goal is not to essentialize women as mothers, but to historicize childbearing and motherhood. I show that the meaning of the body and the ways in which it contributed to perceptions of motherhood were contingent on time, social position, experience, and a host of other variables. The body must be seen as "a fleshly field of dreams," and the purpose of this book is to examine the experiences and fantasies that invested the maternal body with meaning in American society.[30]

Writing a history of the maternal body is in some respects an impossible task. The bodies of which I write have vanished, and most women did not reflect on and write about their embodiment in a conscious way. Even in the abundant cultural representations of motherhood it is not always easy to read between the lines to understand what perceptions of the body shaped the vision an author or artist sought to convey. Looking for the historical body often feels like peering through a heavy veil at a figure just beyond reach. But it is essential for historians to keep in mind the physical dimensions of human experience and understanding. The body is both everywhere and nowhere in the historical record. It existed in the lived experiences of the individual, in encounters between people, and in the articulation of sameness and difference, and it has been the fundamental site of both oppression and resistance. As historians we most often rely on written evidence from the past that allows us to forget that the mind that articulated the words on the page was given form by a body, and that the pen that recorded events and ideas was wielded by a fleshly hand. As historians we tend to bring to life the thoughts and feelings of the women and men of the past, while allowing the flesh to remain dead and forgotten. In order to find the historical body we must peer imaginatively at every source, for inevitably the body is present just below the surface.

# 1 The Tyrannical Womb and the Disappearing Mother

## The Maternal Body in Medical Literature

· · · · · · · · · · · · · · · · · · · · · · · · · · · · · · · · · · · · · · · · · · · · · · ·

Some of the earliest texts that explicitly discussed the maternal body were found in a growing realm of medical literature relating to reproduction and the practice of midwifery. The Western tradition of medicine traces its roots back to ancient Greece, where medical writers such as Hippocrates, Aristotle, and Galen sought to understand human physiology and were much exercised to explain the peculiarities of the female body in relation to the male body, which they perceived as both normative and superior.[1] Medical authorities debated whether women were best defined in terms of their cooler and moister constitutions or in terms of their wombs. By the medieval period many medical writers came to place more emphasis on women's reproductive capacity as their defining feature, and by the early modern period the notion of "woman" was inextricably tied to the womb and to her generative capacity.[2]

With this vision of the female body as predominantly a reproductive body, it is no surprise that the early modern period saw a growing number of medical texts that focused on what we would now call obstetrics and gynecology, though those medical terms were not in use until the nineteenth century. Thomas Raynalde, for instance, is credited with publishing the first English-language midwifery manual in 1540. This text was designed for the instruction of women and their midwives and went through numerous editions through the mid-seventeenth century.[3] The seventeenth century saw an unprecedented proliferation of medical texts, particularly those aimed at a vernacular audience. Nicholas Culpeper's *A Directory for Midwives*, for instance, was first published in 1651 for the benefit of women and their midwives and went through numerous editions.[4] His extremely popular midwifery text helped shape a growing discourse about women's reproductive bodies that also included the writings of female midwives, such as the English midwife Jane Sharp, who first published her *Midwives Book* in 1671.[5]

In England the practice of midwifery remained almost exclusively in the hands of female midwives into the early eighteenth century. Male practitioners were called on only in emergency situations, often to extract a fetus using instruments such as the crochet or forceps. This division of medical labor was reflected in the fact that most early midwifery texts were addressed to women, providing information that female midwives and their patients needed to navigate the perils of childbearing. Midwives received their knowledge primarily through apprenticeship and practice rather than through formal medical education, and writers saw their books as a helpful addition to the midwife's store of knowledge. The English midwife Sarah Stone, for instance, published a collection of case histories in 1737 that she hoped would help "instruct my Sisters in the Profession; that it may be in their power to deliver all manner of Births."[6]

Beginning in the mid-eighteenth century, both the practice of midwifery and its literature began to change as male practitioners—known as manmidwives or accoucheurs—increasingly attended the deliveries of elite women.[7] Thus began a process of professionalization in which male practitioners asserted their authority over midwifery by virtue of their formal medical training. Their newfound (and somewhat tenuous) authority was articulated in a wave of new midwifery texts, such as William Smellie's widely influential *Treatise on the Theory and Practice of Midwifery*, which he published in 1752, followed by an anatomical atlas of the female reproductive body.[8] The professionalization of midwifery also made its way to America, though the process was slightly delayed. British-trained physicians such as William Shippen, who returned to Philadelphia in 1762 and offered the first formal series of lectures on midwifery, carried their training in obstetrics back to the colonies and began to attend elite American women.[9] American practitioners relied on British and European medical texts until the nineteenth century, when prominent American physicians such as Samuel Bard and William Dewees began to publish their own obstetric texts, which borrowed heavily from earlier British and European authors.[10] This chapter therefore examines a transatlantic body of medical literature, encompassing the British texts and English-language translations that were used by American practitioners in the eighteenth century, as well as the nineteenth-century texts produced by American physicians themselves.

The professionalization of midwifery resulted in changes not only in the practice of midwifery but also in the representation of the maternal body in medical literature. Changes in medical literature reflected the fact that the figure of the man-midwife raised the specter of sexual impropriety in the birthing chamber.[11] Sarah Stone, writing in the 1730s, warned that the new fashion of calling for a man-midwife meant that "the Modesty of our Sex will be in great danger of being lost."[12] Another English midwife, Elizabeth Nihell, was even more vociferous in her concerns, and she sought to defend the authority of female midwives in her 1760 treatise by asserting that the presence of the man-midwife sacrificed "modesty and decency." The private parts of women should be accessed only by their husbands, she argued, and medical necessity did not justify allowing another man access to that which was not rightfully his.[13] The discussion of sexual decency continued into the nineteenth century, with both women and men raising concerns about the moral implications of having men in the lying-in chamber. This meant that would-be accoucheurs were forced to justify their presence at deliveries and to develop ways of legitimizing their practice by demonstrating not only their medical competence but also their respect for decency and sexual propriety. This concern came through with particular clarity in the ways that physicians negotiated the female body and their role as man-midwives in the obstetric texts that they produced in increasing numbers.

Beginning in the mid-eighteenth century, physicians found new ways in their medical writings to mitigate the potential for sexual danger in their encounters—both real and textual—with the maternal body. They did this in several ways. First, unlike earlier medical writers who lingered gleefully on women's physiological capacity for sexual pleasure, they began to describe women's sexual organs in ways that evaded any hint of sexual enjoyment. Women's sexual subjectivity disappeared, thus easing the danger of allowing a male practitioner access to the female body. If women did not experience sexual pleasure, they could not be tempted by the ministrations of a man-midwife. Second, medical writers began to turn away from portraying the whole female body in their anatomical illustrations and focused exclusively on the pelvis and reproductive organs. The body, as illustrated, was literally cut to pieces, turning the woman into a series of disembodied specimens that allowed the physician to escape (textually, at least) the moral dangers of physical intimacy with a woman. Third, in their descriptions of the processes of childbearing, medical writers began to efface the presence and agency of the mother. In doing so they made the womb the focus of their studies and eventually a main character in their medical texts. As the womb became textually more prominent, the mother herself became increasingly invisible, easing fears of sexual intimacy.

The invisibility of the maternal body in medical texts had important class and race dimensions. By the nineteenth century, physicians' fixation on the uterus as the primary agent in reproduction contributed to an understanding of childbearing as a pathological process for "civilized" women whose bodies were not vigorous or animal enough to perform the work of pregnancy and childbirth alone. The refined woman—understood to be white and economically privileged—became the normative figure in the medical text. She was the frail patient whose body could not handle the power of the uterus and therefore required the labor of the physician to assist her. In contrast, physicians believed that "savage" (nonwhite) and unrefined (lower-class) women could successfully navigate the perils of childbearing. These women's bodies were robust and could do the work of childbearing without danger. Moreover, physicians did not concern themselves with questions of delicacy and sexual modesty in relation to these women. When they appeared in medical texts their bodies were rendered visible and tangible, and for physicians they represented useful sources of medical knowledge that could be probed with impunity.[14]

The disappearance of the refined mother in medical texts also had implications for the meaning of motherhood and women's work. As physicians began to emphasize the primacy of the womb alongside their own agency as practitioners, childbearing came to seem less a result of women's labor and more the outcome of a tense relationship between the uterus and the man-midwife. In short, over the course of the eighteenth and early nineteenth centuries, the reproductive work of white middle-class and elite women was gradually written out of medical texts. This was directly at odds with women's own view that motherhood was fundamentally defined by the labor of their bodies. However, medical depictions of the refined maternal body as passive and even invisible anticipated a broader cultural trend that highlighted white middle-class and elite women's moral and emotional work as mothers while effacing the labor of their bodies. This vision of motherhood evaded the physical messiness and the sexual implications of the female reproductive body, allowing the mother to emerge as an idealized figure symbolizing virtue and order. Because this vision was predicated on the disappearance of the maternal body, however, it was a vision that excluded poor women and women of color, who were perceived as fundamentally embodied.

These aspects of medical literature highlight the fact that medical knowledge speaks not only to physiological realities but also to a host of assumptions about social roles and relationships. Indeed, the disappearance of the maternal body and the dominance of the uterus in medical literature indicate that these texts can tell us as much about common assumptions regarding gender roles, race and class differences, and sexual ideology as they do about medical knowledge and practice. Medical representations of the female reproductive body reveal that it was perceived as deeply problematic on both a medical and a cultural level. Concerns about sexual propriety meant that eighteenth- and nineteenth-century medical practitioners were never at ease with the mother as a corporeal agent and accordingly turned their attention to plumbing the mysteries of discrete reproductive fragments. Medical writers of course could not simply ignore the whole body and its messiness—they did after all treat living patients—but they could use textual representations to deal with maternal corporeality with greater scientific ease and less embarrassment. Medical practitioners wrote about some of women's most intimate physical experiences, but they were able to create an authoritative narrative that articulated a new, more passive role for the mother that stood in tension with women's lived experiences of childbearing.

· · · · · ·

One of the first significant shifts in medical representations of the maternal body occurred in descriptions of women's anatomy and the processes of sexual intercourse and conception. Sixteenth- and seventeenth-century medical texts, particularly those aimed at a vernacular audience, did not shy away from references to sexual pleasure. Indeed, they seemed to revel in depictions of human sexuality, drawing on popular earthy metaphors to explain physiological facts, as did Jane Sharp when she explained that "the Yard [penis] is as it were the Plow wherewith the Ground is tilled, and made fit for the production of Fruit."[15] In their descriptions of reproductive anatomy, intercourse, and conception, they portrayed both women and men as lusty participants in the enjoyments of procreation. At the same time, however, these authors betrayed a certain degree of ambivalence. They offered disclaimers that the information they provided was for medical instruction alone, not for purposes of titillation. Their fears were perhaps not unfounded, for there was indeed a history of medical texts serving as "a kind of 'ersatz' for hard-core pornography," and some readers must certainly have found certain descriptions and illustrations titillating.[16] Yet these concerns did not ultimately prevent these authors from presenting explicit information about female and male sexuality.

When Thomas Raynalde published an English translation of Eucharius Rösslin's midwifery manual in 1540, he intended to provide readers with a practical guide that included descriptions of female anatomy as well as the process of conception.[17] His text highlighted the importance of sexual pleasure, arguing that if "the God of Nature had not instincted, and inset in the body of man and woman such a vehement and ardent appetite and lust . . . neither man nor woman, would never have been so attentive to the works of Generation and increasment of Posteritie, to the utter decay in short time of all Mankind."[18] Thus both women and men were driven by sexual desire to procreate, so much so, his text insisted, that even women who foreswore intercourse because of their suffering in childbirth shortly thereafter forgot their pain and returned to the pleasures of the marital bed.[19] Women were therefore sexually lusty, and Raynalde made no attempt to apologize for this characterization. He did express some scruples about translating such information into English for laypeople to read, for he feared those who "shall condemn and utterly reprove the whole matter; some alledging that it is shame, and other some, that it is not meet nor fitting such matters to be treated of so plainly in our Mother and vulgar language, to the dishonor (as they say) of Womanhood, and the derision of their wont secrets." Yet his fears centered less on the potentially titillating nature of his text than on the risk that male readers might use the information to mock and disparage women and their bodies.[20]

In general, early vernacular medical writers thought that the benefits of a clear explanation of reproduction outweighed possible risks. Raynalde's popular manual was superseded in 1651 by Nicholas Culpeper's text, *A Directory for Midwives*, which was reprinted for over a century.[21] Culpeper was unabashed in his representations of reproductive bodies, and he focused his anatomical explanations on men's bodies as well as women's, portraying women's bodies as imperfect variations of male anatomy.[22] In his section on female anatomy he specified without apology that the clitoris "is that which causeth lust in Women, and gives delight in Copulation; for without this a Woman neither desires Copulation, or hath pleasure in it, or conceives by it."[23] He insisted, moreover, that lust was more often the cause of procreation than the pious desire to fulfill God's mandate to people the earth.[24] Another text compiled by a group of London practitioners in 1656 presented similarly detailed depictions of men's and women's genitals and made frequent references to copulation and sexual pleasure. The clitoris, these authors noted, "is the seat of Venereal pleasure," and they furthermore invited the reader to peer (in imagination, presumably) within the female body, "that as soon as ever your sight is entred within the female fissure, there do appear to the view, two certain little holes or pits, wherein is contained a serous humour; which being pressed out in the act of copulation, does not a little add to the pleasure thereof."[25] The authors of these texts did not explain their choice to include information about intercourse and sexual pleasure in texts ostensibly intended to help women navigate the perils of childbirth, suggesting that they felt no pressure to justify the presence of such inessential material.

It was not only male practitioners who published explicit accounts of copulation and procreation. Two decades after Culpeper published his midwifery guide, the midwife Jane Sharp published a similar text, borrowing heavily from previous authors.[26] The only English-language midwifery manual to be published by a woman before 1700, Sharp's work offered childbearing women and practitioners a lively and explicit source of information about the female reproductive body and was reprinted in numerous editions.[27] Like Culpeper, Sharp portrayed women's anatomy as an inferior and "not so compleat" version of men's, and the first section of her book was devoted entirely to a minute description of the male and female reproductive organs and their functions during intercourse.[28] Sharp mirrored Culpeper in asserting that "we Women have no more cause to be angry, or be ashamed of what Nature hath given us, than men have."[29] Both Sharp and Culpeper saw shame as an impediment to gaining the knowledge that would aid women in living healthy reproductive lives. Sharp was also quite direct about female sexual pleasure, explaining that the clitoris "will stand and fall as the Yard doth, and makes women lustful and take delight in Copulation, and were it not for this they would have no desire nor delight, nor would they ever conceive."[30] She referred frequently to both women's and men's experience of sexual pleasure throughout her section on anatomy.

Perhaps the text most emblematic of this early modern enthusiasm for sexual matters was *Aristotle's Masterpiece*, which was first published in London in 1684 as a compilation of other texts. It quickly became the most popular English-language guide to sexuality, conception, pregnancy, and childbirth and went through numerous editions in England and America.[31] *Aristotle's Masterpiece* began with a frank discussion of anatomy and the mechanics of sexual intercourse, explaining the nature of men's and women's sexual organs and their specific roles. The author explained that the penis "is covered with a Preputium or Foreskin . . . and by its moving up and down in the Act of Copulation brings Pleasure to both the Man and

Woman."[32] Women's parts were equally implicated in the giving and receiving of pleasure, for the author emphasized the "neck of the Womb . . . which receives the Man's Yard like a Sheath; and that it may be dilated with the more Ease and Pleasure in the Act of Coition, it is sinewy and a little spongy."[33] In case precise anatomical explanations of pleasure were not sufficiently clear, the author also included verses that testified to the delights of the marital state and implied that women were so driven by sexual desire that they were discontented until they married and became mothers.[34] Sexual desire and motherhood, therefore, were two sides of the same coin.

*Aristotle's Masterpiece* proved to be so titillating that it caused trouble in at least one respectable town. In 1744 the celebrated Puritan minister and theologian Jonathan Edwards conducted an investigation into rumors that men in Northampton, Massachusetts, were reading a copy of *Aristotle's Masterpiece* and making lewd comments to women. The men caused trouble with their provocative claim to local women that "we Know as much about ye as you and more too."[35] As Raynalde had feared two centuries before, precise knowledge of female reproductive anatomy could lead men to mock women. Evidently medical writers were right to consider the risks of putting sexually explicit material into their midwifery texts, yet these risks did not prevent early authors from dwelling on the particularities of reproductive anatomy and the sources and functions of sexual pleasure. The maternal body in these texts was indeed a sexual body. More importantly, these authors often evoked the sexual subjectivity of women rather than portraying their bodies as solely the objects of men's sexual desire and the sources of men's sexual satisfaction (though this, too, was an important factor in their representations).

With the professionalization of midwifery in the mid-eighteenth century, a new model of midwifery manual emerged in which discussions of intercourse and sexual pleasure were almost entirely absent. In particular, the professionalization of midwifery prompted the rapid disappearance of women's sexual subjectivity from obstetric texts. By separating women from sexual pleasure, medical writers could ease fears about the sexual impropriety of having men in the birthing chamber. By erasing women's sexual desires, they could erase the possibility that childbearing women and their man-midwives might be tempted into illicit relations, thus desexualizing the encounter and allowing men to participate with propriety in the formerly female domain of midwifery.

William Smellie, one of the earliest and most well-known man-midwives in England, was deeply concerned with legitimizing his profession and the publications that emerged from the pens of physicians. His work was frequently cited by later practitioners in both Britain and America, and his writings reflected deep-seated concerns about sexual propriety. He wrote in his 1752 treatise that the man-midwife "ought to act and speak with the utmost delicacy of decorum, and never violate the trust reposed in him, so as to harbor the least immoral or indecent design, but demean himself in all respects suitable to the dignity of his profession."[36] He included further practical details about how the practitioner ought to behave, shaping a vision of the man-midwife as scrupulously modest and respectable.

Smellie was one of a handful of medical writers who ushered in a new type of midwifery manual to reflect the newly professionalized field. These texts were written in a highly technical style with an emphasis on internal anatomy (as opposed to external genitalia) and aimed primarily at male practitioners and medical students rather than at female midwives and their patients. Smellie wrote his 1752 treatise in a strictly professional manner, unlike the cheerful, anecdotal, and garrulous style of authors like Raynalde, Culpeper, and Sharp, or the mixture of medical knowledge and bawdy verse in *Aristotle's Masterpiece*. He downplayed sexual desire in favor of the objective precision of anatomy. Smellie described the female sex organs and mentioned the clitoris in passing without giving any hint of its role in female sexual pleasure.[37] In his detailed descriptions of the female organs, Smellie gave only two hints of the potential pleasure involved in intercourse, explaining that "the *Uterus* yields three or four inches to the pressure of the *Penis*, having a free motion upwards and downwards, so that the reciprocal oscillation which is permitted by this contrivance increases the mutual titillation and pleasure."[38] He reiterated this idea a few pages later, adding that such movements "produce a general titillation and turgency," resulting in the ejection of fluids.[39] Embedded as these ideas were in highly technical language, they lacked the same ability to evoke a real sense of sexual pleasure. The result was a medical text seemingly devoid of titillating features. More significantly, in Smellie's text the sense of female sexual subjectivity faded away, and internal reproductive anatomy came to the fore.

The English physician, Thomas Denman, demonstrated a similar approach to female sexuality in his treatise from the 1780s. "The *clitoris* is supposed to be the principal seat of pleasure, and to be capable of some degree of erection in the act of coition," he wrote, suggesting with the word "supposed" that he did not entirely credit the information and that it was not relevant enough for him to pursue the question. Later, he insisted that "the clitoris is little concerned in the practice of midwifery."[40] The Scottish practitioner Alexander Hamilton seemed to agree, merely noting in his 1780 treatise where the clitoris was located and the fact that it might differ in size from woman to woman.[41] Women's external parts were rapidly becoming less relevant to the study of midwifery than internal parts such as the uterus and the pelvis, which could be seen only through the process of dissection that so greatly interested practitioners such as Smellie and Denman.

By the turn of the nineteenth century, medical writers displayed even greater reluctance to discuss or even acknowledge women's sexual activity and pleasure as part of the reproductive process. In his course of lectures published in 1800, the American physician Valentine Seaman explained that "the peculiar manner in which conception takes place, being a matter more of curiosity than of real utility, we shall omit at present any attempt to investigate."[42] Samuel Bard, credited with publishing the first American midwifery textbook in 1807, explained that "immediately below the superior angle which unites the labia, rises the *clitoris* C, a pendulous substance, not quite an inch in length."[43] He did not include any description of the mechanics of intercourse or the function of the clitoris. His primary nod to human sexuality was to warn against early marriage, before the sex organs in both men and women could be fully matured.[44] The Scottish surgeon John Burns similarly discussed female anatomy in his 1809 midwifery text without recognizing either female or male sexual pleasure. He described the diseases the clitoris was subject to, but did not explain the mechanics of intercourse or the role of the female genitals in generating sexual pleasure.[45] The eminent Philadelphia obstetrician William Dewees was equally uninterested in sexuality, writing of the clitoris that "it is supposed, but without sufficient proof, to contribute to sensual gratification."[46] Here too the subject was not relevant enough to warrant further investigation. These later medical writers quickly bypassed the issues of intercourse and conception and restricted their representations of the reproductive body to pregnancy and delivery, processes in which the internal reproductive parts might be given a leading role, allowing physicians to avoid the immodest possibilities of sexual temptation.

· · · · · ·

In addition to the shift away from depictions of female sexuality, the mid-eighteenth century also saw a significant transition in visual representations of the female body in medical texts. The new generation of professional man-midwives became increasingly preoccupied with the study of internal reproductive anatomy, and they particularly sought to understand the structure of the pelvis and the functions of the uterus by dissecting bodies and creating highly detailed anatomical illustrations. As Charles White proclaimed with pride in the 1770s, "Bringing the art of midwifery to perfection upon scientific and mechanical principles seems to have been reserved for the present generation. We have been but lately able to explore the secret operations of nature."[47] As their interests turned inward, these medical writers and the artists and engravers they collaborated with shifted the ways in which the female body was represented visually. Whereas earlier visual depictions of the female reproductive body often featured the woman as a whole and animated figure, with anatomical parts such as the uterus displayed in their bodily context, in later texts the figure of the mother was literally cut into pieces. This visual fragmentation of the maternal body resulted in the disappearance of the woman as an animated character in the obstetrical text, allowing the practice of midwifery to be visually articulated as a relationship between the practitioner and impersonal fragments of anatomy. In this way, these anatomical pieces allowed the man-midwife to conduct his explorations of the female body in ways that did not evoke a dangerous intimacy with the childbearing woman. Instead, the intimacy of the physician's gaze turned to fragments of skeleton and organ.

Vernacular medical writers in the sixteenth and seventeenth centuries had a range of conventions to choose from when it came to visually depicting the female reproductive body. Often, their images combined artistic trends with anatomic precision, based on the relatively new practice of human dissection. Indeed, as Jonathan Sawday has shown, the separation between the arts and the sciences was not well established in Renaissance Europe; the science of dissection shaped creative depictions of the human body, and artistic conventions shaped medical imagery. Artists and medical men all strove to arrive at a clearer understanding of the "interior world of the human frame."[48] The dissection of human bodies did not become a significant part of medical practice and knowledge until the fourteenth century, when it spread from Italy to other parts of continental Europe. The practice of teaching human anatomy via dissection did not reach England until the late sixteenth century, but it grew swiftly in importance, and the centrality of anatomical study was firmly established there by the eighteenth century.[49] Dissection made the visual representation of the interior body increasingly important, and medical writers across Europe compiled texts that revealed the inner secrets of the human body in both prose and picture.

The male body predominated in these early explorations of human anatomy. For one thing, male bodies were more readily available for dissection because anatomists frequently worked on the bodies of executed criminals, who were more likely to be men.[50] Moreover, the male body was generally understood to be the norm from which the female body deviated; thus understanding the male body took priority. The female body was interesting only in the ways that it differed from the male body. Andreas Vesalius of Brussels, for example, published a groundbreaking anatomical atlas in 1543 that helped set the stage for a massive effort at mapping the human body.[51] Following in the footsteps of Galen, Vesalius emphasized the need for medical men to learn anatomy by seeing it for themselves via the process of dissection. He provided a comprehensive series of precise drawings of the dissected human form, beginning with the skeleton and moving on to the muscles, nervous system, abdominal organs, heart, and brain. His illustrations featured complete skeletons and flayed figures (nearly all male) in lifelike and active poses. It was only in the section on the abdominal organs, including the reproductive organs, that Vesalius highlighted images of the female body, implying that woman was primarily defined by her reproductive parts: vagina, uterus, ovaries.[52] Anatomical illustrations of the female reproductive body were found in other sixteenth- and seventeenth-century medical texts as well, but almost always in the context of revealing the reproductive organs. The female body was not needed to display other parts such as muscles, heart, or brain, being understood solely in terms of its reproductive parts and generative capacity, while the male body expressed the full range of the human form.

Images of the female body generally appeared in two types. The most common image in sixteenth-century texts was the figure of a whole and life-like woman with the skin and muscles of her abdomen gently peeled back to reveal the inner reproductive organs or a fetus. An anatomical text by the Frenchman Charles Estienne, published shortly after Vesalius's *De humani corporis fabrica*, focused on images of male bodies to show the form of the skeleton, muscles, vessels, and other aspects of internal anatomy, but he also included several images illustrating women's reproductive anatomy. In each of his images the woman appeared as a lifelike figure in various seated or semi-recumbent poses, often gesturing discreetly and with modestly averted gaze toward the part of her anatomy that was on display. With curled hair, small, high breasts, and hairless genitals meant to signify a delicate and pure sexuality, these women represented a widely recognized classical aesthetic of female beauty.[53] At the same time, each figure displayed a particular aspect of women's reproductive anatomy, such as the uterus, the position of the fetus in the uterus, or the genitalia.[54]

This type of image appeared in other works as well, such as Jacob Rueff's 1554 midwifery manual, which was first published in German and Latin and later published in an English translation. Rueff's text included an image of a whole and lifelike woman with her abdomen opened to reveal her reproductive organs and a tiny fetus.[55] As in Estienne's work, this figure represented a recognizable classical ideal—the figure of the woman might have passed for a copy of a Botticelli Venus if it were not for her dissected abdomen. These images persisted through the seventeenth century, appearing with little variation in works such as Jane Sharp's late seventeenth-century midwifery manual (see fig. 1.1). The illustration in Sharp's text offered a vision of the mother as whole, lovely, and sexual (the vagina was suggestively concealed by a flower, drawing attention to the woman's sexual parts even as it partially concealed them), rather than fragmented and faceless, as she would become in later images.[56] These lifelike images made the mother a visible character in anatomical texts and midwifery manuals. Moreover, she was depicted as a participant in the act of dissection rather than merely an object of science: many of these lifelike figures pointed or gestured to their anatomy or met the viewer's gaze with an inviting glance as if complicit in their own dissection.

As an alternative to images of the whole and lifelike woman, some sixteenth- and seventeenth-century medical texts also included truncated versions of the female body that hinted at the lifelike presence of the woman but placed more emphasis on the specifics of her anatomy. Thomas Raynalde and Andreas Vesalius published their texts within three years of one another, and both included truncated images of the female body. Both images depicted a headless and limbless body, displaying only the woman's breasts and her open abdomen with a detailed depiction of her internal parts.[57] These images were essentially abbreviated versions of the lifelike images that appeared in other publications, but by focusing solely on the torso and the contents of the abdomen they were able to emphasize the anatomical interest of the figure over the woman's aesthetic appeal or sense of human subjectivity. Although the woman's head and limbs were cut off in these images, the presence of her high, round breasts and shapely shoulders gestured to the same aesthetic of female beauty found in the more complete images and indicated to the viewer that the anatomized figure represented the body of a once-animate woman. These truncated images also appeared in seventeenth-century texts such as Culpeper's midwifery

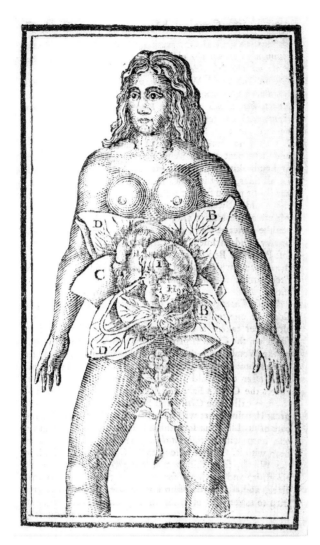

FIGURE 1.1
From Jane Sharp,
*The Compleat
Midwife's
Companion* (1724).
Courtesy of the
Wellcome Library.

manual and the treatise by the French obstetrician François Mauriceau, whose work was translated into several languages and frequently referenced.[58]

Alongside the lifelike and truncated images of the female body, a few of these early medical writers also included detailed images of anatomical fragments such as the uterus, ovaries, and vaginal canal, indicative of an increasingly precise vision of the internal body. These illustrations pictured female reproductive anatomy as detached from the woman's body, but they almost always appeared alongside more complete renditions of the female body. Rueff's midwifery text, for instance, included the image of the whole woman discussed above as well as separate magnified images of the uterus and surrounding parts.[59] Similarly, Mauriceau provided images of the truncated female body with the abdomen open to reveal her inner organs, and he also included multiple enlarged illustrations of these organs with carefully labeled sections.[60] These illustrations of specific organs added a further scientific dimension, indicating that the author's authority as a medical practitioner derived from his precise scrutiny of the internal body via the practice of dissection. Yet virtually all of these authors provided at least some images that presented the female body as more than simply a dissected uterus.

Thus medical writers emerging in the eighteenth century had a range of prior models from which to draw inspiration for their own illustrations. They could choose to depict the female body in a way that paired the study of anatomy with a lifelike figure of a woman, offering not only anatomical knowledge but also an aesthetically appealing (and perhaps titillating) female form. They could also choose to depict a more fragmented female body, either a truncated figure of a woman or precise diagrams of organs that were disconnected from the rest of the body. The new professional man-midwives of the mid-eighteenth century, then, inherited a well-developed visual vocabulary for depicting the female form, but they ultimately took their anatomical illustrations in new directions.

By the second half of the eighteenth century, prominent British practitioners such as William Smellie, William Hunter, Charles Jenty, and James Hamilton were at the forefront of the new specialty of midwifery and were working to take the study of female reproductive anatomy to new heights of precision.[61] In their anatomical illustrations the figure of the woman disappeared entirely, to be replaced by precise, at times almost photographic, renditions of the pelvis and the reproductive organs. This manner of representing the female body was not restricted to midwifery texts. General anatomies also moved away from representing the whole female body, offering only illustrations of the reproductive organs. Whereas the animated male skeletons and flayed figures that walked and gesticulated across the pages of early atlases like those of Vesalius and Estienne continued to appear in anatomy texts into the nineteenth century, their lively female counterparts largely disappeared. In short, the male body continued to enjoy a range of representations, while the female body was reduced to a pelvis and a collection of reproductive organs. For specialists in midwifery, the new single-minded focus on women's reproductive parts allowed them to present a more sophisticated visual understanding of the mechanics of conception, pregnancy, and childbirth. Moreover, the practice of dissection and the anatomical illustrations that resulted offered a less fraught way to interact with the female body. Man-midwives could hardly be accused of sexual impropriety when the female body was cut into pieces that bore little resemblance to a living woman.

William Smellie published an anatomical atlas in 1754 that was one of the first to focus exclusively on the female body. Smellie's text exemplified a single-minded emphasis on the internal body by envisioning the female body as a series of disconnected and neatly presented parts. The first edition of his atlas included thirty-nine plates, but not one of the illustrations so much as gestured to the presence of a complete and lifelike woman. Instead, Smellie first turned his focus to the form and dimensions of the pelvis, which he represented visually in isolation from the rest of the body and without reference to the skeleton as a whole. Smellie and his contemporaries saw knowledge of the shape and dimensions of the pelvis as crucial for understanding the mechanics of childbirth and for identifying potentially problematic deliveries. The other illustrations primarily consisted of depictions of the different positions of the fetus in the uterus and in the process of delivery.[62] Taken together, these illustrations dissociated childbirth from the body of the mother. For Smellie, childbirth involved the pelvis, the uterus, the fetus, and the man-midwife. These illustrations turned childbirth into a mechanical process facilitated by a man-midwife with precise anatomical knowledge, rather than a social experience involving interactions among a laboring woman, her female companions, and the female midwife. In effect, these illustrations suggested that childbirth had very little to do with the woman herself. She provided the necessary parts, but thereafter did not have a significant or visible role to play in the delivery drama.

William Hunter, another renowned British anatomist and accoucheur, followed Smellie with his own anatomical atlas two decades later. *The Anatomy of the Human Gravid Uterus* included thirty-four nearly life-size illustrations by the artist Jan van Rymsdyk, who had done many of the original images for Smellie's atlas as well as the illustrations for Charles Jenty's 1757 dissections of a pregnant cadaver.[63] Hunter's atlas was massive in scale, an expensive and beautiful work of both science and art, and it came to dominate the field. Simultaneously beautiful and gruesome, the fragments of female anatomy were photographic in their realism, revealing the texture of flesh and the full shape of the pregnant uterus. One illustration,

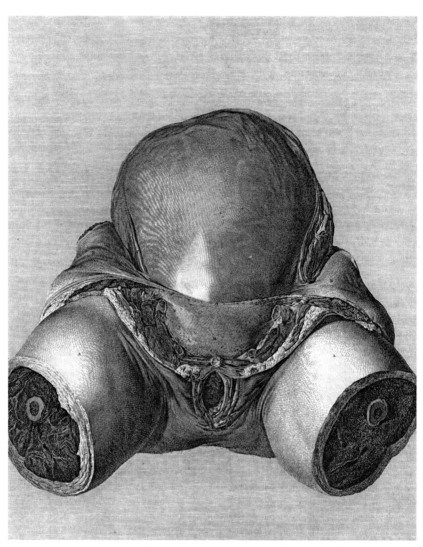

FIGURE 1.2 From William Hunter, *The Anatomy of the Human Gravid Uterus* (1774). Courtesy of the Wellcome Library.

for instance, invited the viewer to peer between the severed thighs of a cadaver and see the surface of the pregnant uterus rising high above the woman's genitals (see fig. 1.2).[64] Hunter's images emphasized the process of dissection by showing the severed stumps of the legs and the flesh of the abdomen as if just peeled away from the uterus. Although some of Hunter's illustrations revealed the shape of the cadaver's buttocks and upper thighs as well as offering close-up images of her genitalia, the fragmented nature of these images made it hard to imagine them as part of a living woman, much less one with the potential to elicit male desire or evince desires of her own. By reducing the maternal body to scientifically useful pieces, Hunter simultaneously highlighted his own authority as a preeminent anatomist and man-midwife and presented a desexualized and scientific vision of the female body.

A slightly later anatomical text by James Hamilton, a professor at the University of Edinburgh, followed in the footsteps of Smellie and Hunter and expanded in some respects the disembodied nature of the reproductive parts. Hamilton copied a number of his images directly from both Smellie and Hunter. His goal, as he explained in his preface, was to present anatomical illustrations on a smaller and therefore cheaper scale than Smellie's or Hunter's publications so that more students and practitioners could have access to the information. Like his predecessors, he began with the structure of the pelvis so that practitioners could understand the mechanics of delivery, and then he included a number of illustrations of the fetus in various positions in the uterus. Finally, he offered illustrations based on dissections of specific organs, including the uterus and the vagina, as well as a diagram of the vascular system of the reproductive organs. In most respects, these illustrations were not noticeably different in content from those in previous atlases, but Hamilton's images went a little further by avoiding recognizable external body parts, such as the thighs or the external genitalia, in almost all of his illustrations. Whereas both Smellie and Hunter presented several images in which the viewer was allowed to peer directly between the splayed thighs of the cadaver, only one of Hamilton's illustrations did this, and it was borrowed from Hunter. Moreover, Hamilton's illustration of the uterus was entirely dissociated from any reference to the rest of the female body. Whereas Hunter included an image of the uterus taken partially out of the abdomen and hanging between a faint sketch of thighs and vulva, Hamilton's illustration depicted the uterus suspended alone on a blank page.[65]

The works of these prominent British anatomists were influential at the time they were published and continued to be referenced and copied well into the nineteenth century. Samuel Bard, for instance, published the first American midwifery textbook in 1807 and copied images from Smellie and others. These mid-eighteenth-century British anatomists provided a new visual vocabulary for depicting the female reproductive body as a scientific specimen rather than as a lifelike figure. They presented their interactions with the pelvis, the uterus, and the fetus, not the woman, therefore there could be no reason to suspect man-midwives of unwarranted intimacy with their patients. In essence, the illustrations in eighteenth-century anatomical texts replaced the social interactions of childbirth with scientific ones, rendering the question of sexual impropriety less urgent.

. . . . . .

As anatomical illustrations shifted emphasis toward the internal female reproductive parts in the mid-eighteenth century, the focus of written medical descriptions also turned inward. Practitioners such as William Smellie and his contemporaries were at first particularly entranced by their growing knowledge of the pelvis, a part that had received little attention in sixteenth- and seventeenth-century manuals. Whereas earlier authors such as Jane Sharp and Nicholas Culpeper had begun their texts with discussions of the sexual organs, mid-eighteenth-century practitioners such as Smellie, John Burton, and Thomas Denman began their treatises with lengthy discussions of the dimensions of the pelvis, followed by generally shorter discussions of the uterus.[66] These practitioners saw the pelvis as the foundational structure in childbirth. They pictured childbirth as a mechanical process and the pelvis as the frame that held the machine together. A well-formed pelvis allowed childbirth to proceed smoothly, while a malformed pelvis (often the result of rickets) brought suffering, medical intervention, and the risk of death for the woman and her infant. This focus on the pelvis set the model for subsequent midwifery texts.

At the beginning of the nineteenth century, however, medical writers began to display a growing interest in the nature of the uterus, and it soon became a central character in medical narratives, an organ with a personality and agency of its own. Unlike the pelvis, which was portrayed as a static frame, the uterus gained a startling degree of power as medical writers began to adopt new language and grammatical patterns. The uterus became the grammatical subject of strong verbs—the womb seemed to *do* a great deal and often appeared imperious or uncontrollable. In their descriptions and in the grammatical structure of their sentences, medical writers began to replace the agency and subjectivity of the mother with that of her womb. In consequence, the labor of the uterus replaced the labor of the mother, making the woman an unnecessary appendage to the process of childbirth.

The idea that the womb was an overbearing and somewhat uncontrollable character in its own right was not new. From antiquity at least through the nineteenth century, the uterus emerged and reemerged in different contexts, being of particular interest to medical men and to philosophers busy pondering the nature of woman and man. Hippocrates had theorized that the womb wandered, raging up and down the body in disappointment and anger when it was not pregnant.[67] Later medical writers rejected the idea that the uterus could actually travel throughout the body but continued to view it as the primary feature of interest in female anatomy. In their eyes, the womb was what distinguished woman from man. It made her anatomically different, it allowed her to reproduce, and it shaped her mind and behavior.

Ideas about the uterus were closely linked to broader cultural trends, and therefore changing views of the female body often reflected larger debates about gender, sexuality, power, religion, and even politics. Mary Fissell, for instance, has argued that the shift to Protestantism in sixteenth-century England transformed ideas about the uterus. Previously, vernacular culture in Catholic England tended to link the female reproductive body to notions of divinity through the figure of the Virgin Mary. English women and men saw the womb as a marvelous organ that participated in the divine work of procreation. But in the seventeenth century the womb "went bad," and English writers emphasized its chaotic properties, including its propensity for producing monsters.[68]

During the period of the Enlightenment, the image of the womb as a fierce and troublesome entity enjoyed even greater attention. The eighteenth century was an era of ideological upheaval in which ideas about the nature of men and women were debated and reconfigured. One of the paradoxes of the Enlightenment was that proclamations of natural human equality went hand in hand with a philosophy of sexual difference that radically divided women and men by highlighting intellectual, moral, and physical difference. Scientific and philosophical debates about woman's nature took center stage beginning in the mid-eighteenth century. Influential Enlightenment thinkers, inspired by a sentimental vision of nature, recast female identity as being rooted in women's reproductive organs.[69]

This philosophical preoccupation with the uterus was not yet mirrored in the midwifery literature of the eighteenth century. Although practitioners of midwifery—those who were most interested in the womb—began to offer more precise descriptions of the reproductive organs, few attributed particular power or agency to the uterus. Their writings tended to focus on precise anatomical description, with few subjective evaluations of the character of different organs. William Smellie, for instance, described the size, shape, and components of the uterus at length, but essentially viewed it as a container like the pelvis, except that the uterus "contracts itself and grows thicker" during labor.[70] John Burton was more enthusiastic than most of his contemporaries; writing in 1751, he described the womb as the "great Nursery of Mankind . . . which may very justly be said, With Regard to its Substance and Structure, to be as extraordinary a Piece of Mechanism as any in the whole Body."[71] Burton expressed a sense of wonder at the functions of the uterus, but did not describe the uterus as particularly powerful or possessing any agency of its own. Charles White noted the ability of the uterus to contract itself, but did not seem to find this ability particularly impressive. Moreover, in his midwifery treatise from 1773, he described natural labor as a combined effort between woman and womb. "After the child is expelled in this gradual manner by the force of the woman's pains," he wrote, "the womb by degrees contracts itself."[72] Here, the woman (grammatically) possessed the pains needed to expel the fetus, while the womb then worked to return to its usual shape. Each character—the woman and her womb—was an active subject in its own way. Thomas Denman seemed more impressed than either Smellie or White with the ability of the uterus to contract during labor. He explained that "it does not seem reasonable to attribute the extraordinary action of the uterus at the time of labour to its muscular fibres only . . . unless it is presumed, that those of the uterus are stronger than in common muscles."[73] Denman posited that there must be something special about the uterus that gave it its physical strength, but it was a question that did not seem significant enough for him to dwell on. For the most part, these eighteenth-century authors gave the uterus (mechanically and grammatically) the power to contract itself, but beyond this it was presented primarily as an object of their anatomical descriptions rather than a subject of its own actions.

In this respect, the uterus was not unlike other organs. Other medical texts in the eighteenth century began to describe with new precision the functions of parts such as the heart, the brain, or the nerves. Medicine became increasingly specialized, with some practitioners focusing on particular diseases, organs, or systems within the body, which was always presumed to be male unless presented in the context of reproduction. The Scottish physician Matthew Baillie, for example, was instrumental in advancing the study of pathology in the late eighteenth century, while the anatomist Charles Bell was renowned for his treatise on the brain and the nervous system, which included detailed illustrations of the anatomy of the brain.[74] In spite of this greater specialization, these medical writings did not imply that a particular organ or process dominated men. The male body was a mechanism with a wide range of components, each with its own role in the system, but none of these single-handedly defined men's subjectivity, behavior, or social roles in the way that the womb defined women.

By the end of the eighteenth century some medical writers began to hint at a growing interest in and a changing perception of the uterus. The Scottish practitioner John Burns signaled a new interest in the womb when he wrote, "I cannot, then, be wrong in maintaining, that the anatomy of the gravid uterus is the very foundation of the art of midwifery."[75] Writing around the same time as Burns, the English midwife Martha Mears hinted at a more extravagant view of the uterus and its powers. She explained with palpable awe that the uterus "has another property, which appears directly opposed to all reasoning on mechanical principles: it does not grow thinner in proportion to its greater stretch, but retrains its thickness through the whole period, to whatever degree it may be distended. *Here our inquiries are for a moment lost in admiration*" (my emphasis). Mears drew her readers' attention to the ability of the uterus to flout mechanical principles (things that are stretched grow thinner). She also highlighted the womb's physical power, writing that "the *human* womb is capable of exerting infinitely greater power, for the expulsion of its contents, than that of any other living creature."[76]

Nineteenth-century medical writers adopted a similar sense of wonderment in their depictions of the uterus, but pushed their descriptions of its powers considerably further. Marie François Xavier Bichat, a French anatomist whose works were translated into English and printed in both Britain and America, described each organ as having an independent life of its own, but then seemed to suggest that the uterus possessed special powers, claiming that "it might be said that the contractile power of the womb has been formed at the expense of the forces of all the other organs." He explained that other organs in women's bodies, such as the heart and the stomach, gave weaker responses than men's organs in experimental situations, suggesting that the womb took more than its fair share of strength from the system as a whole.[77]

Not only was the uterus physically powerful, but medical writers began to give it an impressive degree of agency. Moreover, the early nineteenth century saw the publication of the first American midwifery texts, and these authors seemed to be particularly vociferous in their depictions of the powerful uterus, perhaps as a way of strengthening the importance of the relatively new professional field of midwifery in America. William

Dewees, the first physician in America to offer a full course on the practice of obstetrics, wrote in 1806 that "we cannot fail being struck with the various resources [the uterus] seems to possess, and the wonderful order it pursues, to give the greatest possible chance of perfection to the ovum; to secure it against accident; and finally, to cast it off when it can no longer be useful to it."[78] Referring with awe to the resources of the womb and making it the grammatical subject of decisive verbs such as "pursue," "secure," and "cast off," Dewees granted the uterus extraordinary agency. Similarly, Valentine Seaman wrote in his lectures to New York midwives in 1800, "At the end of the thirty-ninth week [of pregnancy], the womb, from some unaccountable law of nature, exerts itself to get rid of its contents." The active subject of his description was the uterus itself, which had the power and initiative to "exert itself." Furthermore, Seaman's description of labor focused on the actions of the womb rather than on the laboring mother. He explained that after the birth of the fetus, "the womb, having now got rid of so great a proportion of its contents, generally is free from pain for a little while."[79] Here the womb, not the woman, was the subject that experienced pain. The American physician Samuel Bard described the process of natural labor as controlled by the womb: "The womb first begins to contract at the fundus, and hence that subsidence of the belly, which denotes the approach of labour, and proves not only that the womb has begun to act, but that it is prepared to act in a favorable manner."[80] Thus writers such as Dewees, Seaman, and Bard framed their descriptions in such a way that the uterus became the primary agent in childbearing. As the English physician Francis Ramsbotham asserted, "The principal agent in labour is the uterus itself."[81] As a result the mother began to recede into the background of the medical text just as she had disappeared from anatomical illustrations in the mid-eighteenth century.

Although medical writers seemed to marvel at the powers of the uterus, they also betrayed uneasiness. Dewees, for instance, was frustrated by the seemingly mysterious nature of this organ: "There is no organ in the human body, from whose structure so little can be inferred, as the unimpregnated uterus; in it, when laid open by the knife, we see no manifestation of capacity for distention; on the contrary, we observe nothing but dense unyielding walls . . . in it we have no promise of the immense force which it is destined to exert."[82] Unlike the pelvis, which at least had a decipherable structure and could be measured with precision, the uterus, as Dewees saw it, was without clear form and structure, secretive, nothing but dense walls that refused to yield to the probing of science. In pregnancy the form and function of the uterus might become clearer, but it remained a mysterious entity that seemed to conceal its capacity for "immense force."

Physicians also began to portray the uterus as potentially antagonistic to the practitioner. The British physician Samuel Merriman described the uterus as working in opposition to the man-midwife. Explaining when and how the accoucheur should attempt to turn a fetus that was presenting incorrectly, he emphasized that nothing should be attempted as long as the uterus was making strong contractions. He believed the danger of attempting to turn the fetus was greater than the danger of the wrong presentation: "Will there be less hazard in the efforts of the operator to push forward his hand in opposition to the powerful resistance of the uterus?" he asked. "Nay, is not the attempt to introduce the hand likely to excite the uterus to still more inordinate action, and consequently to increase rather than to diminish the danger?"[83] Here, Merriman portrayed the womb as working against the man-midwife and as being incited to greater resistance. He later reiterated the point that it was fruitless and dangerous for the accoucheur to intervene manually "when the uterus opposes so obstinate a resistance."[84] Depicting the womb as powerful, resistant, and obstinate, Merriman seemed to set up an antagonistic relationship between two principal agents: the man-midwife and the uterus. These depictions framed the process of labor as a series of standoffs between these two figures, with the presence of the laboring woman fading away in the face of these confrontations.

The autonomy and power of the uterus were deemed so great that medical writers began to depict it as an imperious and dangerous character. The American physician Charles Meigs, for instance, was emphatic in describing the tyrannical powers of the womb and surrounding reproductive organs, for he wrote that "they are among the most powerful disturbers of the complacency of the organisms. They constitute an imperium in imperio, whose behests are not to be disobeyed. These organs can disturb the brain—the respiration—the digestion—the circulation—the secretions—the nutrition."[85] Here the reproductive organs took on the persona of an imperious ruler whose willful behavior threatened the delicate balance of the body. According to a story recounted by Meigs, this tyrant could also pose a threat to the physician. One day a physician was obliged to insert his hand into the uterus to extract the placenta, and as he did so the cervix closed with such force on his wrist that he could not remove it. "After various unsuccessful attempts to extricate himself from such an unheard-of difficulty," Meigs explained, "he sent for a Bleeder, and, after causing a large quantity of blood to be drawn from the lady's arm, the spasm of the cervix ceased, upon which he was liberated from an imprisonment of two hours. His wrist was marked, as if a cord had been strongly bound round it; the red traces of which impression were visible, even the next day."[86] Such descriptions of the female reproductive organs revealed a profound unease on the part of physicians tasked with the management of the female reproductive body.

Thus, beginning in the nineteenth century physicians took the eighteenth-century emphasis on the interior body a step farther by developing a vision of the uterus as powerful, autonomous, imperious, and potentially antagonistic. As a result, the uterus became the primary agent in reproduction, allowing the woman to become largely invisible and inactive. The labor of the mother seemed to be replaced by the actions and subjectivity of her womb, allowing her to become detached, at least rhetorically, from the messy and dangerous processes of childbearing. Male practitioners were needed to study and manage the obstreperous uterus, thus saving women from almost certain reproductive calamity.

This growing focus on the dangerous and disruptive nature of the uterus revealed that nineteenth-century physicians were increasingly invested in an understanding of reproduction as a pathological process. This had not always been the case. The British physician John Aitken asserted in the late eighteenth century that "parturition, proceeding in the way described, is in every respect an action of health."[87] Some practitioners, like Samuel Bard, continued to view childbearing as a generally natural process. But the trend in the medical profession was to see childbearing as a state of danger and disorder. In his medical notes from 1804 to 1809, for instance, the celebrated Philadelphia physician Benjamin Rush listed pregnancy under the category of pathology.[88] The American Quaker physician Horton Howard noted that "no organ of the female system is perhaps so liable to become diseased, or fail to perform its healthy functions, as the uterus; and hence arise some of the most obstinate and painful maladies to which the sex is liable."[89] Marcia Nichols has argued that by situating women as the victims of their internal organs, physicians were able to represent themselves as the heroes in their own medical narratives.[90] Women were weak and needed to be rescued from the tyrannical womb. As one American physician effused to his fellow practitioners, "On your own resources alone rests the issue of life or death."[91]

But when physicians grappled with the dangers posed to women by their reproductive organs, they were not presuming a universal physiological reality. Instead, they created a close link between their understanding of pathology in childbearing and the concept of civilization. Physicians believed that women whose lifestyles they perceived as primitive did not suffer the same pain and danger in childbirth as "refined" or "civilized" women, nor did lower-class women whose access to the refinements of so-called civilized life were limited. Ultimately, medical writers came to associate purportedly primitive and unrefined women with a robust corporeality, while refined women were represented as generally noncorporeal, their wombs taking over the work of childbearing while they disappeared from the medical text. Ultimately, physicians made it clear that the mother who needed their care throughout the process of childbearing was white and socioeconomically privileged.

The idea that civilization shaped women's experience of reproduction was not new, nor was it unique to the medical profession. Almost as soon as European travelers came into contact with people in Africa and the Americas, they took note of different practices surrounding pregnancy and childbirth. Observing that African and Native American women often did agricultural work while pregnant and returned to work shortly after childbearing, they concluded that these allegedly savage women suffered little in childbirth. This observation allowed them to differentiate Christian women (those who suffered from the curse of Eve) from African and Native American women, whose bodies could be exploited for productive and reproductive labor because they were deemed so robust.[92] The eighteenth-century Scottish explorer Sir Alexander Mackenzie, for instance, observed of the "Chepewyan" Indians of North America that "child-birth is not the object of that tender care and serious attention among the savages as it is among civilized people. At this period no part of their usual occupation is omitted, and this continual and regular exercise must contribute to the welfare of the mother, both in the progress of parturition and in the moment of delivery."[93] Many European observers saw such women as healthier and closer to nature and assumed that their supposedly primitive ways of life made them more robust and therefore less in need of protection and consideration.

What Mackenzie and other European observers did not consider, of course, was the different cultural contexts in which women in different societies gave birth. In a study of Native American communities in eastern Canada and New England, for instance, Ann Marie Plane has proposed that Indian women may have deemphasized the pain of childbirth because they were part of a culture that respected women and men for bearing pain and suffering without complaint.[94] Moreover, in many Native American societies the maternal body was viewed as powerful and life-giving, a site of pride and authority rather than weakness and despair.[95] Such beliefs may have shaped the attitudes with which Indian women anticipated and experienced childbirth. Yet, rather than consider the variety of beliefs and practices surrounding childbirth, observers such as Mackenzie assumed that Indian women experienced childbirth differently because of their purportedly primitive nature. The way women experienced childbearing thus became a measure of their degree of civilization.

Many eighteenth-century medical writers agreed that there was a clear difference between childbearing in European society and in societies that were allegedly closer to the state of nature. But these writers tended to attribute the problems of "refined" women to individual mismanagement rather than viewing reproduction itself as fundamentally pathological. As the Scottish physician William Buchan wrote in 1769, the norms of elite European society kept women indoors and in restrictive clothing, causing their bodies to be weakened by excessive refinement: "The confinement of females, besides hurting their figure and complexion, relaxes their solids, weakens their minds, and disorders all the functions of the body." He praised the robustness of milkmaids in the English countryside and claimed that "we seldom find a barren woman among the laboring poor, while nothing is more common among the rich and affluent."[96] Charles White concurred, describing how smoothly childbirth would go for a "straight healthy young woman, who had never suffered from improper dress, inactivity, or unwholesome diet."[97] Essentially, these physicians blamed difficult childbearing on lifestyle choices made by refined women with respect to habits such as diet, exercise, and clothing. These lifestyle choices marked them as physically deficient, but also worthy of special consideration.

By the early nineteenth century some physicians began to argue that reproduction had become a fundamentally pathological process, no longer solely a matter of individual behavior. Civilization had changed women's bodies, and not for the better. In his essay on the treatment of pain in childbirth, William Dewees claimed that "however easy the act of Child-bearing may be among savage tribes and certain individuals in various states of society, we find it among others an operation of great pain and frequent danger."[98] More particularly, Dewees thought that labor contractions would not be painful were it not for "some change which the muscular fibre has undergone from civilization, refinement, or disease."[99] Moreover, he insisted that "a number of circumstances must concur that a woman carry her child to the full period of utero-gestation, and then give birth to it with the least possible trouble and risk." There were so many conditions necessary for a natural delivery that Dewees deemed problems to be inevitable.[100] By the nineteenth century most of the medical profession agreed that elite women suffered more in childbearing than previously.[101] Refinement had so weakened the bodies of succeeding generations that they could no longer cope with the powerful functions of the uterus.

Although American physicians in the South treated enslaved women when complications arose, and both British and American practitioners often delivered the babies of the urban poor in hospitals, nineteenth-century medical texts nevertheless assumed that the normative patient was an affluent white woman whose weak body required their ministrations. Physicians' differentiation of civilized and uncivilized women exposed how integral notions of race and class were to their understanding of the reproductive body. Physicians assumed that pain was felt differently by refined women, and refined women were by definition white and socioeconomically privileged. Although physicians expressed a certain admiration for the allegedly natural reproductive powers of "savage," rural, or working women, they nevertheless envisioned their work as benefiting refined women, who in their view both required and merited greater concern. These white women needed to be rescued from civilized debility. Pain and pathology thus became markers of social worth and privilege.

More importantly, by linking pain and pathology to notions of civilization, medical writers opened the way for the use of nonwhite and nonelite women's bodies in the development of gynecology and obstetrics. These women were believed to be sturdier and more resistant to suffering; medical men saw them as closer to nature, more like animals and therefore less chaste, so that their bodies could be manipulated by physicians with little impropriety. The American physician Samuel Gregory, for instance, complained that practitioners took greater liberties with lower-class patients, so "there is often too much officiousness and freedom for the physical welfare of the patient, and the moral good of patient, practitioner, and female assistants."[102] He feared that physicians' lack of respect for lower-class women's moral delicacy could compromise practitioners as well as the women in their care. In addition, a great deal of pioneering work in gynecology was done by physicians in the American South because they had ready access to black women's bodies. And, as with the physicians Gregory complained about, they did not feel many scruples about violating the feminine delicacy of their patients. Many of the surgeries and treatments that became routine in obstetrics and gynecology during the second half of the nineteenth century were first practiced on enslaved women in the antebellum South. Marie Jenkins Schwartz has argued that enslaved women's bodies were integral to nineteenth-century medical progress because physicians could operate more boldly and even recklessly on black bodies than on white ones. When gynecological problems occurred, slaveholders had a vested interest in taking extreme measures to restore a woman's reproductive capacity. On the other hand, when a woman's organs were so debilitated as to render reproduction impossible, her body was devalued and therefore became a suitable subject for medical experimentation. Similarly, Deirdre Cooper Owens has argued that impoverished women in northern American cities, often immigrants, came to hospitals to be delivered and treated and in so doing provided needed subjects for medical training and experimentation in the North.[103]

One of the most important examples of the use of women's bodies in medical experimentation was in the work of the American physician James Marion Sims. Sims became renowned for his innovations in gynecological surgery, including the development of a surgical repair for vesicovaginal fistula, a devastating condition that could result from prolonged labors during which the tissue of the vagina was weakened and torn. In his autobiography he recalled his frustration at receiving a number of patients who suffered from this condition, which he deemed utterly incurable. It was not until a chance discovery prompted him to operate repeatedly on several enslaved women that he developed a successful surgical technique. As he later wrote, "I made this proposition to the owners of the negroes: If you will give me Anarcha and Betsey for experiment, I agree to perform no experiment or operation on either of them to endanger their lives, and will not charge a cent for keeping them."[104] His success depended on repeated experimentation without, as he noted, the benefit of anesthesia. Anarcha endured thirty operations over the course of four years, from 1845 to 1849, when Sims finally achieved a cure.[105]

Sims's medical techniques and writings revealed important differences in his handling of black and white female patients. He described two different moments with patients that gave him clues as to how to develop his surgical techniques. One of the first moments that prompted Sims's quest for a surgical cure involved an examination of a poor but "respectable" white woman with a prolapsed uterus. Placing the patient on her knees, covered from sight by a large sheet, Sims inserted one finger to touch the uterus, then introduced his entire hand in an effort to restore the uterus to its proper position, discovering that the vagina and uterus could be opened up in a way that would allow for surgical work.[106] This moment of discovery emphasized the act of "touching" the patient, an approved medical technique for examining the internal organs that was extensively described in medical texts beginning in the eighteenth century.[107] The practice of touching allowed physicians to interact with the female body in a way that preserved modesty by touching only the internal parts, allowing the external (and potentially appealing) female body to remain invisible.

Sims's next discovery occurred in a different way and highlighted sight and the manipulation of the external body. He and two of his students examined an enslaved woman suffering from a vaginal tear. "I got a table about three feet long," Sims later narrated, "and put a coverlet upon it, and mounted her on the table, on her knees, with her head resting on the palms of her hands. I placed the two students one on each side of the pelvis, and they laid hold of the nates [buttocks], and pulled them open."[108] This anecdote reveals important differences from the one featuring the "respectable" white woman. First, while the white patient was covered entirely by a sheet, no such courtesy seemed to be afforded the enslaved woman, who was instead "mounted" onto the table in full view of at least three men. The sight of the female body was problematic in ways that appropriate medical touching was not. Touching focused on information that could be gathered from the internal parts of the body, while sight could take in the external body—breasts, hips, buttocks, thighs, and genitals—that might inspire a more prurient interest in the female form. Second, two assistants were present to manipulate the body of the patient by grasping her buttocks, an act that did not qualify as part of proper touching. Thus, by being exposed to the sight and grasping hands of male practitioners, the body of the enslaved woman was subjected to different treatment, both in the moment and in Sims's textual depictions of the events. Such treatment emphasized her corporeality, while her race and status precluded any claim she might have made to feminine modesty.

The notions of pathology and civilization that were promulgated in nineteenth-century medical texts perpetuated physicians' drive to master the perceived disorder of the internal female body. The refined woman needed to be rescued from her imperious uterus by the heroism of the man-midwife. But these assumptions about the pathology of childbearing permitted and even encouraged the exploitation of enslaved and impoverished women for the development of medical techniques. Their bodies were assumed to be stronger and able to handle the pain of childbearing with ease. They were also assumed to be less chaste, so that male physicians could manipulate their bodies without fear of violating feminine modesty. This meant that the bodies of these women could be used to develop medical techniques intended primarily to benefit the refined women perceived by male physicians to be at risk of being overwhelmed by their reproductive organs.

· · · · · ·

As the womb became the dominant character in medical illustrations and descriptions over the course of the late eighteenth century and into the nineteenth century, the ultimate result was that the labor of the mother in the process of childbearing was written out of midwifery texts. This was particularly striking in descriptions of childbirth. Childbirth was a profoundly embodied experience, and women saw it as a test of their ability to endure pain, fatigue, and fear. But for male practitioners, childbirth was the moment when mother and man-midwife were forced to occupy the same real and textual space in intimate and troubling ways. For the sake of modesty and sexual propriety, physicians had to disguise the female body when it was at its most active, keeping the laboring mother's flesh covered from sight at all times and effacing the work of her body in the process. In midwifery texts the refined mother did not labor—the physician and the uterus did the work for her. Erasing the mother from the scene of childbirth, both textually and in their encounters with birthing women, helped physicians do their work without the risk of sexual impropriety.

Even in the nineteenth century, when man-midwives had been delivering the babies of elite women for decades, concerns about modesty, female delicacy, and propriety resurfaced regularly. In the mid-eighteenth century the outspoken English midwife Elizabeth Nihell had expressed concern that man-midwives might take advantage of their ready access to women's "secrets." She wrote that "a skill in what we call the *Touching*, is not to be acquired without a frequent habit of recourse to the sexual parts whence the indications are taken," and she feared that men would become addicted to the practice.[109] Writers in the nineteenth century perpetuated Nihell's concerns. John Steven presented an entire work to the Society for the Suppression of Vice in which he evaluated the history of man-midwifery and labeled it a profound moral evil, blaming its origins on the "luxury and lewdness" of the French courts.[110] Thomas Ewell, an American physician, was deeply concerned about the risk of seduction in the lying-in chamber and asserted that his purpose in writing was to "wrest the practice of midwifery from the hands of men, and to transfer it to women, as it was in the beginning, and ever should be."[111] The American practitioner George Gregory likewise railed against man-midwifery, inquiring, "What is it but a vast system of legalized prostitution?"[112] In general, concerned practitioners and laypeople agreed that male self-restraint could not always be relied upon and that the woman in childbed was uniquely vulnerable. As the American physician Wooster Beach put it, "The great intimacy and confidence which exist between the physician and the patient, gives the most unbounded liberties and temptations to the unprincipled and licentious to alienate their affections from their husbands."[113] He went on to cite examples of adultery resulting from conquests in the lying-in room, making the link between man-midwifery and sexual misconduct appear indubitable. Such concerns may sound a bit hysterical, but there was occasional anecdotal evidence to suggest that sexual impropriety did sometimes intrude on the sanctity of the birthing chamber. One young southern physician who was attending a young white woman in labor reported that she "imprinted on my lips a voluptuous kiss which shot through my system like electricity."[114] For many, both physicians and laypeople, the potential intimacy of the physician-patient relationship carried real danger.

Based on what we have seen of medical representations of the reproductive female body prior to the professionalization of midwifery, it is not surprising that the mother was more visible and active in early descriptions of childbirth than in later periods. Thomas Raynalde's sixteenth-century manual, for instance, described in detail the actions of a woman in labor. He recommended that "it shall be very profitable for her, for the space of an houre to sit still, then (rising again) to go up and down a pair of stairs crying and reaching so loud as she can, so to stir her self." In his text the laboring woman was loud and active; she kept herself moving and straining to make sure the labor progressed. After she had bestirred herself awhile, he recommended that "also it shall be very good for a time, to retain and keep in her breath, for because through that means, the guts and intrails be thrust together and depressed downward."[115] The woman's physical strength and her agency in deciding when to move, when to rest, and when to hold her breath were essential to the progress of the labor. When the final stage of labor began, Raynalde explained that the mother needed a pallet bed: there she could lie with legs splayed and feet pressed against something solid, shoulders held by two female assistants, breath held and body straining. In this vision of labor the mother was physically strong and fully present, both physically and mentally, in the work of giving birth.[116]

Writing in the late seventeenth century, the English midwife Jane Sharp offered a similarly active description of labor. She explained that "when the Patient feels her Throws coming she should walk easily in her Chamber, and then again lie down, keep her self warm, rest her self and then stir again, till she feels the Waters coming down and the womb to open." The woman's movements were essential to the progress of the labor. Sharp insisted, "Let her not lie long a Bed, yet she may lie sometimes and sleep to strengthen her, and to abate pain, the Child will be the stronger."[117] In Sharp's vision, the laboring woman's activities were not only essential for her own safety by promoting a prompt delivery, but they also enhanced the strength and well-being of the child that was about to be born. Moreover, in Sharp's descriptions the mother was subject to her own authority; she needed to notice the way her body felt and make her own decisions about when to rest and when to move. The functions of the body might be disruptive and messy, but early medical authors did not shy away from describing the mother as active and authoritative, with a body whose labor was at the center of the drama.

With the professionalization of midwifery in the mid-eighteenth century, these descriptions of the active and embodied mother began to fade, though this transition was neither immediate nor complete. In William Smellie's midwifery treatise from 1752, for instance, the scene of the birthing chamber with the woman walking, crying out, marching up and down stairs, or straining on a pallet bed disappeared in favor of a more minute examination of the internal process of labor. Yet even in Smellie's text, the woman's presence and agency did not entirely vanish. In first describing the onset of labor, Smellie explained that the gradual dilation of the cervix created an "uneasy sensation; to alleviate which, the woman squeezes her *Uterus*, by contracting the abdominal muscles, and at the same time filling the lungs with air." As a result of the woman's actions, "the waters and membranes are squeezed against the *Os Uteri*, which is, of consequence, a little more opened."[118] Thus in Smellie's depiction the deliberate actions of the woman advanced the process of labor. But soon the woman began to recede from his descriptions. Smellie noted that after contracting her muscles, the laboring woman became fatigued by pain and effort and allowed her muscles to relax for a short time until "the compression of the womb again takes place, and the internal mouth is a little more dilated."[119] This time, the compression of the womb seemingly took place without the deliberate action of the woman—it simply happened.

Other eighteenth-century writers followed this pattern. The Scottish practitioner Alexander Hamilton explained that during labor "the child advances, and by the astonishing expulsive force of the womb, assisted by the midriff and muscles of the belly, is thus ushered into the world."[120] The womb performed most of the work, and Hamilton made no mention of the woman's efforts to contract her muscles or to position her body in such a way as to advance the process. The British practitioner John Aitken likewise described labor as something apart from the woman herself. Yet he also paused in his description to note that "the mother's cries, during this event, are exceedingly strong, expressive of the racking anguish she suffers."[121] Thus in many midwifery texts from the second half of the eighteenth century the mother was not entirely forgotten, though her role in labor became increasingly unclear. Writers repeatedly described labor as a process that happened *to* the woman, rather than making her actions part of the process.

There were some exceptions to this pattern. Charles White, for instance, did not give the mother much agency in the process of childbirth, but he did make her an animated presence in the lying-in room. He generally recommended to practitioners a noninterventionist approach, placing his faith in the natural process of labor. Accordingly, he explained that he never confined his patients to bed during labor, but allowed them to walk around or lie down as they saw fit. Describing the ideal natural labor, White explained how the mother "would for some time walk about, then sit down to rest, then rise and walk again, till for her own ease, and the safety of the child, she would find it necessary to lie down. During this time the mouth of the womb would be gradually opening."[122] Thus in White's depiction the mother performed little physical work in the process of labor, but she was present and participated in managing herself during the long process. In a similar vein, Thomas Denman explained that the accoucheur should pay attention to the sounds the laboring mother made in order to know where she was in the stages of labor. As he insisted, "The expressions of pain uttered by women in the act of parturition may be considered as complete indications of the state of the process, so that an experienced practitioner is often as fully master of the state of the patient, if he hears her expressions, as by any mode of examination."[123] Thus Denman encouraged practitioners to be attentive to the experience of the laboring woman rather than focus solely on the internal mechanisms of labor. This was an approach that the anti-interventionist physician Samuel Bard would continue to promote in the early nineteenth century, but most nineteenth-century writers would erase even this small role for the mother in their writings.

As the profession of man-midwifery continued to grow and physicians were more regularly called upon to assist even uncomplicated deliveries, medical writers developed increasingly specific recommendations for medical practice that were intended to preserve female delicacy even during the messiness of childbirth. The dilemma of employing male midwives could be mitigated if the female body could be removed, or at least hidden, from the gaze of the male practitioner. By the nineteenth century, some physicians became especially insistent in their discussions of how man-midwives should conduct themselves so as to assist patients with propriety. William Dewees, for instance, taught that all examinations should be done by touch rather than sight, preferably in a darkened room. "The slightest exposure is never necessary," he cautioned.[124] The practice of touching focused on examining the internal body with the first two fingers of the right hand, allowing the physician to monitor the birth process while still maintaining some sense of separation from the woman herself, who was thoroughly covered. Although physicians were allowed to use the touch to gain information about the progress of labor, Dewees insisted that they "beware of officious and unnecessary touching."[125] The American practitioner Joseph Warrington's *Obstetric Catechism* epitomized concerns about improper practice by delineating in great detail the procedure for a blind examination:

> Q: What arrangements should be made in order to conduct the examination most satisfactorily?
> A: The room should be darkened, and the patient lightly dressed, and placed in the suitable position . . .
> Q: What is the rule for carrying the hand under the coverings?
> A: The clothes should be properly raised at their lower edges, by the left hand, and then the right hand with the index finger lubricated, passed cautiously up under the clothes without uncovering the patient.[126]

These medical writers signaled that the sight of the female body was problematic, even during a medical examination. It was the external female body—the shapely limbs, breasts, and soft flesh—that was potentially desirable and titillating, not the internal reproductive parts that anatomists studied with scientific detachment. Thus physicians could examine their laboring patients with propriety as long as they used the utmost caution and consideration. Moreover, the practice of touching made the agency and subjectivity of the mother unnecessary. The physician did not need to listen to the tone of her cries or to ask her questions to ascertain which stage of labor she was enduring. Instead, he had an approved medical technique that would allow him to gather that information in such a way that he could evade the very presence of the laboring woman and instead consult her cervix and uterus. Thus medical knowledge could become detached from the dubious social context of the birthing room.

The birthing positions that physicians prescribed also mitigated their encounters with the body of the mother during delivery. Most British and American practitioners recommended positioning the laboring mother on her left side with knees drawn up. This was quite different from the position described by Raynalde, with the woman bracing herself with her feet against the foot of a sturdy pallet bed. But this side position saved the physician the discomfort of gazing between the spread thighs of a woman. French physicians, as these writers often noted with a hint of disapproval, generally favored delivery with the woman on her back with thighs spread. The American physician Valentine Seaman recommended that the mother "should be properly supported by some of her *female friends*, a few of whom are always welcome companions upon such occasions, not only on account of the assistance they afford in enabling her to bear her pains to more advantage, but also as their cheerful conversation supports her spirits, and inspires her with confidence."[127] The only bodies that could with propriety touch and support the mother in her time of crisis were those of her female attendants. The physician might be allowed carefully to insert his fingers in order to gather information from her internal parts, but the women could use their own bodies to bolster her strength and confidence during labor. As the historian Laurel Thatcher Ulrich has written, "Early American women literally gave birth in the arms or on the laps of their female neighbors," making the childbirth experience a profoundly embodied one for the laboring woman and her female assistants alike.[128] But the man-midwife needed to keep his distance, restricting his assistance to monitoring and guiding the internal process of childbirth.

Once they had positioned the mother in the most seemly way possible, physicians turned their attention to the uterus and allowed the woman to recede into the background of the birth narrative. As the Scottish practitioner John Burns asserted, "Labour, may be defined to be, the expulsive effort made by the uterus, for the birth of the child."[129] The effort of the mother was not an essential part of his vision. Similarly, Valentine Seaman described the stages of labor without mentioning the birthing mother. In the final stage, he wrote, "the membranes being broken, and the waters evacuated, the head now falls down into the cavity of the bason, and by the continuation of the pains, is forced forward."[130] Here, delivery proceeded like clockwork; the physician's role was to monitor the actions of the uterus while the mother played no essential part in the drama. William Dewees similarly explained how delivery occurred without once implying that a woman was also involved, referring to the "body" of the uterus but not to the body of the mother. He explained that "the uterus may be enabled to expel its contents, as we have already said, the fundus and body must contract, while the mouth must relax."[131] Here, the uterus functioned autonomously, doing all of the work of labor. The primacy of the uterus became abundantly clear when he explained how exhaustion in the laboring woman would not slow delivery of the child, for as long as the uterus "preserve its powers," delivery would progress without delay.[132] Even in their unpublished case notes, physicians often cited the powers of the uterus. For example, the American physician Walter Channing noted after a delivery in 1821, "About 2 a.m. the uterus began to act with powerful effect."[133]

Women's personal writings reveal that childbirth was a time of intense emotional and physical labor that birthing women shared with their kinswomen and female friends. But because of fears of sexual impropriety, male practitioners could not participate in the complex social context of the lying-in room in the same way that women could. Of course, physicians' texts do not tell us how they actually behaved in the lying-in chamber. Surely in moments of crisis they did not always manage to keep their patients modestly invisible or maintain a discreet physical distance. Physicians also became part of the social fabric of the lying-in chamber, though in different ways than female companions. But in their writings physicians had to describe their practice in ways that would bolster their medical authority and testify to their moral decency. Thus physicians did their best to conceal the figure of the mother, both in their descriptions of childbirth and in their prescriptions for medical practice in the lying-in room. In consequence, medical writers evaded the presence of the woman and made themselves and the uterus the protagonists in their birth narratives.

· · · · · ·

The practice of midwifery underwent a profound transformation over the course of the eighteenth century as it became a part of the male medical profession. The new generation of man-midwives that emerged in Britain and then America in the second half of the eighteenth century was concerned with legitimizing men's involvement in childbirth. They moved away from the cheerfully bawdy traditions of early vernacular medical writings and developed a new textual realm in which they could imagine applying their medical knowledge to fragments of the female body rather than to complete women. In consequence, women were removed from medical images and narratives of childbearing, and the uterus emerged as the primary agent in reproduction, a powerful character whose dangerous propensities highlighted the need for heroic medical intervention on the part of the man-midwife.

As medical writers made clear, the women they rendered invisible in their texts were assumed to be the "refined" women of the upper classes, those who required and merited the ministrations of a physician. Thus the disappearing mother was white and socioeconomically privileged. As she receded from medical images and writings, she was dissociated from the messiness of childbearing and from the potential moral dangers of embodiment. Without a body, the mother would not find her sexual virtue at risk; without a body, her moral character could not be warped by the pain, fatigue, and fear wrought by pregnancy and childbirth.

By writing the mother out of their texts, medical writers made it possible to envision her as an idealized figure, rising above the taint of the body. At the same time, they separated the mother from the physical work of childbearing, thus making it possible to imagine motherhood as an effortless emanation of maternal tenderness rather than as a process involving grueling physical labor. Medical writers opened the way for an emerging cultural ideal of the mother as an ethereal creature who was defined by her tender emotions and her moral strength. Although this vision of the mother emerged most clearly in the prescriptive and popular print culture of the late eighteenth and early nineteenth centuries, in many respects it was first fostered by medical men grappling with the implications of their new profession in the mid-eighteenth century.

## 2  Writing the Body

### The Work of the Body in Women's Childbearing Narratives

· · · · · · · · · · · · · · · · · · · · · · · · · · · · · · · · · · · · · · · · · · · · · · · · · · ·

Elizabeth Drinker reflected in her diary in 1797, "I have often thought that women who live to get over the time of Child-bareing, if other things are favourable to them, experience more comfort and satisfaction than at any other period of their lives."[1] Having given birth nine times and watched her adult daughters suffer through pregnancies and difficult labors, she concluded that life was best enjoyed when the physical challenges of childbearing had passed. Although most women, like Drinker, seem to have been affectionate mothers who derived satisfaction from raising their children, the bodily trials of maternity forced them to approach motherhood with both joy and trepidation. The physical unwieldiness, discomfort, and suffering wrought by pregnancy and childbirth, as well as the lack of choice and control that many women experienced with respect to their reproductive lives, brought the body to the forefront of women's understanding of motherhood. While physicians evaded the maternal body and its labor in their medical writings, women placed the work of their bodies at the center of their vision of motherhood. Although the lives of the women represented here spanned nearly a century of social, cultural, medical, and demographic changes, the testimonies they left behind attest to remarkable continuity in the importance they placed on the maternal body. Motherhood was hard physical work, and when women weighed in the balance the bodily challenges of childbearing and the emotional rewards of mothering, they were compelled to regard motherhood with ambivalence.

This perception of motherhood unfurled from generation to generation as older women ushered new mothers through their childbearing experiences. As Elizabeth Drinker mused in 1800, "I have never brought a child into the world without thinking how much my dear mother might have suffer'd with me."[2] She in turn bore witness to the suffering of her daughters in childbed. When one of her daughters was in labor in 1799, she noted, "This day is 38 years since I was in agonies bringing her into this world of trouble; she told me with tears that this was her bearth day."[3] In her diary,

Drinker connected three generations of women within a history of their fraught relationship with motherhood. In her experience and imagination, the physical suffering and danger of childbirth linked mothers and daughters, providing a sense of continuity. Indeed, it was not until the second half of the nineteenth century that a significant generational disconnect developed as women began to unmoor childbearing from its association with suffering. Nancy Theriot has argued that the cohort of women who came of age in the late nineteenth century developed a new understanding of motherhood based on confidence and self-control, largely due to the fact that these women enjoyed more certain control over their fertility and a new vision of childbearing as healthy, safe, and potentially pain-free.[4]

This chapter explores the ways in which women portrayed the physical experiences of childbearing and focuses in particular on their remarks about fertility, pregnancy, and childbirth. Middle-class and elite white women left a more substantial archive of first-person accounts of childbearing than did lower-class women and women of color; consequently, their writings form the bulk of my evidence. I have examined the personal writings of women from multiple generations, ranging from women like Experience Richardson of Massachusetts, born in 1705, to Elizabeth Neblett, who began her childbearing years in Texas in the 1850s. Because of the greater population density along the Eastern Seaboard, the majority of these women lived in the Southeast, the mid-Atlantic, or the Northeast, with a few representatives of regions farther west, such as Oregon, Texas, and Louisiana. Some of the women were mistresses of southern plantations, where they found themselves living apart from close friends and family; others lived in urban areas such as Philadelphia or small towns such as Northampton, Massachusetts, where they circulated within a close local network of female companions. Nearly all enjoyed a significant degree of financial security and, in many cases, wealth. This meant that they had access to considerable resources during their cycles of childbearing: physicians to consult, nurses to care for them during and after childbirth, wet nurses to suckle their children if they were unable to breastfeed, and the leisure to recuperate in bed. Most of these women availed themselves of at least some of these options.

These women were also literate and often highly articulate. They bore children with regularity throughout their adult lives, and many of them wrote even more prolifically, peppering their personal writings with comments about childbearing and childrearing. For many, motherhood was the most important aspect of their lives, and they were full of advice, opinions, anecdotes, complaints, and concern for their children and for their child-bearing friends and kinswomen. The language and narrative structures these women used to discuss their childbearing experiences are particularly important. They lived in a culture that increasingly emphasized the virtues of bodily restraint and the primacy of mind and spirit over matter. These women's writings reveal a tension between the broader expectations of the culture in which they lived and their desire to write about their em-bodied experiences. The words they used and the stories they told often reflected this tension. Yet, in the end, their drive to record the bodily ex-periences of motherhood triumphed over the impulse to evade the messi-ness of corporeality.

Although we lack the same richness of documentation for less-privileged women, other types of sources provide important insight into their experi-ences and attitudes toward childbearing. The testimonies of enslaved women, in particular, offer a crucial counterpoint to the narratives of middle-class and elite white women. Published slave narratives provide a glimpse into the lives of these women, although the fact that these narra-tives were written for the public to raise awareness for the antislavery cause means that the experiences articulated in these texts were necessarily fil-tered through a particular ideological lens. Interviews with former slaves collected in the 1930s provide another means of accessing enslaved women's stories. These interviews generally reflect only the recollections of individ-uals enslaved during the last years of slavery, so using information culled from these sources risks conflating earlier and later narratives of childbear-ing in slavery. But because the continuities in women's depictions of child-bearing have proved more striking than the differences, I use these sources carefully with the desire to bring at least the echoes of these women's voices into my narrative.

Enslaved women's stories are particularly significant because they con-firm the centrality of the body to American women's perceptions of mother-hood. But they also reveal that the maternal body meant different things in bondage than in freedom. While more-privileged women emphasized the day-to-day physicality of pregnancy and childbirth, enslaved women's testi-monies tended to focus on the significance of their reproductive bodies within the larger context of their enslavement. Their words suggest that the discomfort of pregnancy or the immediate pain of childbirth was overshad-owed by the knowledge that their bodies were defined as commodities to be bought, sold, and forcibly bred. Moreover, enslaved women understood that their reproductive labors were located at the crossroads between the work they did for their families and the work they did for their owners. Because of this, their ambivalence toward motherhood was profound.

Unfortunately for the historian, the richest expressions of embodiment almost certainly occurred physically and orally between women. Enslaved women tended one another during childbirth and undoubtedly shared advice about negotiating the combined demands of childbearing and forced labor. Middle-class and elite women's writings referred often to their social interactions with their peers, to the times spent together chatting in the lying-in chamber, and to advice sought and received. In 1790 Sarah Logan Fisher, a member of Philadelphia's large Quaker community, noted in her diary that she "went with Coz' Waln to pay a Lying in visit to Becky Waln several were there, & we had a very agreeable afternoon."[5] We can only imagine the kinds of stories those women might have shared. Pregnant for the first time in 1840, Penelope Warren wrote to her husband, "I did not feel so well Thursday, every little pain frightened me . . . whenever I have any strange pains Cousin Annie says I must come to her & she will explain them to me."[6] In this way, women's perceptions of childbearing were shaped by their peers and by the wisdom of preceding generations. Unfortunately, we can never be privy to the conversations between female relatives and friends or between women and their midwives and physicians. We can never see the gestures they made in describing their experiences, nor can we know the intimacy of women who used their bodies to comfort and support one another through repeated reproductive trials.

· · · · · ·

Fertility was one of the factors that defined women's embodied experiences as mothers. The simple count of how often and how many times a woman became pregnant helped define her perception of motherhood as manageable or physically burdensome. Most women cherished the delights and demands of mothering children once they were safely born, but the physical challenges of repeated childbearing pushed many women to feel ambivalent at the prospect of each new pregnancy. Indeed, many women greeted pregnancy with dismay or regret, but once safely delivered they incorporated the new baby into the family with love. Fertility was something that women wished to regulate, but many found that it eluded their control. They lived their childbearing years in tension with their bodies.

The period from the mid-eighteenth century to the mid-nineteenth century is particularly significant for the study of childbearing patterns. Fertility rates in the American colonies peaked in the 1760s and then began a steady decline, nearly a century earlier than in western Europe with the exception of France.[7] In 1800 white married couples had an average of just over seven children, by 1825 this had dropped to just under six children, and by 1850 white couples had an average of 5.42 children.[8] Susan Klepp has located this downward trend within a broader Revolutionary-era emphasis on reason and restraint, which led white American women, particularly those of the middle classes, to engage in careful family planning and to shift their perception of childbearing from pride in a large family to a more negative view of frequent pregnancy. Unlike white women, however, enslaved women experienced an increase in fertility over this period, due to the coercive pronatalist measures that slaveholders employed in order to sustain the domestic slave trade. Not until after emancipation did birthrates among African American women begin to decline.[9]

In spite of the steady decline in rates of childbearing, middle-class and elite women's personal writings remained consistent in their discussions of fertility from the later decades of the eighteenth century through the first half of the nineteenth century. Women presented fertility as a form of accounting. Numbers accounted for the children born to one woman, but they also represented a record of her physical labors as a mother, a record that might be inscribed on the body itself. Susan Klepp has argued that the practice of numeracy became prevalent in the Revolutionary era as American women began to rationalize childbearing through numbers.[10] In 1779, for instance, Sarah Logan Fisher reported that she "walkd down in the morng to see Peggy Howell who is Lying in of her 6th Child, before she is 29."[11] Fisher was also in her late twenties, but had only just given birth to her third child. She frequently reported the pregnancies and deliveries of her friends, but she generally tallied the number of children only in situations when the numbers seemed noteworthy. Similarly, in 1782 Elizabeth Drinker took the time to note in her diary that an acquaintance had given birth to a son. She concluded by remarking that this was "their 10th Child; all living."[12] Not only did Drinker pause to record the safe birth of a new baby, but she emphasized that the woman had now given birth to ten children. When women recorded large numbers of children or children born very close together in time, they often implied awe at such a reproductive feat as well as concern for the well-being of the mother.

Generations of women continued to take note of reproductive histories. In 1841, on the twenty-fifth anniversary of her marriage, Sarah Hale of Massachusetts tallied the results of her childbearing years and recorded in her diary, "I have borne eleven children, and have been permitted to keep until this day seven."[13] Over the years, Elizabeth Perry of South Carolina took stock in her diary of her reproductive past. In 1843 she recorded, "I am now about to be a Mother for the fourth time." In 1848 she noted that she had borne six children, two of whom were stillborn, and that she had endured four miscarriages. Finally, when her childbearing years had passed, she recorded the final score: "7 living children, two still born, & four miscarriages so have been 13 times pregnant."[14] These numbers, tallied over the years, were central to Perry's life history and testified to the work she performed as a mother. Moreover, by tallying in her final sum the number of pregnancies she endured, rather than the living children she gave birth to, Perry emphasized that each pregnancy, whether or not it resulted in a living child, represented a record of her reproductive work.

For enslaved women, fertility was a particularly significant form of accounting because it signified not only the repeated challenges of childbearing but also the coercive circumstances in which they bore children. Frances Kemble, the celebrated British actress and antislavery writer, was the recipient of a host of petitions from enslaved mothers on her husband's Georgia plantation in the late 1830s. Like the written accounts of Sarah Hale and Elizabeth Perry, the verbal accounts of these enslaved women were defined by a simple tallying of numbers—an account of the number of children born, the number of miscarriages endured, and the number of childhood deaths mourned by each woman—but for these women the numbers reflected the uniquely coercive patterns of motherhood in slavery. Kemble recorded the women's histories:

> *Nanny* has had three children; two of them are dead. She came to implore that the rule of sending them into the field three weeks after their confinement might be altered . . . *Sarah*, Stephen's wife—this woman's case and history were alike deplorable. She had had four miscarriages, had brought seven children into the world, five of whom were dead, and was again with child. She complained of dreadful pains in the back, and an internal tumor which swells with the exertion of working in the fields . . . *Sukey*, Bush's wife, only came to pay her respects. She had had four miscarriages; had brought eleven children into the world, five of whom are dead.[15]

These women presented long histories of difficult childbearing and forced labor that took a terrible toll on their bodies. They begged Kemble for lighter workloads and for more time to rest after childbirth, forcing her to acknowledge that childbearing was hard physical work that became debilitating when combined with fieldwork. For these women, reproductive accounting referred to a history of simultaneous reproductive and productive labor.

For enslaved women, moreover, fertility represented a literal form of economic accounting that defined their status as commodities in a way that was different from that of enslaved men. Fertility signified the growing value of women and their children, and slaveholders both encouraged and enforced high fertility rates.[16] Hattie Rogers, a former slave in North Carolina, recalled that "Marster didn't care who our fathers was jest so the women had children. . . . If a woman was a good breeder she brought a good price on the auction block. The slave buyers would come around and jab them in the stomach and look them over and if they thought they would have children fast they brought a good price."[17] Josephine Howell, whose family had been enslaved in Tennessee and Arkansas, testified that her grandmother bore twenty-one children in slavery and was highly prized as a result. She was a "breeding woman." She also emphasized that when her own mother was still very young, her owner had "forced motherhood upon her."[18] Enslaved women lived with the awareness that slave owners regarded them as commodities of greater or lesser value depending on their reproductive histories and childbearing potential.

As commodities to be bought, sold, and bred, enslaved women were acutely conscious of their lack of control over their reproductive lives. Indeed, this lack of bodily integrity was central to their understanding of motherhood. Thus, when they accounted for the number of pregnancies they had experienced, they simultaneously accounted for a repeated history of forced breeding and sexual vulnerability.[19] Indeed, references to sexuality and sexual coercion were more common in slave testimonies than were references to pregnancy or childbirth, suggesting that, at least in retrospect, women may have been more profoundly affected by the systemic trauma of sexual vulnerability than by the day-to-day challenges of pregnancy and childbirth. Elizabeth Keckley, for instance, recounted that she was "persecuted" for four years by a white man. "I—I—became a mother," she confessed and explained that "if my poor boy ever suffered any humiliating pangs on account of birth, he could not blame his mother, for God knows that she did not wish to give him life."[20] Keckley's attitude toward motherhood was distinctly ambivalent, torn as she was between love for her child and her horror of the system that forced motherhood upon her and entrapped her son. Another former slave, Ida Hutchinson, told a more unusual story of forced childbearing that had been passed down from older relatives. "Once on the Blackshear place," she recounted, "they took all the fine looking boys and girls that was thirteen years old or older and put them in a big barn after they had stripped them naked. They used to strip them naked and put them in a big barn every Sunday and leave them there until Monday morning. Out of that came sixty babies."[21] The account of the births of those sixty babies was important enough to have been passed down from family members and eventually to a WPA worker in the 1930s. Thus, when enslaved women discussed childbearing, they also emphasized a parallel history of repeated sexual coercion and exploitation that undermined their bodily integrity.

When women, both free and enslaved, paused to account for a mother's reproductive history, they gestured to the reality that each pregnancy and each delivery were fraught with risk. Indeed, women who bore many children often suffered an accumulation of problems that could become debilitating. Because of the limits of medical knowledge and technology, all childbearing women, regardless of social position, risked complications such as infections, uterine rupture, perineal tears, chronic incontinence, and abdominal and back pain. These complications could be compounded by hard physical labor, particularly in the case of enslaved women and lower-class women. Plantation records, for instance, show that many enslaved women suffered from uterine prolapse, mostly likely caused by a combination of debilitating work and too frequent childbearing.[22] But reproductive injuries and chronic ailments were not unique to enslaved and working women, though they may have been more common. Wealth could not protect women from the dangers of childbirth, and even the best physicians that money could procure might make dangerous situations worse. Forceps might provide needed assistance to deliver a child in cases of maternal exhaustion or a difficult presentation of the fetus, but they could also cause irreparable tears in the vagina, leaving women permanently incontinent. Such bodily marks accumulated with each pregnancy and birth and followed women throughout their lives, perennial reminders of the inescapably corporeal dimensions of motherhood.

It is not surprising, then, that when middle-class and elite women commented on fertility they often expressed concern for women who bore what they deemed too many children. They knew firsthand the dangers of childbearing and, in spite of the delight that a new baby might bring, desired above all safety and health for the mother. Abigail Adams, future First Lady, worried in 1790 that "Sister Shaw was likely to increase her Family. I wish her comfortably through, but shall feel anxious for her feeble constitution."[23] In 1813 Rosalie Calvert of Maryland fretted about the well-being of her sister, writing, "I heard with much sorrow that my sister was so ill, and I hope that this will be her last child. After what she wrote me I did not think she would have this one."[24] The illness Calvert referred to was a difficult labor, and she therefore viewed any ensuing pregnancies as undesirable and potentially dangerous. These women feared for the health and safety of their female friends and relatives as they saw them increase their families, and they looked with trepidation at the risks involved in the long months of pregnancy and the "fiery trial" of childbirth.[25]

Some women were eager to bear their first children, but experienced a change in attitude with subsequent pregnancies. While pregnant with her first child in Texas in the early 1850s, Elizabeth Neblett saw motherhood as the ultimate fulfillment, writing, "I feel that my joy is not yet replete, that my cup of happiness is not yet quite full the time is not yet come, when I hope to feel a Mothers joy, a mothers love." Yet by 1860, when she anticipated the birth of her fourth child, she lamented to her husband, "I have suffered ten times more than you have and ten times more than I can begin to make you conceive of . . . I feel different and am more afflicted now than ever before, and think it probable, (tho' I fear not,) that my desire to die will be gratified, but oh the suffering that lies between me and the port of death."[26] Although Neblett's growing horror of motherhood was unusually extreme, she poignantly illustrated how the physical and mental suffering wrought by repeated childbearing could turn women from happily anticipating motherhood to desperately hoping to avoid further suffering.

Although middle-class and elite women generally stopped short of describing the suffering that they feared, there were times when they could not escape the recognition that for many women, the rigors of their reproductive lives were inscribed in gruesome ways on the body itself. Frances Kemble recounted with shock her interaction with an enslaved woman whose body was ravaged by childbearing and fieldwork: "She was the mother of a very large family, and complained to me that what with childbearing and hard field labor, her back was almost broken in two. With an almost savage vehemence of gesticulation, she suddenly tore up her scanty clothing, and exhibited a spectacle with which I was inconceivably shocked and sickened."[27] The woman's body exposed a long and terrible history of childbearing under the most coercive circumstances. Kemble could not bring herself to describe exactly what it was that she saw, yet she acknowledged the mute testimony of the woman's body. Although such dramatic anecdotes were rare, even women who bore children under less dire circumstances carried on their bodies the marks and scars of their reproductive histories.

If bearing many children seemed dangerous, or at least exhausting, women worried even more about the problem of spacing. Middle-class and elite women expressed particular concern for women who bore children close together in time. Logically, of course, spacing pregnancies further apart would also help accomplish the goal of bearing fewer children overall. In 1790 Abigail Adams implicitly criticized women who bore children too quickly when she hoped that a friend would "not have children as fast as Mrs. Smith. It is enough to wear out an Iron constitution."[28] Around the same time, Elizabeth Drinker mourned the stillbirth of a grandson, not only because she was deprived of a "sweet, little grandson," but also because she feared her daughter would become pregnant again a year sooner because of the lack of a baby to breastfeed.[29] Mary Hubbard of Boston was more specific in her definition of good timing when she sent a message to her niece in 1799, hoping that "she may not have another in less than two years from the date of this."[30] Many women seemed to agree that a two-year interval was reasonable, although longer might be better. Laura Randall, struggling to keep house in Florida in the 1830s, complained to her friend that "three babies in less than three years are enough to make one tired of babies, I think." She wrote that she was worn out by the combination of housekeeping and repeated cycles of childbearing, but apologized for her complaints, explaining: "I feel as if I were ungrateful in repining at the only thing really hard in my lot. The rapid increase of their number."[31] Many women understood the challenges of bearing children in such quick succession. Mary Lee of Massachusetts, a mother of six children, hoped rather sardonically in 1833 that babies would not become an "annual blessing" for her daughter; that, she suggested, would be a "calamity."[32] In accounting for rates of fertility, women insisted that bearing children without periods of rest undermined their health and strength.

Thus fertility was something that all women endeavored to control, though with varying degrees of success. Married women and enslaved women all lacked the legal right to refuse sexual intercourse (though for very different reasons), but they had other options that might help them limit their fertility. Women shared information among themselves about medicines and herbs that might prevent or abort a pregnancy. Plants such as savin, cotton root, tansy, rue, and pennyroyal, for instance, were thought to be abortifacients and were readily available to women with a little botanical knowledge, so much so that advice manuals for slaveholders warned about the common use of such remedies among enslaved women.[33] In fact, some scientific studies have confirmed that a substance found in the cotton plant is effective at suppressing fertility.[34] Moreover, thanks to a growing public dialogue about the benefits and methods of restricting fertility, by the 1830s literate women had increasing access to print information about the theory and practice of family limitation.[35]

Women also shared information about the efficacy of breastfeeding in limiting fertility, and there is evidence to suggest that women often relied on it as one of the most accessible means of controlling their childbearing.[36] Elizabeth Drinker noted that she had reassured her thirty-nine-year-old daughter, in the throes of labor in 1799, that "this might possibly be the last trial of this sort, if she could suckle her baby for 2 years to come."[37] In 1843, shortly before her marriage, Caroline Dall noted that "after Sarah came we had a strange but earnest talk in regard to the law of increase," and they puzzled over the fact that "Mrs. ___ is nursing and yet in the family way."[38] Not only did Dall reveal that the "law of increase" was a subject for earnest discussion among women, but she also intimated that women generally thought that breastfeeding would prevent pregnancy. Breastfeeding was often fraught with difficulty, but many women seemed to agree with Margaret Manigault, who wrote to her daughter in 1809, "I think it is less fatiguing to the constitution to nurse this one, than to bring forth another."[39]

Although women might strive to use breastfeeding strategically, there were many obstacles that stood in their way. For enslaved women, work schedules made consistent breastfeeding almost impossible. George Womble, a former slave, recalled that on his plantation "those children who were still being fed from their mother's breasts were also under the care of one of these old persons. However, in this case the mothers were permitted to leave the field twice a day (once between breakfast and dinner and once between dinner and supper) so that these children could be fed."[40] Breastfeeding with such infrequency most likely undermined the women's supply of milk and their ability to breastfeed long-term, thus lessening the potential effects on fertility. In addition, breast problems such as abscesses and damaged nipples might prevent women of all walks of life from continuing to nurse, and husbands sometimes made the decision to employ a wet nurse or to wean the child. Even in the matter of breastfeeding, women's bodies were not their own.

Other methods available to women included sexual abstinence, though, as with breastfeeding, the choice to avoid sexual relations was not exclusively in women's hands. Rosalie Calvert wrote to her sister about her pregnancy in 1811, complaining that "it is a prospect which does not please me as I want no more children, and after this I believe I will adopt your way of not having any more."[41] Calvert referred to her sister's use of abstinence as the only certain way to prevent pregnancy, though the fact that both sisters continued to bear children suggests that abstinence was difficult to maintain. Some women suggested that husbands ought to be and often were cooperative partners in the effort to limit fertility. Calista Hall, living in upstate New York in the 1840s, offered an oblique reference her husband's cooperative measures, writing, "The old maid come at the appointed time. I do think you are a very *careful* man." The old maid she referred to was menstruation, and she complimented her husband for the care he took to prevent conception. She did not specify her husband's method (most likely withdrawal),[42] but she followed up her remark by telling her husband that he should do his friend a favor and "take Mr. Stewart out one side and learn him [how to prevent conception]."[43] No doubt she had Mrs. Stewart's well-being in mind. As the marked decline in fertility among white women during this period shows, many women were able to limit their fertility to a certain extent. Yet the efforts of all women to control their fertility were constrained by circumstances such as enslavement, coercion, lack of cooperation from their sexual partners, the pressures of social expectations, and the lack of accurate medical knowledge and effective contraceptive technology.

It is important to recognize that women's efforts to limit their fertility did not mean that they wished to reject motherhood as an experience and an identity. For one thing, most women were pragmatic and knew that motherhood was their "common lot" in life.[44] But more importantly, children provided women with a source of affection and pride. As Katy Simpson Smith has argued, motherhood also afforded women a potential source of power in a society that largely restricted their autonomy and authority. As mothers, women were responsible not only for giving birth, but for feeding, clothing, healing, teaching, and protecting the interests of their children. These mothering activities garnered women considerable respect and authority in their families and communities.[45] Even as mothers dreaded exhausting cycles of childbearing, they also recognized the emotional, intellectual, and social rewards of becoming mothers.

Even enslaved women, who bore children under the most coercive and physically brutal circumstances, often welcomed motherhood as a role that helped them resist the worst aspects of enslavement.[46] The sparse records suggest that some enslaved women bore large families out of choice. Interviewed by WPA workers in the 1930s, former slave Josephine Howell spoke matter-of-factly of her enslaved mother's distress when she could no longer bear children: "Mother married then and had five children. . . . Dr. Goodridge stopped her from having children, she raved wild."[47] How and why the doctor rendered her unable to bear children is unclear, but this woman's despair attested to the importance of childbearing in her life. Children could be a practical asset to slave families, as with any other family, as well as a treasured part of the social and emotional fabric of the family and community. Their presence could mitigate the most inhumane aspects of slavery.[48] Finally, some enslaved women might have seen large families as a kind of insurance against extremely high rates of infant mortality and against the terrible knowledge that some of their children could be sold away from them at any time.[49]

Moreover, in spite of coercive pronatalist practices, enslaved women were sometimes able to control the circumstances in which they became mothers. In this respect, childbearing may have provided a small feeling of autonomy to counteract the depredations of slavery. Some enslaved women managed to postpone childbearing until they deemed circumstances to be more favorable. Former slave Mary Grayson of Oklahoma recounted a story about her mother, who did not bear children until much later than was desired by her owners. She was bought in quick succession by at least three different owners and "married" to one of their slaves each time, but she did not bear any children until the third time, at which point she and her husband produced ten children.[50] We cannot know whether Grayson's mother did not initially bear children because of her own wishes, or whether other factors such as youth or poor nutrition and health prevented conception. It is possible, however, that she was able to control her fertility until such time as she saw fit to bear children. Similarly, Mary Gaffney recollected with some pride that "Maser was going to raise him a lot more slaves, but still I cheated Maser, I never did have any slaves to grow and Maser he wondered what was the matter. I tell you son, I kept cotton roots and chewed them all the time but I was careful not to let Maser know or catch me."[51] After emancipation, Gaffney began bearing children. The fact that these two stories were remembered and repeated to subsequent generations suggests that they carried an important message: they represented women's triumph of will over the coercive pronatalist practices of slave owners. Such accounts demonstrate that for many enslaved women the tension between coercion and bodily control was at the center of their understanding of motherhood.

When women discussed rates of fertility, they alluded to an entire reproductive history that for many included pain, debility, and loss of control. It is no wonder that women, both enslaved and free, felt ambivalent toward the prospect of a new pregnancy. They cherished their living children and watched over them with pride and anxiety, but they also knew that repeated childbearing was a physical burden. In keeping accounts of their reproductive lives and those of friends and family, middle-class and elite white women emphasized the desire to ease the physical burden of motherhood. Enslaved women, too, kept careful track of their reproductive histories and even passed them down to subsequent generations, and in doing so testified to the coercive pronatalist system of slavery that transformed their reproductive bodies into commodities. No doubt many women, enslaved and free, would have sympathized with Rosalie Calvert, who rejoiced in 1819: "My little Amelia is two years old and a charming child. Don't you deem me fortunate indeed to think that she is the last? I believe I am safe now from having any more children, and I am greatly delighted."[52] For Calvert there was no contradiction in expressing delight in her child while simultaneously hoping never to have another. Motherhood was defined by the tension between women's love for their children and the ever-present fear of the physical consequences of childbearing.

· · · · · ·

In 1844 the writer and social activist Caroline Dall recorded her first pregnancy in her diary: "For the first time the conviction presses itself upon me—that I am myself a mother."[53] Though she had not yet given birth or raised a child, Dall made the physical fact of pregnancy the foundation of her new identity as a mother. The recognition of a new pregnancy marked the beginning of a period in which a woman's body became increasingly central to her daily life and sense of self. Unfortunately, the testimonies of enslaved women are silent on their experiences of individual pregnancies, focusing instead, as we saw earlier, on the meaning and cumulative impact of repeated cycles of childbearing. Middle-class and elite women, however, sprinkled their letters and diaries with frequent discussions of pregnancy. These women's personal writings were marked by a peculiar combination of explicitness and modest evasion that seemed to reflect their overall perspective on pregnancy.

In their letters and diaries, middle-class and elite women explored the boundaries of what bodily details they felt could properly be expressed. Some women were comfortable confiding the messy particulars of childbearing on paper; others felt a greater need for modest evasiveness while still seeking to record and share important information. Many women must have considered the fact that their letters and even diaries might be shared among friends and family. After keeping a diary for many years, Elizabeth Drinker explained that "as I don't lay out for any one but some of my Children to read my silly writings, am the more free to mention bowels and obstructions, than I otherwise would do."[54] Clearly Drinker felt that bodily details could be shared within the family circle, though perhaps no further. Indeed, Drinker left quite a detailed record of personal and family health, and as she grew older she must have found more time to write, for she included lengthy records of her daughters' childbearing experiences.

Other women seemed to experience greater difficulty in committing to paper the intimate physical details of their lives. In 1797 Esther Cox of Philadelphia, a contemporary of Elizabeth Drinker, wrote to her daughter, Mary Chesnut, in South Carolina, "This day two weeks ago I wrote you a long letter—to that I refer you for my opinion respecting your coming here, should a certain event call for peculiar attentions, which might not be easily had where you are—I will add no more on that head, seeing 'tis so difficult a talk for you to repose even in a Mother's breast, the confidence of saying you are, or you are not in the way to become a Mother yourself. Your last [letter] left me as uncertain as I was before."[55] Cox's daughter, pregnant with her first child, was evidently reluctant to put into writing the fact of her pregnancy. Yet even as Cox asked her daughter to be more explicit, she also shrouded the subject of pregnancy in layers of innuendo. As an experienced mother, she was perhaps more confident in asking for reproductive news, but still couched her inquiries with delicate evasion. In 1826 Eleanor Lewis offered a similarly veiled announcement of her daughter's pregnancy when she wrote to her friend, "My Beloved Parke is much improved in health & strength, but (*entrenous*) I fear she will have more cares than she anticipated. She hopes not, but Mrs Gains thinks, *that in 5 months*."[56] Her coy "between ourselves" and strategic use of italics must have conveyed a clear message to her friend while emphasizing the desire to be discreet. Margaret Gregg indicated similar discretion when she inquired of a friend in 1857, "Dont Mary expect to be confined Soon also, I thought Mary intimated as much but I did not like to ask any more questions."[57] These correspondents perhaps found discussions of pregnancy better suited to intimate conversation among women. Indeed, their written exchanges lacked the knowing gestures, touches, and sights that might have eased the communication of reproductive news.

Other women, however, felt that the exigencies of childbearing justified discussions of bodies, bellies, and bowels. In 1833 Mary Lee of Boston responded to a letter from her daughter in New York, who was pregnant with her first child: "You seem to apologize for its being a *medical* letter as you term it. . . . Our correspondence for the present must certainly be of this character." She went on to reassure her daughter that the physical sensations she had described in her letter were "nothing unusual" and took the opportunity to offer some advice for regulating her bowels.[58] Most women's writings forged a middle ground between the circumspection of women like Esther Cox and her daughter and the explicit attention to bodily functions exhibited by women such as Elizabeth Drinker and Mary Lee and her daughter.

In their personal writings women rarely referred to pregnancy as such. Instead, they used a coded vocabulary to signal news of pregnancy that seems to have been readily adopted by both women and men. Although medical texts during this time referred to "pregnancy," and women occasionally let slip the word in their personal writings, overwhelmingly they used oblique phrases that obscured the corporeal nature of pregnancy.[59] Hearkening back to an older and more corporeal vocabulary that evoked the changes a woman's body underwent during pregnancy, women did very occasionally report being in a thriving condition, in the increasing way, or in a growing condition, but such phrases were uncommon by the late eighteenth century.[60] Instead, the preferred vocabulary for pregnancy gestured vaguely to a predicament, a certain matter, a particular complaint, a situation, or even a peculiar situation.[61] As Ebenezer Pettigrew wrote to his wife Nancy in 1818, "Write me in your next whether our suspicions as to your situation are correct." Twelve years later, he again relied on this coded vocabulary, writing, "I should have been pleased to hear whether my *lovely wife* was in the situation which we both suspected."[62] This coded vocabulary evaded the concreteness of corporeality (of bigness), but nevertheless allowed women to convey their news to friends and family. Moreover, it may suggest a more circumspect view of pregnancy. Whereas earlier colonial descriptions of women as teeming, flourishing, growing, or thriving suggested a vision of pleasant abundance and good health, later remarks about being in a situation or having a particular complaint implied a dimmer view of pregnancy that may have reflected women's growing desire to limit their fertility.

Although coded references to pregnancy were enough to communicate to friends and family the news of a baby on the way, such oblique phrases were inadequate when it came to articulating the bodily experiences of pregnancy. Women consistently pushed the boundaries of propriety by describing their bodies and the sensations wrought by pregnancy. Generally, women seemed to agree that being pregnant was unpleasant, often worrisome, and sometimes debilitating, and they commiserated openly with one another about their experiences. Exposing the physical burden of pregnancy, women complained often of the various unpleasant sensations they experienced and of the general awkwardness imposed by a growing belly. Whether writing in their diaries or corresponding with loved ones, women became more explicit in their personal writings as the physical symptoms of pregnancy increasingly intruded on their daily lives.

In the earlier stages of pregnancy, women made frequent note of morning sickness. Certainly there was nothing surprising about this symptom of pregnancy, nor was there much they could do about it, but it was evidently important to women to monitor the progression of their pregnancies through these symptoms. During several of her pregnancies, Sarah Logan Fisher recorded almost daily remarks about how she felt, particularly in the early and late stages of a pregnancy. In January and February 1781 she noted several days of morning sickness, remarking, "Very sick indeed" or "Very Sick all day, kept up stairs."[63] Her diary became a means of keeping track of the changes in her body, and she wrote sometimes with resignation and sometimes with concern about her symptoms. Esther Cox wrote to her daughter in 1805, "I wish I could tell you your Sister Kitty was well but she is in the family way again, & has been far above three months in a very distressing state with Sickness of Stomach added to many other complaints."[64] Communicating these kinds of concerns was just as important to women as simply conveying the news of a new pregnancy. Women could sympathize with one another and perhaps offer helpful tips for ameliorating symptoms. Pregnant in 1804, Rosalie Calvert complained to her mother about morning sickness interfering with her duties: "I have thought of writing you every day since the beginning of April, but something has always prevented it. For some time my house has been full of houseguests and before that, I was so sick *every morning* that I couldn't do anything."[65] Two years later, she was pregnant and suffering again, and she complained to her sister, "I am so uncomfortable and sick every morning that I don't know what to do, and I can't eat anything. I hope this won't continue for long, because it is most unpleasant and makes me good for nothing."[66] Women like Calvert acknowledged their physical discomfort openly to other women and in the privacy of their diaries, testifying to the ways in which their pregnant bodies intruded on their lives and shaped everything from their daily activities to their personal writings.

Women also highlighted the changing shape and feel of their bodies when they complained of the swelling and discomfort they experienced later in pregnancy. Pregnant in 1787, Sarah Logan Fisher recorded in her diary, "My Ancles Swell exceedingly which makes me uneasy."[67] Fisher found such symptoms important to track, as they provided her with a view of her overall well-being during pregnancy. By August she was feeling even worse, and noted, "Very Warm—felt very poorly all Day, the Air so trying, my Legs & Feet swell very much indeed four Weeks to Day since I was down Stairs, except one Morng a very few Minutes."[68] Fisher moved beyond the mere discomfort of swollen legs to record how the symptoms of pregnancy had interfered with her daily life. It was a common scenario. In 1837 Matilda Henry wrote to her friend about the progress of her pregnancy: "Everybody remarks it," she complained, "I seem to fatten all over—my feet and legs swell considerably, and heartburn and acid continue, otherwise I feel pretty well. . . . You never saw such a sight as Mrs. Anderson is in your life. She says she knows she will have two. Her feet swell till she can't stand on them."[69] Clearly, symptoms such as swelling and heartburn were problems that childbearing women frequently thought and wrote about—no doubt Henry and her friend Mrs. Anderson shared many such details when they visited one another. Women wrote of these physical sensations sometimes with concern, sometimes with resignation, but it was important to them to communicate how they were feeling and the ways in which their bodies were changing and challenging them.

As the weeks of pregnancy wore on, women became increasingly aware of their changing shape, and in the later months of pregnancy they frequently commented on the size and unwieldiness of their bodies. In August 1781, Sarah Logan Fisher was seven months pregnant and was still busy washing, ironing, visiting, and tending her children. She noted feeling "very poorly, heavy & painfull."[70] Two years later, pregnant again, she complained of feeling very anxious, for "I feel so very heavy & uneasy to myself, more so I think than ever I did by far."[71] Judging by her diary, the unwieldiness of her pregnant body had by this time engrossed her thoughts, and she wrote of little beyond the immediate concerns of her body. Her complaints of heaviness and discomfort became a familiar refrain, and with each pregnancy she seemed to suffer more. Ellen Coolidge revealed the extent to which these changes could disturb women's equanimity when she complained of the suffering she endured during her pregnancy in 1830: "You may imagine how I get along under such circumstances with my three little ones, all babies together and so helpless and unwieldy as I am from my situation. Oh it is a 'chien de métier que le mien'[72] and I know not from what cause that at five months I am as great a sufferer as I usually have been at seven or eight."[73] Referring to motherhood as a "dog of an occupation," Coolidge exposed the frustration she felt with her heavy and uncomfortable body. No doubt she spoke for many mothers when she revealed that childbearing was marked by irritation and suffering. As Eliza Robertson remarked in 1855, "I am getting so clumsy and uncomfortable."[74] Women may have felt obliged to circumvent the fact of pregnancy with vague phrases about their situation, but by the later stages of pregnancy their heavy corporeality intruded so fully on their physical and emotional lives that they abandoned conventional phrases for more individualized descriptions of the symptoms of pregnancy. At such times, women's bodies became the main focus of their attention and concern.

Although middle-class and elite women seemed to feel comfortable articulating the physical sensations of pregnancy in writing, the reality of appearing pregnant in public sometimes posed a greater challenge to their sense of modesty. Catherine Scholten has noted that in the seventeenth and early eighteenth centuries it was quite normal for women to appear in public when obviously pregnant.[75] Yet by the second half of the eighteenth century, women's writings reveal that they were often self-conscious about being visibly pregnant, reflecting a growing culture of bodily restraint in American society.[76] Many women were reluctant to be seen by anyone beyond their circle of family and intimate friends. For example, Elizabeth Drinker noted in 1807 in her diary, "Poor Molly . . . has a fire upstairs as she is asham'd, she says, to be seen, she cuts such [a] figure."[77] Caroline Gilman of Massachusetts similarly commented in 1827 that she was "ashamed to put her head out of doors."[78] Remaining in the privacy of the upstairs was one way women with spacious homes could avoid the knowing eyes of friends and neighbors. Other women worried about being visibly pregnant in public. Penelope Warren, pregnant for the first time in 1840, wrote to her husband, "In two or three weeks my appearance will not be such as to admit of my going anywhere—for you know I am exceedingly particular & if I thought I showed hardly at all nothing could induce me to go out, but it is beginning to be quite perceptible what is the matter with me."[79] Yet a month later she was still going out to visit her friends, suggesting that practicality had won out over modesty. Many women were simply strategic in their use of clothing to conceal their pregnancy. In 1857 Tryphena Fox, a transplant from Massachusetts to the Deep South and eventual mother of ten children, rejoiced that she had so far hidden her pregnancy from public view: "You know one can dress admirably with, hoops & crinoline and I went to town feeling that I was not exposing myself in the least."[80] These women were motivated by a strong, yet conflicted, sense of propriety to keep their pregnancy hidden from public view, even as they strove to live their lives as usual.

Other women, however, indicated that the desire to conceal pregnancy was neither necessary nor universal. Esther Cox wrote to her daughter in 1809, "I have this day seen Mrs. Sumpter and am quite charmed with her easy agreeable manner. . . . I am very glad she consented to come, French Ladies don't keep out of company, as ours do, when they are rather clumsily shaped."[81] Matilda Henry seemed to concur that being pregnant in public should not be seen as shameful, complaining to her friend in 1837 that she was unable to leave home because family opinion dictated that "it is shameful (in this mighty refined they think part of the world) for a lady to go out so soon before her confinement." Her rather sarcastic comment on their pretensions to refinement suggests that she found their scruples excessive, and she openly regretted missing out on the season's social amusements. But she bowed to popular opinion, noting that "I went to church till I heard of people laughing and now I stay at home all together."[82] Similarly, Eliza Robertson seemed unconcerned about visiting friends while pregnant; her diary revealed that she frequently walked out to visit friends even in the later months of pregnancy.[83] Caroline Dall's attitude toward the matter in 1845 was more anguished and morally complex. She believed it was her God-given duty to her unborn child to get healthful exercise during her pregnancy—yet her mother, her husband, and acquaintances repeatedly insisted that she should remain indoors to avoid "attracting observation" because of her size. She was criticized for impropriety, yet she felt that her first duty was to promote the health of her child. In anguish at what she viewed as lack of support from her family, she wrote in her diary, "When will my own sex learn—that the child within their bosoms—is as precious and pure in his sight as that they lead by the hand?"[84] Viewing pregnancy as a physical state blessed by God, Dall could not understand why being visibly pregnant in public should be construed as improper.

Although the evidence is sparse, these scraps of women's writings suggest that the imperative for women to conceal their pregnant bodies from public view may have grown stronger over time. Whereas women writing in the late eighteenth century and the beginning of the nineteenth century seemed to suggest that staying at home was an option rather than a necessity, women living with pregnancy later in the nineteenth century seemed to experience greater pressure to keep their bodies out of view. This trend may have reflected the evolving vision in genteel print culture of the mother as a disembodied figure, which will be explored in subsequent chapters. If the ideal mother was increasingly defined as an ethereal and transcendent creature, then a parade of pregnant bellies would have posed significant ideological problems. Moreover, as succeeding generations of women began to bear fewer children than their foremothers (and thus spent less of their lives pregnant), it was perhaps more feasible to obey increasingly stringent notions of propriety. Yet what did not change over time was women's ambivalence toward this imperative to conceal their bodies. On the one hand, middle-class and elite women sought to conform to the social norms of their peers and to present an image of feminine modesty by downplaying their physicality; on the other hand, they were distinctly practical about being pregnant and carrying on with their lives. Women's personal writings reveal that they were often out and about when heavily pregnant, even though they may have felt embarrassed about being in public view.

Whether desired or not, pregnancy was a recurring part of life for most married women in the late eighteenth and early nineteenth centuries. When referring to pregnancy, they used a coded vocabulary that obscured the bodily changes involved; but at the same time, they frequently discussed and recorded the physical symptoms of pregnancy and commiserated with one another over their bodily discomfort. Women might hesitate to go out in company when visibly pregnant, but they still wrote letters to friends and family detailing their symptoms and complaining about problems such as swollen ankles and the general awkwardness of a growing belly. Their depictions of pregnancy were thus constrained by propriety but were also driven by a real desire to articulate their experiences and to receive advice and consolation, a trend that also characterized their descriptions of childbirth.

· · · · · ·

Over the course of the late eighteenth century American women began to experience gradual changes in childbirth practices. Prior to this time, childbirth was an exclusively female realm. Women gave birth at home with the assistance of female family and friends and a female midwife who relied on herbal remedies and a noninterventionist approach. But in the second half of the eighteenth century male physicians gradually began to enter the lying-in chamber. Between 1750 and the early nineteenth century

Americans began to see childbirth as the purview of both female midwives and male physicians. Midwives oversaw normal births, while doctors attended those with complications. By the early decades of the nineteenth century, the medical profession came to see childbirth as requiring greater intervention, and some middle- and upper-class women concurred, demanding the expertise of formally trained physicians.[85] Judith Walzer Leavitt has estimated that in 1800 roughly 20 percent of births were attended by physicians, while by 1900 that proportion had risen to roughly 50 percent.[86]

This shift toward male practitioners was experienced unevenly, depending on a woman's socioeconomic status, whether she lived in proximity to a doctor, her beliefs about childbirth practices, and the advice of family and friends. Access to doctors was more readily available to women who lived in towns and cities, where wealthy women and poor women were the most likely to encounter male practitioners, the former because they could afford the services of medical experts, the latter because they sometimes gave birth in hospitals for the poor rather than at home.[87] Enslaved women also sometimes encountered physicians in cases of complicated or prolonged deliveries.[88] Nevertheless, the majority of births through the 1850s were attended by a female midwife. Thus most women continued to give birth much as their foremothers had, in a female-centered environment. Even when a physician was present, he was often there in case complications arose, and most of the support for the laboring mother came from female friends and kinswomen. Although references to developments in medical practice and technology appear in some women's personal writings, these changes seem to have had little impact on the ways in which women recounted their childbearing experiences. While doctors made themselves the heroes of their own medical narratives, women placed the labor and the sensations of the mother at the center of their birth narratives.

As with pregnancy, some middle-class and elite women were torn between their sense of modesty and their desire to relate the circumstances of childbirth. For example, Agnes Cabell wrote to her stepdaughter in 1825, "I should have taken a great interest in learning the particulars of your accouchment, but as they cannot well be committed to paper I must wait until I see you."[89] Ellen Coolidge's attitude was somewhat more ambiguous when she wrote at some length of the pains and rewards of childbirth in response to her sister's queries. She concluded her letter by exclaiming, "What an abominable letter! Throw it in the fire & drive away all your blue devils."[90] Her sense of propriety required such an exclamation, yet it did not prevent her from responding to her sister with considerable candor. Other women were more comfortable sharing information about childbirth. When Rosalie Calvert wrote to her sister in 1807 to describe the recent birth of her daughter, she explained, "You asked me, dear Sister, for a complete account of the birth of my little Eugénie."[91] For Calvert and her sister, sharing reproductive news was normal, and frankness was appreciated. Matilda Henry was similarly direct when she inquired of her friend, recently brought to bed of a daughter, "Well how do you come on? . . . What sort of a time had you?"[92] Such questions were essential for ascertaining the well-being of loved ones.

Just as pregnancy could be signaled through coded language, childbirth had its own vocabulary that alluded to the panoply of experiences revolving around labor and its aftermath. Variations of the phrase "brought to bed" were particularly common in the eighteenth century and offered a comforting way of referring to an anxiety-inducing experience.[93] Mehitable Amory noted in 1812 that she was "most *Gratefully* & most *Comfortably* put to bed."[94] This phrase also highlighted the fact that women who could afford to do so might spend as much as a month in bed recuperating from their ordeal—they were brought to bed first to suffer and then to heal. By the nineteenth century, references to a woman's "confinement" were more common and provided a quick reference to a lengthy and complex experience. A woman's confinement referred both to childbirth and to the time she spent in bed recovering, suggesting that women continued to place childbirth within a broader context of rituals of recovery and healing. In addition, women consistently used terms such as "unwell," "sick," or "ill" to refer to a woman in labor, highlighting the fact that women saw childbirth as worrisome and even dangerous.[95]

Some women simply listed in their letters and diaries the friends and relatives who had been brought to bed, but many gave more detailed accounts of childbirth. In doing so, they relied on stock phrases to convey a wide range of meanings. In 1788 Abigail Adams reported that her daughter "Mrs. Smith & my young Grandson are as well as usual at this period." Mary Hering used similar language when she reported to her daughter that her sister had delivered a baby and "both Mother and Child are as well as we could possibly expect at this time." In 1839 Sarah Lindley Fisher, daughter-in-law of Sarah Logan Fisher, reported that a younger kinswoman had given birth and was "as well as could be asked, under the circumstances . . . no other difficulty than what is necessarily connected with such occasions attended her." Persis Black wrote of her own confinement in 1856 and announced, "I was dreadfully sick for some hours after the birth—but since then I have got along as well as common in such cases."[96] These oft-repeated phrases referred obliquely to the pain and messiness of childbirth, something with which most adult women would have been familiar. To announce that a woman was "as well as could be asked" conveyed a successful outcome but also hinted rather grimly at the difficult experiences that were an expected part of the childbirth process. Such stock phrases both alluded to the body and permitted it to remain veiled, allowing women to decide how far they wished to go in elaborating the physical experiences of childbirth.

In addition to using stock phrases to announce the outcome of a birth, women often followed a consistent narrative structure. This basic narrative was the most common description of childbirth to appear in middle-class and elite women's personal writings throughout the period in question. When women announced a birth they tended to focus on three key points: the outcome for the mother, the outcome for the infant, and an assessment of the birth in terms of its duration and the severity of suffering (often in that order). Sarah Logan Fisher, for instance, recorded in her journal in 1779 that she "was poorly all the morning & taken worse about Noon, & in between 8 & 9 was favord to be deliverd of a very fine Son, after a very hard difficult Labour, yet I was safely put to bed & everything right, which was a mercy I wish to be thankful for."[97] Martha Dyer of Virginia recorded a very succinct memorandum in 1824, noting, "I had a severe chill & fever before day sent for Mrs. Harrison I kept about all day till an hour by sun was taken & presented by the decrees of a kind providence with a fine daughter at quarter past 6 and as well if not better than usual."[98] In 1826 Georgina Lowell of Massachusetts sent a more detailed account to her closest friend, to whom she often wrote in French, announcing: "Il faut que je vous dise que notre cousine Catharine Codman a donné naissance samedi dernier à quatre heure du matin, à une petite fille. Ella n'a souffert que très peu: elle ne fut malade que quatre heures, et l'enfant vint au monde [sans] qu'aucune personne de la famille excepté Mme Stevens sa nourrice, eut appris ce qui se passait. Elle se porte à present très bien: la petite demoiselle est fort petite, mais se porte à merveille."[99] Lowell's announcement offered a bit of extra detail—she noted that one woman attended the birth—but followed the basic narrative structure. In these brief narratives many women noted with considerable relief that they were recovering from the trials of childbirth. Rachel Lazarus, a Jewish woman in North Carolina, wrote to her friend in 1828, "You do not yet know that my illness was subsequent to the birth of another daughter (my 3rd child). I was for some days at the point of death, and my infant was also despaired of; but through the goodness of the Almighty, it has nearly recovered, and I find myself, too, happy in being restored to my beloved husband and family."[100] Similarly, in 1850 Mary Fox recorded: "I was very very sick until the 6th March when my son was born at 10 o'clock. He was a very thin delicate baby he received the name of his Grandfather Joseph M. Fox. I did not suffer much and my recovery was gradual, but very sure."[101] The brief memorandums written by Fisher, Dyer, Lowell, Lazarus, and Fox were typical.[102] They did not evoke the physical intensity of the birth experience, but they did communicate the key results and characteristics of the delivery. In such textual moments, the sensations of the mother's body receded into the background of the narrative while the focus shifted to the outcome of her reproductive work.

Some women, however, employed very different narrative strategies in describing birth experiences. Instead of focusing solely on the outcome of a delivery, they described the series of events as they unfolded, noting moments of surprise, fear, pain, and triumph. These detailed birth narratives were highly individualized, but they shared a strong focus on the physical sensations of childbirth. Moreover, these detailed narratives became more common by the end of the eighteenth century. There are a number of possible reasons for this, the simplest being that we have more examples of women's personal writings at this time to draw from, and these writings tended to be more detailed in many respects. Yet it may also show that women were becoming more insistent in their depiction of childbearing as difficult and dangerous physical work. In their work on the Virginia gentry, Jan Lewis and Kenneth A. Lockridge have argued that women began to discuss childbearing with more trepidation and with more individualized detail beginning around the 1790s.[103] My findings likewise reflect some of these patterns, yet it should be emphasized that the more formulaic language and the basic narrative remained strongly in evidence into the nineteenth century.

Young and inexperienced women in particular sometimes described their experiences in greater detail. For instance, Mary Walker, one of several missionaries in Oregon, wrote candidly of her first birth in 1838, during which she was attended by two women and a physician. She began her birth story with a tone of surprise and a frank recognition of her body's functions: "Awoke about five o'clock A. M. As soon as I moved was surprised by a discharge which I supposed indicated approaching confinement. Felt unwilling it should happen in the absence of my husband. I waited a few moments. Soon pains began to come on & I sent Mrs. Smith who lodged with me to call

Mrs. Whitman."[104] Walker's explicit reference to the discharge of fluid that was a part of many women's birth experiences was unusual. But this was Walker's first child, and her birth story evoked the surprise, uncertainty, and anticipation of a woman going through this event for the first time. The moment when Walker's waters broke was an important physical memory, for it marked the moment of no return. Her birth narrative was remarkably complete in that it combined a sense of both the emotional and the physical experience of birth. She concluded her story with the sequence of emotions that marked her first delivery: "Almost nine I became quite sick enough—began to feel discouraged. Felt as if I almost wished I had never been married. But there was no retreating, meet it I must. About eleven I began to be quite discouraged. I had hoped to be delivered ere then. . . . But just as I supposed the worst was at hand, my ears were saluted with the cry of my child. A son was the salutation. Soon I forgot my misery in the joy of possessing a proper child."[105] Walker's narrative ended on a triumphant note, showing her transition from suffering and discouragement to the satisfaction of giving birth to a healthy infant. Walker eventually recorded five more deliveries, but with each subsequent birth she used the more basic narrative structure to simply announce the outcome and the nature of the birth. No doubt she had less time to write as her family grew, but her diary also illustrates that for many women the first childbearing experience warranted more extensive commentary. Women who were living through their first pregnancy and delivery (often in their early twenties) were, in a sense, encountering their bodies as adults for the first time, and many found it important to record the experience.

More extreme corporeal experiences also prompted women to push the boundaries of narrative convention. Indeed, women's most explicit representations of childbirth centered on intense experiences of suffering. In 1794, for instance, Elizabeth Drinker narrated the circumstances of her daughter-in-law's labor. Focusing on the woman's physical suffering, Drinker narrated the birth as a dramatic sequence of events that began when "John came in for liquid ladanem for his wife." Drinker then recounted her own participation in giving her daughter-in-law several doses of laudanum, "in hopes it would still those useless pains that she suffer'd—it appear'd to have little or no effect." The drama of the birth became more intense, and Drinker recorded that "the mid-wife inform'd me that le enfant est fort grand, et la mere bien pitit, it was her opinion que l'enfant [sont] [sic] mort,[106] that she wish'd I would send for a Doctor I wrote a note to Dr. Bensal of Germantown and sent Sam with the Chaise for him. . . . I left John and Hannah . . . and went with the Doctor to poor Mary—terrible was the succeeding hour to me, how must it have been to the poor sufferer?" Finally, continuing in the same hasty and scattered style that evoked the intensity of the situation, Drinker recounted the denouement of the scene: "The Doctor confirm'd what the mid wife had said, et avec ses instruments et beaucoup de deficility, ill la delivera d'enfant mort,[107] the first male child of seven, a very fine lusty baby—6 of the 7 dead born—Je n'etoit pas dans le chamber a le moment Cretical,[108] poor Mary appear'd very thankful that all was over—I think her a patient well inclin'd woman."[109] The immediacy of the passage appears in Drinker's initial focus on the suffering mother and her quest for relief from pain. Next Drinker highlighted the medical urgency of the situation—the concern of the female midwife, the arrival of the doctor, and the use of the instruments (forceps) both dreaded and welcomed by laboring women. Only then did Drinker reveal the final outcome—the death of the baby and the survival of the mother. This was childbirth at its most dramatic, and it warranted a different kind of story-telling, one that brought the physicality and danger of childbirth closer to the surface of the text.

Indeed, Elizabeth Drinker was often more frank than many of her peers in describing the physical challenges of childbirth, although this may have been partly due to the fact that she seemed to encounter more than her fair share of difficult births. According to her estimation, she and her daughters were prone to difficult deliveries and regularly sought the aid of physicians. Her narratives were more explicit when describing her daughters' labors than her own—in part at least because she had more time as a grandmother to write in her diary, and the longer entries in later years reflected as much. But she also wrote about her daughters' deliveries with empathy generated by the recollection of her own difficult experiences with childbirth. As Drinker recorded when her daughter Sally was in labor in 1799, "This day is 38 years since I was in agonies bringing her into this world of trouble."[110] Drinker was quick to record the suffering her daughters experienced. When her daughter Molly endured an agonizing birth in 1797 due to the wrong presentation of the child, Drinker noted that "Docr. Way said her labour was very severe indeed, that he never knew a young woman pass through so much, with equal fortitude and patience."[111] The next day Drinker reported that she had found her daughter the next morning "awake and feverish—she lay very still most of this day, but very sore, and complain'd of her left side being brused by lieing so long on it, and straining so hard—the blood was settled in the ends of her fingers, by hard pulling, and her nails blue."[112] This was a picture of struggle and physical anguish that cut to the heart of women's experiences of childbirth.

Roughly half a century after Elizabeth Drinker's daughters had suffered in childbed, Caroline Dall eloquently recounted her own agonizing birth experiences. "I was just on the point of preparing my bed, when I felt a sudden relief—from the breaking of the water," she recalled in 1848. "I undressed & threw myself hastily on the bed, from which I was not destined to rise again, till all was over. . . . Two pains rending—splitting—tearing me asunder—with inconceivable rapidity, followed quick upon the first, and while my girl went to the head of the stairs, to call Mrs. P. I fell back exhausted by agony and my child was born."[113] Although she recorded this birth experience five weeks after the fact, Dall was clearly preoccupied with evoking the immediacy of pain. She recounted her next childbirth in 1849 in a similar fashion: "I slept quietly till a little after eleven when I woke with pains so severe that they drove me out of bed like a rocket. I bore them quietly as I could till ten minutes of twelve when I hurried Mr. Dall to wake Mrs. Rowe and Mrs. Gardiner. There was no interval between my pains, they overlapped, and my agony was almost too great for human nature. Thank Heaven, they did not last long."[114] With that, her second living child was born. Dall's evocation of pain was more urgent than in most women's birth narratives; yet other mothers would have recognized the consuming nature of the physical suffering she depicted.

For enslaved women, the unique trauma of giving birth in slavery was another factor that could shift the pattern of storytelling. We lack sufficient numbers of childbirth narratives from the lips or pens of enslaved women to trace narrative patterns in the same way that we can for middle-class and elite white women, but two powerful stories from Harriet Jacobs's memoir intimate that the social trauma of childbearing in slavery may have held greater resonance in the minds of enslaved women than either the outcome of the birth or the physical suffering of the mother. Jacobs told the story of her first pregnancy and delivery in considerable length: "For some weeks I was unable to leave my bed. I could not have any doctor but my master, and I would not have him sent for. At last, alarmed by my increasing illness, they sent for him. I was very weak and nervous; and as soon as he entered the room, I began to scream. They told him my state was very critical. . . . When my babe was born, they said it was premature. It weighed only four pounds; but God let it live. I heard the doctor say I could not survive till morning. I had often prayed for death; but now I did not want to die, unless my child could die too."[115] Jacobs's narration emphasized two key facets of her experience: her terror of being in the presence of her owner and tormentor and her view of death as a means of escape for both her and her infant. Of secondary importance in her narrative was the actual outcome of the birth—the survival of both herself and her infant. Rather than offer narrative resolution, Jacobs evoked unresolved tension between life and death in the context of enslavement. Because this childbirth story was published as part of Jacobs's larger narrative condemning slavery, it is perhaps not surprising that she should emphasize the social conditions surrounding her reproductive experiences as a way of furthering her argument against slavery.

Another birth story recounted by Jacobs further highlighted the ways in which social conditions could supersede physical experience in enslaved women's narratives. Jacobs wrote: "I once saw a young slave girl dying soon after the birth of a child nearly white. In her agony she cried out, 'O Lord, come and take me!' Her mistress stood by, and mocked at her like an incarnate fiend. 'You suffer, do you?' she exclaimed. 'I am glad of it. You deserve it all, and more too.'" As with her own delivery, Jacobs emphasized the emotional trauma of giving birth in slavery. She again highlighted an understanding of death as escape from servitude rather than as a personal and family loss: "The girl's mother said, 'The baby is dead, thank God; and I hope my poor child will soon be in heaven, too.' 'Heaven!' retorted the mistress. 'There is no such place for the like of her and her bastard.' The poor mother turned away, sobbing. Her dying daughter called her, feebly, and as she bent over her, I heard her say, 'Don't grieve so, mother; God knows all about it; and HE will have mercy upon me.'" Jacobs consistently portrayed death as a welcome release from slavery, a common trope in antislavery literature, but she also used the physical suffering of the young mother to underscore the immorality of slavery. She described how the young mother's sufferings "became so intense, that her mistress felt unable to stay; but when she left the room, the scornful smile was still on her lips. Seven children called her mother."[116] Jacobs used the intensity of the mother's suffering to show how the institution of slavery destroyed what should have been an empathic community of mothers. For her, the corrupting influence of slavery appeared in the fact that a loving white mother of seven children could not empathize with the physical anguish of another woman passing through the throes of childbirth. These two birth stories told by Jacobs signal that, at least in the more public context of the published slave memoir, the narrative patterns developed in white women's private writings were less useful in conveying the experiences of enslaved mothers. Jacobs used maternal suffering not to highlight the dangers of motherhood but to make a broader point about the failure of American social relations.

But the physical suffering of women in childbirth was nevertheless a constant theme in all childbirth narratives. Women's testimonies revealed that pain was often at the heart of their understanding and experience of childbirth. In many women's minds, the maternal body was above all a vessel for suffering. Hannah Heaton wrote passionately in her diary of her fears of pain when giving birth in the mid-eighteenth century. "Now there came a turn of extreme fear and terror upon me about the hour that i cannot escape and now it draws near," she wrote. "I got into a fit of extream crying. i was alone begging for mercy. O how fraid i am of the pain tho i believe i shall not die till i have seen them promises fulfild in the building up of zion."[117] Heaton was a deeply religious woman, yet her fear of the pain of childbirth temporarily overwhelmed her faith. Sarah Logan Fisher, another pious woman, recorded a fervent prayer in her diary in anticipation of childbirth that revealed her anticipation of suffering: "Be a stay & support to my mind during this fiery trial, which sometimes appears to be more than my nature can support & in the painfull Hour that is approaching, sustain & strengthen me by thy Love."[118] For Fisher, pain was a regular companion throughout repeated cycles of childbearing, and she noted it consistently but with varying degrees of resignation and anguish in her diary. Other women were less inclined to bear pain with resignation. In 1804 Jane Williams described her daughter as an extremely fond mother, but reported that "Hill declares she does not think she could or would undergo the same Pain that brought it to save its life, it so far exceeded her belief or expectation."[119] For Williams's daughter, the pain of childbirth was shocking and impossible to bear, and she refused to regard it with resignation. Similarly, the physician James Anderson described how Mary Owens, whose child he delivered in the Philadelphia almshouse, was overcome by the pain of labor. He noted in his records that she exclaimed that "she could not support herself thro' the gloom, and that death would inevitably release her from these sufferings, which had become unsupportable."[120] For many women, the pain of childbirth seemed more than they could bear, yet it was an experience they could not avoid.

For many first-time mothers in particular, pain loomed especially large in the imagination. Ellen Coolidge replied to her sister's queries in 1826 by explaining, "To your question whether the birth of a baby is as bad as having all your teeth drawn at a sitting I can only remind you of what Napoleon said to O'Meara, that the worst of all pains is the one under which we happen to be suffering." Her sister was pregnant with her first child at the time and anxious about impending childbirth. Coolidge continued to reassure her, "I do not attempt to deceive you as to the *pain*, but upon the whole you get through it infinitely better than you could possibly conceive without having experienced the strength & support that is granted to a woman even in the hardest part of the operation."[121] Coolidge was calm and confident from experience, but she admitted to her sister that pain was at the heart of childbirth. Sidney Carr, like Coolidge's sister, had concerns about pain. Pregnant for the first time, she wrote plaintively to her sister in the 1820s, "My dear Jane how can I ever get through[.] I feel as though I would rather die than bear so much pain."[122] In 1853 Elizabeth Neblett counted the days until the birth of her first child and wrote, "I know I have no conception of the pain nor can have none, until I feel and experience it."[123] For many women, pain defined their expectations of childbirth and caused them to regard impending motherhood with fear.

Even for experienced mothers who had survived childbirth before, pain was foremost in their thoughts when they anticipated childbirth. In 1837 Matilda Henry wrote to her friend, "I sometimes wish it could have been ordered that women could bear children easily but then I remember it is a decree of Heaven to be otherwise and I no longer repine. . . . All I want is to be well over it and *never, no never* be so *again*."[124] Henry's emphatic wish never to be pregnant again spoke volumes about women's fear of pain. Even when childbirth passed smoothly, women still highlighted pain in their recounting of the events. Mary Scott reported to her sister in 1826 that "my confinement which as you may have perceived I dreaded exceedingly was a more fortunate one than I ever had. My child was born *almost* without pain."[125] To give birth almost without pain was indeed an occasion worthy of note, and other women also noted with pleasant surprise when the event passed with less suffering than expected. Pain was assumed to be part of the birth experience. As Mary Middleton wrote to her daughter in 1840, "God grant you may not suffer more than Mothers usually do!"[126] Most women understood the pain of childbirth to be inevitable, as decreed in the Bible and made real by experience.

By the 1850s, however, medical technologies began to evolve, and some women and their physicians began to question the inevitability of pain. On January 19, 1847, the Scottish obstetrician James Young Simpson administered ether to ease the delivery of a woman with a deformed pelvis. This was the first known use of anesthesia in childbirth, and it quickly prompted debates on both sides of the Atlantic about the advisability of tampering with the pain of childbirth. Physicians such as Charles Meigs thought that anesthesia interfered with the natural process of childbirth, but such ideas were soon overshadowed as physicians such as Walter Channing became proponents of anesthetized childbirth and women became vocal in demanding it.[127] On April 7, 1847, Fanny Longfellow was the first American woman to give birth under the influence of ether, and she immediately became a champion of anesthetized birth. After the birth she wrote to family, explaining, "I am very sorry you all thought me so rash and naughty in trying the ether. Henry's faith gave me courage, and I had heard such a thing had succeeded abroad, where the surgeons extend this great blessing much more boldly and universally than our timid doctors. Two other ladies, I know, have since followed my example successfully, and I feel proud to be the pioneer to less suffering for poor, weak womankind. This is certainly the greatest blessing of this age, and I am glad to have lived at the time of its coming."[128] Longfellow identified suffering as the essence of women's childbearing experience and declared that anesthetized childbirth was surely the greatest blessing for women. Many women seemed to agree. The physician Samuel Butler, for instance, recorded a case in 1857 in which "the labor was protracted, and the pains severe. The mother was very desirous to take chloroform, but I did not think best to administer it."[129] Although Butler chose not to administer chloroform, his record reveals the mother's knowledge of available treatments and her strong desire to transform her experience of childbirth. The enthusiasm for anesthetized childbirth on the part of women and some physicians suggests that this new technology may have prompted a turning point in perceptions of childbirth. Indeed, Nancy Theriot has argued that women who bore children in the late nineteenth century came to have a more optimistic view of childbearing than their foremothers. They enjoyed a greater degree of control over their fertility, and they incorporated the possibility of painless childbirth into their vision of motherhood.[130] Further research in women's personal writings beyond the 1850s might reveal gradual changes in the ways women represented the physicality of childbearing as the possibility of painless birth became more common, influencing both the lived experience of childbirth and women's attitudes toward it. But throughout the period in question here, pain was an expected and feared aspect of childbirth.

As if the fear of pain were not bad enough, childbearing women were also acutely aware of the dangers of childbirth and the ever-present possibility of death. In their diaries and letters women regularly reported the survival or death of friends and relatives in childbirth. Elizabeth Ball wrote to her friend in 1760, "It gives me reall pleasure to hear you are the living Mother of a living Child the Lord has now been kinder to you then your fear." Her friend, she noted, had been preserved by God from the "dark borders of the grave."[131] Other women were not as lucky. Rebecca Shoemaker recorded in 1785 that "Becky Jones, Late Waln, was removed almost as Suddenly, to the great grief of her frds. She was ill but 48 hours & died yesterday in child Bed."[132] Similarly, Hannah Sansom noted in her diary in 1785 that "this day died Rebecca Jones, wife of Esra Jones, a young woman with her first child."[133] Eleanor Lewis most likely spoke for many women when she wrote in 1826 that "death has ever been more terrible to me in *that* shape than in any other."[134] So fearful was she of the dangers of childbirth that upon her daughter's marriage she earnestly prayed that the latter would never become a mother.[135] The threat of death was particularly gruesome in the context of childbirth. Death might come during the agonies of a difficult childbirth or sneak up on a mother in the following days. A woman's body could become her greatest enemy.

Childbearing women in the eighteenth and nineteenth centuries left a wide variety of birth narratives, some following long-established conventions, others depicting highly individualized experiences of childbirth. Across the generations women employed familiar phrases and narrative structures to announce the outcome of childbirth while maintaining a genteel distance from the messiness of the body in labor. At the same time, women giving birth for the first time or experiencing or witnessing extreme suffering wrote more individualized accounts. Pain in particular forced the body to become more prominent, and it shaped women's attitudes toward motherhood. Pain and death also connected women from one generation to the next. As Maria Flagg noted in 1793: "I can't reflect without pain, that I was the innocent cause of her death. I always thought & think now, that if I am ever married, what she suffer'd for me, I shall for *another*, believe me in such a case it will comfort me to think I am paying the debt I owe."[136]

· · · · · ·

The textual evidence illuminating women's physical lives as mothers in the eighteenth and nineteenth centuries is often fragmentary at best, offering fleeting glimpses of a panoply of experiences that shaped the life cycles of most adult women. Women's narratives of childbearing reveal the complex situations in which they found themselves as mothers. The testimonies of enslaved women emphasized that their bodies represented a battleground on which they fought for bodily integrity and struggled to embrace or reject motherhood on their own terms. For these women, their reproductive labor was only one facet of the demands made on their bodies, and their testimonies reveal that they understood motherhood as part of the broader context of their enslavement.

Middle-class and elite white women, on the other hand, lived with the expectations of a culture that valued white feminine purity, physical delicacy, and moral superiority. Beginning in the late eighteenth century, genteel society increasingly valued restrained and orderly bodies that retreated into the background and allowed the soul and the intellect to shine forth.[137] In short, mothers lived and labored in a society that increasingly privileged the ethereal over the material. The tension between lived experience and cultural prescription appears in the language and patterns of middle-class and elite women's personal writings. They gave accounts of their reproductive lives by deploying a conventional vocabulary that veiled the corporeality of childbearing. They wrote discreetly of being in a particular situation and wrote hopefully of the emotional pleasures of motherhood. But then the physicality of childbearing broke through the barriers of convention, and women described the daily annoyances and discomforts of pregnancy that seemed at times to dominate their lives and thoughts. Less often, but with more drama, women also wrote about their fears of pain and death, and they described scenes of suffering in childbirth. Although these women often embraced the idealization of motherhood that began to emerge in the second half of the eighteenth century, they ultimately took their own physical experiences as the foundation for their perception of motherhood.

In spite of the often incomplete nature of women's childbearing stories, taken together, women's letters, diaries, and testimonies provide a rich well of information that reveals the extent to which they understood their lives to be shaped by the repeated rhythms of pregnancy, childbirth, and childrearing. They saw their life histories in the number of pregnancies endured, the number of children born, and the changes these experiences wrought on their bodies. For some women these events represented a history of joy and completion, but many women became mothers under the shadow of fear, suffering, danger, and coercion. By recognizing the centrality of the body to women's understanding of maternity, we also acknowledge the ambivalence that shaped many women's attitudes toward motherhood.

3   **The Highest Pleasure of Which Woman's Nature Is Capable**

Breastfeeding and the Emergence of the Sentimental Mother

· · · · · · · · · · · · · · · · · · · · · · · · · · · · · · · · · · · · · · · · · · · · ·

Pregnancy and childbirth posed significant challenges to the idealized images of motherhood that began to emerge in the eighteenth century. The implications of sexuality, pain and danger, and the simple messiness of the physical body seemed to contradict the increasingly powerful cultural vision of motherhood as primarily a moral and emotional role. The imagined figure of the sentimental mother was defined by her virtue, her piety, and her tender maternal affections, a vision that left little space for exploring the challenges posed by the reproductive body. Physicians struggled to reconcile their encounters with the maternal body with notions of female virtue and delicacy, while childbearing women themselves confronted the tensions between their emotional and physical lives as mothers. The issue of breastfeeding, however, provided a unique context in which some of these tensions could be worked out by prescriptive writers who created an ideological realm in which the maternal body and maternal virtue merged around the act of breastfeeding. By the end of the eighteenth century breastfeeding came to be idealized as the sentimental mother's greatest joy and pleasure, fostering a vision of motherhood that erased more problematic aspects of the maternal body and replaced them with a celebration of the nursing mother as the epitome of female virtue and moral influence.

The second half of the eighteenth century saw the appearance of a significant volume of advice literature intended to instruct women in the art of childrearing.[1] Both practical and ideological in nature, these texts provided detailed advice on infant care while also offering interpretations of the moral and emotional duties of mothers. Breastfeeding figured prominently in these discussions both as a topic that demanded practical advice and as a primary ideological vehicle for articulating the attributes of the sentimental mother. Most of these advice manuals were written by British authors and were then circulated in America, shaping a rich transatlantic discourse on the nature and responsibilities of motherhood. The majority of these early advice manuals were written by physicians and the occasional minister, though a handful of treatises by female midwives or mothers also appeared. By the nineteenth century American physicians and moralists began to produce their own body of advice literature for mothers, and it was also at this time that significant numbers of women began to put their ideas and expertise as mothers into print in advice manuals and shorter didactic writings for women's magazines, combining practical advice for childrearing with a deeply sentimental appeal to the shared experiences of motherhood.[2]

In their discussions of breastfeeding, prescriptive authors generally agreed that infants should be nursed by their mothers rather than be suckled by a wet nurse or fed by hand. Two primary types of argumentation in favor of maternal breastfeeding emerged in this advice literature. Eighteenth-century authors primarily sought to persuade mothers to breastfeed their own children by emphasizing the benefits of nursing for infant and maternal health, by levying harsh criticism against women who failed to nurse, and by offering practical advice to help women manage nursing. A second strain of argumentation also tentatively emerged that emphasized maternal breastfeeding as a physically and emotionally pleasurable experience for women. By the end of the eighteenth century, prescriptive writers began to place greater emphasis on maternal pleasure as their primary argument in favor of breastfeeding. By shaping their discussions of breastfeeding around images of physical and emotional pleasure, advice manual authors transformed the messiness and danger of the maternal body and reimagined the maternal breast as the locus of sensibility, sentiment, and maternal virtue.

Breastfeeding provided a unique context in which the maternal body could be presented as neither frightening nor disruptive. Representations of the breast as the principal site of maternal and familial pleasure simplified and refined the complexity of the female body, resulting in a narrowly idealized space in which maternal corporeality could be safely celebrated. Of course, in real life breastfeeding could be physically difficult and disruptive. Lactating breasts leaked fluid, an unavoidable reminder of unrestrained corporeality. More devastatingly, breastfeeding could lead to excruciating conditions such as abscesses and cracked nipples. For many mothers there was little that was ideal about the daily practice of breastfeeding, though they understood its importance as one of their maternal duties. But women's lived experiences did not diminish the fact that breast-feeding became a primary symbol of the good mother.[3] As the Scottish physician and popular medical writer William Buchan effused, "In the language of love, women are called angels; but it is a weak and a silly compliment; they approach nearer to our ideas of the Deity: they not only create, *but sustain their creation*, and hold its future destiny in their hands" (emphasis mine).[4] Breastfeeding represented the pinnacle of maternal virtue and influence, and in this context the problematic maternal body was made to disappear in favor of an idealized vision of the wholesome maternal breast.

As sentimental images of maternal pleasure came to the forefront in discussions of breastfeeding, they created a picture of motherhood as effortless and delightful, a role that women fulfilled naturally. Though women's personal testimonies revealed the diligence and fatigue involved in breastfeeding an infant for twelve months or more and the complications that could arise throughout the process, prescriptive authors (while occasionally acknowledging the practical challenges facing nursing mothers) evoked the sense that breastfeeding was not work, but pure delight. The sentimental mother was inherently tender, affectionate, and dutiful, therefore she could experience no greater pleasure than in suckling her infant. Moreover, depictions of the nursing mother suggested that the broader work of raising a virtuous child was mainly accomplished by maternal influence rather than the labors of the mother. By breastfeeding, the sentimental mother imbued her child with virtue and piety, thus solidifying the infant's future as a virtuous citizen and a pious Christian. The complicated physical, intellectual, and emotional work of childrearing was time and again reduced to a single act—an intimate physical connection—that filled both mother and child with delight and led them together down the path of virtue.

· · · · · ·

The idealization of breastfeeding in prescriptive literature emerged in the context of a growing emphasis on motherhood and domesticity in eighteenth-century literary and intellectual life.[5] Enlightenment-era discussions of virtue and men's and women's respective roles in society led to a new view that the essence of womanly virtue was to be found in the figure of the sentimental mother. In this period sentimentalism came to define a new understanding of virtue and influence in which emotions were seen as a force for good in human life. Prior to this, women had been perceived to be driven by passion, excessively sensitive, and therefore lacking in reason, but in the eighteenth century emotion came to be viewed positively as a force for moral and social good.[6] Women thus gained a unique claim to moral power and influence. Although the Enlightenment took different forms in France, Britain, and America due to their respective political and cultural contexts, sentimentalism was a common denominator in political, social, and cultural life. Enlightenment thinkers, whose writings traveled across the Channel and across the Atlantic, saw feelings such as compassion and sympathy as natural and inherent to human nature and as the necessary foundation for a virtuous society. Sensibility, the acute physical and emotional ability to feel (pain, pleasure, sorrow, joy) and to empathize with the feelings of others, was a corollary to sentimentalism. These concepts were particularly important in America in the late eighteenth century as a component of nation-building in the new republic, for sentiment, sensibility, and sympathy were seen as the emotional glue that bound Americans together as part of a single virtuous community.[7]

Sentimentalism and sensibility permeated political and philosophical discourse in Europe and America, and it also found its way into the popular literature and culture of the eighteenth century. The English author Samuel Richardson's best-selling novel *Pamela*, for instance, was first published in 1740–41 and illustrated the importance of sentiment and sensibility in expressing and sustaining feminine virtue. Richardson located virtue in the simplicity, sincerity, and sensitivity of the young Pamela's emotions, while he explored Mr. B.'s evolution from a man of base passions to a man of wholesome sentiment. More importantly for this discussion, *Pamela* was one of the first widely read literary texts to locate female virtue in maternal sentiment and sensibility. Popular in England and America and on the Continent from the 1740s on, the novel anticipated an emerging understanding of motherhood as women's principal contribution to society and a growing perception that women were especially defined by their sentimental nature and extreme sensibility.[8] Two decades later, a similar conception of motherhood was articulated by the French philosopher Jean-Jacques Rousseau in his popular and highly influential work *Emile,* which highlighted the mother's unique moral duty to her children and to society.[9] As Rousseau wrote, "When mothers deign to nurse their own children, then will be a reform in morals; natural feeling will revive in every heart; there will be no lack of citizens for the state."[10] This notion of moral motherhood gained particular prominence in America during the Revolution and became increasingly significant with the formation of the republic as writers began to draw a connection between the virtuous citizenry necessary for a stable republic and the moral influence of mothers. As Margaret Cox explained in her writings on motherhood, "To American mothers . . . is then committed, in a special manner, the solemn responsibility of watching over the hearts and minds of our youthful citizens, who are soon to take their places on the public arena."[11] Women were understood to possess a special aptitude for personal Christian virtues that made them particularly suitable for raising children and creating a wholesome home environment, while men were seen as better suited for the public virtues of service to the state and patriotic self-sacrifice.[12]

The Enlightenment was not the only source of new ideas about motherhood and women's social roles. Evangelical Christianity in both England and America supplied a new emphasis on emotion, female piety, and motherhood that began to emerge during the religious revivals of the eighteenth century and flowered more fully in the early decades of the nineteenth century. The notion of female influence, particularly in the context of motherhood, became central to religious rhetoric, granting women a significant claim to moral authority within the family, the church, and society.[13] Ruth Bloch has suggested that this Christian vision of female and maternal influence most likely enjoyed even broader popular support than Enlightenment ideas, for evangelical and nonevangelical Protestants alike adopted the ideal of the tender and moral mother whose Christian influence would transform the domestic sphere, and eventually society at large, into a haven of piety.[14] As the American minister, historian, and prescriptive writer John Abbott intoned: "O mothers! Reflect upon the power your Maker has placed in your hands. There is no earthly influence to be compared with yours. There is no combination of causes so powerful, in promoting the happiness or the misery of our race, as the instructions of home. In a most peculiar sense, God has constituted you the guardians and the controllers of the human family."[15] Although this Protestant vision of women's moral authority, particularly as mothers, differed from Enlightenment discussions of motherhood in that it deemphasized reason in favor of piety, both visions highlighted the importance of sentiment and sensibility in describing and enacting motherhood. It was the sentimental mother's ability to be physically and emotionally attuned to her child that granted her unmatched influence over its character. More specifically, many prescriptive writers suggested that virtue was literally passed from mother to child via breast milk, making maternal breastfeeding essential to good mothering. Thus the sentimental mother was defined by her virtue, by her ability to feel deeply as a mother, and by her ability to create an emotional bond with her child that would fundamentally shape its character.

. . . . . .

Discussions of breastfeeding provided prescriptive writers with a particularly compelling context in which to develop and explore the core attributes of the sentimental mother. It was in the act of breastfeeding that her sentimental nature and her sensibility appeared most clearly. But this vision of the sentimental mother did not emerge immediately in the maternal advice literature of the eighteenth century. Early authors of maternal advice manuals agreed that breastfeeding was a central duty for responsible mothers, but they focused more on moral and pragmatic arguments in favor of maternal nursing than on sentimental rhetoric. They represented motherhood as a natural and instinctive role, but in spite of this characterization these early authors mistrusted women's ability and willingness to perform it. Nature made women mothers, yet some women evidently did not know how to mother properly. As one physician insisted, women lacked a "Philosophic Knowledge of Nature, to be acquired only by learned Observation and Experience, and which therefore the Unlearned must be incapable of."[16] In this view, women were uneducated in natural philosophy and other profound subjects generally reserved for the consideration of men, therefore they needed to be taught and supervised by men in order to ensure proper maternal devotion and correct parenting practices. Mixing criticism with hints of sentimentalism, early prescriptive authors wrote manuals to correct, educate, and encourage mothers.

Eighteenth-century prescriptive authors shaped their arguments in favor of maternal breastfeeding in a practical vein by emphasizing the health benefits of nursing for both mother and child. Medical writers in particular insisted that mother's milk was the only natural, and therefore wholesome, food for infants. As the British surgeon William Moss wrote in the 1780s, "There can be no doubt that the mother's milk is the only sustenance nature has designed for an infant at birth."[17] The English physician William Cadogan served as the governor of the London Foundling Hospital in the 1750s and was particularly concerned about what he perceived as dangerously low rates of maternal breastfeeding. His text on childrearing was one of the first and most influential of such texts, and it circulated in numerous editions in both England and America in the mid- and late eighteenth century. He was particularly concerned by high rates of infant mortality and saw maternal breastfeeding as the solution to the problem. Asserting that the mothers and infants of the working classes enjoyed better health because they could not afford to hire wet nurses, Cadogan made his case for maternal breastfeeding by emphasizing that the key to maternal and infant health lay in the respect of nature. "If we follow Nature, instead of leading or driving it," he insisted, "we cannot err. In the Business of nursing, as well as Physick, Art is ever destructive."[18] Artificial methods of infant feeding flouted the laws of nature and therefore ruined health. Cadogan also made his case for maternal breastfeeding by identifying it as essential to good maternal health: "If she be a healthy Woman, it will confirm her Health; if weakly, in most Cases it will restore her."[19] Moreover, he insisted that breastfeeding provided a cure for the psychological disturbances that he believed sometimes accompanied childbearing: "The Mother would likewise, in most hysterical nervous cases, establish her own health by it . . . as well as that of her offspring."[20] The British physician Hugh Smith, writing in the 1760s, was likewise concerned with high rates of infant mortality and explained that those who suckled their own infants had greater success than those who hired nurses or fed by hand, for "nature is always preferable to art." Moreover, he insisted that mothers who failed to breastfeed were more likely to suffer from fever, tumors, breast cancer, asthma, and other serious health problems. On the other hand, he claimed, "Many instances have I known of weakly and delicate women, who, at my particular request, have suckled their children, and thereby obtained a much better state of health."[21] These arguments about infant and maternal health were apparently so common that the British physician Alexander Hamilton, writing in the 1780s, concluded that "the important advantages derived from *Nursing*, both to the mother and child, are so universally known, that it would be needless, in this place, to give a detail of them."[22]

Early advice writers also based their arguments in favor of maternal breastfeeding on notions of moral duty and natural law. As Jean-Jacques Rousseau complained, "Since mothers have despised their first duty and refused to nurse their own children, they have had to be entrusted to hired nurses."[23] These writers criticized women for thwarting their God-given duty by refusing to nurse and stressed how essential this practice was. Hugh Smith described breastfeeding as the "first great trust which is reposed in them" and complained that humans were the only animals that abused natural law by refusing to nurse their young. Moreover, he asserted that "nothing but a strange perversion of human nature could first deprive children of their mothers milk."[24] *The Nurse's Guide*, an advice manual published in England in the early eighteenth century, emphasized that "the Duty of a Mother does not consist in conceiving, or bringing a Child into the World, but in bringing it up."[25] The first essential step in bringing up a child was to breastfeed it, and the author insisted that "every Mother that is in perfect Health ought to nurse her own Children herself, because she will be sure to take more Care of them than a Nurse. . . . Nay, further, a Mother will not fail to instruct and bring up her Child every Way better than a Country-Nurse can possibly do, who is very often given to Drinking, and all Sorts of Vice."[26] Not only were mothers presumed to be more diligent caregivers than hired nurses, but prescriptive authors also assumed that only a good mother (that is, one who was not tainted by the presumed vices of poverty and ignorance) could transmit appropriate moral values via her breast milk. Mothers who failed in this duty were severely criticized based on the belief that "a Woman must be very unnatural, who can part with her own Child."[27]

Prescriptive authors particularly vilified elite mothers for their alleged inattention to sacred maternal duty. As Alexander Hamilton asserted, "Women are to be considered but as half mothers who wantonly abandon their children as soon as born."[28] These writers believed that elite women were perpetually out paying calls, enhancing their wardrobes, going to parties, and attending the theater rather than remaining in the nursery to watch over their children. Sophia Hume, an early American religious writer, complained that fashionable women declined to breastfeed for the most frivolous reasons. For fear that breastfeeding might "prevent some little Delicacy in our Shape or Dress, or detain us from making unedifying and impertinent Visits, etc. we consign the poor Innocent into the Hands of a Stranger, to be foster'd by Women, often-times, of savage Tempers, and vile Affections."[29] Prescriptive writers harped on the neglectful tendencies of elite mothers, who in England did in fact often send their children to be wet-nursed in the countryside throughout the eighteenth century.[30] "Compare the opulent with the rustic," Hugh Smith urged his readers, "the success is still exceedingly different. How many children of the great fall victim to prevailing customs, the effects of riches! How many of the poor are saved by wanting these luxuries!"[31] One midwifery textbook suggested that practitioners issue vague threats about the greater prevalence of breast cancer in women who did not breastfeed in order to convince their elite patients to do their maternal duty.[32] Although these authors were openly critical of elite women, viewing them as selfish and frivolous, their criticisms implicitly acknowledged that breastfeeding was hard work. Nursing a child for twelve months or more required time, diligence, physical effort, and a degree of knowledge and skill. The commitment of so much time and energy would necessarily interfere with women's ability to accomplish other activities, frivolous or otherwise.

While criticizing elite mothers for neglect, prescriptive authors also romanticized the natural mothering they imagined prevailed in the more rustic homes of country folk and among the working classes. In their estimation, these were women who were not afraid of work and whose limited resources demanded that they use their own bodies to accomplish the labor of childrearing. William Cadogan insisted that "the Mother who has only a few Rags to cover her child loosely, and little more than her own Breast to feed it, sees it healthy and strong . . . while the puny Insect, the Heir and Hope of a rich Family lies languishing under a Load of Finery . . . abhorring and rejecting the Dainties he is crammed with, till he dies a Victim to the mistaken Care and Tenderness of his fond Mother."[33] Such remarks revealed a common contradiction in maternal advice literature regarding the convergence of good mothering and socioeconomic class. On the one hand, writers argued that elite women should not consign their infants to the care of working-class women, whose bad morals and uncouth ways made them unfit to nurse. In particular, they worried about the dangerous effects of wet nurses, whose "savage Tempers, and vile Affections" they feared would corrupt the constitutions and morals of the infants in their charge.[34] On the other hand, in the same breath these writers vilified elite mothers as unnatural and incompetent and praised the wholesome mothering that took place among working-class women. These prescriptive writers saw good mothering as occurring only within very specific circumstances. The elite mother's dissipated lifestyle made her a poor nurse and therefore a neglectful or at best incompetent mother. The poor woman who sold her milk out of economic necessity was likewise a monster, damaging her own infant by neglect and corrupting the infant she was hired to nurse with her bad morals and diseased milk. As Rousseau insisted, "The woman who nurses another's child in place of her own is a bad mother; how can she be a good nurse?"[35] Thus it seemed that only women who occupied the vague middle ground between fashionable excess and economic deprivation could possibly embody the perfect mother. It is perhaps not surprising, given the rising prominence of the bourgeoisie in eighteenth-century England and America, that prescriptive authors tended to elevate the virtues of middle-class women over the extremes of either poverty or wealth.

In addition to criticizing mothers and emphasizing the healthful effects of breastfeeding, early and mid-eighteenth-century advice manual authors began to hint at the concept of pleasure that was to become a central method of persuasion by the end of the eighteenth century. The author of *The Nurse's Guide* acknowledged that "there is a considerable deal of Trouble to be undergone in the bringing up of a Child," but insisted that the "trouble is sweeten'd and rewarded by a Pleasure and Satisfaction not to be conceiv'd."[36] The author summarized four key arguments in favor of maternal nursing: first, by breastfeeding mothers provided their infants with both nutritious milk and good morals; second, by breastfeeding mothers created a lasting sense of obligation and duty on the part of their children; third, breastfeeding was women's duty; and fourth, the good mother should breastfeed "because she is thereby put into a Capacity of receiving the greatest Pleasure and Satisfaction in the World."[37] Pleasure was not the first argument in this author's arsenal, but it was emphatically expressed. William Cadogan, writing at midcentury, explained that women who refused to nurse their children did not understand that "were it rightly managed, there would be much Pleasure in it."[38] Hugh Smith's 1767 manual perhaps best represented the transition toward a greater focus on pleasure and sentiment in advice literature for mothers. Although writing as a medical authority, Smith eschewed medicalized discussions of breastfeeding and focused instead on highly moral and sentimental discussions of women's duties as mothers. He evoked an emotional understanding of pleasure when he worried that the few women who were physically unable to nurse were "thus deprived of a happiness, only known to those who enjoy it."[39] These authors illustrated the transitional nature of ideas of motherhood in this period. They combined a pragmatic approach in their arguments in favor of maternal breastfeeding with a modest dose of sentimental rhetoric that emphasized that maternal virtue would be rewarded by pleasure and delight.

Prescriptive authors writing at the end of the eighteenth century and into the nineteenth century deployed some of the same practical arguments as their earlier counterparts. They insisted that breastfeeding was crucial for both infant and maternal health. The English midwife Martha Mears, writing in the 1790s, argued that nature made the mother's "health and happiness, and very often her life dependent on the discharge of this most sacred of all duties."[40] The well-known medical writer William Buchan claimed in his 1803 text that failure to breastfeed would result in "a great degree of fever in the whole system" and was dangerous to the mother, while the midwife Mary Watkins asserted that "fewer women die while they are nursing, than at any equal period of their lives."[41] These later authors also emphasized women's moral duty to breastfeed. Mrs. Dawbarn, for instance, insisted that when a woman becomes a mother "it will be her indispensable *duty* to suckle her child, if she be able, for it is *nature's law*, and cannot be violated without injury to both mother and child."[42] The English writer Louisa Barwell agreed, writing that breastfeeding "is a duty which may be attended with some degree of inconvenience; but this is amply compensated in the delightful feelings which are developed in the course of the nursing period, and the consciousness of performing a duty of the greatest importance to one in whom she feels the deepest interest."[43] Like their earlier counterparts, these writers were also critical of women, believing that the ability and desire to breastfeed was a part of human nature that had been corrupted by fashion. As one early nineteenth-century author exclaimed, "How dead to the finest feelings of our nature must that mother be who can voluntarily banish her infant from her bosom, and thus forego the exquisite delight attending the first development of its rational faculties. O fashion! Arbitrary tyrant, of what hours of heartfelt bliss dost thou deprive thy votary."[44] Similarly, the British minister Thomas Searle lamented the fact that some women gave up breastfeeding in favor of frivolous pastimes: "But alas! there are some, who, without any reason but their own indolence, the indulgence in other scenes and occupations, unnaturally assign the care of their infants to other hands."[45] The American reformer and physician William Alcott asserted with horror that "there are some mothers who seem to have a perfect hatred of children; and if they can find any plausible apology for neglecting to nurse them, they will."[46] Like their predecessors, such authors were certain that women who neglected to breastfeed must be unnatural mothers and were deserving of chastisement. As the prominent American physician William Dewees proclaimed in his 1825 guide to childrearing, those "women who may stifle this strong maternal yearning . . . have ever been the subject of the satirist's lash, and the object of the moralist's declamation."[47] These authors assumed that breastfeeding was natural and instinctual, and mothers who failed to breastfeed were therefore monstrous and unnatural.

Alongside these long-standing arguments, criticisms, and practical hints, later prescriptive writers also developed a vision of motherhood that emphasized the sentiment and sensibility of the ideal mother. As one author pointed out, mothers who refused to breastfeed displayed a "most shameful degree of selfishness and unnatural insensibility."[48] To be sensible was to be a good mother—to be insensible was an affront to female virtue. It is important to note that by the nineteenth century an increasing number of maternal advice manuals and magazine articles for mothers were being published by women and nonmedical men (often ministers and reformers), which could provide a possible explanation for the shift away from more pragmatic arguments in favor of maternal breastfeeding toward a more sentimental framework. Yet nineteenth-century medical writers frequently used the same kinds of sentimental language and moral arguments as laypeople, suggesting that the vision of breastfeeding as a crucial part of sentimental motherhood was a widely accepted framework. As William Dewees expressed it, "God has declared almost in every part of his living creation, that the female, for a certain time, is the natural protector of her offspring; to the human female he has been particularly emphatic, implanting in her affections, which are rarely subdued; and by giving her an organization most wonderfully fitted for the exercise of her best and most enviable feelings."[49] Although his interest in maternal and infant health was ostensibly medical, Dewees framed his advice in sentimental terms, emphasizing the strength and purity of maternal feeling in language that was similar to that of prescriptive writers coming from a nonmedical background.

In the context of this sentimental vision of motherhood, the language of pleasure became a primary vehicle for promoting maternal breastfeeding. Advice manual authors regularly evoked the emotional pleasure of the good mother as she suckled her child. The midwife Mary Watkins suggested that one of the consequences of women failing to nurse their children was that "the mother is deprived of a very high source of pleasure, of the most tender and endearing kind, which also remarkably strengthens her attachment to the infant of her bosom."[50] William Buchan mingled criticism and sentimentalism when he argued that nursing was "an obligation so strongly enforced by nature, that no woman can evade the performance of it with impunity. But cheerful obedience to this sovereign law is attended with the sweetest pleasures of which the human heart is susceptible."[51] The American physician Thomas Ewell similarly evoked the naturalness of the desire to breastfeed when he wondered "how any woman could be so lost to the feelings of nature, as to give up the pleasure of this undertaking."[52] In his view, women's feelings were naturally maternal, and therefore they found their greatest fulfillment in nursing their infants. The beloved American writer Lydia Sigourney exhorted women to fulfill their natural role in order to bask in the joys of motherhood: "Were I to define the climax of happiness which a mother enjoys with her infant, I should by no means limit it to the first three months. The whole season while it is deriving nutriment from her, is one of peculiar, inexpressible felicity. Dear friends, be not anxious to abridge this halcyon period. Do not willingly deprive yourselves of any portion of the highest pleasure of which woman's nature is capable."[53] This was high praise for breastfeeding indeed. Sigourney placed the experience of nursing at the center of women's happiness and encouraged mothers to embrace and extend this source of joy.

By highlighting pleasure as an inherent part of nursing, proponents of maternal breastfeeding naturalized a portrait of the sentimental mother whose happiness depended on an intimate physical connection with her infant. In their view, breastfeeding was natural, instinctual, and a profound source of pleasure and happiness. If breastfeeding was a mother's first and most important duty, it also guaranteed that motherhood would be defined by delight rather than by toil and difficulty. John Abbott summarized this view by asserting that "the human heart is not susceptible of more exquisite pleasures than those which the parental relation affords. Is there no joy when the mother first presses her infant to her heart? Is there no delight in witnessing the first placid smile which plays upon its cheek? Yes! The very earliest infancy of the babe brings 'rapture a mother only knows.' The very care is a delight."[54] Abbott's enthusiastic description of maternal joy suggested that the act of mothering was most profoundly defined by rapture.

These representations of maternal pleasure culminated in an emphasis on the physical mother-child bond, for only by nursing, cradling, and embracing a child could a woman be a true mother. As one author noted, "Happy the mother who *can* suckle her infant; she who has not the power to do so is deprived of one of the greatest maternal pleasures, while her toils and anxieties are more than doubled."[55] This author acknowledged the challenges of childrearing, but viewed the physical ability to breastfeed as not only pleasurable but also an escape from childrearing difficulties. William Buchan emphasized that the mother who could not breastfeed "is to be pitied in being thus deprived of the greatest pleasure of life, the pleasure of feeding and rearing her own offspring."[56] Prescriptive authors delighted in describing the intimate physical connection between mother and child, made more potent by the sensibility of the good mother. William Dewees focused his discussions primarily on the physical pleasure of the fond mother and insisted that she "*must not delegate to any being the sacred and delightful task of suckling her child.*"[57] These depictions also revealed that women's pleasure in nursing was not merely emotional—the joy of fulfilling a sacred duty—but also a fundamentally physical sensation of delight and satisfaction resulting from the act of nursing. As one woman wrote in 1805, "What a delightful employment it is to *suckle a beloved child,* who repays the kindness it receives with the sweetest caresses!"[58] If pleasure was an inherent part of nursing, then good mothering must be by definition a pleasurable experience. A popular women's magazine corroborated this idea in a sketch of the ideal mother: "She takes her child to her breast, and imparts that nourishment which the Creator has designed for its sustenance; and in so doing she is conscious of a new principle of delight, physically and morally. The turbulence of love is past, and she has now that tranquil enjoyment best adapted to her health and her moral and intellectual growth."[59] In obeying the dictates of God and nature, the good mother derived a new form of joy that permeated her body and spirit. No longer tossed about by the passions of romantic love, she attained the highest state of womanhood and could enjoy the physical and emotional pleasures of maternity.

In spite of the overwhelming emphasis on pleasure, prescriptive authors occasionally acknowledged that breastfeeding could involve discomfort and difficulty. The body of the nursing mother was not always as cooperative in life as it was on paper. The physician Thomas Bull explained that "the period of suckling is generally one of the most healthy of a woman's life. But there are exceptions to this; and nursing, instead of being accompanied by health, may be the cause of its being materially, even fatally, impaired." The problem, he argued, was not breastfeeding itself, but continuing to breastfeed too long or when the mother was too weak.[60] Tackling the issue of pain, American mother Ann Allen described breastfeeding as "a pleasing, although a painful sensation," but urged women not to be deterred, for, "if you would be a happy mother . . . be a faithful mother, and you will be rewarded daily."[61] William Dewees, whose text contained an entire section on breastfeeding "as a pleasure," referred briefly to the "fatigue and anxiety of nursing," indicating that breastfeeding might be more complicated than his other glowing depictions suggested. Fortunately, he stressed, these challenges would be overcome by the deep affection of the good mother for her offspring.[62] The popular domestic author Catharine Beecher asserted grimly that "many a mother will testify, with shuddering, that the most exquisite sufferings she ever endured, were not those appointed by Nature, but those, which, for week after week, have worn down health and spirits, when nourishing her child."[63] The pangs of childbirth were natural and of short duration, she suggested, but there was something particularly terrible about the experience of unnecessary suffering while breastfeeding. Even William Buchan, who rapturously promoted the pleasures of breastfeeding, acknowledged the possibility of discomfort. But, he argued optimistically, "a little pain is easily surmounted, and is followed by lasting pleasure."[64] Pleasure and pain converged in the maternal breast, signifying that mothering represented both a sacrifice and a peculiar privilege for women. More importantly, perhaps, these texts assured women who persevered in spite of pain or difficulty that they had attained the height of maternal virtue; pain was of little consequence when good mothering guaranteed lasting rewards.

Late eighteenth- and nineteenth-century depictions of breastfeeding as a pleasure contributed to a widespread vision of the good mother as a figure of sentiment and sensibility. She was compelled to breastfeed by her natural maternal affection and by a sense of moral duty, and her experience of breastfeeding was defined by extreme emotional and physical sensibility. In effect, these visions of the nursing mother transformed the messy and troublesome body—the one that might suffer breast infections, cracked nipples, fatigue, or poor milk supply—into a refined source of moral and emotional influence. A verse in a poem by Lydia Sigourney suggested how the physical work of the maternal body was reimagined as emotional labor. In her poem the voice of God spoke to a mother, telling her that "thou hast a tender flower/ Upon thy breast—fed with the dews of love."[65] Here the nourishing properties of breast milk were transformed into the more ethereal "dews of love." The physical link that breastfeeding created between mother and child was elevated far above a merely nutritional transaction. Moreover, these idealized depictions of nursing mothers defined the work of mothering as effortless and natural. As Lydia Sigourney illustrated in her *Letters to Mothers*, the maternal role came as naturally to women as the growth of beautiful plants in a natural setting: "You are sitting with your child in your arms. So am I. And I have never been as happy before. Have you? How this new affection seems to spread a soft, fresh green over the soul. Does not the whole heart blossom thick with plants of hope, sparkling with perpetual dew-drops? What a loss, had we passed through the world without tasting this purest, most exquisite fount of love."[66] The botanic images in Sigourney's portrait of maternal bliss emphasized the naturalness of motherhood. Maternal happiness grew like woodland flowers, watered with fountains of love. Indeed, the phrase "fount of love" was a particularly apt metaphor, for the lactating breast was consistently described as abundant and fount-like, a site where, as William Cadogan wrote decades earlier, milk "is poured forth from an exuberant, overflowing Urn, by a bountiful Hand, that never provides sparingly."[67] Thus Sigourney's emphasis on the fount of maternal love also echoed images of the nursing mother who symbolized the height of maternal virtue, influence, and delight.

· · · · · ·

At the same time that late eighteenth- and nineteenth-century prescriptive writers effused about the pleasures of maternal breastfeeding, they also developed a secondary and more provocative realm of imagery that raised the possibility of sexual pleasure centered on the act of breastfeeding. Historians of motherhood and breastfeeding have identified a long-standing cultural tension between visions of the maternal breast and the sexual breast in Western culture.[68] As Ruth Perry has argued, in the eighteenth century "maternity came to be imagined as a counter to sexual feeling."[69] The good mother was too moral to be driven by sexual passions. More pragmatically, in the seventeenth and early eighteenth centuries it was believed that sexual intercourse was detrimental to the flow and quality of breast milk, so that abstinence was considered the appropriate choice for lactating mothers. In this view, sexual activity could literally damage a woman's physical ability to be a good mother.[70] Although this tension between the maternal and the sexual is well documented by scholars in many social and cultural contexts, descriptions of breastfeeding in maternal advice literature suggest a more complex picture of the relationship between motherhood and sexuality. In fact, I would argue that beginning in the late eighteenth century, prescriptive discussions of breastfeeding allowed the maternal and the sexual to converge in the breast of the sentimental mother. The pleasures of breastfeeding at times took on sensual and even erotic tones, connecting the joys of motherhood to a broader realm of erotic enjoyment and romantic love.[71] Enthusiastic descriptions of pleasure in prescriptive literature located both maternal virtue and sensual pleasure in the act of breastfeeding, revealing a complex understanding of the relationship between maternity and sexuality.

Scholars have tended to treat motherhood and sexuality as separate phenomena with distinct histories, despite the obvious link between sex and childbearing. Perhaps one reason for this disinclination to consider sexuality and motherhood in tandem is our own cultural uneasiness with anything that allows for slippage between that which is maternal and that which is sexual. Americans today do not like to think simultaneously about motherhood and sex. Yet the body that gives birth and nourishes an infant may also be the body that experiences and creates desire, receives and gives pleasure. Another reason that it is so difficult to understand maternity and sexuality in tandem is that scholars have tended to cling to an understanding of sexuality in terms of (primarily heterosexual) intercourse, without exploring the complex play of desires and sensations that constitute the human experience of sexuality. Focusing on evocations of sensual pleasure in discussions of breastfeeding brings motherhood and sexuality together and adds a new dimension to our understanding of the trope of sentimental motherhood that came to dominate American cultural visions of womanhood by the nineteenth century.

Scholarly debates about the history of sexuality in the eighteenth and nineteenth centuries reveal a complex and often contradictory set of ideologies that emerged and coexisted in the period in question, making it difficult to clearly situate discussions of maternal pleasure in the broader context of sexual ideology.[72] Just as scholars have shown that the period from the late eighteenth century to the early nineteenth century was a transitional moment for ideas about motherhood, historians have argued that this period also saw changes in sexual ideology in European and American societies. Nancy Cott was one of the earliest scholars to posit a change in sexual ideology that began in the late eighteenth century in America. Prior to that period, women were defined as particularly lustful and driven by sexual passion, but by the beginning of the nineteenth century this view had all but vanished, and more weight was given to women's moral nature, while their capacity for sexual desire was deemphasized by a rhetoric of "passionlessness."[73] Like Cott, many scholars have marked the beginning of the nineteenth century as a turning point in the history of sexuality in America, signaling a period of increased emphasis on restraint in sexual ideology and practice.[74]

While there is good evidence for this interpretation, other scholars have rightly questioned what Michel Foucault has referred to as the "repressive hypothesis." In his influential study of nineteenth-century bourgeois sexuality, Foucault has argued that rather than being an era of repression, the nineteenth century in fact saw a vast multiplication of sexual discourses, behaviors, and identities.[75] More recent scholarship has followed Foucault's lead and shifted from an emphasis on sexual ideology to a greater focus on diverse sexual practices and attitudes, revealing much greater openness and enthusiasm for sexuality than previously suspected. For instance, John D'Emilio and Estelle Freedman's comprehensive survey of American sexualities argues that in the nineteenth century "the reproductive moorings of sexual experience gradually gave way to a new constellation of meanings, in which both love and intimacy became increasingly important." As married couples began to exercise control over childbearing, sexuality came to have a life of its own apart from reproduction, although women's lives continued to be shaped by the work of childbearing and rearing. Moreover, D'Emilio and Freedman argue that "during courtship and in marriage, sexuality came to be more deeply associated with the emotion of love and the quest for interpersonal intimacy."[76] More recently, Karen Lystra has taken up the question of romantic love and sexual intimacy. Exploring the attitudes of women and men toward one another and toward love, marriage, and sex, Lystra argues that in the nineteenth century "both men and women saw sexual desire as the natural physical accompaniment and distillation of romantic love. . . . Under the right circumstances, sex might be viewed as a romantically inspired religious experience, a sacrament of love."[77] In this view, sex enhanced the affective bonds that were at the heart of the domestic sphere, suggesting that locating female sexual pleasure in the context of motherhood was not perhaps as anomalous as it might initially seem. Pleasures, both maternal and conjugal, could be seen as blending and merging to reinforce the strength of family bonds.

Thinking about motherhood and sexuality in tandem pushes us to think more flexibly about the category of sexuality and what we mean when we speak of sexual pleasure. Most adult women in the eighteenth and nineteenth centuries could not separate sexuality from motherhood in the way that we do in twenty-first century America, where the widespread availability of effective contraception has largely decoupled sex and parenthood. In earlier eras sexually active women almost invariably became mothers at some point, and women who survived until menopause spent a large percentage of their lives either pregnant or lactating. Their sexual lives were thus inextricably entwined with their experiences as mothers, a fact that should push us to examine what it meant to have a simultaneously maternal and sexual body. Kathryn Schwarz has signaled the need to view the maternal breast as a possible site for female sexual pleasure, in the context of the "erotic dyad of mother and child," and, "still more disruptively," to consider the ways in which "the eroticized maternal breast might always prove to be *self*-satisfying, self-contained in its economy of desire."[78] Her analysis suggests that it is important to read eighteenth- and nineteenth-century prescriptive discussions of breastfeeding with an eye toward the maternal breast as a locus of female pleasure while also considering it as a center for the pleasures of both infant and husband.

Advice manual writers linked women's joy as mothers to the bodily experiences of maternity by portraying the mother-child bond created by breastfeeding as a profoundly physical experience that provided the mother with sensual pleasure. By focusing on the physical sensations of breastfeeding, writers at times described nursing as a sensual and even erotic experience. Although these advice manuals were certainly not intended to be read as erotic texts, their descriptions of breastfeeding veered toward erotica, which Karen Harvey usefully defines as "material about sexual pleasure which depicted sex, bodies and desire through illusions of concealment and distance: bodies were represented through metaphor and suggestion, and depictions of sexual activity were characterized by deferral and silence"[79] The concepts of suggestion, deferral, and silence are particularly useful here in considering the erotic in maternal advice literature. To notice in representations of breastfeeding the suggestion and deferral of sexual pleasure between husband and wife, the silence surrounding the possibilities of autonomous female pleasure centered on the breast, and the satiety of the nursing infant as a possible metaphor for or displacement of sexual satisfaction is to comprehend the enormously complex possibilities with respect to sexuality and motherhood in the eighteenth and nineteenth centuries.

By the end of the eighteenth century, when the rhetoric of pleasure emerged in maternal advice manuals, there was already a well-established tradition of print erotica in English and American culture. These explicitly erotic texts sometimes created a link between breastfeeding and sexual desire, suggesting that there was an existing cultural impetus to view the maternal breast and the sexual breast as one and the same. For instance, Thomas Stretzer's *A New Description of Merryland* (1740) was part of a genre of geographic erotica that portrayed the female body topographically and dwelled fondly on its charms, including the lactating breasts: "There are two other pleasant little Mountains called BBY, which tho' at some Distance from MERRYLAND, have great Affinity with that Country, and are properly reckoned as an Appendage to it. These little Mountains are exactly alike, and not far from each other, having a pleasant Valley between them; on the Top of each is a fine *Fountain*, that yields a very wholesome Liquor much esteemed, especially by the younger sort of People."[80] Stretzer's text indicated that the breasts and their fine fountains of milk (much esteemed by infants) were as much a part of the erotic topography of the female body as any other part, showing that in the erotic imagination at least there was little distinction between the maternal breast and the sexual breast. However, this type of depiction of the maternal/sexual breast was different from those that would appear in maternal advice manuals in that here the breast was subject to the desiring male gaze (and, presumably, touch), whereas advice manual writers first of all centered their discussions of pleasure on the sensations of the maternal body itself.

Alongside erotic texts, some early medical writers also offered discussions that linked sexual pleasure and breastfeeding. The sixteenth-century French surgeon Ambroise Paré described the act of breastfeeding as explicitly sexual, for he explained that "as the breast is tickled, the womb is aroused and feels a pleasurable titillation, since that little tip of the breast is very sensitive because of the nerves that end there." This titillation provided an incentive for "the female to offer and exhibit her breasts more willingly to the child, who tickles them sweetly with its tongue and mouth, from which the woman derives a great delectation."[81] Paré was obviously aware, at least to a certain extent, of the physiological link between suckling and sexual arousal.[82] Writing in the mid-eighteenth century, the British physician John Burton was more physiologically specific, describing how the sexual organs were connected by nerves to other parts of the body and using this fact to explain "why some [women] are so fond of giving Suck, and why Tickling the Nipples occasions an agreeable Sensation in the *Clitoris*."[83] These medical texts differed from prescriptive texts in that they framed their discussions in terms of anatomy rather than in the context of broader discussions of motherhood and maternal duty.

The large body of prescriptive literature for mothers that emerged starting in the eighteenth century provided a new realm for exploring the sensual aspects of motherhood in a context that was neither explicitly erotic nor solely medical. As the rhetoric of pleasure emerged in their discussions of breastfeeding, these prescriptive authors did not shy away from the sensual pleasures of the lactating mother and her nursing infant. The midwife Martha Mears, writing in the 1790s, waxed poetic on the physical pleasures of nursing and claimed that "the act itself is attended with a sweet thrilling, and delightful sensations, of which those only who have felt them can form any idea."[84] This description of the thrilling physical sensations of nursing was evidently so compelling that William Buchan included it in his own book in 1803.[85] He also gushed that "the mental raptures of a fond mother at such moments are far beyond the powers of description or fancy."[86] Breastfeeding was indeed a stimulating subject, prompting Buchan to refer on two separate occasions to the "thrilling sensations" of breastfeeding.[87] Buchan's references to thrilling sensations and mental raptures clearly exhibited the influence of Enlightenment ideas about sensibility, invoking the belief that the physical stimulation of the nerves would also prompt a similarly intense emotional response.[88] Thus the physical pleasures of breastfeeding stimulated corresponding emotional pleasures, fueling the affections of the good mother. Sensual pleasure and maternal feeling were mutually reinforcing.

While Mears and Buchan focused primarily on the pleasures of the nursing mother, other authors described the ways in which breastfeeding became a sensual experience for both mother and infant. Writing in 1825, William Dewees first offered a strikingly erotic description of the physical pleasures of lactation for the mother. He insisted that "if we can believe the *fond mother* upon this point, there is no earthly pleasure equal to that of suckling her child—and if any reliance can be placed upon external signs, she is every way worthy of belief." Dewees did not specify exactly what external signs might testify to the woman's experience of pleasure, but in case the reader did not quite catch the fact that this pleasure was profoundly physical, he went on to explain that "this pleasure does not seem to be the mere exercise of social feeling while the mother is witnessing the delight of the little hungry urchin, as it seizes upon the breast . . . but from a positive pleasure derived from the act itself; for most truly it may be said, when 'The starting beverage meets its thirsty lip, / 'Tis joy to yield it, as 'tis joy to sip.'" Thus women's pleasure was not simply the result of maternal affection or the sense of a duty well done; it was a pleasure specifically occasioned by the physical act of suckling an infant. Moreover, in the midst of Dewees's exuberant description of maternal pleasure, he noted the pleasure of the infant and the delight with which it "seizes upon the breast." He referred furthermore to "the rapturous expression of its speaking eye" and "the writing of its little body from excess of joy."[89] If Dewees was to be believed, breastfeeding was a physically pleasurable experience for both mother and infant that was tinged with sensuality and even eroticism. The raptures and writhing of the mother and her infant centered on the breast and signified a deeply sensual experience, superior to any other "earthly pleasure."

Other writers focused more specifically on the sensual pleasures enjoyed by the nursing infant. The American physician Frederick Hollick offered a tactile description of "the graceful swell of the fully developed breast" and suggested that the beauty of the breast was not merely aesthetic, but "a matter of positive utility, as well as of beauty, because it better adapts it to the use of the child, and probably also adds to its *pleasure*, as anyone may readily conceive who will observe the delight with which an infant, even when not nursing, will often caress it."[90] Here, the infant's delight in its mother's breast was not simply a matter of nutrition, for it took pleasure in caressing the breast at other times as well. Hollick's description echoed the vision set forth by the eighteenth-century English scientist and poet Erasmus Darwin in his popular and frequently excerpted set of poems in which he described the nursing infant as a plunderer of his mother's charms:

> So when the Mother, bending o'er his charms,
> Clasps her fair nursling in delighted arms;
> Throws the thin 'kerchief from her neck of snow,
> And half unveils the pearly orbs below;
> With sparkling eye the blameless plunderer owns
> Her soft embraces, and endearing tones,
> Seeks the salubrious fount with opening lips,
> Spreads his inquiring hands, and smiles, and sips.[91]

These verses dramatized the act of breastfeeding as a moment of unveiling in which the woman's charms were exposed to view and to the plundering mouth and hands of the infant. Darwin's and Hollick's descriptions slipped subtly between references to the beauty of the female breast (which could be appreciated by the male gaze as well as the infant's) and the pleasures of touch, here enjoyed by the infant but also imagined by the male authors. Darwin and Hollick both seemed to hint at what Sigmund Freud would much later make explicit in his work on child sexuality—that the experience of sexual satisfaction begins with taking nourishment from the breast. As Freud wrote, "No one who has seen a baby sinking back satiated from the breast and falling asleep with flushed cheeks and a blissful smile can escape the reflection that this picture persists as a prototype of the expression of sexual satisfaction in later life."[92] Although pre-Freudian prescriptive writers did not explicitly explore this avenue of thought, their descriptions of the sensual pleasures of breastfeeding for both infant and mother paralleled notions of sexual pleasure and satisfaction experienced by adult men and women.

Some texts also drew more specific parallels between the sensual pleasure of the suckling infant and the sexual pleasure of the fond husband. A didactic article in a ladies' magazine included an excerpt from the *Philosophia de l'univers* (1796) by the French economist and writer Pierre Samuel Du Pont de Nemours that described the ideal woman's physical attributes and explicitly attested to the fact that the maternal breast was always also a sexual breast. Exploring the intersection of motherhood and sexuality, the author proclaimed: "Let her enchanting bosom represent the celestial globes, of which a rose-bud shall form the magnetic pole. Let it offer to desire its first enjoyment—its first nourishment to infancy; and let man ever remain in doubt whether it has most contributed to the happiness of the father or the son."[93] Here, the infant's pleasure and that of the husband (and perhaps the mother too) intertwined around the enchanting breast. The author emphasized that the breast both fueled desire and provided nourishment, thus satisfying the infant and the father. Which of the two functions was more important the author could not quite decide, but his coy conclusion suggested that male sexual desire may have been foremost in his thoughts. Whatever his primary interest in the female breast, he brought together motherhood and sexuality in one clear image.

Alongside these parallels between infant desire and adult male desire, advice manual authors emphasized the link between maternal breastfeeding and marital happiness. Hugh Smith, writing in 1767, was one of the earliest authors to evoke the significance of breastfeeding for the marital relationship. Rapturously describing how a husband must feel upon seeing "a dear little cherub at your breast," he insisted that "how ardent soever such an one's affections might be before matrimony, a scene like this will more firmly rivet the pleasing fetters of love."[94] Moreover, he asserted that "though a beautiful virgin must ever kindle emotions in a man of sensibility, a chaste, and tender wife, with a little one at her breast, is certainly to her husband the most exquisitely enchanting object upon earth."[95] For Smith, breastfeeding enhanced female beauty and desirability and strengthened the bonds between husband and wife. These descriptions ran counter to an older belief that breastfeeding interfered with the enjoyment of female beauty and marital pleasures. Samuel Richardson, for instance, merged new ideas with old when his fictional heroine Pamela argued with her husband for the right to breastfeed her own child. Representing the new idealization of motherhood, Pamela insisted that it was her duty to nurse her infant, while her husband clung to older ideas when he told her in no uncertain terms that he believed breastfeeding would interfere with his enjoyment of her physical charms.[96] Thus Smith's depiction of the desirable mother represented a new vision of femininity in which motherhood defined the peak of women's moral, emotional, and physical appeal. Rather than allowing motherhood and marital relations to remain in tension, Smith skillfully melded the two around the enchanting maternal breast.

Smith was not alone in his assessment of the desirability of the good mother. As the nineteenth-century American phrenologist Orson Squire Fowler demanded, "Who but a flint-hearted gelding, emasculated of every manly virtue and feeling, can ever cease to love her who has borne him even but one child, and love her more and more by every new object of parental love? Certainly, who not riddled of every masculine feeling, but will be doubly enamored of her maternal charms, and chant anthems of perpetual love to her, while carrying within her the sacred casket of all his joys and treasures?"[97] Drawing a connection between true masculinity and passion for maternal charms, Fowler made it clear that maternity only enhanced feminine appeal and masculine affections. In this view, motherhood did not thwart male desire, but increased it. Mrs. Dawbarn shifted this vision slightly by depicting the pleasure that the good mother experienced in witnessing the enjoyment of her husband. She proclaimed that "there is no enjoyment in nature which affords such exquisite pleasure as is felt by a tender mother, when she is nourishing her infant at her breast, and beholds her husband smiling in approbation."[98] Although in this scene the husband ostensibly communicated approval of his wife's virtue as a mother, the gaze of the husband and the "exquisite pleasure" of the mother signaled other dimensions of their relationship. Overall, prescriptive writers agreed that women only became more appealing when they became mothers, and that the passion created by parenthood (properly experienced within marriage, of course) represented the pinnacle of heterosexual love. As Fowler put it, it is "after they have *become parents* together—that they can be completely enamored of each other; because it is her *maternal* relations which most of all endear the wife to her husband, besides making her love him inexpressibly more for being the *father of her idolized children*."[99] Motherhood and romantic love were therefore fundamentally compatible, even mutually dependent.

By mingling references to the pleasures of mother, infant, and father, advocates of maternal breastfeeding accentuated the parallel pleasures invoked by the touch and the gaze. Whereas descriptions of the mother and infant emphasized the importance of reciprocal touching, in other depictions the gaze of the husband took center stage and intimated that the sight of breastfeeding might provide as much pleasure as the physical experience itself. The husband took pleasure in watching his wife, while the wife took pleasure in physical contact with her infant *and* in her husband's gaze. Karen Harvey has explored the notion that visual connoisseurship was a specifically "masculine endeavor," especially when concerned with the female form. The sight of a woman breastfeeding was presented as a particularly appealing scene for the male gaze, and it contained erotic possibilities. The mother's flesh was evocative of both motherhood and sexuality, and the gaze of her husband encompassed and enjoyed both aspects of her corporeality. Thus in the descriptions of advice manual authors, breastfeeding became a three-way site of familial pleasure. The maternal breast became the focal point of the scene in which mother and infant enjoyed the tenderness of mutual caresses while the husband bore rapturous witness to their pleasures. The erotic possibilities revealed in these sources suggested that maternity and sexuality were meant to go hand in hand in the context of marriage.

Yet prescriptive authors' descriptions of breastfeeding also attested to a certain ambivalence toward erotic pleasure. While describing the pleasures of breastfeeding in rather exuberant terms, they also portrayed the mother as chaste and tender, a figure clearly untainted by base passions. Images of the mother as modest and restrained yet simultaneously swept by pleasurable sensations implied a drive to embrace pleasure while remaining within the safe bounds of appropriate feminine virtue and modesty. However, prescriptive authors seemed to be more explicitly concerned with the restraint of male sexuality. In their descriptions of the beauty, desirability, and virtue of nursing mothers, writers also claimed that breastfeeding created important familial ties that restrained men's potentially dangerous passions. Hugh Smith urged women to breastfeed their children as a way of preserving mutual ties of affection between themselves and their husbands, for, "by these powerful ties, many a man, in spite of impetuous passions, is compelled to continue the prudent, kind, indulgent, tender husband."[100] William Buchan asserted that by breastfeeding the good mother would ensure "the steady attachment of her husband."[101] By insisting on the respect and affection due a virtuous mother, these authors envisioned a way of controlling men's carnal urges, keeping men's sexual activities and affections within the bounds of marriage.

Acknowledging the potentially erotic dimensions of maternal advice literature raises conceptual challenges for historians. At first glance there seems to be a fundamental incompatibility between the maternal ideology that celebrated women as uniquely moral, chaste, and virtuous, on the one hand, and depictions of breastfeeding as a sensual pleasure, on the other. One possible resolution of this conflict could be to read the sensual descriptions of breastfeeding as a way of concealing female sexual pleasure within the more chaste physical enjoyment of maternity, as well as viewing it as a means of controlling men's sexual appetites by emphasizing the devotion due the pure mother. Yet to assume that advice manual authors sought only to disguise and restrain sexuality too readily falls in line with long-standing assumptions about sexual repression in this time period.[102] Instead, we might view the pleasures of breastfeeding as part of the ascendancy of romantic love in American culture, by which sex became an acceptable and even sacred component of a loving relationship. Karen Lystra writes that "properly sanctioned by love, sexual expressions were read as symbolic communications of one's real and truest self, part of the hidden essence of the individual." Moreover, she argues that Americans saw children as precious symbols of romantic love.[103] Representations of breastfeeding and its connection to loving marital relations hinted at this evolving attitude toward sexuality and romantic love in the late eighteenth and early nineteenth centuries. Thus we might see the eroticized triad of mother-infant-father as a means of retaining sexual desire and expression within the bounds of the home, offering a safe realm of sexual expression for virtuous women while drawing men away from the world of vice and into the bosom of the family. Descriptions of the nursing mother's sensual enjoyment opened an avenue for acknowledging women's physical pleasure while still remaining within the proper bounds of sentimental and domestic imagery. Motherhood and sexuality were not necessarily incompatible, for sexual enjoyment could be sanctified by romantic love and by parenthood. The erotic tones in advice manuals implied willingness, eagerness even, to explore women's capacity for sensual enjoyment in the context of sentimental motherhood.

These erotically charged descriptions add important nuance to our understanding of the trope of the sentimental mother. While historians might be inclined to ask whether the script of sentimental motherhood could be ideologically reconciled with visions of a robust female sexuality, perhaps a better question might be, did maternity and sexuality *need* to be reconciled? The language of pleasure employed by advocates of maternal breastfeeding performed important work in the cultural production of the sentimental maternal ideal by emphasizing the role of breastfeeding in cementing familial bonds and demonstrating maternal virtue. But descriptions of breastfeeding also valorized sensual pleasure and eroticized the figure of the mother without tarnishing her claims to virtue. It seemed that maternity and sexuality could coexist easily and naturally. Seamlessly invoking the joys and duties of motherhood *and* wifehood, William Buchan perhaps best summarized the multiple rewards of good mothering. In

Buchan's view, the nursing mother "ensures the fulfillment of the promises made by the best writers on this subject—speedy recovery from child-bed, the firm establishment of good health, the exquisite sense of wedded joys, the capacity of bearing more children, the steady attachment of her husband, the esteem and respect of the public, the warm returns of affection and gratitude from the objects of her tender care, and after all, the satisfaction to see her daughters follow her example and recommend it to others."[104] Buchan's ideal maternal script connected the "exquisite sense of wedded joys" to other facets of motherhood and marriage such as good health and filial affection. Thus he tied together the (exquisite) sexual enjoyment of the husband and wife and the satisfaction of the good mother. The concept of maternal sexuality was thus not the contradiction it might seem, but an important part of the sentimental maternal ideal. In the context of breastfeeding, advice manual authors created a vision of desire and pleasure that could flourish within the safe confines of motherhood and matrimonial affection, and these relations were in turn strengthened by the pleasures of breastfeeding.

· · · · · ·

In many ways, these advice manual authors were exceptional in acknowledging the potential for physical, even erotic, pleasure while breastfeeding. Their positive outlook on the convergence of motherhood and sexuality was eventually overcome by a suspicion of maternal sexuality, and it was not until the late twentieth century that a few American women, particularly feminist writers, began to embrace and explore in an explicit way the many pleasures implicated in the act of breastfeeding. The American feminist poet Alicia Ostriker was one of the first women in the twentieth century to openly discuss sexual arousal during breastfeeding. Ostriker described breastfeeding in the following verses:

Greedy baby
sucking the sweet tit
your tongue tugging the nipple tickles your mama
your round eyes open appear to possess understanding
when you suckle I am slowly moved
in my sensitive groove
you in your mouth are alive, I in my womb.[105]

The feminist writer Adrienne Rich explored similar connections between breastfeeding and sexuality. "The act of suckling a child," she wrote, "like a sexual act, may be tense, physically painful, charged with cultural feelings of inadequacy and guilt; or, like a sexual act, it can be a physically delicious, elementally soothing experience, filled with a tender sensuality."[106] But in the United States today any hint of sexual pleasure in the context of a maternal act conjures up the specter of sexual abuse in the public imagination, and the consequences for women who have admitted to feeling physical pleasure have been dire. Marilyn Yalom describes a case in which a child was taken away from its mother because she admitted to feelings of arousal during breastfeeding.[107] It seems likely that an eighteenth- or nineteenth-century audience would have been perplexed and outraged by the actions of the court. In the framework that prescriptive authors created, it was important for women to experience breastfeeding as pleasurable, as this experience was understood to strengthen maternal and marital bonds. Moreover, women's experience of physical and emotional pleasure was a testament to their sensibility, an essential trait of the sentimental mother. But now at the beginning of the twenty-first century most Americans recoil at the thought that breastfeeding can afford the mother any pleasure other than the satisfaction of a duty well done. In contrast, eighteenth- and nineteenth-century prescriptive authors created a rhetorical framework in which women could experience physical pleasure as an integral part of motherhood.

Embracing women's physical pleasure, however, was not meant as a form of female sexual liberation. This was not a nineteenth-century sexual revolution. Instead, notions of pleasure were an essential part of the emerging vision of the sentimental mother. This vision assumed that mothering was natural and instinctual and that all good mothers would want to breastfeed because it was best for their infants and themselves. Moreover, the pleasures of breastfeeding helped create a vision of motherhood as pure and delightful, unencumbered by the messy problems of the body. Breastfeeding was effortless and defined by emotional and physical pleasure, meaning that motherhood was not work, but pure delight. Furthermore, by locating physical pleasure within that most symbolic act of mothering, prescriptive authors bound women to a single identity. The biology of women's bodies made it possible for women to bear children and nurse them, and popular representations of motherhood in the late eighteenth and early nineteenth centuries likewise came to equate *woman* and *mother*. Women were meant to find their greatest pleasure in their capacity as mothers. As the popular author Lydia Sigourney explained, "The love of children, in man is a virtue: in woman, an element of nature. It is a feature of her constitution, a proof of His wisdom, who, having entrusted to her the burden of the early nurture of a whole race, gave that sustaining power which produces harmony, between her dispositions, and her allotted tasks."[108] Prescriptive authors described the experience of mothering as one of unmitigated joy and importance for the individual, the family, and society. Women were meant to derive pleasure—even erotic pleasure—from the maternal role, but this pleasure was circumscribed within very clear limits. Women, or at least *good* women, fulfilled naturally and instinctively the role of the sentimental mother, who exemplified "true domestic bliss, / The fountain of maternal love, / Welling with happiness."[109] To step beyond this role was to leave the safety of the sentimental maternal ideal and to expose oneself to the scorn and derision of society—to become unnatural and monstrous.

# 4 Good Mothers and Wet Nurses

Breastfeeding and the Fracturing of Sentimental Motherhood

Just as the maternal breast was at the center of prescriptive discussions of motherhood, the experience of childrearing for many mothers initially revolved around the pleasures and challenges of breastfeeding. Middle-class and elite women wrote often in their journals and correspondence about breastfeeding, but their discussions rarely imitated the expressions of maternal pleasure that filled advice manuals from the late eighteenth century on. Instead, women balanced their sense of duty and the occasional pleasures of breastfeeding with the pain and frustration that often attended the practice. Women's perceptions of breastfeeding were more complex than their attitudes toward pregnancy and childbirth. Most women agreed (often emphatically) that childbearing was an unpleasant and sometimes terrifying process, a physical trial that was the foundation of their identity as mothers. Breastfeeding, on the other hand, could be alternately difficult, delightful, tiring, satisfying, and painful—and sometimes all these at once. Nursing could be one of the "privileges of motherhood," for many women enjoyed the intimate connection with their infants and drew satisfaction from the knowledge that they were fulfilling the responsibilities of a good mother.[1] But even the pleasures of such intimacy could not always compensate for the physical discomfort that was a regular part of nursing for many women or for the fact that breastfeeding was quite simply hard work.

In spite of their ambivalence toward the act of breastfeeding, women agreed that it was practically and ideologically crucial to good mothering. On a practical level, maternal breastfeeding promoted the health and survival of infants more surely than either wet nursing or hand feeding. Most middle-class and elite women agreed that wet nurses would not care for infants with the same tenderness and dedication that a mother would, and they saw from experience that infants who were hand-fed liquids such as animal milk, pap (typically a mixture of flour, water, and milk), or broth often suffered digestive problems and infections that could prove fatal. Maternal breastfeeding was thus the surest choice for infant health. On a symbolic level, women also knew that breastfeeding had become perhaps the single most important way to demonstrate maternal virtue and dedication. Middle-class and elite women were surrounded by cultural injunctions to attain virtue and joy as mothers by breastfeeding. With both the practical and ideological nature of breastfeeding in mind, women passed judgment on themselves and other women based on the practice of breastfeeding.

Because the act of breastfeeding was so important both to the practical work of mothering and to the construction of sentimental motherhood, by the beginning of the nineteenth century it became a central issue around which the very definition of the mother became fractured along lines of race and class. Any woman who bore a child was, in a literal sense, a mother. Yet culturally and socially the category was far more nuanced, and not all women who bore children were considered true mothers. In white middle-class and elite women's private writings, fissures in the category of the mother appeared most clearly in their discussions of hired wet nurses, whom they gradually came to perceive as reproductive and productive bodies rather than as true mothers. A wet nurse produced a valuable commodity which, in the case of a free woman, enhanced her ability to support her family. But in doing so she forfeited her claim to true motherhood by breaking the physical and affective ties that were supposed to bind her to her own infant. Because wet nurses were generally lower class, immigrant, or enslaved women, the definition of the good mother came to have a clear race and class location in the writings of more privileged women. By the beginning of the nineteenth century, middle-class and elite white mothers began to articulate a distinction between women who were true mothers and women whose bodies produced a valuable commodity. Although middle-class and elite white women saw their corporeal experiences as the foundation of their identity as mothers, they did not see themselves as solely defined by their corporeality; lower-class and nonwhite mothers, however, they perceived to be nothing but bodies, and socially and ideologically disruptive ones at that.

Most scholarship on breastfeeding in the late eighteenth and early nineteenth centuries has focused either on changing practices of infant feeding, including the use of wet nurses, or on the meaning of breastfeeding and the role it played in prescriptive discussions of motherhood as a social role.[2] The work of defining the ideal mother was conducted by women and men alike in diverse venues such as medical texts, prescriptive literature, and popular literary and visual culture. Yet childbearing women also had strong opinions about breastfeeding—both as a bodily function and as a practice imbued with meaning—that they shared in their personal writings. Few scholars have probed the complexity of women's experiences with breastfeeding to highlight their ambivalence to the act of breastfeeding and their simultaneous reliance on it as a measure of maternal virtue. This chapter seeks to explore more fully the nuances and contradictions that characterized women's attitudes toward breastfeeding and to show how their understanding of breastfeeding helped shape a maternal culture that excluded many childbearing women.

. . . . . .

In spite of the practical and ideological importance of breastfeeding in the eyes of mothers, some of the time it was a part of women's lives that required neither dramatic commentary nor sentimental expression. Elizabeth Drinker of Philadelphia wrote complacently in 1763 that she "began this Morning to Ween my Sally,—the Struggle seems now (April 2) partly over.—tho it can scarcely be call'd a Struggle she is such a good-natur'd patient Child."[3] Eliza Haywood of North Carolina recorded the same sentiment in a letter to her husband in 1800, writing, "Betsey has nearly forgot how to Suck already and has freted very little for being weaned and is quite in health."[4] Caroline Laurens of South Carolina wrote in her diary with more detail but similar tranquility about weaning her son in 1825: "John was weaned from his mother's breast. She, finding herself 4 months gone in pregnancy, was obliged to do—he was easily weaned. Whenever he woke at night, he would ask for 'tee tee' his mother would tell him it was all gone. He would repeat the words 'all gone' . . . and go quietly to sleep."[5] Physicians often advised women to cease breastfeeding if they became pregnant, for they believed that pregnancy could contaminate or decrease the quality of the breast milk, so it was not uncommon for women like Laurens to cease breastfeeding only when they found themselves pregnant again. This meant that many women's lives were defined by nearly continuous cycles of pregnancy and breastfeeding. For many women the processes of breastfeeding and weaning went smoothly and caused little complaint. Narcissa Whitman, a pioneer and missionary to Oregon, wrote of the birth of her daughter in 1837 and commented with pleasure that the infant "sleeps all night without nursing more than once sometimes not at all."[6] Such casual references to nursing showed that breastfeeding and weaning were important enough for women to make note of but warranted little fuss or ceremony as long as things went smoothly.

Often, however, women indicated that their experiences with breastfeeding were difficult, painful, and damaging, far from the pleasurable practice that maternal advice manuals promised. In 1771 Mary Holyoke of Massachusetts recorded several terse entries about breast infections. One day she noted a "violent pain in my breast," and a week later reported that "the Dr opened my Breast." Her trials continued for at least another week, when she reported, "Left off the poultice. Put on a frog Plaister. In a good deal of pain."[7] Holyoke's other diary entries tended to include relatively few details about herself, suggesting that the problems with her breast were particularly significant to her and needed to be recorded. Holyoke was not alone in her afflictions, for infections and abscesses in the breasts were complaints that appeared often in women's private records, alongside extremely painful conditions such as sore and cracked nipples that could make it agonizing to breastfeed. Breast problems were so significant for maternal and infant health that even men sometimes commented about the challenges of breastfeeding. John Campbell of Virginia reported to his adult son in 1804 that "your sister Polly had a young daughter now three Weeks old a fine Child and seems healthy. She seems to come to streangth herself but slowly but she has had no back-set since she had her Child except sore breasts which keeps her weak."[8] Breast infections had the potential to be life-threatening to both the mother and the infant, so it is perhaps not surprising that men as well as women took an interest in women's health as they nursed. Women, however, commented much more regularly about breastfeeding and often in greater detail. Catherine Read of South Carolina wrote to her sister in 1821: "Poor Cornelia after having gone thru her confinement . . . was afterwards afflicted with a gather'd Breast it was nearly well when I left . . . but a letter I have recd from her since I have been here mentions that it has gathered in another place which distresses me greatly, tho she says the Boy thrives well on feeding what she has to give him."[9] Following the birth of her child, Mary Walker, a native of Maine and a missionary to Oregon, recorded on a daily basis the pain and difficulty she experienced attempting to breastfeed with her first child in 1838. "Nipples very sore. Worry with my babe. Get all tired out," she wrote one day, only to continue the next with "Milk so caked in my breasts, have apprehensions of 2 broken breasts." By the end of the week, she complained of "very little strength on account of suffering so much with my breasts."[10] For several weeks, Walker continued to write of her discouragement and ill health. Although she had greater success with her next child, breastfeeding rarely went smoothly for her, and her later diary entries continued to expose the grim difficulties faced by many nursing mothers.

Occasionally women reported extreme examples of suffering as a result of breastfeeding, and they wrote in gruesome detail about their experiences, evoking the messiness and danger involved in childrearing. In 1803 Eliza Haywood reported to her mother: "Dr. Williams lanced my Breast on that Day week on which you left me, I had suffered great Pain from the rising with Fevers, Cough, and Inflammation, I had Excruciating pains in my Shoulders, Breast and Stomach—the Discharge of Matter was great with much Blood, it still runs a deal twice a Day Night and Morning."[11] Although the grim picture Haywood painted seems shocking to the modern reader, such narratives of the painful and messy consequences of lactation were all too common. In 1822 Laura Randall of Florida described the plight of a friend who had recently given birth and suffered from a *gathered breast.* "It had been lanced repeatedly," she reported, but *"mortification* had taken place. . . . One of her breasts is *entirely* off, leaving nothing but the bare ribs. . . . And the other is in a dreadful state. Pieces of flesh as thick as your three fingers will sometimes drop off."[12] The woman did not survive much longer. Such gruesome cases reminded women that the physical dangers of motherhood did not end with childbirth.

Because complications with breastfeeding were common, women frequently sought and shared remedies that might ease the process. Maine midwife Martha Ballard, for instance, spent much of her time in the late eighteenth century delivering babies and tending to the health of new mothers whose breasts became painful and inflamed. On one such occasion she recorded in her diary: "I was Calld Early this morn to See thee Revd mr Fosters Lady who is very unwell; her Breast is Likely to Break. I aplyed a Poltis of Sorril & reeturnd home."[13] Abscesses, cracked nipples, and general pain were common complications that prevented women from enjoying nursing. These conditions were often treated with poultices and salves that women recommended to one another based on experience or word of mouth. Mary Chesnut, for instance, corresponded frequently with her mother, who sent her advice on how to manage her tendency to develop lumps and infections while nursing. In 1800 her mother expressed concern over Chesnut's health and wrote, "I wish you had a Plaster from New York, which is a fine remedy—I brought some of it from there last year . . . & gave it to Emily Cuthbert who received great benefit from it—the hardness was all dispersed by it & she soon got well."[14] In 1801 her mother excitedly announced that another remedy had been discovered by Chesnut's sister: "Tis the salve, which she says you must have spread thin upon a linnen or leather & lay all over that breast that has the hardness in it soon after you are brought to bed—I believe I told you before what great things it had done for her, & that by experience she can advise your trying to Suckle with both breasts."[15] But when the child was born Chesnut's trials did not abate, and breastfeeding continued to be a painful and difficult process. Women often shared new remedies or tried and true recipes, hoping to find something that would relieve the sufferings of their friends and kinswomen. Future First Lady Abigail Adams remarked in a letter to her sister that in her experience "a Bath of Hot Herbs was the most salutary means made use for me. A poultice of Camomile flowers is also very good."[16] In spite of these shared remedies, many women struggled time and again to breastfeed each of their children and were sometimes defeated by chronic breast problems. For women such as Mary Chesnut, breastfeeding never became the physically pleasurable duty that advice manuals promised it would be, and they alternated between hope that a new remedy would solve their problems and disappointment when it did not.

Although mothers who could not breastfeed were often disappointed by this fact, they rarely expressed guilt, suggesting that in their estimation physical incapacity did not render them bad mothers. In their eyes only the willful rejection of maternal duty defined the unnatural mother. Indeed, although most mothers hoped to breastfeed successfully, they were practical in recognizing insurmountable difficulties. Elizabeth Drinker was disappointed in 1771 when her ill health made it necessary to substitute a wet nurse: "Dr. D. says I must wean my little Henry or get a nurse for him, either seems hard—but I must submit." Several days later she found a nurse for him, but noted that she felt "lost without my little dear."[17] Although she longed to breastfeed her child, she recognized and submitted to her physical condition. Esther Cox wrote to her daughter in 1797 expressing her hope that "you may be able to perform the Mother's part by Suckling her yourself." But, she continued, "sometimes the Pain, in instances like yours is too much to bear, and then it must be given up."[18] Such cases reveal that although physicians and family members emphasized the healthful effects of breastfeeding and encouraged women to persevere, they often swiftly changed their minds in the face of complications and strongly recommended that women stop breastfeeding for the sake of their own health. Thus women may have been able to make the decision to stop breastfeeding without guilt, knowing that they were supported by their physicians and family members who generally prioritized the mother's health over the infant's. Other women needed only their own reasoning and observations to feel confident in their decision to stop breastfeeding. Mary Walker, who had endured so much pain attempting to breastfeed, wrote plaintively one day in 1838, "Try very hard to invent artificial nipples. Do not succeed. Feel very much unreconciled to the idea of being unable to nurse my babe." But by the next day she indicated satisfaction with her decision to try hand feeding instead: "Find my health in a good measure restored. Babe in good health, no appearance of sore mouth. Nurse him mostly with a bottle. Feel more reconciled than I did yesterday. Tho the dispensations of Providence often appear dark, yet they are in the [end] for the best. How do I know but the want of means to nurse my babe may be the greatest of blessings?"[19] Walker noted the improvement in her own health and the continuing good health of her infant and was satisfied that she had made the right decision in switching from breastfeeding to bottle feeding. Women were practical, and they made compromises calculated to optimize their own health and that of their infants, showing that making good decisions for themselves and their children was an important part of motherhood, even if it meant going against the prevailing enthusiasm for maternal nursing.

In their discussions of breastfeeding women often openly contradicted the idea, frequently professed in maternal advice literature, that breastfeeding was beneficial for maternal health. Instead, many women portrayed breastfeeding as draining and even debilitating. Weakness and weight loss were particularly common complaints. Agnes Cabell wrote to her stepdaughter in 1824, "I am distressed to hear that you are so much reduced in flesh, and that you are 'injuring' by suckling the baby." She emphatically recommended that her stepdaughter stop breastfeeding, lest she put her life at risk.[20] Eleanor Lewis expressed similar concerns when she reported in 1827 that her daughter "is better and I trust improving rapidly—she has been very weak and thin, and almost destroy'd herself by nursing."[21] Sarah Hopkins of South Carolina chided her husband in 1836, writing, "In your last letters you appear to think I have not been as well as was represented. Now you forget the *drain* that has been upon my system, and now nursing this dear *great* Boy is enough I think, to keep anyone weak for some weeks."[22] These comments reflected the fact that it could be challenging for women to receive the nutrition they needed to remain hearty while breastfeeding.

Many women also reported that breastfeeding was draining physical work. Margaret Brooke reported to her husband in 1843 that "Bunny is so hearty that he sucks me too much—I feed him a great deal he is very good and does not disturb me at night . . . I get very tired nursing."[23] Her remarks suggested that her infant was thriving at the expense of her own sense of well-being. Eliza Fisher reported to her mother in 1844 that she was unable to breastfeed without diminishing her own strength, writing, "I am sorry to find by yr last letter that you are making yrself unhappy at my indisposition—which I assure you is nothing serious, but Dr Meigs says entirely owing to the exhausting process of nursing—which he has strongly urged me to discontinue."[24] Many women (and their physicians) agreed that breastfeeding could be exhausting, particularly when prolonged. Frances Kemble, the celebrated British actress and unwilling plantation wife, criticized a plantation mistress for continuing to breastfeed her child after two and a half years and concluded: "I attribute much of the wretched ill health of young American mothers to over nursing; and of course a process that destroys their health and vigour completely must affect most unfavorably the child they are suckling."[25] Kemble insisted that prolonged breastfeeding was a drain on women's health and was therefore unconscionable. Moreover, her remark seemed to imply that American women actually became bad mothers, allowing their children to suffer from their mistaken insistence on breastfeeding. In her view, breastfeeding was a practice that could be taken to dangerous extremes.

Women also not infrequently made a rather implausible connection between breastfeeding and problems with their eyes, suggesting that they viewed nursing as having potentially widespread physical consequences. Elizabeth Drinker recorded in her diary in 1802 that "Molly Rhoads was here forenoon, she has made a beginning to wean her Son, having a great weakness in her Eyes . . . she has been told it is owning to her suckling such a strong lusty boy—and was told of a person who lost her sight by it—that after her child was wean'd, her sight was restored."[26] Jane Bernard of Virginia similarly complained of weakness in her eyes when she wrote to her husband in 1819 that "for some days the great quantity of milk which flowed gave me considerable alarm but I hope, by great attention, to prevent a return of the long suffering I encountered before. As my eyes are a little weak I must stop for the present."[27] Bernard seemed to draw a link between the large amount of milk she had produced and the weakness in her eyes that prevented her from keeping up with her correspondence. Although with today's medical knowledge it seems improbable that breastfeeding could damage women's eyesight, such remarks implied that women saw breastfeeding as a powerful process, capable of affecting multiple systems of the body, not just the breasts.

Only when the body did not intrude with pain and debility did women think about breastfeeding in less grim and more sentimental terms. By the early decades of the nineteenth century, when sentimental representations of motherhood had reached their height, women sometimes employed the language of sentimental motherhood to highlight the joy and pleasure they received from the act of breastfeeding. Georgina Lowell of Boston echoed the descriptions of prescriptive writers when she enthused in 1827 that "no one who has not tried can tell what delight it is for a mother to nurse her own offspring—I am more grateful for the blessing every day—for as the child increases in age & size, the pleasure increases."[28] Some women emphasized the importance of the physical connection between mother and infant that was an inherent part of breastfeeding. Writing in her diary in 1857, southerner Rebecca Turner expressed her attachment to nursing when she wondered, "How am I to relinquish so sweet an office—that of giving nourishment to my darling? Are these foolish tears that dim my eyes when I think of the times, when he will no longer nestle in my bosom through the silent watches of the night?"[29] Women sometimes combined sentimental rhetoric with discussions of complications, creating a sense of unfulfilled ideals. Esther Cox referred to breastfeeding as a pleasure when she wrote to her daughter about the latter's problems breastfeeding: "I rather think you . . . will be forced to relinquish the pleasure of giving Nourishment from your own breasts to the dear little Sally."[30] Judging from previous and subsequent letters, breastfeeding had never been particularly delightful for Chesnut, for it had always brought pain and difficulty, yet her mother still deployed the sentimental trope of pleasure, showing that it had at least some rhetorical currency with women even when their lived experiences did not quite meet their ideals. Similarly, Mary Peabody noted in 1831 that to be unable to breastfeed was to miss out, noting that a friend of hers was "perfectly well now, and if she could enjoy all the privileges of motherhood, nothing would be wanting to her happiness—but she is obliged to see her babe 'inhale life' from others."[31] No doubt the act of nursing a beloved infant was often a source of gratification and joy when the process proceeded smoothly—but women's sentimental depictions of breastfeeding were few in comparison to their complaints.

Such sources show that representations of breastfeeding in the personal writings of white middle-class and elite women rarely imitated the depictions of maternal nursing that were presented in prescriptive literature. Breastfeeding was a repeated and prolonged physical experience with which mothers were intimately acquainted—more so certainly than male advice writers—and women writing between the mid-eighteenth and mid-nineteenth centuries remarked frequently on nursing, weaning, and wet nursing and the effects of these practices on the bodies of mothers and infants. They harbored no illusions about the ease and pleasure with which they might nurse their children, for experience told them that the reality might be grim. Yet just as nineteenth-century prescriptive literature became more effusive and sentimental about breastfeeding, women letter writers and diarists in the nineteenth century were also more likely to deploy sentimental depictions of breastfeeding than their eighteenth-century foremothers. Even so, sentimental comments were almost always tempered by discussions of women's difficulties. Women in both the eighteenth and nineteenth centuries wrote with greatest frequency about the difficulty, discomfort, and frustration attending nursing. In this sense, women's references to breastfeeding remained remarkably consistent over the century in question. Although breastfeeding was an allegedly natural and simple act, women's bodies did not always cooperate. The physical work of nourishing and then weaning an infant could be difficult and taxing. Occasionally, women indicated that they derived pleasure from the practice, but more often they recorded matter-of-fact statements of the daily cares of a nursing mother or enumerated their struggles and their suffering.

Although women were intimately aware of the challenges posed by breastfeeding, they nevertheless used it as a measure for judging other women, much as prescriptive writers praised or castigated women in their published writings. A woman's ability to breastfeed, or her failure to do so, could provoke either praise or criticism from those around her. Women who breastfed successfully epitomized the ideal mother, but those who would not—or could not—might find their maternal virtue in question. In 1798 Gertrude Meredith exemplified maternal virtue by sacrificing her health to that of her infant, writing to her husband that she was "better than I have been this summer, but extremely thin notwithstanding, Mama tells me this is owing to my suckling my child—she is very anxious that I should wean her, but this I cannot think of doing, as I am confident that if I did, I should sacrifice her health which is infinitely dearer than my own."[32] In both her words and actions, Meredith identified herself as a good mother, although her own mother's wish that she wean the child signaled that there were reasonable limits to what mothers needed to do for their children. Not all mothers were as exemplary as Meredith, as Sarah Cary intimated in an inquiry to a friend in 1785: "Tell me, my dear, if you intend, like other town ladies to sacrifice the pleasure of nursing the dear one to *fashion?* If you do I pity you, for you are possessed of too much sensibility to do it without giving yourself great pain."[33] Just as some advice manual authors criticized women for caring more for the comeliness of their bosom than for its nurturing capacity, Cary identified fashion as a destructive influence that prevented mothers from fulfilling their duty. Indeed, a truly maternal body could not be a fashionable body, for tight stays might deform the breast and nipple. As the physician Samuel Bard insisted, "Above all things, a loose dress is absolutely necessary; and particular care should be taken not to press the nipple into the breast, by which it has been sometimes really obliterated, so as to render it impossible to suckle."[34] Moreover, Cary emphasized the trait of sensibility that defined the sentimental mother, claiming that her friend had too much sensibility to abandon the practice of breastfeeding. Other women could be even more critical than Cary of mothers who did not or could not nurse their children. "She has a sweet good babe," wrote Eleanor Lewis of her niece in 1827, "but she is a helpless Mother, she cannot suckle it, and knows very little about the care of children. I hope you will see *my* little treasure next autumn, and his *devoted* Mother."[35] Lewis drew a clear connection between breastfeeding and maternal devotion, contrasting the incompetent mother who could not breastfeed with her own role as the devoted and capable mother. Her statement also implicitly questioned the purportedly natural and instinctual nature of motherhood—apparently mothering was a learned skill that some mothers mastered more quickly or more thoroughly than others. Even if breastfeeding was often destructive to the mother's body and peace of mind, women saw it as central to the performance of good mothering. Although women may have felt ambivalent about the physical experiences of breastfeeding, they believed that good mothers nourished their children from their own bodies, a form of both pleasure and sacrifice that marked a woman as virtuous and competent in the maternal arts.

The corporeal nature of maternal virtue was so important that some women in the nineteenth century found a means of visually highlighting breastfeeding as both a practical and a symbolic act. A few daguerreotypes from the mid-nineteenth century exist that depict mothers in the act of breastfeeding (see figs. 4.1 and 4.2).[36] Although mother-child portraits were common with the advent of photography in the late 1830s, most photographs displayed the mother with her child in her arms or at her side. The frank

FIGURE 4.1 *Portrait of Unidentified Woman Breastfeeding a Baby* (ca. 1848). Courtesy of the Schlesinger Library, Radcliffe Institute, Harvard University.

display of the mother's bare breast in portraits from this era is surprising to the twenty-first-century viewer, yet by visualizing the intimate physical connection between mother and child, these portraits privileged the same physical mother-infant bond that prescriptive literature idealized and that many women treasured. The mothers in these daguerreotypes demonstrated

FIGURE 4.2 *Portrait of Unidentified Woman Breastfeeding a Baby* (ca. 1850). Courtesy of the Schlesinger Library, Radcliffe Institute, Harvard University.

their maternal virtue by nursing, speaking to the symbolic importance of breastfeeding at this time. Unfortunately, the identities of the women in these breastfeeding images are lost, and with them the possibility of knowing the thoughts and emotions behind these photographs. We cannot know whether it was the mother herself who chose to pose in this way or if her husband or the photographer might have influenced the decision to breastfeed for the camera. Moreover, we cannot know what it meant to her to have a permanent image of the act of nursing. Perhaps it was a reminder of duties faithfully fulfilled, of maternal love, of past pleasures and intimate moments. But perhaps it was also a reminder of the trials of maternity, of hard work, lack of choice, and self-sacrifice. Whatever the story behind these daguerreotypes, it is significant that these images captured women in the very act of performing the maternal duty that, more than anything, legitimized them as good mothers by showcasing the appropriate use of the maternal body.

· · · · · ·

If the definition of a good mother was one whose body provided life and nourishment for her children, the very function of a wet nurse was antithetical to good mothering. As noted earlier, prescriptive writers frequently castigated both women who employed wet nurses as well as the women who sought this kind of employment. Of course, most advice manual authors and women agreed that a mother who was so unfortunate as to be unable to breastfeed—because of infections, lack of milk, or other complications— could not be blamed for hiring a wet nurse, as long as she had done everything in her power to protect and promote her ability to breastfeed. In hiring a nurse, she simply fulfilled her maternal duty by proxy. The wet nurse, on the other hand, became by definition an unnatural mother because she sold her milk instead of devoting it to her own infant. The commodification of breast milk went against all notions of the sanctity of the maternal body and of maternal duty by placing a literal price on the lactating breast.

Throughout the eighteenth and early nineteenth centuries breast milk was in high demand. Ernest Caulfield has argued that in the eighteenth century, "breast milk was the most frequently advertised commodity in American newspapers."[37] Advertisements for wet nurses abounded in local newspapers, announcing, with little variation, that "a certain person wants a wet nurse into the house, to suckle a child."[38] Many women also advertised their own services, proposing that "a young woman with a new breast of milk, wants a place in a genteel family, as wet nurse."[39] These advertisements did not specify the reasons for which a woman's services were needed or offered, but they did expose the economic value of mothers as producers. The wages offered to wet nurses meant that providing such a service generated needed income for lower-income mothers. Wet nursing was an economic exchange based on the maternal body. Indeed, descriptions of the wet nurse's body were at the heart of such advertisements, which sought or proposed the services of a "hearty" and "perfectly healthy" nurse with a "fresh" or "good" breast of milk, or even a "good full young breast of milk."[40]

Interestingly, until roughly 1820, American newspaper advertisements for wet nurses tended to highlight the quality of the lactating breast in question, whereas subsequently they were more likely to focus on the overall health or heartiness of the wet nurse. Such a shift most likely reflected growing concerns about immigration, the health of the poorer inhabitants of urban areas, and the perceived risk of bringing purportedly unsanitary lower-class bodies into the middle-class home.

The challenging realities of childbearing and childrearing meant that wet nursing was a common aspect of family life in America from the early colonial era through the late nineteenth century, though it has been marginalized in historical studies of motherhood. It is difficult to calculate the extent to which middle-class and elite American mothers relied on wet nurses in the eighteenth and nineteenth centuries. Maternal mortality, illness, breast infections, and the numerous stresses on mothers that could prevent their milk from flowing all contributed to the need for a substitute feeding method.[41] Sometimes a wet nurse was only needed for a short period of time while the mother recovered from illness or from childbirth complications, or she may have been needed only sporadically to supplement a mother's scant supply of milk. In an era without refrigeration, it was difficult to keep a baby alive on animal milk or other liquid mixtures, which were often full of bacteria as well as being nutritionally inadequate, and it was also a challenge to feed infants enough using spoons, pap boats (small vessels with a spout), or bottles that were also likely to be contaminated with bacteria. Thus hand feeding was an even less desirable method of infant nurture than wet nursing.

Rates of wet nursing most likely corresponded to a certain extent to maternal mortality rates. In cases when a mother died during or after delivery, but the infant survived, an informal or hired wet nurse would have to be found. In the North, maternal mortality rates were relatively low. In Newport, Rhode Island, for instance, between 1760 and 1764 the Reverend Ezra Stiles recorded ten deaths out of sixteen hundred deliveries, while the midwife Martha Ballard delivered nearly one thousand babies between 1778 and 1812 and recorded only five maternal deaths that each occurred after delivery and during the lying-in period.[42] Most mortality studies have focused on specific communities or small regions, so it is difficult to generalize about the whole of British America in the eighteenth century, but the historian Janet Golden suggests that maternal mortality rates probably ranged from six to twenty deaths out of one thousand births, with higher rates occurring primarily in the South, due at least in part to complications from exposure to malaria.[43] In the nineteenth century, overall rates of mortality climbed in urban areas, particularly among the urban poor. The 1850 census shows that the proportion of white women's deaths that occurred during childbirth ranged from more than 5 percent in Georgia and Florida to just over 1 percent in New Hampshire and Rhode Island.[44] As a point of comparison, a recent report that compiled global data on maternal mortality recorded twenty-eight maternal deaths out of one hundred thousand live births in the United States in 2013, a high rate compared to other developed nations and more than double the rate in 1990, but still significantly lower than in the eighteenth and nineteenth centuries.[45]

Although prescriptive literature in both England and America from the eighteenth and the nineteenth century routinely criticized "fashionable" mothers for neglecting to breastfeed their own children, it seems that most well-to-do mothers who survived childbirth were generally the primary nurses for their children, though they may have received temporary assistance from a friend, relative, or hired or enslaved wet nurse shortly after delivery or in cases of breast pain, infection, or scarcity of milk. Maternal mortality and debility—not disinclination to nurse—most likely drove the demand for wet nurses. Daniel Blake Smith has argued in his work on eighteenth-century plantation society that "most women, except when ill, seem to have continued to nurse their own children."[46] Likewise Sally McMillen has argued that in the antebellum South, even in the case of elite mothers who had ready access to enslaved wet nurses, about 20 percent employed them, leaving a substantial majority who nursed their own infants.[47] Sylvia Hoffert has shown that women in the antebellum North saw breastfeeding as an important source of authority and self-worth and a central part of mothering.[48] Thus advice manuals that insisted on the merits of maternal breastfeeding were most likely preaching to the choir, but the very real dangers and difficulties of childbearing and childrearing ensured that there was always a market for wet nurses.

Economic necessity drove women to seek employment as wet nurses, which usually paid them more than they could earn for other kinds of domestic labor.[49] As one newspaper advertisement for a wet nurse promised, "a wet nurse with a good Breast of Milk . . . will receive good wages."[50] Some nurses were employed by families and generally earned higher wages, while others were paid by cities or institutions to nurse orphans and foundlings of the poor. Some wet nurses had lost their infants and thus had superfluous milk; others had an abundant supply of milk and were able to nurse more than one infant at the same time; but many were forced to leave babies behind or to wean them prematurely so as to give the majority of the milk to the privileged child. At a time when hand-fed infants died in much greater numbers than those who were breastfed for at least twelve months, it is not surprising that mortality rates were high for the infants of wet nurses. This created a trap for poor women who, in turning their breast milk into needed income for their families, lessened their infants' chances of survival and undermined their own claims to respect as virtuous mothers.[51]

Hired wet nurses were of course not the only mothers to be commodified in American society and culture.[52] The most significant commodification of maternal bodies occurred in the context of American chattel slavery. A rich and abundant literature has sprung up around the perception and use of the enslaved body in the antebellum South. Much of this scholarship has highlighted the ways in which women experienced the commodification of their bodies differently than men because of their ability to reproduce. Enslaved women's bodies provided labor, but they also produced new laboring bodies and breast milk.[53] In spite of the emphasis slaveholders placed on enslaved women's ability to bear children—their capacity to "breed"—they did not emphasize enslaved women's identity as mothers in the fullest sense of the word. Instead, their bodies were forced to produce three key commodities: labor, infants, and breast milk, and they were never awarded the social and cultural capital that American society granted to white mothers. This is not to say that enslaved mothers did not engage in the emotional and social work of mothering, for historians have shown that enslaved mothers struggled on a daily basis to maintain the integrity of their affective relationships and, on a more practical level, to protect the health and happiness of their children.[54] But in spite of the extraordinary emotional and physical work these women accomplished, their humanity and their claims to motherhood were articulated and defended only in abolitionist literature and propaganda. In the social context of slavery, these women were simultaneously valued as commodities and discounted as mothers on the basis of their corporeality.

Unfortunately, we know little about enslaved women's attitudes toward breastfeeding and wet nursing, but we do know that the seemingly basic practice of nursing an infant became extraordinarily difficult for enslaved mothers. The system of slave labor demanded that women work long hours at their appointed tasks and simultaneously expected them to raise healthy children to bring increased wealth to the slaveholder. Weakened by heavy labor and nutritional deficiencies during pregnancy, and unable to breastfeed at sufficient intervals during the work day, enslaved mothers faced immense difficulties in their efforts to raise their children through the first year of life. Anecdotally, we know that rates of infant mortality among enslaved populations were high. Frances Kemble's journal of antebellum plantation life, for instance, recorded a litany of petitions from desperate slave mothers seeking some small alleviation of their burden of labor during pregnancy and after delivery. Collectively, ten women had borne a total of sixty-five children and lost nearly half of them.[55] One statistical study of a large slave population on a South Carolina plantation found a 35 percent infant mortality rate between the 1830s and 1861, less than the anecdotal rates found in Kemble's narrative but still very high, especially when compared with mortality rates for white and free black children in South Carolina for 1850, estimated at 5.7 percent for children under one year of age and 12.9 percent for children up to five years of age.[56]

It is hard to say to what degree insufficient breastfeeding contributed to these high rates of infant mortality, but the references to breastfeeding made by former slaves attest to the fact that for many enslaved mothers it was nearly impossible to provide adequate nutrition for their infants. Emily West and R. J. Knight have suggested that enslaved infants may have been more likely to be bottle-fed, a method that would have freed up the woman's body for labor or for wet nursing, but that would likely have been both unsanitary and nutritionally deficient for the infant.[57] Even for enslaved women who were allowed to breastfeed their children, problems abounded. Willie Wallace, a former slave, recalled, "My father was crippled and couldn't work in the field, and I remember he used to carry the children out to the field to be suckled."[58] In this case the slave mothers were able to feed their children without leaving work, but it is unlikely that they were allowed to stop often enough or long enough to give sufficient nourishment. Many other enslaved mothers did not have the advantage of having their children brought to the fields. Another former slave, Celia Robinson, recalled stories her own mother told her: "I 'member how mother tole me de overseer would come ter her when she had a young child an' tell her ter go home and suckle dat thing, and she better be back in de field at work in 15 minutes. Mother said she knowed she could not go home and suckle dat child and git back in 15 minutes so she would go somewhere an' sit down an' pray de child would die."[59] The image of this mother praying for the death of her child put the act of breastfeeding in a very different light than the discussions of breastfeeding recorded by white women. In such dire situations breastfeeding was of little practical utility because the slave mother could not have enough time to give sufficient nutrition to her child, nor could breastfeeding be envisioned as an act of sentimental or affective importance because it only prolonged the uncertain and unhappy existence of the infant. Unlike the white mothers discussed earlier, breastfeeding could not as easily become a source of pride or maternal identity for many enslaved women because they could not dictate the uses to which their bodies were put.

For many enslaved women, the demands of maternity and forced labor collided when they were required to nurse white infants in addition to, or instead of, their own. The former slave Jeff Calhoun remembered, "My massa had 15 chillun and my mamma suckled every one of dem, 'cause his wife was no good to give milk."[60] In such cases, enslaved mothers provided a valuable and life-giving commodity for a child who was not their own, but in doing so they most likely undermined the well-being of their own infants. For enslaved women, wet nursing was predicated on a refusal to recognize their claims as mothers. As West and Knight have noted, "White women's use of enslaved wet nurses provides evidence of both spatial closeness and racial distance between black and white women."[61] The fact that enslaved women wet-nursed white infants should not be sentimentalized, nor should the more surprising instances when white slaveholding women served as wet nurses for their own slaves. Sim Greeley, a former slave, recalled how "Miss Viny Cannon suckled me and her son Henry at de same time, me on one knee and Henry on t'other."[62] Lucy Cocke of Virginia, whose infant was stillborn in 1850, likewise served as a wet nurse to an enslaved baby as a way of dealing with her surplus milk. She explained in her diary, "My chief trouble is having such a quantity of milk, I am forced to have one of the servant's children to nurse. I fear I shall become too much attached to the little fellow! He is a sprightly little fellow of 3 Months old *perfectly black*. . . . My children seem much astonished to see me with the little *Ebony fellow*, but they are becoming very fond of him."[63] A surprising reversal of the role of wet nurse, such instances can be understood in different ways. On the one hand, these scenarios demonstrated that while wet nursing was frequently an act that turned the maternal body into a literal commodity with specific economic value, it could also in special circumstances be a practical gesture that spoke less about the politics of the body and more about the exigencies of daily life at a time when breastfeeding needed to be managed carefully for the sake of both infant and maternal health. On the other hand, these examples testified in multiple ways to the commodification of the black body. In the first example we cannot know why the slave infant was suckled by the white mother, but it could have been to promote his survival if his mother was unwell or lacked an adequate milk supply, thus ensuring future profits for the slaveholding family. In the second example, Lucy Cocke was able to use an enslaved infant to help preserve her own health. Although the baby may have benefited nutritionally from her actions, the infant's mother no doubt had little choice but to hand over her infant for Cocke's use and benefit. Her needs or desires as a mother would have had little place in this process of exchange.

As these more unusual examples of white women nursing enslaved infants suggest, hired or coerced wet nursing was by no means the only context in which a woman might nourish a child who was not her own. Informal, that is, unpaid, wet nursing also occurred between friends and relatives in both the eighteenth and nineteenth centuries. Sometimes a mother simply needed a little assistance while she recovered from childbirth or from an illness, or sometimes a woman's milk was slow in coming in or was not quite sufficient in quantity. In such cases a friend or sister who was lactating might take over suckling the child sporadically or for a short period of time. Southern mother and grandmother Caroline Clitherall, for instance, found herself in the position of acting as wet nurse to her own grandchild. As she explained in her diary, when her daughter Eliza's child was born, "my Alexr was a baby; Eliza was so ill, I performed for Georgena the office of *Wet-Nurse*—it does not often occur, that the G[rand]d-child is suckled by the Gr[an]dmother."[64] Clitherall was not the only grandmother to nurse her own grandchild. Caroline Gilman reported a curious story to her sister in 1821: "The mother of Mr. Blois, whose youngest child is 12 years old, finding it very difficult to procure a nurse for her little grandchild, conceived the project of nursing it herself, & after ten days of persevering application, actually procured for it an abundant supply of milk, & performs for the little creature all the offices of a mother! This circumstance though wonderful, is not, I believe, unprecedented."[65] Although it would have been more common for sisters or friends to share the task of suckling a new baby rather than a grandmother, these anecdotes reveal the ways in which female friends or relatives stepped in to share the burden of infant nurture on an informal basis.

The practice of wet nursing arose in a variety of contexts for a host of different reasons, testifying to the complexities of childrearing at a time when breast milk was the only safe option for infant feeding. Although the evidence is sometimes difficult to pin down, it seems clear that the majority of American women in the eighteenth and nineteenth centuries planned to breastfeed their children and were prevented from doing so only because of complications. As we have seen, however, breastfeeding often did not go as smoothly as women might have hoped, thus making the practice of wet nursing widespread and complex. Wet nursing most likely occurred on an informal basis more frequently than the historical record reveals, but when Americans discussed the issue of wet nursing they almost always had in mind the paid (or coerced, in the case of enslaved women) use of women's bodies. Thus wet nursing was fundamentally a process of commodification by which maternal bodies were valued based on their ability to produce wholesome breast milk.

· · · · · ·

Although the practice of wet nursing remained a part of American childrearing practices through the nineteenth century in both formal and informal ways, attitudes toward wet nurses underwent an important transition around the turn of the nineteenth century. Scholars such as Janet Golden have examined a subtle shift in the discussions of wet nurses in prescriptive literature that revealed a growing fear of wet nurses as a source of moral and physical contagion. But there was also much that remained consistent in prescriptive portrayals of wet nurses from the eighteenth to the nineteenth century. The ways in which middle-class and elite women wrote about their encounters with wet nurses, however, changed dramatically from the eighteenth to the nineteenth century. Whereas the women who employed wet nurses in the eighteenth century tended to see their nurses as part of their community of friends and acquaintances, by the early decades of the nineteenth century women were more likely to define their wet nurses as troublesome laboring bodies, exposing the race and class biases that played an increasingly important role in the way women defined themselves as mothers and how they viewed other women.

Eighteenth-century mothers often mentioned their wet nurses by name and included them in their roster of friends and acquaintances, indicating a sense of social proximity, if not necessarily equality. They also sometimes acknowledged the affections of wet nurses toward their own children and toward the children they nursed, thus implying that these women had claims to the affective bonds of motherhood. If the ideal mother was defined by her sentiment and sensibility, wet nurses had the potential to meet these standards. Elizabeth Drinker noted in her diary in 1765 that "Molly Worrel with Sitgreaves's Baby who she Nurses, were also here," signaling that her social circle included women who worked as wet nurses as well as more well-to-do friends.[66] Janet Golden has used the relationship between Elizabeth Drinker and the wet nurse Nanny Harper to explore the close and cordial relations between employer and hired nurse. After nursing her daughter Ann (Nancy) for six months, Drinker sent her to be nursed by Nanny Harper, the wife of a blacksmith. Drinker called often to visit and even sent her carriage to fetch Harper and the baby for visits home. Even after the baby was weaned and returned home, Drinker continued to exchange visits with the Harper family, showing that their relationship extended beyond the economic ties of the employer-employee relationship. Yet even in this friendly relationship, Drinker remained apparently blind to or unconcerned by the fact that by tending Ann, Harper may have been jeopardizing the health of her own infant, Benjamin.[67] Thus formal long-term nursing arrangements—even when they occurred between respected acquaintances—almost always created a hierarchy of importance between the two mothers and their children. Still, it is significant that eighteenth-century mothers and their nurses saw themselves as part of the same community of women who frequented one another's homes.

In spite of the fact that both formal and informal wet nursing were common and necessary practices, from the eighteenth century through the nineteenth prescriptive authors consistently looked with a suspicious eye on both wet nurses and the mothers who employed them. Both were deemed unnatural mothers, though for different reasons. Yet eighteenth-century prescriptive writers tended to have a more positive view of wet nurses than later authors. Maternal nursing was ideal, they argued, but in cases of maternal death or debility, a kind nurse with an abundant breast of milk could mean the difference between life and death for an infant. According to prescriptive literature, it was theoretically possible to find a good wet nurse, "who may be known to be such by her Health; by the good Habit and make of her Body; by her Age; by her Breasts; by her Lying-in; by the Time since her Lying-in, and by her Milk."[68] Her character and her sexual habits were of particular concern because writers feared that intemperate passions could affect the infant, and a nurse with venereal disease was believed to infect the home with immorality and contagion.

The physical appearance of the nurse was crucial in determining her wholesomeness and suitability, and medical and prescriptive writers offered advice about how to choose a wet nurse based on a host of physical characteristics. The tradition of describing the ideal wet nurse stretched back much earlier than the eighteenth century. In the seventeenth century the English midwife Jane Sharp recommended a "Nurse of a sanguine Complexion."[69]

She defined the ideal nurse in terms of a litany of physical characteristics: "Her Milk will be good, and her Breasts and Nipples handsome, and well proportioned . . . not fat, but well flesht; of a ruddy, merry, cheerful, delightsome Countenance, and clear skin'd that her Veins appear through it; her hair is in a mean between black, and white and red, neither in the extream, but a light brown, that partakes somewhat of them all."[70] Sharp also explained that all of these desirable physical traits would add up to a pleasant and cheerful disposition, ideal for someone entrusted with the care of young children. Roughly a century and a half later, the American physician William Dewees offered a nearly identical description. He quoted another authority as saying that the wet nurse should be between the ages of twenty and thirty-five, "she should neither be too fat nor too lean; she should be fresh-colored . . . her hair should not be too black, nor too deep a red . . . her breast should be of moderate size, with a nipple sufficiently projecting and irritable, and yielding milk upon the slightest force."[71] Added to these physical attributes, the ideal wet nurse of course needed to have a good character.

These minute descriptions of the age, hair color, breast size, and nipple quality of the prospective wet nurse exposed an important inconsistency in prescriptive discussions of breastfeeding. Nowhere did prescriptive writers suggest that *mothers* who failed to live up to these standards should not be trusted to breastfeed their own children. Not a single writer implied that women with hair too dark or breasts too large should forbear from marrying and bearing children because they would be poor nurses. These physical standards evidently applied only to wet nurses, not to the middle-class and elite mothers to whom prescriptive writers offered their advice. No mother was ever subjected to the same intrusive physical evaluation as her potential wet nurse.[72] Thus wet nurses were defined by their utilitarian physicality, while middle-class and elite mothers were described in terms of their morality, sensibility, and sentimentality.

Although prescriptive literature in the nineteenth century continued many of the same themes as earlier texts with regard to the use and character of wet nurses, it also took on a more ominous tone. Nineteenth-century prescriptive authors such as William Alcott were generally skeptical as to the existence of a truly good wet nurse. As Alcott explained, "If a nurse could always be procured whose health, and temper, and habits were good, who had no infant of her own, and who would do as well for the infant, in every respect, as his own mother, it would be preferable to have no feeding by the hand at all. But such nurses are very scarce. Their temper, or habits, or general health will often be such as no genuine parent would desire."[73] Janet Golden has argued that as motherhood was reconfigured in the post-Revolutionary era, the figure of the wet nurse took on a new and more dangerous image. The fear of wet nurses as a source of danger and contagion derived from a growing sense of embattlement on the part of the white middle class, which reacted to growing urbanization, immigration, and poverty by withdrawing to the safety of the nuclear family and genteel domestic culture. In particular, nineteenth-century depictions of wet nurses served as a means of articulating class differences and emphasizing the virtue of middle-class mothers in contrast to the presumed vice and incompetence of poor women.[74] A cartoon from a popular nineteenth-century comic almanac illustrated the visions of intemperance and vice attached to the figure of the wet nurse by portraying her as drunk and dangerously neglectful (see fig. 4.3). The caption, "Wanted—A *Dry* Nurse," used humor to imply that wet nurses were universally vice-ridden and dangerous. Drunk, slovenly, and neglectful of the infant in her care, this wet nurse epitomized the fears of middle-class Americans.[75] Representations of wet nurses helped to reinforce the divide between the true mother and the poor, diseased, and depraved women whose disorderly bodies allegedly populated the slums of the nation's largest cities with new generations of inferior women and men.

Although prescriptive writers developed a long-standing tradition of defining wet nurses differently than mothers by focusing on their physical attributes, it was not until the nineteenth century that middle-class and elite women betrayed in their writings a clear perception of wet nurses as a distinct class of mothers who were in fact not real mothers at all, but simply reproductive and productive bodies. Writing in 1813, Peggy Craig revealed a subtle distinction in her view of elite mothers and hired nurses when she remarked that her daughter "is the best Nurse (of a lady) that I ever saw—she is fat and hearty and much improved in her looks."[76] Craig betrayed a degree of surprise that her daughter, "a lady," should prove such an excellent nurse and that her body should prove robust in the ways that wet nurses were expected to be, indicating that she viewed elite women and lower-class women as different in terms of their physical abilities. Unfortunately for the historian, women did not often leave extensive comments about their wet nurses in their letters and diaries, but when they did, they evinced the belief that these women lacked the tender and sentimental instincts of true mothers. They portrayed wet nurses as a separate class of women, and even depicted them as more animal than human. Lydia Russell wrote of her use

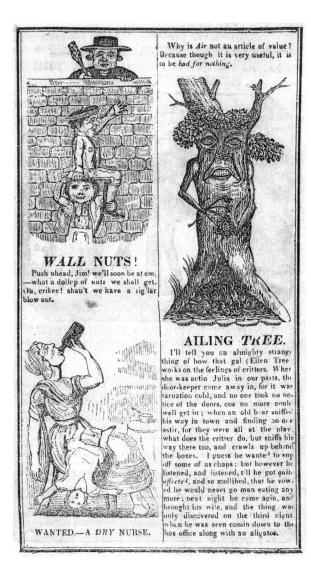

FIGURE 4.3 "Wanted—A *Dry* Nurse," *Turner's 1839 Comic Almanack.* Courtesy of the Library Company of Philadelphia.

of wet nurses while traveling in Sweden in 1818, "I had a kind of jealous repugnance to have my child take anything but from me, but of all animals the human was most obnoxious to my feelings."[77] It seems unlikely that Russell would have thought of herself as a human "animal." In the personal writings of privileged women, the wet nurses' bodies were seen as more capable than those of mothers who could not breastfeed, but this very capability shifted the focus away from their moral and affective role as mothers and toward the function of their bodies. In short, wet nurses were defined by the abilities of their bodies, and their bodies (or the milk they produced) were commodified in a way that was antithetical to sentimental motherhood. The wet nurse was not a mother, in this view, but merely an occasionally useful and always problematic body.

The case of Eliza Fisher and the Irish wet nurse she engaged in Philadelphia in 1844 is strikingly illustrative of the ways in which privileged women in the nineteenth century othered their wet nurses, defining them by the functions of their bodies and denying them the emotional privileges of sentimental motherhood. Fisher wrote to her mother that, owing to her problems with breastfeeding, she had at last hired a wet nurse. "She is such a remarkably nice looking, good humoured person, & brings from Ireland such high recommendations, that I trust she will suit me well & make a faithful nurse for my little darling," Fisher enthused, and went on to reassure her mother that the nurse "appears perfectly healthy, & the Dr, after examination pronounces her *sound* in every respect." Although Fisher's description of her wet nurse was complimentary in the sense that she described the woman as good-natured and trustworthy, she dwelled on the woman's physical attributes in such a way as to render her animal-like. She emphasized the nurse's health and soundness (a term frequently associated with animals and slaves) and seemed to think that there was nothing out of the ordinary in having a male physician inspect the woman, though middle-class and elite women would likely have found such an examination intrusive and indecent. Moreover, alongside her fixation on the woman's body, Fisher also devalued the nurse's emotional role as a mother. She noted that "the only objection to her is that she has an infant of her own, 3 months old, from whom she was very reluctant to part—but she now consents to leave it under the care of her cousin—& will I hope remain several months with me—so that I shall now have a good chance of recovering my strength—by having both mind & *body* relieved."[78] The only problem with the nurse from Fisher's perspective was that she was reluctant to abandon her own child. Although Fisher was herself a fond and watchful mother, it did not seem to occur to her that the Irish wet nurse might entertain the same feelings of devotion to her own infant. Fisher seemed unable or unwilling to empathize with the hired nurse. The implicit boundary she drew between the two mothers demonstrated that, in her worldview, one woman truly merited the name "mother," while the other was merely a body that could replace Fisher's feebler one.

Several months later Fisher wrote again at some length about her wet nurse and revealed even more clearly the distinction she saw between mothers like herself and lower-class women. This distinction was based on a hierarchy that placed emotionality over corporeality, making emotional mothering more important than physical mothering. Referring to her own little daughter, Fisher wrote, "The little monkey is beginning to love her Nurse so much better than me that I am quite mortified—which I ought not to be as the preference is as yet purely physical, and when her *morale* is more developed, I need not fear the continuance of it—therefore as long as she continues to thrive so well with the Alderney I must therefore not let my *jealousy* get the better of me."[79] Fisher tellingly exposed her insecurity that, in spite of her best efforts, she was perhaps not perfectly fulfilling her maternal role because her little daughter seemed to prefer the Irish wet nurse. Yet she quickly corrected herself by asserting that the infant's preference was purely physical, not emotional, and that therefore Fisher herself was still the true mother. Indeed, the wet nurse was nothing more than an Alderney, a dairy cow, whose bounty allowed the infant to thrive. But this did not make her a real mother, only a commodity that could be purchased and then dismissed when no longer needed. In Fisher's estimation *she* was the real mother who had borne the child and then set aside her own preferences so that her daughter could be sufficiently nourished. Though she could not do the physical work of nursing the child, her emotional investment served to sustain her maternal virtue.

Eliza Bellows had a similar blind spot in the way she understood her own role as a mother as compared to that of her wet nurse. She bore a daughter in 1845, who unfortunately found "no sufficient nurse in her Mamma, but is so fortunate as to have her deficiencies supplied in a most satisfactory personage."[80]Although Bellows could not breastfeed her own daughter, she was in all other respects a doting mother whose diary focused almost exclusively on the activities and welfare of her children. A few months after the birth of her daughter, Anna, Bellows noted that she "went to town with Anna & her nurse, on account of the illness of nurse's child. Found the little creature very low. Remained in town until nearly morning, the poor little child having been released from suffering during the preceding night."[81] It is impossible to know why the nurse's child died, but its access to its mother's milk had been curtailed by her employment as a wet nurse, and this most likely lessened the infant's chances of survival due to imperfect nutrition and a potentially weakened immune system. Although Bellows expressed pity for the deceased infant, she wrote nothing of the bereaved mother. The death of an infant was hardly uncommon in the mid-nineteenth century, yet if one of her own children had died Bellows would have been distraught.

Tellingly, she did not consider the emotions of the bereaved wet nurse to be worthy of note.

An exchange between Mary Lee of Massachusetts and her daughter in 1834 revealed a similar inability to consider the emotional aspects of motherhood for working-class women. Lee's daughter employed a wet nurse for her infant, and when the woman's own child fell seriously ill Lee wrote to her daughter: "I feel extremely sorry that you should be called to so great a trial in this your first experiment with a wet nurse. If the child should recover, you will have a continuance of it I fear, for after such an alarm Mary will feel it almost wrong I suppose to pass a day without seeing her child, & it is . . . difficult to oppose a feeling so natural & proper in itself, though situated as she is poor soul, there is an opposing duty."[82] Although the life of the nurse's child was at stake, Lee framed her commentary in terms of the inconvenience for her daughter. She did at least recognize that the wet nurse, Mary, would be moved by anxiety to pay special attention to her child, and she noted that such maternal affections were natural and proper. Yet she presented the woman's maternal devotion as a distraction from her duty as a wet nurse. A few days later she wrote, "By this time I presume the fate of the poor little child is decided, & if its pilgrimage is closed, you may perhaps be more comfortable, for Mary's sorrow tho at first I doubt not sincere will be transient, & I shall consider *you* better off than you have been before."[83] Here Lee was even more dismissive of the emotions of the wet nurse, suggesting that the woman's sorrow at the loss of her infant would be sincere but of short duration, implying that such a woman could not feel deeply about her child. Moreover, she felt certain that her daughter and new grandchild would be better off if the wet nurse's infant died. Three days later Lee responded to the news that the wet nurse's child was expected to survive its illness by commenting that "nurses are certainly troublesome creatures."[84] As it turned out, however, the infant died shortly thereafter, and Lee suggested that the loss would ultimately prove a blessing for its mother.[85] Lee's disregard for the affections and distress of the wet nurse was callous and reflected prevailing attitudes at the time. Women such as Lee understood the emotional experience of motherhood to be different depending on women's class identities.

Although many women who procured wet nurses, especially those living in the urban North, hired white women from the lower classes and from immigrant populations, race could often be a compounding factor in the ways they differentiated true mothers from (re)productive bodies. In 1805 Rosalie Calvert of Maryland wrote to her sister that she "had planned so much pleasure this summer breast-feeding my little Louise," but she discovered that she was pregnant again and felt that she should stop nursing lest it take strength away from the growing fetus. "It is hard to get a wet nurse whom you really know," she lamented, and insisted, "I never want to have a black one again—they are not capable of attachment to a child."[86] By labeling black women (most likely enslaved) as incapable of emotional attachment, Calvert created an impassable divide between women who could fulfill the affective role of a true mother and those who purportedly possessed only the physical capacity to feed a child. Other women's remarks were less explicit but equally dismissive of nonwhite women. Mary Walker procured a Native American woman to nurse her first child when it became apparent that she would be unable to breastfeed the baby. She remarked in her diary in 1839, "Am glad my babe can be supplied with milk tho it comes from a black breast."[87] Although appreciative of the service the woman provided, she essentialized the nurse both in terms of her race and in terms of the physical attribute that was most significant to Walker—the breast. Such a description left no room for the personhood of the Native America woman, for she was simply a useful body. Emily Judson, wife of an American missionary to Burma, similarly wrote of her wet nurse as if she were less than human, defined entirely by her physical nature and with no capacity for intellect or emotion. "I am all alone," wrote Judson in 1848. "All alone? Bless me, how indifferent we can be brought to feel to the presence of humans! There is Granny Grunter (alias wet-nurse, alias Mah Bya), who does nothing but eat and sleep alternately (she is eating now) during the twenty-four hours, and who would invent a machine to lift the child and carry it to her breast if she were a Yankee."[88] In spite of the presence of the wet nurse, Judson saw herself as alone, negating any possible sense of companionship between the two women. She further othered the wet nurse by defining her only in terms of three bodily functions: eating, sleeping, and suckling. Moreover, she implied that the woman had so little maternal feeling that she would have happily mechanized the labor of breastfeeding. In Judson's view, the wet nurse lacked the traits of a sentimental mother—even her personhood seemed questionable—and Judson joined other middle-class and elite women such as Fisher and Bellows in representing her wet nurse as defined exclusively by her physicality.

Although women rejoiced when they hired a wet nurse whom they found wholesome and agreeable, by the nineteenth century they generally echoed prescriptive literature in seeing wet nurses as a necessary evil. For example, Ellen Coolidge wrote after the birth of her twins in 1830: "The arrival of the young gentlemen has compelled me to add a domestic to my establishment, in the person too of a wet-nurse, the most troublesome of all inmates. I am tolerably supplied, having a country girl, strong healthy & good-humoured, whose *fall from virtue* is a less grievous offence in my eyes than the airs & insolence of an *honest woman*."[89] In Coolidge's view, the wet nurse was not a mother, but a mere "country girl" whose principal virtue was her robust health and, perhaps, the robust sexuality that had put her in a position to take work as a wet nurse. Viewing wet nurses as "the most troublesome of all inmates," Coolidge echoed the attitudes of prescriptive authors and her peers who, by the nineteenth century, consistently viewed wet nurses as immoral, diseased, and lacking in the virtues of sentimental motherhood.

· · · · · ·

Maternal advice authors writing in the eighteenth and nineteenth centuries were consistently suspicious of wet nurses, though earlier writers tempered their suspicions by acknowledging the benefits a good wet nurse could bring to an infant and its family. By the nineteenth century, however, growing urbanization, immigration, and geographic and economic separation between the middle and upper classes and the poor contributed to a shift in perceptions of the wet nurse. She came to be seen as a contaminant, threatening the sanctity of the genteel home with her immorality and her diseased body. As sentimental motherhood became increasingly important to notions of ideal womanhood, the wet nurse no longer had any place as a wholesome partner in the work of mothering. Women's own reactions to their hired wet nurses roughly followed this trend in the prescriptive literature. Middle-class and elite women writing in the eighteenth century were matter-of-fact about the use of wet nurses and saw them as part of the community. In fact, they often seemed less suspicious of nurses than did advice manual authors, most likely because the women they hired were often acquaintances and even friends. By the nineteenth century, however, women were more likely to hire wet nurses from very different social circles and even from different parts of town, and women's remarks about their wet nurses became even more blatant than prescriptive texts in defining wet nurses as useful bodies rather than as mothers.

Women's personal writings revealed the full extent to which the identity of the mother became fractured around the issue of corporeality in the early nineteenth century. A woman who bore a child did not necessarily qualify as a mother under the tenets of sentimental motherhood; she had to exhibit emotional and moral virtues as well as physical dedication to claim that status. The physical act of breastfeeding provided a focal point around which women defined and judged one another as mothers. Middle-class and elite mothers drew a line between women who were mothers in the fullest sense—physically and emotionally present for their children and revered for their tender maternal love—and those women whom they deemed nothing but reproductive bodies. Breastfeeding could be both a physical and an affective act for women who fulfilled the ideals of senti-mental motherhood, but for other women it was a bodily function that could be bought and sold. Breastfeeding thus became more than a practical ne-cessity and the focal point of sentimental motherhood; it allowed women to fracture the community of mothers along lines of race and class.

## 5 The Fantasy of the Transcendent Mother

The Disembodiment of the Mother in Popular
Feminine Print Culture

· · · · · · · · · · · · · · · · · · · · · · · · · · · · · · · · · · · · · · · · · ·

The script of sentimental motherhood emerged tentatively in the late eighteenth century in a range of cultural forms, including medical, moral, and prescriptive literature, but it reached its fullest expression in the realm of popular print, which was rapidly expanding in volume and variety by the early decades of the nineteenth century. This ephemeral print culture was different from the previous world of print, in which volumes of essays, religious matter, and even occasionally novels had been understood as the most legitimate material for respectable readers. Instead, this growing realm of popular print matter was characterized by the rapid production of daily, weekly, monthly, and annually published material, providing American readers with a constantly varying literary and visual feast. For the first time in American history much of this print culture—particularly texts such as magazines and giftbooks—was marketed for women, constituting a new feminine sphere in American culture. Combining didactic fiction, essays, poetry, and, increasingly, beautiful and expensive images, this emerging ephemeral feminine print culture promulgated a rich vision of feminine "beauty, piety, and morality."[1] At the heart of this vision reposed the figure of the sentimental mother.[2]

Both texts and images were notable for their use of sentimentalism, a mode that emphasized sympathy and sensibility in the construction of the self and in the act of storytelling.[3] Sentimental print culture played a much larger role in American society than simply enriching the affective lives of readers; it was also instrumental in creating and defining the emerging American middle class.[4] As the United States evolved in the first half of the nineteenth century into a more ethnically diverse, individualistic, geographically mobile, urban, and market-driven society, the middle class increasingly relied on sentimental culture to create and regulate its identity.[5] Middle-class Americans (particularly those newly arrived to genteel prosperity) lived with anxiety about the volatility of their economic fortunes, and this sense of vulnerability meant that they clung even more tenaciously to cultural (rather than monetary) markers of class identity.[6] Sentimental culture and the printed objects that disseminated its values provided a means of creating and communicating cultural belonging based on a constellation of virtues that by the 1850s came to be known simply as "gentility." Gentility signified inner qualities of integrity, restraint, taste, and virtue that could be best cultivated by interacting with appropriate cultural forms.[7] By reading emotionally and morally uplifting poetry aloud with friends and family, by arranging elegantly bound giftbooks on parlor tables, or by framing magazine embellishments on the parlor wall, women in particular could send a clear message about their virtue, sensibility, and taste.[8] The language of sentiment was understood to generate a particular way of feeling and being in society that communicated a sense of mutual belonging and a conviction of moral and cultural authority among those who participated in its values and emotions.[9] Sentimental culture fostered a sense of morality and gentility that was understood to exist in tension with the perceived vices of the poor and the excesses of the rich. By placing the good mother at the heart of sentimental print culture, these texts marked the sentimental mother as a white middle-class icon.

The values of middle-class sentimental culture overlapped in important ways with the religious revivalism that emerged in the late eighteenth century and reached new heights in the first half of the nineteenth century. Having gained considerable momentum in the 1820s and 1830s, driven particularly by members of the middle class, the Second Great Awakening swept the nation and gave new purpose to those seeking a higher spiritual realm.[10] This surge in religious enthusiasm was paired with the notion that human labors could perfect society and bring about the millennium, which would be followed by the second coming of Christ.[11] As part of this millennial optimism, this period saw a growing body of religious writings that praised the influence of women in achieving a more Christian society.[12] In particular, evangelical religion promoted a vision of the mother as the moral and emotional center of the family whose duty and joy was in assuring the spiritual salvation of her husband and children. Large numbers of pious middle-class women acted on this vision by forming maternal associations and writing and consuming advice about how to rear Christian children.[13]

The feminine sphere of popular print culture merged explicitly religious goals and more secular sentimental imagery in the figure of the mother. In the realm of print culture, artists and writers could fully embrace the idealization of sentimental motherhood and create—unfettered by the complex lived experiences of maternity—a vision of the mother as the epitome of white middle-class beauty, morality, and piety. Images and poems, often working in tandem, were particularly central to the formation of this image of the sentimental mother. Indeed, by the 1830s images and poems worked together to create a remarkably consistent image of the sentimental mother that was marked by a particular vision of the maternal body. While women's personal depictions of motherhood consistently dwelled upon the messy and challenging physicality of motherhood, in sentimental print culture the figure of the mother became divorced from the more embodied aspects of maternity. The maternal body was refined, passive, and unobtrusive in its textual form. Instead of depicting the work that women performed as mothers, these images and verses highlighted the more nebulous concepts of maternal virtue and maternal influence.[14] Whereas earlier depictions of the mother in print culture often explored the bustling activities required by childrearing, by the 1830s mothering seemed to become less a form of labor and more a way of being. The good mother simply *was*, and her very existence allowed her to transform the lives of her children.

This move toward the noncorporeal mother was part of a broader cultural trend toward emphasizing the power of the sentimental mother. In order for mothers to be powerful, they had to be released from the constraints of their material lives so that their moral influence could be boundless, allowing them to shape the moral course of their children (and, consequently, their nation). As sentimental images and poems sought to deemphasize the physicality of the mother and to celebrate her emotional and spiritual attributes, the good mother was elevated to "a higher place in the scale of being," a position of nearly deity-like power by which she surpassed the limits of ordinary human existence and influence.[15] This vision particularly emerged in poetry, which developed an extreme version of sentimental motherhood that I call the *transcendent mother*. Whereas maternal advice literature celebrated a refined vision of maternal embodiment that was centered on the act of breastfeeding and its sentimental importance, the transcendent mother was refined to such an extent that her body simply disappeared. She became defined not by her materiality, but by her spirituality. As one poet effused about the ideal maternal figure: "Often, in my dreams, she stands, an angel to my sight, / Glowing in all the nameless charms of Heaven's eternal light."[16] She was also transcendent in the sense that her most important traits—her love and Christian influence—were not limited by time, space, or mortality. While childbearing women were rooted in their daily lives by the repeated physical challenges of childbearing and childrearing, the transcendent mother was freed from the constraints of her body so that her pious influence on her family could extend across time and space and from beyond the grave.

· · · · · ·

By the 1830s visual depictions of motherhood were abundant in popular feminine print culture, but this had not been the case in earlier decades. The sphere of feminine print culture itself was only just emerging in the late eighteenth and early nineteenth centuries, and so the choice of publications treating subjects such as motherhood was limited. Moreover, the technology for the mass reproduction of high-quality images was also just developing at this time. Thus American women's magazines, which tentatively emerged in the 1790s with *The Lady's Magazine and Repository of Entertaining Knowledge*, initially presented few visual "embellishments," making it difficult for historians to assess the ways in which the mother may have evolved in the popular visual imagination prior to the 1830s.[17]

Children's books, however, which enjoyed a growth in popularity in the last decades of the eighteenth century and often included illustrations, provided one source of images of motherhood in the late eighteenth and early nineteenth centuries. Early children's books hardly offered the same visual abundance that would characterize later magazines and giftbooks—their illustrations tended to be small and rough—but they did portray interactions between mothers and children. Children's books often depicted mothers actively engaging with their children in different activities and frequently highlighted the importance of the mother's role in educating her children. By the late eighteenth century, most Americans agreed that one of women's most important roles was as an educator for her children, and it was a role that middle-class and elite mothers themselves took seriously.[18] For instance, the letters of Rachel Lazarus, who raised siblings, stepchildren, and her own children in North Carolina in the early nineteenth century, reveal a woman deeply committed to finding the best teaching materials and the best pedagogical practices.[19] She worked hard to become a capable teacher, and other sources suggest that she was not alone in this endeavor. It is perhaps not surprising, then, that early images of mothers and children often highlighted not only the mother-child bond, but also the teacher-student relationship. One rather rough image from the title page of *A Present for a Little Girl* (1804), for instance, depicted a mother and her two children studying nature under the shade of a tree. The mother held the younger of the two children, who gestured to the other with an open book, while the older child appeared to be studying a family of birds and reporting back to mother and sibling.[20]

Education was just one of the many mothering activities portrayed in illustrations for children's books. Another book from 1816, this one in verse, included illustrations highlighting the stages of a child's development. One such image depicted the mother sitting under a tree in a cottage garden and stretching out her arms to assist her toddler as he learned to "go alone."[21] Ann Taylor, a popular British children's author, published a number of works that were printed in Great Britain and America. Her poem "My Mother" appeared in varying forms through the early decades of the nineteenth century and included small illustrations of the mother engaged in various activities, from breastfeeding, to assisting her toddler after a fall, to teaching her daughter how to play.[22] Another book of children's verse included images of the mother instructing her children, as well as a poem in which a child enumerated the work of her mother in guarding, washing, soothing, healing, and teaching her children.[23]

What these early children's illustrations had in common was an emphasis on the different kinds of activities involved in mothering, from caring for an ailing child, to helping a toddler learn to walk, to facilitating a child's moral and intellectual education. Many of these children's books depicted different stages in children's physical and mental development, and in doing so they also represented the evolving activities involved in mothering children as they grew. The mother in children's books tended to be an active figure; she used her body to support her children, and she employed her mind to advance their education. These texts and images showed mothers and children as busy creatures, facing new tasks and surmounting new challenges together. In short, these images of the mother suggested that motherhood was work—charming and delightful work, perhaps, but work nonetheless. These types of images continued to appear in children's books beyond the early years of the nineteenth century.[24]

Putting children's book illustrations side by side with images from the feminine print sphere of magazines and giftbooks that grew increasingly popular by the 1830s risks conflating images intended for different audiences. Illustrations created for children did not necessarily seek to convey the same vision of motherhood as those intended for older viewers. Moreover, by portraying the activities of children, they also necessarily portrayed the activities of the mothers who assisted these childish pursuits. But putting these images side by side does at least allow us to see the different possibilities available for the visual depiction of motherhood. Comparing portrayals of the active mothers in children's literature with the images of mothers intended for older readers helps us recognize the choices that were made and the different meanings that were generated when visual depictions of motherhood became common in popular magazines and giftbooks.

By the 1830s print technology had advanced to a degree that made the mass dissemination of images more feasible, and this visual abundance became one of the factors that propelled the growing enthusiasm for relatively expensive texts such as annual giftbooks (ranging in price from three to fifteen dollars) and increasingly elegant illustrated periodicals (around two to three dollars for a subscription).[25] *Godey's Lady's Book*, for instance, was one of the earliest American women's magazines and became enormously popular for its beautiful hand-colored fashion plates, which were joined over time by engravings of paintings paired with stories and poems.[26] By the 1840s *Godey's* was joined by other illustrated magazines such as *Graham's Lady's and Gentleman's Magazine* and *Miss Leslie's Magazine*.[27] Although these magazines were produced in the large urban centers of the Eastern Seaboard, such as Philadelphia and New York, they targeted a national audience and provided a means of connecting Americans across the nation via a shared literary and artistic experience.[28] Giftbooks, those elegantly bound volumes of prose and verse that were often exchanged at Christmas and the New Year, were also increasingly filled with images, often engravings of paintings by well-known European and American artists that depicted historic events, elegant portraits, and domestic scenes.[29] These pictures were the main attraction for many readers, though the poems and stories that accompanied them were also popular.[30] But the beautiful graphics in magazines and giftbooks were not simply for viewing pleasure. Their beauty was understood to facilitate moral and spiritual uplift, and they were viewed as sources of instruction and inspiration, providing an enticing means of conveying to women in particular how best to cultivate virtue and gentility.[31] Mothers and children were common subjects in these volumes, sending a clear message that female virtue was most profoundly anchored in motherhood.

By the 1830s, as sentimentalism became the dominant mode in popular print culture in both its literary and visual forms, the mother emerged as a figure meant to convey virtue and emotion. The paintings reproduced in nineteenth-century magazines and giftbooks were drawn from a range of artists, time periods, and genres, but they nevertheless collectively presented a coherent vision of the sentimental mother. First and foremost, the sentimental mother was uniformly young, white, and socioeconomically privileged—the occasional images of mothers who did not embody these three traits generally signaled to the viewer that this was *not* a sentimental mother to be revered by the viewer, but a deficient mother presented to elicit pity or horror.[32] Although the sentimental mother could not be pictured as a disembodied figure in images, which clearly necessitated some kind of visual corporeal presence, her body could be refined, concealed, or deemphasized in favor of exploring her emotional and spiritual influence. The ideal mother in sentimental imagery was not composed of fertile round belly, full breasts, and busy hands; instead, she was physically restrained and passive, but emotionally and spiritually potent. The illustrations of the mother that appeared in increasing abundance in magazines and giftbooks tended to represent four main types, which I label the *mourning mother*, the *fond mother*, the *Madonna*, and the *rustic mother*. The first three types shared important characteristics in that they depicted the mother as young, white, beautiful, and surrounded by the trappings of a genteel home. She was usually depicted holding or watching over a single infant, or at most one infant and one small child, suggesting that her maternal cares were intensively focused on just one or two small "treasures." These images of motherhood were curiously static—the mother (and her preternaturally well-behaved children) seemed to *do* very little. She was not busy with the many activities of mothering such as bathing, dressing, feeding, healing, teaching, and playing, which we know occupied women's time. Instead, often with the assistance of an accompanying poem or story, the portrait of the mother conveyed a deep emotional realm of maternal devotion and piety.

Images of the mourning mother were among the most common to grace the pages of women's magazines and giftbooks, echoing the reality that infant mortality rates were high and that many mothers faced the loss of at least one child. Portraits of genteel mothers grieving over their dead or dying infants and the verses that often accompanied them must have resonated with readers. In these mourning images the physicality of the mother and of her relationship with her child were downplayed. Instead, viewers were compelled to imagine the sentiments of the mother as she drooped pensively over the dying child or the empty cradle. Although we know that women were often the primary medical caretakers for ailing family members, these images rarely depicted the mother laboring to heal her child; instead they focused principally on her grief and resignation. One such image was accompanied by a short text combining poetry and prose that idealized the faith and submission of grieving mothers. In this image the mother's bent posture, bowed head, and lowered gaze spoke to her sorrow and submissiveness alike. She was weighed down by grief, physically as well as emotionally, but it was a grief that Christian piety demanded she accept with resignation. The listlessness of her body, her left arm hanging softly down at her side, her bonnet lying forgotten on the floor, and her workbag hanging untouched from her chair, emphasized the passivity of one who is lost in spiritual realms, one who "lives in the past, so sweet with human love and hope—in the future, so glorious with heavenly love and joy."[33] She did not live in the now of the empty cradle beside her, but in a larger and more enduring realm of sentiment and pious submission (see fig. 5.1). A similar image featured the grieving mother in an almost identical posture as she drooped over the bed of her "dying babe."[34] In this case, the mother reached out one hand to hold that of the child, providing a small physical connection symbolic of the mother-child bond. Living, yet lost in reverie, the grieving mother's body was useful only to the extent that it could convey her sense of loss and her quiet resignation.

Even more common than images of the mourning mother were portraits of the "fond mother" and her offspring. These images often portrayed scenes of greater beauty, even opulence, compared to images of the mourning mother, presenting the mother-child dyad as if it were a jewel in a beautiful setting. They also tended to highlight the beauty of mother and child. Mothers with luxurious curls and children with cherubic faces populated the pages of elegant magazines and giftbooks, seeming to suggest that motherhood lifted women to new heights of inner and outer beauty that could best be evoked by glowing eyes, smooth cheeks, glossy hair, and tender smiles. Most often in these images the mother held an infant or toddler, thus romanticizing the affective bonds formed by the young mother and her new offspring. Less often, these images also included an older child as part of a trio. These images suggested that mothering was envisioned as intensive rather than extensive. The good mother poured her love and devotion on just one or two treasured children. One such engraving, based on a painting by the American artist Robert Walter Weir, presented a richly attired young mother with an infant in her lap and her young daughter at her side (see fig. 5.2).[35] The artist celebrated the cherished relationships within this elegant trio and visualized the connection between them: the infant resting on its mother's lap, the older child's hand lying softly on the baby, and the mother and older daughter exchanging a steady and affectionate gaze that provided the emotional weight of the image.

FIGURE 5.1 *The Empty Cradle,* in *Godey's Lady's Book* (1847). Courtesy of the Library Company of Philadelphia.

FIGURE 5.2 *Maternal Affection*, in *The American Juvenile Keepsake* (1834). Courtesy of the American Antiquarian Society.

Images of the fond mother almost invariably emphasized the mother's countenance rather than her body. In most images, the mother's form was subsumed by the folds and puffs of her gown, or her body was largely excluded from the framing of the image. These images were not meant to suggest the abundance and fecundity of the maternal body, but to emphasize instead her inner qualities and emotional connections. Against the backdrop of rich fabric or, occasionally, a natural scene, the mother's face and the faces of her children shone forth with increased emphasis. If, as many writers suggested in the nineteenth century, a beautiful countenance reflected inner virtue, there could surely be no question of the inner substance of these mothers and their offspring. One image of a "Mother and Infant" evoked a particularly disembodied vision of maternity.[36] In this image the only distinct elements were the mother's face and the infant's head, both brightened against the dark fuzziness of the forest that engrossed most of the scene.[37] The mother was almost as swaddled in indistinct garments as her infant, and the only aspect of her physical presence that stood out clearly was her face, which gazed down with a slight sweet smile at the infant in her arms as it reached one plump hand toward her cheek. The accompanying poem spoke of "true domestic bliss" and fountains of maternal love, and indeed the emotional bond between the two was evidently the focal point of the image. Such depictions of mothers were intended to draw in the interest of the viewer not because of any compelling action or personality, but because of the emotional weight of the scene and what it signified for the enactment of ideal womanhood.

Images of motherhood in popular print culture also at times drew on religious iconography by echoing images of the Madonna. Some were direct reproductions of paintings of the Virgin Mary, such as an engraving based on the painting entitled *Madonna and Child* (1638) by the Spanish artist Bartolomé Esteban Murillo. In this case, the image was retitled *The Christian Mother*, thus eliding associations with Catholicism in the interest of appealing to a majority Protestant readership in America.[38] The accompanying poem helped the reader understand the image, in which

The mother watches o'er her only child
With that long, earnest, and impassioned gaze
Which so much hope, which so much fear betrays.[39]

Other references to the Madonna were less direct, as in an image titled *The Young Mother* that appeared in a giftbook in 1845. This young mother presented the easily recognizable pose of the Madonna, face turned partly to the side and tilted slightly toward the infant, eyes gazing downward, head modestly covered with a light veil, and a blank background that evaded contextual specificity, suggesting the timelessness of maternal virtue. Isabelle Lehuu has argued that popular images of mothers and children reflected a "softening of American Protestantism" and a new emphasis on more feminine sensibility usually associated with Catholicism.[40] Images that mirrored the figure of the Madonna reaffirmed the links among sentimental culture, feminine virtue, and Christian piety.

Like the women pictured earlier, sentimental visual culture commonly represented mothers as refined and detached from the world around them, intimating that they lived in a rich interior emotional realm. At a time when American society was rapidly changing and Americans were increasingly gravitating to bustling, diverse, and impersonal urban areas, it is easy to imagine how these images of domestic tranquility might have provided a reassuring reminder of the enduring benefits of maternal influence. Sitting quietly amid the activity of others, gazing gently into space, or looking fondly at her child, rather than engaging directly either with the viewer or with her own world, the sentimental mother was young and beautiful, but her most compelling quality was her aloof passivity and her air of grave contemplation, which gave the impression that she lived in but was not entirely of the everyday world.

There were occasional exceptions to this visual trend of the restrained and passive mother. One image that appeared in *Godey's* in 1845 depicted a mother in the act of instructing her young daughter to read, a more elegant version of a scene that would have been familiar to readers of children's books (see fig. 5.3).[41] Another picture in a giftbook featured a mother showing her tiny daughter how to kneel down to pray.[42] A more unusual image featured a mother apparently in the midst of a little dance with both arms raised above her head as if to snap her fingers and one foot outstretched as if to tap the floor, her baby looking on from a plush chair.[43] This particular engraving presented the mother as unusually active, as very few other images depicted the mother standing, much less actually in motion. Alongside these unusually active mothers, there were also occasional images that broke with the trend of portraying the mother as uniformly young and beautiful. One such image depicted a daughter and her aged mother begging for money. The mother's face was delicately wrinkled, and her hands were misshapen, as if poverty had aged her prematurely.[44] The mother's age and her poverty set her apart from the usual depictions of ideal motherhood. Such exceptions were rare, however, and the visual shock of finding an active or aged mother presented in the pages of a magazine or giftbook attests to the overwhelming similarities in images of motherhood in this period.

The only common exceptions to the young, beautiful, and passive mother were those images that fell into the fourth category, that of the rustic mother (so named because she appeared in front of a quaint country cottage or in an agricultural scene). The rustic mother was more active than the other maternal types, or at the very least she was surrounded by activity. She was most often portrayed with three to six children around her, suggestive of a bustling household and many demands upon the mother's time and energy. In one such image, the mother was presented in a wooded scene with four children. The children collected vines into a large basket while the mother was in the process of placing a garland on one daughter's head.[45] Another image, printed in different iterations throughout the mid-nineteenth century, was based on a painting by the eighteenth-century British artist Thomas Gainsborough.[46] *The Cottage Door* featured a mother standing outside the door of her cozy cottage with an infant in her arms and five other children playing at her feet. Although the mother appeared calm and detached as she gazed into the distance, the lively figures of the children

FIGURE 5.3 *Maternal Instruction*, in *Godey's Magazine and Lady's Book* (1845). Author's collection.

evoked the babble and bustle of a large family. Another rustic cottage scene, based on a painting by the early nineteenth-century British painter Louisa Sharpe, displayed a husband's "unlooked for return" from war (see fig. 5.4).[47]

FIGURE 5.4 *The Unlooked for Return*, in *The Keepsake* (1833). Author's collection.

His wife, seated with a baby in her lap and two older children nearby, lifted her hand to her face in astonishment and emotion, and even the infant seemed so surprised that it turned away from nursing, leaving her left breast exposed. This image eschewed the restraint and passivity of the other maternal types. Catching the mother in the act of breastfeeding in the midst of a crowded household, this image suggested that she was a good mother devoted to the many essential tasks of childrearing. In fact, visual depictions of breastfeeding mothers were quite rare in popular magazines and giftbooks, and when the act of breastfeeding was featured it was almost invariably in a rustic setting.

These engravings of rustic mothers were nearly always based on paintings dating from an earlier period. The fact that they were reproduced in the nineteenth century suggested a certain degree of popular nostalgia for the figure of the busy rural eighteenth-century housewife with a baby at the breast and a cluster of children around her. She was robust, lively, and affectionate, and these popular images seemed to mirror the common view in medical and prescriptive literature that rural women enjoyed better reproductive health than their urban counterparts and therefore were particularly robust and suitable as mothers. In spite of this nostalgic and romantic view of the countryside, however, the rustic mother appeared far less often in visual culture than did the more passive figures of the mourning mother, the fond mother, and the Madonna, suggesting that the internal virtues of the sentimental mother held greater ideological weight for antebellum viewers than did the bustling activities of the attentive rustic mother.

• • • • • •

The vision of the sentimental mother that developed in visual culture was pushed to greater extremes in the poems that peppered women's magazines and giftbooks. Often these poems were paired with images, adding to the emotional experience of viewing an image and helping readers interpret it. Enjoying a wide readership, such poems were read aloud to friends and family, transmitted in letters, and adapted and preserved in diaries and albums by avid readers. These poems were so popular that they even inspired numerous amateur poets to try their hand at verse.[48] In spite of its sheer abundance and its importance in the daily lives of nineteenth-century Americans, sentimental poetry has garnered relatively little scholarly attention, especially when compared with the number of works devoted to the canon of nineteenth-century literary greats. As Paula Bennett has noted, magazine poets in particular have typically been dismissed as "an eminently forgettable horde whose contributions to the enrichment of American literature were negligible at best."[49] Yet there can be no doubt that sentimental poetry claimed an important place in American culture and society. Sentimental poetry evoked situations and emotions that belonged to everyday life and offered readers both elevated ideals and messages of comfort. They helped readers cultivate the inner virtues of piety, restraint, and sensibility that were so prized in genteel culture. Moreover, popular literary forms opened new avenues for women to participate in the production and consumption of literature, particularly in the context of popular magazines. Sarah Josepha Hale, for instance, sought to reshape women's writing by promoting emotionally difficult and socially significant themes in *Godey's*. Rather than publish tales of romantic love, much of the poetry and fiction she chose focused on themes such as motherhood, death, family strife, and religion.[50] Readers—often men as well as women—turned to sentimental poetry to have their emotions stirred by tender scenes and melancholy reflections, and they saw in these poems a source of moral inspiration and regeneration.

These poems moved the mother one final step toward transcendence by portraying her as an entirely disembodied figure whose innate virtue transformed her into more of a spiritual force than a human agent. It was the combination of piety and maternal love that made the good mother so potent. As one moralist put it: "The influence of a pious mother is untold and boundless. It spreads from generation to generation—it stretches into eternity."[51] This pious influence was elaborated more fully in poetry, which explored through sentimental imagery the ways in which mothers shaped the emotional and moral worlds of their children. Emphasizing the potency of intangible concepts such as love and influence, by the 1830s sentimental poems about motherhood were remarkable for the consistent and nearly perfect disembodiment of the mother. Unlike images, which demanded some kind of corporeal presence, verse offered the ultimate means of freeing the good mother from the constraints of the body. Sentimental poems portrayed the mother as a spirit, a smile, a memory, a voice, an essence of everlasting and infinite love and piety; only occasionally did she arrive at a moment of corporeality when her hands, lips, or breast connected to the body of her beloved child in a perfect gesture of maternal affection. The mother's power and influence depended on the timelessness and inexhaustibility of her virtues. Thus the ideal mother as she was imagined in popular poetry became more of a spirit than a living and laboring woman.

The literary figure of the mother was not always so ethereal and noncorporeal as she would become by the 1830s. Indeed, until the early nineteenth century, British and American authors tended to embrace and play with maternal corporeality. Although the mother was not as central to genteel literary culture in the eighteenth century as she would become, early English novels as well as magazine articles, stories, and poems did explore motherhood alongside more popular subjects such as nature, romantic love, marriage, and history. Next to love and female virtue, for instance, motherhood was a central theme in Samuel Richardson's enormously popular epistolary novel *Pamela* (1740–41), which was enjoyed by British and American readers well into the nineteenth century. Pamela, a young servant whose surpassing beauty, purity, and piety made her an ideal heroine, began as an object of lust for her master, the illustrious Mr. B., but ended by overcoming his rakish tendencies with her virtuous example. The first part of Pamela's adventure was rife with heaving bosoms and thwarted sexual escapades, but by the third volume she was safely married to her erstwhile tormentor and pregnant with their first child.

As the saga of Pamela's turbulent courtship and eventual marriage unfolded, Richardson introduced the theme of motherhood—and with it a new tension between Pamela's moral nature and her physical body. It was Pamela's maternal body that exposed her to impertinent and embarrassing comments as the characters around her made ribald jokes about what it was that she must have done to be in such a growing condition. As her sister-in-law joked, "What is done in Secret, shall be known on the Housetop."[52] Pamela, of course, rose above it all with her virtue and gentle humility intact. At times her spiritual nature even seemed to transcend her body. Her husband once exclaimed, "You have no Body just now . . . your Spirit has absorb'd it all."[53] Pamela claimed motherhood as a state that enhanced her virtue and her selfless dedication to others. Yet the problem of the body still remained at every turn in Richardson's novel. Was the female body a sexual body (subject always to dubious humor)? Or was it a reproductive body, subject to suffering and medical catastrophe? Was it a mirror to reflect the internal beauty of the soul? Richardson never resolved the problem of the body, but simply allowed his heroine intermittently to transcend her corporeality.[54]

Another of Richardson's massive novels, *Clarissa* (1747–48), also highlighted the appeal of the maternal body while simultaneously placing motherhood and sexuality in tension. Robert Lovelace, who attempted to force the virtuous heroine to marry him by drugging and raping her, effused to his best friend, "Let me perish, Belford, if I would not forego the brightest diadem in the world for the pleasure of seeing a twin Lovelace at each charming breast, drawing from it his first sustenance; the pious task, for physical reasons, continued for one month and no more!"[55] Ostensibly focusing on the pleasure that the sight of the maternal body would grant him (anticipating the somewhat voyeuristic depictions of breastfeeding that would become common in maternal advice literature beginning in the late eighteenth century), Lovelace also referred to more corporeal pleasures to be gained from Clarissa. Wishing to reclaim his right to sexual intercourse with her, he praised the delights of lactation while limiting them to one month. After that, he implied, Clarissa's body ought to be returned to him. Such passages suggested that the maternal body was indeed a very tangible object in eighteenth-century popular literature. In the mid-eighteenth century literary world, the figure of the good mother began to take shape as a symbol of female virtue, but not yet a disembodied one.

By the turn of the nineteenth century, readers encountered motherhood more often as it became a popular topic in magazines and volumes of poetry. Poems focusing on the charms, duties, and moral influence of the good mother became standard fare. One poem that was reprinted in various publications at the turn of the century offered a sensual portrait of motherhood that underscored its corporeal dimensions and allowed the reader to explore the body of the mother:

> So when the Mother, bending o'er his charms,
> Clasps her fair nursling in delighted arms;
> Throws the thin 'kerchief from her neck of snow,
> And half unveils the pearly orbs below;[56]

Excerpted from the eighteenth-century English poet and scientist Erasmus Darwin's set of poems, *The Botanic Garden*, these verses playfully unveiled the mother's physical charms and emphasized the enjoyment that mother and infant could gain from their mutual embrace. The infant in this poem displayed a proprietary pleasure in caressing the mother's breast, implying a greater emphasis on her physical attributes as a mother than on her moral or emotional influence. Another poem that was reprinted in several periodicals in the 1820s also evoked a sensual vision of breastfeeding with the words of a mother to her firstborn:

> What! do thy little fingers leave the breast,
> The fountain which thy small lips press'd at pleasure?
> Couldst thou exhaust it, pledge of passion blest![57]

Translated from the verses of Madame de Surville, a fifteenth-century French poet whose works were first published in the early nineteenth century, the poem repeatedly evoked the tender physical bond between mother and infant and made reference to the passion between husband and wife that resulted in the birth of a child.

But not all poems at this time were so sensual in their exploration of the maternal body. Poets also described the diligence of the good mother in caring for her children. Another poem from around the turn of the nineteenth century explored the corporeal work of a mother in protecting and entertaining her many children, giving a more pragmatic, if still sentimental, evocation of the daily activities of a mother:

> While one with fondness she caresses,
> Her gentle hand his little brother

Softly to her bosom presses,
And her knee supports another.
See him climb:—her arms extended
Gives the feeble urchin aid;
While her outstretch'd foot suspended
For his sisters seat is made.[58]

The "Good Mother" of this poem was occupied literally hand and foot with the activities of her children. Although the poem gave a sentimental portrait of a mother's duties, appealing to the reader to sympathize with her loving gestures and feel the depth of her maternal love, it also hinted at the real and tiring work involved in mothering a large family. Another poem offered a rarer reference to the bodily suffering of childbirth with a doting mother speaking to her child:

Welcome, thou little dimpled stranger,
O, welcome to my fond embrace;
Thou sweet reward of pain and danger.[59]

Juxtaposing the pain of childbirth with the pleasure of the maternal embrace, this poem offered readers a glimpse of the contradictory physical experiences of motherhood.

As time passed, these embodied depictions of motherhood became less frequent, although they could still occasionally be found into the 1830s and beyond. Sentimental poets continued at times to encourage readers to imagine the mother's body by offering glimpses of motherly actions such as cradling, nursing, and embracing a child. One poem highlighted the mother's Christian influence, but also evoked poignant visions of the mother-child bond by describing the infant's "cheek, now soft reposing / On thy tender mother's breast."[60] Occasionally a poem gestured to the work the mother did as a caretaker, for the good mother was always there to "wipe the cold sweat from off the brow; / The suffering form most gently move."[61] Indeed, one poem about a stepmother emphasized her caretaking role in order to identify her as a true mother, though not a biological one: "She sweetly kisses me, and smooths each straggling curl, / And makes me love her when she says, 'You are my own sweet girl.' "[62] These moments of physical intimacy generally focused on a single point of physical connection, such as a kiss, between mother and child that served to evoke the sincerity and selflessness of maternal love.

But by the 1830s, as poems about motherhood became increasingly popular, the mother developed into a newly disembodied character whose spiritual nature transcended the bounds of material existence. Motherhood poems generally came in two types at this time, the elegiac and the celebratory. The elegiac poem was the most common, a narrative of sacrifice and loss that memorialized the debility and death of the mother in order to arrive at a spiritualized vision of maternal perfection and influence. The poetic fantasy of the good mother took the most extreme forms of maternal sacrifice—death and the act of dying—and showed that they were the means to a more powerful end. Such poems participated in a larger culture of death and mourning that characterized nineteenth-century American society, in which elegies, portraits, and even items made with the hair of deceased loved ones all attested to a continuing link between the living and the dead.[63]

The celebratory and joyful evocations of motherhood, on the other hand, lauded the influence of the Christian mother, the joy that mothers and their children gained from one another, and the power of maternal love and influence. In these literary depictions the mother was young and lovely, as in the images examined above, but her physical attributes were overshadowed by her moral and spiritual virtues. Or perhaps it is more accurate to say that her beauty was defined by her internal spirit. As the well-known educator and reformer William Alcott wrote, "There can be no doubt that beauty, or at least, a set of features that interests us, as somewhat agreeable, is generally connected with virtue and piety." Thus the "morality of beauty," as Alcott called it, moved beauty away from the specific characteristics of the body, such as those seen earlier in Erasmus Darwin's sensuous verses, toward a beauty defined by interiority.[64] This was an essential part of the culture of gentility that privileged internal character above all else. For instance, one celebratory poem gestured briefly to the mother's physical traits before quickly invoking her interior virtues:

Young mother! On thy fair, majestic brow!
And, amid all its loftiness, revealing
Thy soul's rich tenderness and depth of feeling.[65]

Thus her high forehead, a sign of intellect and virtue, rapidly shifted from being a significant feature of the mother's physical beauty to being the primary signifier of her inner beauty.

In both elegiac and celebratory poems about mothers, the focus usually fell not on her physical charms or the work of her body, but on more ethereal and disembodied qualities such as her smile, her voice, and her enduring love. Her "ethereal noncorporeality," to borrow a phrase from Marianne Noble, manifested itself in a number of ways and identified her as a transcendent mother, the pinnacle of sentimental motherhood.[66] In one poem, aptly titled "A Mother's Smile," the mother was simultaneously absent from the poem and constituted its structural and rhetorical anchor:

> There are scenes and sunny places
> On which feeling loves to dwell,
> There are many happy faces
> Who have known and loved us well;
> But 'mid joy or 'mid dejection,
> There is nothing can beguile,
> That can show the fond affection
> Of a mother's welcome smile.[67]

Enumerating in general terms the grief and trials that characterized adult life, the poem insisted that the key to hope and resilience was the radiance of a mother's smile. Anchoring the end of each stanza, the mother's smile shimmered like that of a sentimental Cheshire cat, appearing as needed and unattached to any tangible maternal figure. A disembodied smile could beguile and reassure but had little agency and no personhood, suggesting that the mother was not so much an active participant in the world as she was a cherished influence.

The trope of the mother's voice offered a similarly noncorporeal vision of maternal influence, although it did offer the literary mother some possibility for self-expressive agency. Existing always as an echo, a memory, or a fantasy, the mother's gentle tones guided loved ones toward greater piety, evoking the notion of women's religious influence that had become a centerpiece of evangelical religion. In one poem the author remembered how a mother's "voice of gentle love first led me up in prayer / To the pure fount of bliss, and bade me quench my longings there."[68] Thus the mother was remembered and revered for her pious influence on her children. The mother's voice could also be a persistent presence, even from beyond the grave:

> I might forget her melting prayer,
> While pleasure's pulses madly fly;

But in the still, unbroken air,
Her gentle tones come stealing by—
And years of sin and manhood flee,
And leave me at my mother's knee.[69]

For this poet the voice was as abstract as "healing sent on wings of sleep," yet it held more power and was more enduring than the memory of the mother's prayer. The mother's exact words were inessential and easily forgotten; the influence of her voice alone was eternal. Coming from beyond the grave, a mother's voice, like her smile, was a memory that brought comfort to the sorrowful, for

It was a mother's gentle voice
Communing with a daughter's heart,
While bidding that sad one rejoice,
And every sorrowing thought depart.[70]

The trope of the mother's voice gave her the ability to speak even after death, thus transforming her into a powerful spiritual presence that transcended the bounds of mortality. Her voice served as a guide, leading loved ones along a path of piety and pure living: "a voice is in my heart," as one poet mused.[71] Indeed, such poems seemed to suggest that the mother had more influence as a spirit than as a living member of the family.

The most abstract element of the transcendent mother was her "mother's love": "A noble, pure, and tender flame / Enkindled from above," it was the essence of sentimental motherhood.[72] The mother's love was not merely an emotion—it was divinely ordained, and it had a presence of its own. As one poet mused:

We felt the atmosphere of love,
A mother's presence brings,
And safe, as if an angel form
Had wrapped us with his wings.[73]

A mother's love could have a powerful agency of its own and constituted the most potent aspect of the mother's presence. As the Reverend E. P. Dyer of Massachusetts wrote for an issue of the *Mother's Assistant*:

In the golden days of childhood, there was one who loved me well;—
One, whose love had mighty power with me, and bound me like a spell;

. . .

When the shadows round the sunset fall, as day retires to rest,

Then it glitters, like a diamond-pin, upon the evening's breast;—
With the beauty of that queenly gem, before its beams depart,—
Shines the jewel of Maternal Love, in thee a Mother's Faithful Heart.[74]

Syntactically, this poem elided the presence of the mother by making love the grammatical subject, which held "mighty power," before shifting quickly to ethereal visions of maternal love as a jewel, creating vivid associations with the heavens. The mother's love acted powerfully in life, but it gained a new and more heavenly power after death. In essence, maternal love was next to divine love. Another poem specifically repudiated the body of the mother in favor of her love and piety:

A Mother's Love!—Oh! never, sure
Did sweeter, or more holy feeling
A flame from earthly dross so pure,
On this our sinful earth find dwelling;
A coin so free from base alloy:
A love so near to that above;
Angels might covet to enjoy
A pious Mother's tender Love![75]

Developing the binary between flesh and spirit, earth and heaven, the poet elevated maternal love by drawing a parallel with divine love. Thus a mother's love—"free from earthly dross"—was the secret to her everlasting power and influence, but only if she were a pious and virtuous woman whose influence emanated from her Christian example.

The abstract symbols of maternal virtue—the mother's smile, voice, and love—emphasized the ethereal and spiritual nature of the mother and represented her with metaphors of abundance and endurance. The transcendent mother was everlasting in her virtue and influence, for her highest qualities could not be tarnished by time or death. As one poet wrote, "My mother pressed my hand, and *looked* a sad, a last farewell, / And shed a tinge upon my thoughts that time can ne'er dispel."[76] While the mother herself was gone, she persisted in the thoughts of her children. Another poem was more specific about the mother's enduring presence:

There's music in a mother's voice,
More sweet than breezes sighing,
There's kindness in a mother's glance,
Too pure for ever dying.

The most cherished qualities of the good mother were everlasting. More-over, as the next verses suggested, the qualities of the good mother were infinite and could never be depleted:

There's love within a mother's breast,
So deep 'tis overflowing,
And care for those she calls her own,
That's ever, ever growing.[77]

The metaphor of flowing water and fountains became the standard trope for evoking infinite maternal affection. As one poet mused:

Beautiful, is it not—this sketch,
Of true domestic bliss,
The fountain of maternal love,
Welling with happiness?[78]

Such metaphors brought images of nature—water, fountains, and ever-renewing growth—to the forefront, associating maternal virtue with natu-ral abundance and eternal growth. But these secular sentimental images were always tinged with religious meaning—the fountain of maternal love provided the key to heaven, for maternal influence was the conduit linking the human and the divine.

Thus in spite of her associations with nature—reminiscent of Enlighten-ment ideology that associated virtue with the natural world—the Christian impulse was the single most important characteristic of the transcendent mother. It was this impulse that transformed her from "earthly dross" to a spiritual figure in sentimental poetry, giving her infinite and enduring qual-ities a divine aspect. It was also in the context of Christian piety that the nineteenth-century literary mother possessed the most agency and the strongest voice. One poem, entitled "A Mother's Prayer, on the Birth of Her Child," offered up the mother's own voice in prayer for the future piety of her infant:

Let me, while thy features viewing,
Breathe to heav'n my fervent pray'r.
Ev'ry worldly thought subduing,
Make an int'rest for thee there.[79]

This was a common theme in poems about mothers: the mother gained a voice through prayer, and by praying she and her loved ones were drawn up into the spiritual realm. Another poem used the dying mother's "good-by" to stand in for a whole constellation of Christian teachings:

> My mother's "good-by"—it comes to me
> Like a peace-be-still to the troubled sea;
> And when passions would sway, or temptations entice,
> I hear the sound of a warning voice,
> "My son, this world is a world of sin,
> And there's many a tempting vice therein,
> But shun them all, and their presence fly,
> And God will protect thee—Good-by, good-by!"[80]

In the context of prayer or pious didacticism the mother gained a voice, but only for the dissemination of Christian sentiments. Her individual personhood and subjectivity disappeared in the spiritual essence of her "good-by," which reminded her children to mind their ways and follow her pious teachings.

The feelings and utterances of the Christian mother in sentimental poetry were most often bound up with death and the process of dying. In many poems it was the mother whose "sands of life were ebbing—/Ebbing—ebbing fast away," or whose grave formed the centerpiece of the poem, but it could also be the death of a child that gave the poem its emotional weight.[81] Poems about dead and dying mothers were at the heart of poetic depictions of motherhood. Indeed, roughly one-third of all the motherhood poems published in *Godey's* between 1830 and 1850 featured deceased or dying mothers.[82] In poems about deceased mothers, the body of the mother was literally absent—replaced in the text by a gravestone or by a specific memory or location. The poem "My Mother's Grave," for instance, described the sentiments aroused where

> A mound of waving grass was near,
> A grave, made in the clay,
> A holy spot to memory dear,
> Beneath, my mother lay.

In this particular case, nature replaced the maternal body, for it was Nature who embraced the narrator and "pillowed in her tender arms / My sad and tearful face."[83] Yet it was the memory of the good mother that made the spot holy, joining together personal sorrow and pious reverence to highlight the enduring influence of the mother.

Maternal death poems often featured the wasting and disappearance of the mother's body, which revealed the process by which she became a spiritual figure, unfettered by corporeality. Maternal mortality was, of course, a devastatingly real aspect of life in the nineteenth century, and many women had friends and kinswomen who had died in childbirth or from related complications. We can imagine that one way of making sense of these losses and of the fears women faced when they anticipated the trials of childbearing was to sentimentalize death and spiritualize the mother. If the essence of the mother was in her spirit rather than her material form, then she could never wholly perish, nor would she ever be wholly absent from her children. Motherhood poems emphasized that as the mother herself wasted away, her piety and influence on her children grew. The mother's enduring influence could be fully realized only in death. A poem by Lydia Sigourney featured the mother's deathbed and her last conversation with her children, who could not understand why

> Their mother in such feeble whisper spake,
> Broken with sighs and why her wasted cheek
> Was pale as marble.

The mother's feeble voice, her pallor and wasted figure, and her glowing eyes all spoke to the slow, genteel disappearance of the body. When the body disappeared, her soul could take flight:

> With a wondrous lustre in her eye,
> The last, bright sunbeam of a mother's love,
> Ere it became seraphic, the freed soul,
> High o'er the bondage of all earthly ties,
> Went forth with hallelujahs, at the call
> Of its Redeemer.

The heart of the poem was the mother's transformation from mortal woman to spirit, from "emaciate hand" to "freed soul."[84] Indeed, at the center of maternal death poems was the sought-after release from the trials of the flesh. Such poems presumed that the lot of the mother was one of suffering, though such suffering was rarely linked specifically to the physical challenges of childbearing. One poem told of the hurried baptism of an infant just before the death of his mother; the fact that her death came so soon after his birth signaled that her demise was related to complications in childbirth, but such scenarios were rare in sentimental poems, and poets never alluded to the specific physical complications that led to death or debility.[85]

Thus it was that through death the mother was transformed into a spirit, a figure of surpassing virtue who had greater power and influence from on high than ever she possessed on earth. As one contemporary put it, "A mother is, next to God, all powerful."[86] Her memory and the echoes of her voice in prayer could lead loved ones along the path of righteousness, and her grave remained as a symbol of the transformation from flesh to spirit. What was perhaps most remarkable about this ostensibly powerful spiritual figure, however, was her passivity; the transcendent mother *did* almost nothing. As one contemporary women's rights activist critically noted of American society, "'Woman's influence' . . . is held to be of far more importance than woman's self—her influence being regarded as the end of her being, and herself as an incident only."[87] The transcendent mother was the object of other forces—illness, grief, pain—but she was rarely an active subject. Disembodied, often voiceless, her mere existence and her moral nature were what made her powerful.

The tropes that characterized sentimental poetry appeared frequently in prose pieces as well, although these texts showed less uniformity in their focus and imagery. One short piece, for instance, tapped into the image of the praying mother as a powerful memory and influence in the lives of her children: "I have a vivid recollection of the effect of maternal influence. . . . I seemed to hear the very tones of her voice; and when I recollected some of her expressions, I burst into tears, arose from my bed, and fell upon my knees just on the spot where my mother kneeled."[88] Like the sentimental poems that evoked the voice of the pious mother, this piece envisioned her as a potent memory, an influence that was stronger in death than in life. Similar testimonies appeared regularly, evoking the memory of a mother's voice or touch as a talisman against vice later in life.[89] Another short piece created an image of perfect maternal love by comparing it to the abundance of flowing water: the mother "folded the happy babe to her warm and throbbing breast. She felt a gush of pure enjoyment in that sacred moment, such as flows from no spring save that of a *mother's* heart."[90] Such images were virtually identical to those found in sentimental poems, but they were often mixed with a diverse array of pragmatic advice about mothering, didactic stories, or dogmatic pronouncements about maternal duty. Indeed, what makes sentimental poetry uniquely interesting is the consistency in the imagery used to depict the transcendent mother, which resulted in a particularly potent message about women's spiritual power and influence.

Sentimental poetry condensed an array of ideas and images of motherhood into one densely emotional form.

· · · · · ·

Depictions of white genteel motherhood in images and verse offer a fascinating window into the evolution of the transcendent mother as the pinnacle of feminine virtue in popular sentimental print culture. The frequency with which the trope of the transcendent mother appeared suggests that she filled an important need in American society. Existing in a class- and race-specific location, the transcendent mother demonstrated that white middle-class culture was rooted in Christian piety and genteel values. This must have been comforting at a time when many middle-class Americans felt buffeted by rapid economic and social changes and by the dislocations of growing individualism and geographic mobility. The transcendent mother reconnected individuals to domestic and Christian values and to a vision of a more enduring emotional and spiritual realm separated from the bustle of the world. Envisioning motherhood in these terms allowed readers to cherish an enchanting vision of order and morality in a rapidly changing society and to elide the aspects of maternity that challenged feminine ideologies of virtue, restraint, and maternal devotion.

Of course, this fantasy of transcendence created a script that was impossible for women to follow. As Marianne Noble writes, "The ideal of female noncorporeality promises the true woman a social position of the first importance . . . but leaves that position ever vulnerable to the incessant assault of her own body."[91] Childbearing women—even those who were young, white, genteel, and lovely—could never actually transcend their bodies. Motherhood as women lived it was not easy or unproblematic, and they could not accomplish the work of mothering by simply wafting about their maternal love and moral influence. Swollen ankles, unwieldy bellies, and leaking breasts provided constant reminders of the physicality of motherhood, and the fatigue and frustrations of mothering must have made many women feel at times as if their influence as mothers was negligible at best and that it was a poor return for the physical trials of maternity.

But these literary and visual representations of transcendent motherhood were meant to inspire and uplift readers and viewers, helping them cultivate inner virtues and understand their work as mothers from a more expansive spiritual perspective. Unfortunately, we know little of the specific reactions women might have had to these depictions of motherhood. These images and texts were enormously popular, but what did they mean to the mother who paused in the middle of her busy day to contemplate a beautiful image of a mother and child? Isabelle Lehuu has argued that we should not read these depictions as actual representations of women's self-image as wives and mothers, but view them "rather as texts that the reader-viewers were appropriating, enjoying, and approving."[92] Based on women's own writings about motherhood, this assessment seems accurate. Women were under no illusions about the challenges and the hard work involved in motherhood, but as they tended their children and managed their own reproductive bodies, they could also enjoy the imagined tranquility and the powerful influence of the transcendent mother.

# 6 Imagining the Slave Mother

## Sentimentalism and Embodiment in Antislavery Print Culture

· · · · · · · · · · · · · · · · · · · · · · · · · · · · · · · · · · · · · · · · · · · · · ·

At the same time that the vision of the transcendent mother was developing in sentimental print culture, the figure of the enslaved mother was also being imagined in antislavery literature and visual culture. As the antislavery movement gained momentum in the 1830s, giftbooks such as *The Liberty Bell* and *Autographs for Freedom* were sold to raise money for the antislavery cause, while newspapers such as the *North Star*, the *Liberator*, and the *National Anti-slavery Standard* circulated information and inspiration to supporters throughout the northern states and even abroad.[1] These publications included letters and essays by prominent activists as well as stories, poems, and pictures that helped draw readers in and engage their emotions on behalf of the cause. At the same time, pamphlets, antislavery almanacs, novels, volumes of poetry, and slave narratives also circulated among sympathetic readers, and antislavery literature appeared regularly in many religious and literary periodicals, contributing to a vibrant realm of literary and visual culture focused on depicting the experience of enslavement and presenting moral and emotional arguments in favor of abolition.

Much of this antislavery print culture followed broader cultural trends by drawing on sentimentalism. Whereas early abolitionist writings emerging in the eighteenth century had focused primarily on moral and religious argumentation, by the late eighteenth century some writers were already beginning to appeal to readers on an emotional rather than an intellectual level, and this strategy became particularly important in the nineteenth century.[2] As one eighteenth-century writer commanded, "Awake! Ye whole hearts are attuned to sympathy!"[3] The role of antislavery literature was to stir readers' emotions in the hopes of generating action, and writers increasingly sought to generate sympathy and outrage on behalf of enslaved people. By the 1830s antislavery literature and visual culture drew on a variety of familiar sentimental themes intended to arouse the emotions of readers and make them viscerally aware of the injustices of slavery. In this way they were able to speak to many middle-class readers who were already immersed in popular sentimental print culture, speaking to them with language, imagery, and themes that were already familiar. Although by this time many middle-class northern readers had little direct experience with slavery, their moral sensibilities might be stirred by depictions of attacks on the sanctity of family bonds and feminine virtue. Placing antislavery arguments within the cultural framework of sentimentalism made antislavery rhetoric both appealing and functional for white middle-class readers. Such appeals became an essential part of what Julie Husband has called the "family protection campaign," which was pioneered by activists, particularly middle-class women, beginning in the mid-1830s. This campaign marked a shift away from arguments based on the Bible or rooted in the vision of natural rights enshrined in the Declaration of Independence and the Constitution. Highlighting the destruction of family life under slavery and the sexual vulnerability of enslaved women, the family protection campaign especially sought to appeal to white women and was responsible for increasing support among white northerners for the antislavery cause.[4]

These direct appeals to the sympathies of a predominantly white population of northern readers ostensibly brought forth a universal vision of human emotion intended to forge a sympathetic connection between the victim of slavery and the reader, with particular emphasis on the bonds of womanhood and motherhood. Antislavery print culture, particularly sentimental poems and images, seemed to suggest that if an enslaved woman could feel the anguish of a true mother at the loss of her child, then she must share an essential emotional connection with white mothers. Because sentiment and sensibility were qualities that defined feminine virtue, the emotions of the enslaved mother allowed her to claim the mantle of virtuous womanhood. In turn, the feeling of sympathy on the part of the white female reader provided a way for her to demonstrate her feminine virtue. The experience of feeling allowed individuals, in theory at least, to reach across the racial divide. Thus sentiment seemingly transcended differences of race or class, making way for a common identity based in sentimental womanhood and motherhood.

Drawing on these expressions of shared feeling, scholars have emphasized that one of the essential functions of sentimental culture was to create a universal vision of humanity based on shared emotion. Michael Chaney has suggested that sentimentalism particularly appealed to antislavery writers because it "always implied a universal application."[5] In this way sentimentalism facilitated antislavery arguments by calling on Americans to recognize the common humanity of the enslaved. Celeste-Marie Bernier has explained that in antislavery writing, "it is man's capacity to exhibit feeling towards his fellow man that justifies his rights to be considered within the realms of universal humanity and which make it possible for him to award subjectivity to the otherwise objectified and shackled status of the slave."[6] Thus sentimentalism reaffirmed the humanity of both free and enslaved through the process of feeling. For writers who sought to forge a connection across social boundaries, the universalizing potential of sentimentalism was a powerful tool that seemed to efface, or render negligible, the specificities of social hierarchies. In this way, dynamics of power and oppression could be erased in favor of an idealized realm of human emotion in which questions of equality or difference became moot. For instance, Lauren Berlant has explored the ways in which sentimentalism worked to create a vision of universal womanhood, for "the sentimental abstraction of the values of 'woman' from the realm of material relations meant that interactions among classes, races, and different ethnic groups also appear to dissolve in their translation into sentimental semiosis."[7] Sentimentalism appeared to offer a universal realm of language and feeling to which anyone could belong simply by marshaling the correct emotions and modes of expression. In doing so, the sentimental subject defined his or her humanity in terms of feeling.

Few scholars have challenged this vision of sentimental culture, permitting nineteenth-century sentimentalism to stand as a cultural form that both intended to and succeeded in transcending social power structures and markers of social difference. Yet a close analysis of representations of enslaved mothers in antislavery poetry and visual culture reveals significant problems with this vision. I do not wish to diminish the importance of the ways in which antislavery print culture incorporated enslaved women into the sentimental realm, a strategy that took the important step of creating a sense of shared humanity and subjectivity across socially constructed boundaries of race. But I would argue that the ways in which antislavery print culture developed sentimental depictions of enslaved women ultimately served to reproduce rather than transcend racial hierarchies.

The persistence of a racial hierarchy appeared most clearly in the different ways in which the bodies of the white mother and the enslaved mother were represented in verse and visual culture. Unlike the transcendent mother of mainstream print culture, whose body disappeared, thus freeing her spiritual influence, in antislavery texts the enslaved mother was firmly bound to her corporeality. Antislavery poems drew on sentimental language and imagery to define enslaved women as good mothers, yet these verses also emphasized the ways in which the physical and emotional violence wrought by the slave system thwarted their claims to sentimental motherhood. Visual culture was more extreme in its emphasis on embodiment, tending to present the enslaved mother as an anguished body suffering under the lash or futilely resisting the physical control of the slaveholder. Moreover, her body was often exposed in ways that would have been unimaginable for depictions of white mothers; instead of being shrouded in filmy fabric, the enslaved mother might be stripped to the waist, her bare flesh exposing the realities of exploitation and sexual vulnerability.

Thus in poetry and visual culture scenes of force and violence highlighted the corporeality of the enslaved mother, threatening to overwhelm her claims to sentimental subjectivity. It may be true, as Julie Husband writes, that at the center of antislavery literature was "sentimental identification, when bodily suffering, tears, or the loss of a loved one provide transcendent moments of understanding across dramatically different race, gender, and class experiences."[8] But fleeting moments of sympathy explored in verse or picture could hardly obliterate the entrenched racial boundaries that permeated both social relations and cultural worlds of imagination in antebellum America. In short, the universalizing tendencies of sentimental culture broke down over the issue of black embodiment. In American society and culture, enslaved women were so profoundly defined by their bodies—sexual bodies, productive bodies, reproductive bodies—that even in the realm of antislavery print culture they were denied the same spiritual and emotional transcendence as the white mother in sentimental print culture.

Antislavery visual culture and verse combined to create a broadly coherent vision of the enslaved mother that was intended to convey to northern readers the depredations of the slave system. Rhetorically, then, antislavery texts needed the sentimental vision of enslaved mothers to be incomplete in order to make their point about the horrors of slavery and the need for reform. The gaps and failures of sentimentalism demonstrated for readers the evils at the heart of slavery. Antislavery print culture deployed the enslaved mother as a symbol of disorder. Her frantic emotions and her tortured body expressed to readers the ways in which slavery destroyed all that middle-class sentimental culture held most dear—feminine virtue and spirituality, maternal influence, and the sanctity of the domestic sphere. The enslaved mother in antislavery print culture was not meant to be revered for her ethereal influence; she was meant to elicit sympathy, moral outrage, and action.

· · · · · ·

The sentimental mode in antislavery writings emerged particularly clearly in poems, which sought to express "the subjective experience of slavery."[9] Between the 1830s and the 1860s a substantial body of sentimental poetry was published by both black and white authors who sought to evoke the crimes of slavery, highlight the subjectivity of the enslaved, and appeal to the moral and emotional sensibilities of readers.[10] Antislavery poetry reached fewer readers than the sentimental poems featured in more mainstream publications such as *Godey's Lady's Book*, but antislavery writers were able to use the widespread popularity of sentimental verse to launch an effective appeal to northern readers.[11] In spite of the frequency with which antislavery verse appeared in American print culture, poetry has generally fallen by the wayside in scholarly analyses of antislavery literature. More attention has been paid to slave narratives and antislavery novels, sermons, essays, and pamphlets.[12] Yet poems were an integral part of the antislavery movement's print culture, and they were particularly important for appealing to a female readership. Black female literary societies, for instance, often encouraged their members to write and publish poetry and prose to further the work of antislavery in a way that was deemed appropriately feminine.[13] Women made up a significant portion of antislavery supporters, and so it was essential for the movement to appeal to women's concerns and to present antislavery arguments in ways that would speak to them. Women created an extensive network throughout the towns and rural communities of the North, where they formed antislavery societies, engaged in fund-raising activities, organized sewing circles to equip escaped slaves, and even spoke in public against slavery.[14] Antislavery poetry helped to create a community of shared feeling among supporters when it was read aloud at meetings and in family parlors and when it was collected and shared in letters, diaries, and scrapbooks.

Antislavery poems frequently relied on the figure of the mother to expose the horror and degradation of slavery and to appeal explicitly to mothers in the North. A poem published in the *Liberator* in 1835, for instance, described the plight of enslaved mothers and exhorted women to intervene:

Mothers! for mothers intercede.
Tell me not your voice is weak—
Speak! 'tis all I ask you, Speak![15]

Another poem, set to a popular melody and published in a volume of other antislavery songs, called on mothers specifically to contemplate the loss of a child to sale:

> Ah! Mother! hast thou ever known
> The pain of parting ties?
> Was ever infant from thee torn
> And sold before thine eyes?[16]

Drawing on sentimental tropes of maternal affection and moral and religious feeling, poems featuring the enslaved mother highlighted the violence inherent in the system of slavery and sought to elicit sympathy and outrage by evoking such horrors as the severing of the sacred bond between mother and child.

Poems about enslaved mothers did not demonstrate the same uniformity of message and imagery found in verses about white mothers, making them more difficult to categorize. The majority of poems about enslaved mothers featured the separation of mother and child, either by death or by sale, but this moment of trauma was articulated through a variety of images and emotions. One common feature among these poems, however, was the pairing of sentimental language and imagery, which placed the enslaved mother in a familiar emotional space that appealed to the reader's sympathies, alongside deeply unsettling depictions of physical and emotional violence. What is particularly striking about many of these poems is that they often expressed a degree of raw emotion and frantic action never seen in mainstream motherhood poems, which featured tranquil resignation, effaced the rawness of grief, and disallowed despair.

By placing enslaved women within sentimental discourse, antislavery poems redefined them as legitimate sentimental subjects and connected them to a shared vision of womanhood. A poem in the religious publication *Zion's Herald* in 1837, for instance, articulated an emotional appeal from the enslaved mother to the white mother:

> O! bid the streams of feeling flow;
> To darker sisters yield a part;
> And let the golden law of love,
> Guide the decisions of thy heart
> Believe, that in our torn hearts rise
> The mother's tenderest sympathies.[17]

Allowing the enslaved mother literally to speak in sentimental language as she appealed to the white woman's "streams of feeling" served to bring her into the same affective realm as white mothers and permitted her to demand a corresponding emotional response from them. This was a significant rhetorical strategy because it asserted the humanity of the enslaved, demanded that other women step forward to acknowledge a shared sisterhood, and challenged enslaved women's commodification as human chattel by insisting on the power of their emotions rather than the value of their bodies. The enslaved mother in this poem insisted that the "mother's tenderest sympathies" were not solely the purview of privileged white women. Enslaved women were not simply (re)productive bodies; they also had feeling hearts. Another poem began by acknowledging the enslaved mother's status as property, for "crushed by rude slavery's iron hoof, / She stood, a branded *thing*, aloof," but went on to show that a powerful emotional tie "twined round her soul," for "she had a son, / A pretty playful boy."[18] Her love for her son contested her *thingness*. In case readers were not yet convinced of her humanity, the author went on to emphasize her maternal love and the terrors that slavery forced upon her as a mother. Poems emphasizing the love enslaved women bore their children and the sacrifices they made as mothers placed them firmly in the realm of the sentimental mother: they were tender, dedicated, and self-sacrificing. By locating the enslaved mother within sentimental discourse, antislavery writers created a common ground of language and feeling that justified and enhanced their appeals to white Americans on behalf of the enslaved. The slave mother, too, could be a sentimental subject. This was an important move in a culture that habitually defined nonwhite women and men as less intellectual, less spiritual, more embodied, and therefore less sentimental than white Americans.[19]

In spite of the important ways in which enslaved mothers were welcomed into the sentimental fold, much of the emotional power of antislavery poems came from thwarted sentimental tropes that underscored the ways in which slavery destroyed the sentimental order. A number of poems gestured to the enslaved mother's capacity for proper emotion, but then twisted the imagery to show how those emotions were defeated or distorted by slavery. One poem in *The Anti-slavery Harp*, published by the activist and former slave William Wells Brown, highlighted the enslaved mother's infinite capacity for emotion, which was a common theme in motherhood poems in mainstream sentimental print culture:

O who can imagine her heart's deep emotion,
As she thinks of her children about to be sold;
You may picture the bounds of the rock-girdled ocean,
But the grief of that mother can never be known.[20]

Yet instead of evoking the more usual image of infinite maternal love—the "soul's rich tenderness and depth of feeling"—here the author substituted grief to emphasize the perverse consequences of slavery.[21] For readers steeped in sentimental imagery, these verses would have felt simultaneously familiar and unsettling. Similarly, grief was the only possible emotion in "The Slave Mother's Lament for Her Children," for the mother was left with "a heart that spurn'd all *human* relief, / For its cords had been sunder'd forever."[22] In the sentimental realm in which it was essential for the cords of one's heart to vibrate with emotion, slavery rendered this mother, in essence, heartless, though through no fault of her own. Thus the central emotion of sentimental culture—maternal love—could be twisted into grief or fear for greater emotional impact on the reader.

Other poems drew on treasured images of the intimate bond between mothers and children to reveal the ways in which slavery thwarted the sanctity and power of this relationship. One poet gestured to the connection experienced by a mother and child when the infant's "little arms steal upward, and then upon her breast / She feels the brown and velvet hands that never are at rest." Here the author gave a charming view of the intimate connection between a mother and her beloved child. But the next lines destroyed the image, for in spite of the charm of the child's soft hands, "no sense of joy they waken, but thrills of bitter pain,— / She thinks of him who counteth o'er the gold those hands shall gain."[23] The poet built a picture of the fond relationship between mother and child and then ruthlessly destroyed it, just as maternal affection was thwarted by the greed of the slave owner. The sentimental image of the mother-child bond made the reference to greed and cruelty all the more shocking. Similarly, a poem published in the *Liberator* in 1835 lulled the reader with a tender description of mother and baby:

As a tendril to a vine,
Lo, a prattling babe is thine;
turn thy mourning into joy,
Smile upon thy lovely boy.

Yet the next verse turned this pleasing picture on its head. "Smile?" the poet asked bitterly, " 'tis but the smile of wo; / Ah, the tears begin to flow."[24] This mother knew that her child was not her own; this tendril that twined about her heart brought despair instead of hope. Unlike poems that evoked the infinite tenderness in the white mother's heart, antislavery poems highlighted the emotional devastation inflicted on enslaved mothers in order to make their moral argument. To reveal the full consequences of the slave system, the emotions of the enslaved mother had to be warped by her circumstances.

Antislavery poems also drew on the same natural metaphors that populated mainstream sentimental poetry, but used them to underscore how slavery blighted even the purest and most natural of affections. The beloved poet Lydia Sigourney made the transcendence of "a mother's love" her refrain when she inquired:

> *What was it?* Ask a mother's breast
> Through which a fountain flows
> Perennial, fathomless and blest,
> By winter never froze.[25]

While the transcendent mother's love was infinite and everlasting, antislavery writers set out to show that the fountain of maternal love flowing from the enslaved mother's heart was doomed. One poem begged pity for the enslaved mother specifically because of the emotional devastation wrought by slavery:

> The mildew of slavery has blighted each blossom,
> That ever has bloomed in her path-way below;
> It has froze every fountain that gushed in her bosom,
> And chilled her heart's verdure with pitiless woe.[26]

The botanic imagery and recurring trope of the fountain of maternal love wrapped the enslaved mother in the mantle of sentimental motherhood, but by emphasizing the destruction of these sentimental tendencies the poem exposed the maternal prerogatives that were denied the enslaved mother. Thus the literary enslaved mother was brought into the realm of sentimentalism, but was ultimately defined both within the institution of slavery and within sentimental culture by her status as a slave rather than by her affective life as a mother. Contrary to the real-life examples of many loving enslaved mothers, in this literary context the fountain of maternal affection simply could not continue to flow under the brutality of slavery. Such sentimental imagery worked powerfully on the emotions of the reader who was already familiar with the ideals of sentimental motherhood, but they did not communicate the same fantasy of emotional and spiritual transcendence used to imagine white mothers.

The ultimate betrayal of sentimental motherhood was revealed in the many antislavery poems that depicted an enslaved mother praying for the death of her child. Whereas mainstream poems often featured the grieving mother, mourning the illness or death of an infant, in the case of antislavery poetry the refrain of the tormented mother was "God grant my little helpless one in helplessness may die!"[27] The white mother worked toward pious resignation when faced with the death of a beloved child; the enslaved mother wished for death as a safe haven for her child. Whereas poems about white mothers suggested that maternal love was powerful enough to conquer all evils, this was not the case for the enslaved mother. Maternal tenderness, these poems suggested, was not powerful enough to protect a child or to combat the horrors of slavery; only by ascending to heaven could the enslaved mother or child find peace. As one poem intimated, in death the slave child could maintain its sentimental virtues, for "never will thy heart be blighted, / In its op'ning bloom."[28] Numerous poems played with this notion that a mother might prefer to see her child dead rather than enslaved. As the imagined voice of one enslaved mother intoned in a poem published in the *Ladies' Literary Portfolio* in 1829:

> Then, ere the nursling at my breast
> Shall feel the tyrant's rod;
> O, lay his little form at rest
> Below the quiet sod![29]

The pairing of the "nursling" and the "tyrant's rod" would have been shocking to the reader more accustomed to descriptions of an infant cuddled at its mother's breast. Under slavery, the truly loving mother could do nothing but wish that death would offer her child the protection that she could not. Such jolting images and seemingly monstrous sentiments sought to disrupt the complacency of the reader by demonstrating that even maternal love was necessarily diverted in perverse directions by the institution of slavery.

In addition to the images of maternal love that was warped by slavery, the mother herself presented a very different figure in antislavery poetry. Depictions of the wild and raving enslaved mother provided a striking foil to the passive white mother of mainstream poetry. Indeed, the word "wild" appeared with frequency in antislavery poems, but almost never in poems about white mothers. Numerous antislavery poems deployed the figure of the frantic and raving mother in order to underscore the horrors of the sale of human chattel. Juxtaposing the cold rationality of the white spectators and the frenetic despair of the enslaved mother at an auction, one poem that was published in the *Philanthropist* in 1841 offered a terrible picture of the abuses of slavery:

> 'Twas there was seen a woman sold,
> A mother parted from her child;
> All hearts around were hard and cold,
> While she was raving, frantic, wild.[30]

This poem set the mother apart from the cold-hearted spectators, for unlike them she demonstrated her humanity through her feelings. Yet the wildness of her emotions made her seem crazed or even animal-like, setting her apart from the pure and tranquil emotions privileged by sentimental culture. The poem also sought to draw the reader's sympathy through a visceral awareness of the mother's anguish, translated as it was through the dramatic movements of her body when "she threw herself upon the ground, / In agony and keen despair."[31] Another poem, published in the *Liberator* in 1835, began with a similar image of frantic emotion manifesting itself on the body:

> Close she hugs him to her breast,
> Sighs and moans like one distrest,
> And lifting high her streaming eyes
> To the God of mercy cries.[32]

The image of agony and fierce emotion in this poem was powerfully evoked by the mother's body itself—the way she clung to her child, the tears that covered her cheeks, and the audible cries torn out of her by grief and fear. The poem told of her oppression under the institution of slavery, but in spite of her lack of power she was not a passive figure. Unlike the literary white mother whose emotions were strung somewhere on a continuum between maternal tenderness and gentle grief, the literary slave mother cried out with anguish and strained her body against the impossible cruelties of slavery. Thus while her emotions helped to make the enslaved mother part of the sentimental realm, they also set her apart as wilder, more unpredictable, and less spiritual than the tranquil and piously resigned white mother in sentimental poems.

Just as the voice of the transcendent mother was an important feature in mainstream poems, the voice of the enslaved mother was also heard in verse; but her tones were anything but gentle or passive. In one poem published in the *Boston Recorder* in 1834, the narrator bore witness to an enslaved mother's troubles, writing,

> I saw the burning tear
> Run down her dark brown cheek;
> It told of wo and care.

But the poem quickly moved from the voice of the narrator to the voice of the mother herself, who frantically cried out her tale of loss.[33] While the voice of the transcendent mother was a gentle echo or memory that guided listeners toward greater piety, the voice of the enslaved mother was a shriek that reverberated with horror. One poem used the echoes of these cries to evoke the depredations of the slave auction:

> The harsh auctioneer, to sympathy cold,
> Tears the babe from its mother and sells it for gold;
> While the infant and mother, loud shriek for each other,
> In sorrow and woe.
>
> . . . .
>
> At last came the parting of mother and child,
> Her brain reeled with madness, that mother was wild;
> Then the lash could not smother the shrieks of that mother
> Of sorrow and woe.

Although the refrain of "sorrow and woe" that ended each stanza in this poem partially restored a sense of sentimental order, what stood out in these verses were the images of frantic struggle and violence inflicted in a vain attempt to control the shrieking mother. The poet sought a visceral response from readers who could feel in their own bodies the shrieks of horror, the sense of madness, and the futile straining of the mother. The poem ended with the mother raving, bereft of reason, and finally dead. But instead of evoking her spiritual ascension, the poem kept its focus on the land of the living, imploring, "O, list ye kind mothers to the cries of the slave."[34] The mother's shrieks were not a distant memory or echo, but a vivid and terrible reality meant to rattle the complacency of the white reader.

Perhaps even more unsettling to readers than the ravings of the mother who was driven to despair by the crimes of slavery was the fact that even death failed to bring a proper sentimental resolution. As we have seen, popular print culture taught white mothers that they could console themselves with the thought that even in death their influence as mothers would never dim—in fact, their power would only grow. One of the central narratives in mainstream poems about motherhood was the death of the mother and her transformation into an everlasting and infinite spiritual influence. The essence of the transcendent mother was in her ability to rise above her materiality to obtain greater virtue and influence. Maternal death was also featured in antislavery poems, yet these poems did not underscore the enslaved mother's spiritual influence after death. Even in death, she remained bound to earthly matters. One particularly gruesome poem published in the *Liberator* in 1833 described the murder of an enslaved child by his owner, "who angrily had caught the boy / And dashed him to the ground." The child's mother "wildly raised to heaven her eye, / And shrieked aloud and fell," a powerful image of despair that was located in the reactions of the body. The poem concluded with the death of the mother:

> Her spirit took its flight—
> And mother and child together lay,
> For beasts to eat at night.[35]

A reader accustomed to the conventions of sentimental poetry might have reasonably expected a tender and uplifting description of the mother and child's spiritual reunion in heaven. Instead, the reader was left with the image of desecrated corpses, a spectacle intended to reinforce the inhumanity of the slave system. But the image of these corpses simultaneously reinforced the corporeality of the enslaved mother and child—in the end they were nothing but bodies. This mother, it seems, could not transcend the horrors of slavery even in death.

A few antislavery poems did draw on references to the spiritual realm, though these poems were less common, and their spiritual messages tended to be incomplete. One poem in the *Liberty Bell* created a dichotomy between the corrupt world of the "coiling whip, / Whose cruel lashes drip / With gore," and the world above, "where all is joy, and peace, / And love that cannot cease." The dying mother in this poem received a vision of heaven and cried out in the last verse, "My Boy, I fly to thee!"[36] The reader can imagine that she was welcomed into the spiritual realm by her lost loved ones, but her spiritual journey remained incomplete. The reader cannot *know* of her transformation from flesh to spirit. Thus she arrived at the threshold of immortality, but unlike the white mothers of mainstream poetry, her transcendence of the material world and the triumph of her spiritual influence remained outside the scope of the poem. Instead, these verses conveyed the enslaved mother's longing for transcendence while leaving its achievement in question. The literary slave mother could never arrive at complete spiritual transcendence because she was so profoundly defined by her corporeality. In order to make fully visible the depredations of slavery to potential allies in the antislavery movement, the enslaved mother could not be allowed to escape to the spiritual realm, for her body and its sufferings needed to remain in focus. It was her body that signified the moral disorder wrought by slavery; her inability to transcend her corporeality reminded Americans of their failure to root out a system that seemed to prey most tragically on female virtue and maternal influence.

Antislavery poems further highlighted the inability of the enslaved mother to transcend her material circumstances by combining images of maternal love and forced labor, underscoring the conflict between proper maternal feeling and the physical demands of slavery. One poem, published in the *National Era* in 1855, began with the shocking image of a mother forced to labor at digging a grave for her own child:

> And thou, a woman, scooping out its grave!
> The heart of mercy bleeds to see thee fling
> The broken earth o'er one thou'dst die to save.

The author emphasized the power of the scene to generate sympathy in the viewer—to make hearts bleed—but the shock of the image also served to question her maternity. The very idea of a mother flinging clods of earth over the corpse of her child represented the height of impossibility: "Yet not thine own!" the poet exclaimed; "no mother could be here, / Interring her own dead."[37] The work the mother was forced to do wrought such violence on notions of maternal tenderness and female sensibility that the witness could scarcely believe the scene: surely she *could not be* the mother of the deceased child. Her labors threw her maternity into question. The narrator did not consider that there might be some consolation for the bereaved mother in the knowledge that her child would never be forced to labor in such a way. Instead, the poem focused on displaying the shocked emotions of the narrator and contrasting them with the physical and emotional labor demanded of the woman.

Other poems emphasized the ways in which the work demanded of enslaved women prevented them from being good mothers. They were not allowed to perform the sacred work of motherhood, for their emotional power as mothers was deemed by the slave system to be less useful than the power of their working bodies. One poem, published in the *Liberator* in 1844, drew out to an excruciating degree the tension between the needs of a dying infant and the demands of field labor. "God gave me babe—a precious boon," the weary mother recounted, "But massa called to work too soon, / And I must needs depart." From morning to night the mother experienced the horror of working in the fields while imagining the sufferings of her dying child:

> I work'd upon plantation ground,
> Though faint with woe and dread,
> Then ran, or flew, and here I found—
> See, massa, almost dead.[38]

In each stanza the mother evinced proper maternal feeling and devotion, yet each moment the demands of her owner drove her away from her maternal role and reasserted her status as human chattel. Expressions of sentiment, such poems suggested, had no power against the immediate demands of slavery. Thus the enslaved mother's claims to sentimental motherhood were rendered impossible. Though she might be capable of proper maternal emotion, she would never be defined by her affective ties as long as she remained a slave.

Even more shocking to sentimental sensibility than depictions of forced labor were the scenes of physical violence that antislavery writers used to underscore the immorality of slavery. As Elizabeth B. Clark has shown in her analysis of the rhetoric of pain and suffering in antebellum American culture, "The gruesome tribulations of the body became a staple of antislavery literature."[39] For many writers, violence was the most potent way to express the inhumanity of the slave system, and they dwelled on narratives of punishment and torture. These kinds of spectacles formed part of what Karen Halttunen has called the "pornography of pain." She has argued that it was not until the eighteenth century that the culture of sensibility redefined pain as unacceptable and repulsive, and this new understanding led to views of pain as "obscenely titillating" because of the very fact that it was taboo.[40] Descriptions of slavery used physical pain and punishment to make readers viscerally aware of the injustices of the institution. But at the same time these portrayals could become obscene and potentially titillating by exposing the body of the slave and depicting the very moment of violence.

The lash was ubiquitous in antislavery poetry as the most potent symbol of the violence inherent in the institution. It represented the horrors of slavery—the violation of individual bodily integrity and the corrupting influence of absolute power—but it also highlighted the corporeality of the enslaved, presenting the mother as a battered body rather than a vessel of emotion and maternal virtue. One poem made violence the direct result of maternal nurture by describing how a mother was punished for breastfeeding her child:

At noon—O, how I ran! And took
My baby to my breast!
I linger'd—and the long lash broke
My sleeping infant's rest.[41]

This poem told a frenzied tale of labor and abuse interspersed with a few stolen moments of maternal tenderness. Defining the enslaved mother's body in terms of both its maternal capacity to nourish and its victimhood, this narrative of violence and loss emphasized the physicality of the mother and the corporeal nature of her suffering. Her maternal virtue was displayed in her desire to suckle her infant, while her oppression was underscored by the lash. In another poem, a mother was sold at auction and separated from her child:

The cruel whip soon made her rise;
And on the table take her place;
While from her wild and blood-shot eyes,
The scalding tears streamed down apace.[42]

The whip turned this mother into a spectacle, a physical specimen whose worth was shaped by market values and finalized on the auction block. The whip, more than anything else, provided a clear symbol for the desecration of motherhood.

These images of violence highlighted both the corporeality of the slave mother and the vulnerability of her body. Representations of violence inflicted on the mother provided powerful fuel for antislavery arguments, for the maternal body offered a perfect site for underscoring the immorality and social disorder wrought by slavery. In a culture that revered the influence of the transcendent mother, the exploitation of enslaved women and the destruction of the sacred bonds of motherhood provided uniquely powerful arguments against slavery. But antislavery print culture also offered up the enslaved maternal body as a spectacle for the consumption of white Americans, creating what Carolyn Sorisio has called, "a public exhibition of the female slave's embodied wrongs."[43] By envisioning the physical anguish of the enslaved, such images appropriated pain experienced by the individual and repackaged it as a shocking yet enticing form of argumentation.

Antislavery poetry contained myriad contradictions when it came to redefining the enslaved mother. On the one hand, these poems used sentimental language and imagery to evoke the love of the enslaved mother for her child and to connect her to the values associated with the sentimental mother. They sought to create a realm of shared emotion that would draw women together, regardless of social status. By redefining the enslaved mother as a sentimental subject, these texts made an important statement about universal humanity. On the other hand, by dwelling on the physical and emotional violence wrought by slavery, antislavery poems reopened the divide between the enslaved mother and the idealized white mother. The enslaved mother was raving and wild, evoking disorder with her body; she was physically controlled and violated by slave owners and traders; and when she died, she was unable to achieve spiritual transcendence. In the end, antislavery poems failed to grant the enslaved mother the same kind of moral and spiritual transcendence granted to the white mother, and in doing so they created a gulf that could potentially prevent white northern readers from fully identifying with the enslaved.

· · · · · ·

Alongside literary efforts, the visual depiction of slavery was an essential part of the broader antislavery movement. Visual artifacts were seen by antislavery activists as a particularly effective means of reaching the public, for the eye was understood to provide a direct route to the heart. Moreover, as Teresa Goddu writes, "The image's immediacy, along with its perceptual capacities and emotive power, successfully turns its viewer into an 'eye-witness' to slavery's cruelties as well as a 'partaker' of the slave's woes."[44] Thus antislavery images were understood to create an imaginary connection between the viewer and the viewed, while also giving the viewer an uncomfortable sense of complicity in the system of slavery. The American Anti-slavery Society alone circulated thousands of visual depictions of slavery each year throughout the 1830s, taking advantage of the rise of new technologies for the mass reproduction of images and of the new enthusiasm Americans demonstrated for the vividness of what they understood to be visual truths.[45] High-quality images were expensive to produce, so antislavery print culture tended to take advantage of cheaper forms of print. Much of antislavery visual culture was made up of relatively rough woodcuts that lacked the same elegance or intimate detail as the fine engravings in more expensive mainstream publications.[46] The *American Anti-slavery Almanac*, for instance, was first published by the American Anti-slavery Society in 1836 and provided a popular and cheap (at around six cents) platform for disseminating images and texts depicting the evils of slavery as well as the crimes of slaveholders against antislavery activists.[47] Rough woodcuts, engravings, the occasional fine portrait, and expansive panoramas all worked together to stimulate the eye and the emotions of the viewer.

Even more than antislavery poetry, the images generated by antislavery proponents underscored the corporeality of the enslaved mother. Indeed, in these images the body of the enslaved mother seemed to supersede her subjectivity. In scenes of slavery the roughly sketched bodies and gestures of each character grabbed the viewer's attention and told the story, sometimes with the assistance of a brief text that provided an anecdote illustrating the moral evils of slavery. But the lack of detail and personal expression in depictions of individuals made it difficult to access the subjectivity of the enslaved mother. Whereas fine images of white mothers in expensive gift-books and magazines presented highly detailed and intimate portraits of women and children, the coarser and more indistinct images in antislavery publications represented figures as types rather than individuals. This was true of course for both slaveholder and slave in these images—different types were indicated by their respective clothing, skin color, and role in the scene rather than by unique individual features—but this lack of individualization necessarily fell more heavily on the enslaved figures, who were already assumed by the institution of chattel slavery to be lacking individuality and subjectivity. The enslaved mother's body represented a type intended to elicit sympathy for the collectivity of slave mothers; the specifics of her own personal history and sense of self, however, remained obscure unless they were articulated by an accompanying text. Thus, as Michael Chaney has written, these depersonalized images ultimately "replicated and amplified the process by which the slave was reduced to an object of commodification."[48] The indistinctness of visual depictions of enslaved people cast a veil between the potentially sympathetic viewer and the subjectivity of the enslaved mother; the only thing left to view, then, was her body.

Furthermore, while images of white mothers were frequently paired with sentimental poems or stories that showed viewers how to understand the image and guided their emotions, it was less common for images of enslaved mothers to be paired with sentimental verse. The texts that did accompany images were more likely to be factual anecdotes about the workings of the slave system or about particular instances of abuse. As a result, viewers had less emotional instruction and greater flexibility in their interpretation of images. Without a poem or story to further explore the subjectivity of the enslaved mother and to elicit sympathy and a sense of shared humanity, the viewer might instead fixate on the power of the slave owner or trader who forcibly sought to separate a mother from her child. Thus, while antislavery images dealt with many of the same issues that appeared in poems—the separation of mother and child, the perpetration of physical violence—they did not create the same kind of direct link between the (white) viewer and the subjectivity of the enslaved mother. Instead, the viewer's indignation might be roused by the use of violence against the female body, but this indignation might not be paired with a corresponding sense of sympathy and identification on the part of the viewer. Thus in visual culture the enslaved mother became more closely identified with her body than with her emotions; she was rooted visually in the grim physicality wrought by her status as human chattel.

Because antislavery images tended to present a scene with multiple characters viewed from a distance—as opposed to, for example, the more intimate proximity of a mother-child portrait—they allowed viewers to imagine or inhabit the perspectives of a variety of characters rather than foregrounding a particular perspective. In this way, even as they purported to tell a detailed visual truth about slavery, these images allowed for a range of interpretations and viewing experiences. Whereas antislavery verse highlighted the intimate emotions of a single individual and often explicitly demanded certain feelings of the reader, images offered more varied possibilities. Because of this, such images simultaneously presented a tragic sense of the wrongs of enslaved people as well as an uncomfortable ability for viewers to align themselves with the perspectives of power by regarding the enslaved mother as an object. In her analysis of the "omniscient viewpoint" of the antislavery panorama, with its perspective of overlooking numerous scenes that all added up to a seemingly comprehensive truth about slavery, Teresa Goddu has argued that "the panoramic perspective provided the white Northern viewer access to a position of specular dominance over the landscape of slavery as well as the body of the slave."[49] These images invited the viewers to sympathize with the enslaved, even as they might see in the spectacle of enslaved bodies the reinforcement of their own position of privilege and authority. The body of the enslaved mother, then, could elicit sympathy, but it also constituted a spectacle that highlighted the power of the implicitly white viewer.

As in antislavery poetry, the forcible separation of the enslaved mother from her children was a common scenario in antislavery visual culture.[50] But in these images the focus shifted away from the subjectivity of the mother and toward the drama itself as it played out on the page. In consequence, the viewer's attention might become distracted from the bond of sympathy that antislavery activists hoped to draw between the enslaved mother and the viewer. An image of a mother and her children being separated by sale was included in the *American Anti-slavery Almanac for 1838*, for instance, and was accompanied by two short stanzas of verse. The poem guided readers to feel the sorrow of the fond mother:

> Ev'n her babes, so dear, so young,
> And so treasured in her heart,
> That the cords which round them clung,
> Seemed its life, its dearest part;
> These, ev'n these, were torn away![51]

But an almost identical image also appeared in a broadside, entitled *Views of Slavery*, this time without an accompanying text to instruct the viewer how to understand the scene by focusing on the emotions of the mother (see fig. 6.1).[52] This image first drew the viewer's eye to the figure of the wealthy slave owner, whose social stature was evoked by his physical dominance over the scene. In his elegant clothes and top hat, he towered over the other figures and gazed with the detachment born of self-assurance and power at the scene unfolding before him. Although the composition of the image clearly showed that he wielded the power in this scene, he was physically distanced from the perpetration of violence; the only hint the viewer might have perceived of his role in the scenario was the whip that he held casually in his hand. Next the image directed the viewer to the emotional heart of the scene, where a slave mother knelt, restrained by the heavy grasp of a slave dealer, reaching out in supplication toward her children as they were marched away from her by a man wielding a whip in one hand and her infant in the other. This image depicted the emotions of the mother being overwhelmed by power—the power over her body wielded by the three white men and perhaps wielded too by the viewer, who could be impelled to see the mother as an object of violence rather than as a sentimental subject. Her distress was potent and almost tangible, but the disorder of her body had the potential to make her emotions seem foreign rather than serve

FIGURE 6.1 *Views of Slavery*. New York (ca. 1836). Courtesy of the Library Company of Philadelphia.

as a means of forging a connection between viewer and viewed. Although such images must have been effective at eliciting outrage in the viewer, the physicality of the mother divided her from the revered figure of the sentimental mother.

These visual scenes highlighted the moment of physical rupture and loss for mother and child, but they also underscored the mother's corporeality by exposing her body's desperate force and the physical restraint imposed on her by the white men around her. Unlike the images of passive white mothers whose bodies seemed to retreat from notice, in these images of the distraught enslaved mother it would have been impossible for the viewer not to notice her body and the force applied to it. An image from the *American Anti-slavery Almanac for 1840* depicted another scenario featuring the separation of a mother and her infant (see fig. 6.2). This image showcased the force of the white man who grasped the mother firmly around the waist with one arm and pulled her away from the scene, a gesture that was disturbing in its perverse intimacy. This pair, the mother reaching out desperately toward her child and the man pulling her away, formed the heart of the image, allowing the viewer almost to feel the weight of their physical encounter.[53] Almost in mirror image, on the far left of the scene, the illustration also depicted a white man restraining the woman's infant in an identical grasp, highlighting the perpetuation of physical control over the enslaved body from generation to generation. Although this image invited the viewer to react in horror to the separation of mother and child, it was the sense of physical power enacted by the white men in the scene that was most palpable. Moreover, the image was accompanied by a text consisting of anecdotes recounted by slave traders who had been involved in the separation of families, thus shifting the viewer's attention to the moral crimes—and the power—of the white men in the scene and away from the subjectivities of the enslaved mother and infant. Thus the fact that images of enslaved mothers were only sometimes accompanied by sentimental poems allowed for a much greater flexibility in the interpretation of these images. Without sentimental verse or narrative to guide them, viewers might be drawn to a variety of perspectives. Viewers could imagine the experiences of the tormented mother and sympathize with her plight, but they might also connect with the perspectives of power that allowed the white men in these images to observe, manipulate, and own the enslaved body.

Symbols of power were at the core of antislavery visual culture, shifting the weight of these images away from sentimentalism. The power of the slaveholder was most often signified by the lash, just as it was in antislavery poetry. In these visual scenes, however, the power of the lash seemed to carry more weight than the emotions of the victim. Poems often employed the lash in metaphorical ways, using it to represent the mingled physical and emotional cruelties of the slave system. As one poet wrote, "The lash of the master her deep sorrows mock, / While the child of her bosom is sold on the block."[54] Visual depictions of slavery, however, highlighted the con-

FIGURE 6.2

"Selling a Mother from Her Child," in *American Anti-slavery Almanac for 1840.* Courtesy of the New York Public Library.

crete threat and perpetration of violence, showcasing unbridled power over the enslaved body. The broadside discussed earlier, *Views of Slavery*, offered a series of six scenes of slavery, two of which used the threat of whipping as the center of the drama (see fig. 6.1). These images used physical violence to stand in for the full range of slavery's horrors. Some images of violence were more symbolic, however. A cover image of the *American Anti-slavery Almanac* for 1843, for instance, depicted an enslaved mother prostrate on the ground and attempting to shield her infant while an enormous eagle, nearly as large as the mother herself, viciously grasped her buttocks in its talons. In the background of the scene sat the U.S. Capitol with the flag flying high.[55] Here, then, the perpetrator of violence was the nation, which permitted the violence of slavery to persist even in the nation's capital.

Perhaps the most provocative aspect of antislavery visual culture was the sexualization of the enslaved female body. Carol Lasser has argued that the antislavery movement was defined, particularly in the 1830s, by a voyeuristic tendency in both visual and written texts. Antislavery writers produced explicit discussions of the sexual immorality fostered by the slave system in order to generate moral outrage and activism, especially among women. Although this tendency declined, she argues, after 1840, when the antislavery movement began to put more emphasis on politics and gave less attention to the methods of moral suasion that had proved so effective in generating support among northern women, it is nevertheless possible to see the sexualization of the female body as a common thread running throughout much of antislavery print culture.[56]

It was a common convention in antislavery visual culture to present both enslaved women and men as scantily clad, often with just a bit of fabric forming a short covering from waist to thigh. George Bourne's *Picture of Slavery in the United States of America*, for instance, included images of women naked to the waist being whipped or sold, alongside his excoriations of the sexual immorality of slaveholders.[57] The nakedness of the enslaved women served to enhance the power of the white men in each scene by highlighting the vulnerability of the women and their objectification by the white male gaze, which was typically multiplied by at least two or three male participants or spectators. In the image from the broadside *Views of Slavery*, described above, the distraught mother in question was naked to the waist, and her legs were bare, a fact that added to the shocking nature of the image while further bringing her corporeality to the forefront of the scene (see fig. 6.1). Her nakedness posed a stark contrast to the men in the scene, who were clothed from the tops of their heads to their heels. The clothed bodies exuded power and order; the half-naked enslaved female body signaled vulnerability and disorder. The physical disorder of the woman's body would have made her figure foreign to genteel viewers, drawing a stark line between the virtuous sentimental mother and the vulnerable and disordered enslaved mother.

Alongside the exposure of enslaved women's bodies, the forcible manipulation of those bodies by white men also signaled the sexualization and vulnerability of the female slave. Images of enslaved women being restrained by white men or tied up with ropes to be flogged offered visual proof of the absolute control white men held over enslaved women's bodies. When viewed by readers who were steeped in discussions of mixed-race slaves and the perceived sexual immorality of southern slaveholders, these images no doubt also raised the specter of sexual coercion and exploitation. As George Bourne asserted in his lengthy testimony against slaveholding, "The slave plantations are a scene of promiscuous uncleanness, of the most abhorrent character, which defies all attempts to preserve the existence of decency, personal or social."[58] White northerners were thus alerted to the full implications of the unlimited control exerted by slave owners. Through these images the enslaved mother became associated with physical force, violence, and sexual vulnerability, experiences that created distance rather than fostering a sense of affinity between the white viewer and the enslaved subject.

Thus antislavery images offered more extreme visions of embodiment than did antislavery poems. Although these images drew on some of the same themes and scenarios as sentimental verse—the separation of families and the emotional devastation wrought by slavery—they did so in ways that highlighted the physicality rather than the subjectivity of the enslaved. Antislavery images depicted the enslaved mother as a disorderly body, half-naked, straining and wild with despair, manipulated and exploited by slave owners and traders. These images made it difficult to draw parallels between the enslaved mother, whose body seemed to supersede her subjectivity, and the sentimental mother, whose corporeality retreated in order to liberate her spiritual and emotional influence. The soft emotions of motherhood had little place in antislavery visual culture, which instead implied a stark divide between the white transcendent mother and the enslaved mother who was bound to her body by the violence and commodification inherent to chattel slavery.

· · · · · ·

Antislavery poetry and visual culture worked together to create a complex set of meanings around the figure of the enslaved mother, combining sentimentalism with a voyeuristic focus on the physical and emotional torments perpetrated by slaveholders. By articulating the deep emotions of enslaved mothers, antislavery poems asserted the humanity and the maternal virtue of enslaved women. Viewed in this light, these poems worked to elicit sympathy on the part of the white reader/viewer by redefining the enslaved mother as a legitimate sentimental subject whose maternal feelings could foster a sense of connection between white women and enslaved women. The use of sentimental language and imagery in antislavery verse signaled that the enslaved mother belonged to a higher emotional realm, in spite of her social status, and her emotional outpourings forced recognition of her humanity and her status as a sentimental mother. At the same time, however, these same poems bound the enslaved mother within a more corporeal framework than her white counterpart by emphasizing the physical abuses of slavery and the spectacles of grief and suffering exhibited by the maternal body itself. The enslaved mother might express the proper emotions of a sentimental mother, but she was never allowed to transcend her body.

At the same time, visual depictions of mothers being torn away from their children tugged at the heartstrings of viewers and invited them to enter into the image and feel the plight of the enslaved mother. But the visual conventions of antislavery print culture ultimately served to further emphasize the corporeality of the enslaved mother by making a shocking visual spectacle of her body, highlighting the power and force exerted on the enslaved mother, rather than her emotions. Images of force and violence could serve to arouse the sympathy and indignation of the viewer, but they could also allow the viewer to focus on the perspectives of power that objectified the enslaved body. In these images the subjectivity of the enslaved mother became subordinate to the action playing out on the page, requiring the viewer to work harder to inhabit the emotions and perspective of the enslaved woman.

Thus in these cultural forms the enslaved mother *almost* came to be defined by her emotions and her claims to sympathy. But the sentimental redefinition of the enslaved mother was incomplete. In the end, her inclusion in sentimental discourse stopped short of allowing her access to emotional and spiritual transcendence. Instead, important differences in the ways white and black mothers were represented in print culture reinforced a racialized spirit/body association that granted the white mother access to a higher spiritual identity while relegating the enslaved mother to base corporeality. Antislavery print culture promoted a sympathetic sisterhood of mothers, but it was an inherently unequal sisterhood. Although the sentimental tropes used in antislavery print culture brought the enslaved mother within the same cultural framework as white mothers, they failed to allow her to fully inhabit the sentimental realm. Sentimentalism might seem to create a universal space of feeling and being that anyone could access, but for enslaved mothers that access was always limited by the ways in which they were defined by their bodies.

The emphasis on the corporeality of the enslaved mother in antislavery literature and visual culture is consistent with what we know about broader discussions of race, gender, and embodiment in the nineteenth-century United States. William Etter writes that "in the ideology of American slavery disembodiment was figured as the condition of intellectual power and embodiment as the condition of physical subjugation; whiteness and blackness, respectively, were figured as corresponding to each of these poles."[59] Nineteenth-century science used biological essentialism to explain and perpetuate race- and gender-based inequalities, making the body of the white man the implicit norm against which all others were defined and judged.[60] Privileging the mind over the body, nineteenth-century intellectuals insisted that the superiority of the white man was evident in the scope of his morals and intellect, while the inferiority of women and nonwhites was evident in their childish intellects and their disorderly bodies. White women were redeemed from their corporeality when sentimental poems and images transformed them into spiritual entities, but antislavery print culture consistently mixed sentimental imagery with troubling depictions of embodiment.

The fact that the enslaved mother was not allowed to become a transcendent figure in antislavery print culture meant that she could never access the cultural power and influence attributed to the white mother. While the transcendent mother was credited with perpetuating virtue and morality and strengthening the social order, the enslaved mother was used to display the disorder caused in American society by the institution of slavery. The antislavery message in these texts depended on illustrating the ways in which slavery destroyed what middle-class Americans held dear: female virtue, maternal love, and the sanctity of the domestic realm. Antislavery print culture called upon them to defend these pillars of genteel society and thus shore up their own claims to moral rectitude and influence. In the end, the enslaved mother was culturally useful only to the extent that her body could be made to reveal the cruelties of slavery and convince white northerners that their moral outrage demanded action.

The emphasis on enslaved women's corporeality in print culture challenges us to reconsider the universalizing power that has been attributed to sentimental culture. Although the intentions of antislavery authors were surely reformist, race-based assumptions about what it meant to be an ideal mother showed through in the ways in which slave mothers were incompletely enveloped in the sentimental sisterhood. In this way, differing depictions of the white and black maternal body challenge scholars to see the cracks in the appealing fantasies of a universally inclusive sentimental culture. More broadly, the ways in which white and black mothers were portrayed in print culture reveals that by the nineteenth century the maternal body had become culturally useful. It served as an essential vehicle for articulating race and class identity, and it was insistently deployed to signal notions of virtue and refinement or vice and corruption. Repeatedly, print culture inscribed the maternal body with the fantasies and fears of American society.

# Conclusion

## In Search of the Maternal Body Past and Present

Visions of the maternal body in eighteenth- and nineteenth-century America were complex and contradictory, marked by both change over time and profound continuity. The ways in which women placed the work of their bodies at the center of childbearing and childrearing changed little over the course of a century. They saw motherhood as hard physical work, and in their personal accounts they dwelled on the rhythms of pregnancy, childbirth, and childrearing that dominated much of their adult lives. For example, Esther Burr of Massachusetts wrote to her best friend in 1756: "Now I write with the Son at the Brest—When I had but one Child my hands were tied, but now I am tied hand and foot. (How I shall get along when I have got ½ dzn. or 10 children I cant devise)."[1] For Burr, the constant physical demands of mothering limited her autonomy and defined her sense of self in ways that were at times claustrophobic, and she anticipated the ways in which the work of mothering would continue to structure her life. Hannah Heath echoed Burr's thoughts when she wrote in 1796: "I have hardly been from home since you left Brookline,—my child is very troublesome! Does not like to have me gone at all. She is in my arms now; will not lay in the cradle,—I have put her in at least ten times this evg. & all to no purpose."[2] Women consistently made the labor of their bodies central to their perception of motherhood, and the discomfort, pain, fatigue, and frustration wrought by childbearing and childrearing, intertwined with the love they bore their children, caused them to regard motherhood with ambivalence. Sarah Hale was a fond and devoted mother, but she complained in 1822 of the "quarreling and screaming of so many little ones constantly about me" and noted, "My cares are never ceasing, and I sometimes think how comfortably it must be to have a moment to oneself."[3] At times, motherhood consisted of the "sweetest bliss & diversion" and pure "earthly bliss."[4] At other times, it was quite simply "very fatiguing indeed."[5] Women frequently expressed through both words and deeds their love and devotion as mothers, but they also emphasized the physical burdens of motherhood.

Cultural depictions of motherhood existed in tension with the lived experiences of childbearing women. Between the 1750s and the 1850s representations of motherhood in print culture gradually refined and even effaced the maternal body, portraying motherhood as moral and emotional work performed by an ethereal figure. In the mid-eighteenth century, medical descriptions of pregnancy and childbirth began this process of disappearance by replacing the reproductive labor of the white and socioeconomically privileged mother with the work of the uterus and the man-midwife, thus distancing the figure of the mother from the taint of sexuality and from the messiness of the reproductive body. By the late eighteenth century, advice manuals for mothers began to develop the ideal of the sentimental mother around the practice of maternal breastfeeding. The maternal breast was refined into a symbol of maternal virtue by erasing the very real physical challenges of breastfeeding. Describing the joy and pleasure that women derived from breastfeeding, prescriptive authors transformed childrearing from physical work into an effortless and delightful process that showcased the moral and emotional influence of the good mother. Finally, by the early decades of the nineteenth century, the disembodiment of the sentimental mother became complete in the popular poetry and images that permeated feminine print culture. Popular print culture erased the physicality of the mother, replacing the maternal body with more ethereal symbols of affection and piety to create the image of the transcendent mother whose spiritual power superseded her earthly labors.

Much was at stake in these varied depictions of the maternal body, for corporeality became a way of defining social value by identifying some women as good mothers and others as disorderly bodies. Cultural depictions of the ideal mother, whether in medical texts, advice manuals, or popular print, identified her as white and socioeconomically privileged, with a body so pure, lovely, and delicate that it could be refined away in order to free her more important moral and emotional qualities. At the same time, nonwhite and lower-class women became defined by their corporeality. Elite women who employed lower-class women as wet nurses began in the early nineteenth century to describe their nurses as animal-like, defined by their (re)productive bodies rather than by their capacity for maternal love and devotion. Similarly, antislavery print culture defined the enslaved mother in terms of her body and the violence done to it by the slave system. Although these texts were meant to elicit sympathy for enslaved women, the emphasis on corporeality also served to define them as symbols of disorder in American society. Above all, nonwhite and lower-class mothers came to be defined as laboring bodies that disrupted notions of womanly virtue and sentimental motherhood.

Although I have chosen to conclude this study in the 1850s, the history of the maternal body cannot properly be said to have an ending. The 1850s provide a logical end point, for this decade marked the beginning of a gradual transition into a time when women's childbearing experiences and opportunities in life began to change more rapidly than ever before. These changes brought about new perceptions of the maternal body, both in American culture and in women's private writings, although many older ideas and attitudes remained. As Judith Walzer Leavitt and Nancy Theriot have shown, the women who began to bear children in the 1860s and beyond, as well as the medical practitioners who tended them, gradually created a different reproductive world than previous generations had experienced. During the second half of the nineteenth century, anesthetized childbirth became increasingly available, particularly for middle-class and elite women, and childbearing women did not hesitate to demand relief from pain. The possibility of evading the pain of childbirth helped to reshape women's perceptions of childbearing. Simultaneously, a better understanding of contraceptive methods and a growing emphasis on family limitation made it possible for women to restrict their childbearing more effectively than their foremothers had done. Average birthrates for white native-born Americans continued to drop, from roughly 5.42 children in 1850, to 4.24 children in 1880, to 3.56 children in 1900, so that many women no longer spent the majority of their adult lives pregnant and caring for young children. It is important to emphasize, though, that immigrant women and African American women continued to experience higher rates of fertility than native-born white women, suggesting diverse attitudes toward family limitation and varying access to contraceptive methods depending on region, race, ethnicity, and socioeconomic status.[6]

Ideas about women's bodies also began to change. A growing culture of health and physical education pioneered by college-educated women in the late nineteenth century spread to the population at large and offered a new view of women as healthy rather than inherently diseased.[7] Emphasizing that motherhood was natural and healthy, one female physician wrote in the 1880s, "If woman was made for maternity, then it is evident that the proper exercise of this function should be attended by the highest health, enjoyment and happiness."[8] Few Americans questioned the fact that women were biologically formed to be mothers, but they did begin to think about motherhood, particularly its physical aspects, in new ways. Women increasingly believed that they should claim control over their bodies and reproductive lives. As one woman complained in the 1870s, "Strange that, while the law recognizes rape as a crime punishable by severe penalties, there is no recognition whatever of a married woman's right to control over her own person."[9] Supported by the moral arguments of feminist advocates of "voluntary motherhood," women increasingly asserted the right to make their own decisions about if and when to bear children.[10] Assertions of women's right to refuse intercourse, combined with greater awareness and wider availability of contraceptives, made such control increasingly possible.[11]

Women writers, reformers, and medical practitioners were at the forefront of many of the changes that occurred in ideas about reproduction and women's bodies, but personal writings show that in the privacy of their own lives and homes women were also beginning to think about and describe childbearing in different ways. For over a century women had made the physical aspects of childbearing central to their understanding of motherhood, and this remained largely true. But whereas previous generations of mothers had written tersely of the suffering they anticipated and endured, indicating a somewhat bitter acceptance of circumstances they could not change, by the second half of the nineteenth century women wrote more explicitly and more evocatively of their physical experiences. As one mother wrote of her birth experience in 1885, "Between oceans of pain there stretched continents of fear; fear of death and dread of suffering beyond bearing."[12] Perhaps as women came to feel that they had the right to bodily control, they also became more insistent in describing the physical sensations of childbearing. Elaborating the experience of pain helped explain the need for greater control over their reproductive experiences. In 1866 the wife of a physician wrote to the *Boston Medical and Surgical Journal* on behalf of childbearing women: "One great reason for the aversion to child-bearing is the thousand disagreeable and painful experiences which attend the long months of patient waiting, and the certain agony at the end—agony which is akin to nothing else on earth—agony which the tenderest susceptibilities and sympathies of the noblest physician can but faintly imagine—agony which, in not one case in a hundred, is mitigated by anesthesia."[13] Relentlessly emphasizing the pain and suffering of childbearing, this woman boldly articulated the physical trauma that women faced, but suggested that it did not have to be inevitable if the medical profession would step in to do its part. It seems likely that frequent medical discussions of pain in childbirth and the possibility of painless deliveries created a culture in which pain could be discussed more openly, and women vociferously demanded freedom from physical suffering and harm in the process of childbearing.

The words and experiences of such women illustrate that since the late nineteenth century women have increasingly challenged the assumption that biology is destiny. In the late nineteenth century women began to question whether motherhood was inevitable; today, many American women choose not to bear children and find inspiration and fulfillment in aspects of life that were formerly reserved for men. Yet the figure of the mother continues to be a potent symbol in American culture. Conflicts about the appropriate qualities, use, and visibility of the maternal body have demonstrated time and again that diverse perceptions of the maternal body continue to shape our view of women's role in society. Indeed, we are haunted in America today by the same vision of the maternal body as simultaneously virtuous and disruptive that characterized eighteenth- and nineteenth-century American culture and society. On the one hand, the figure of the mother represents everything that is wholesome. Bright images of (predominantly young, white, middle-class) mothers fill magazines, advertisements, films, and television programs and signal to the viewer that all is well with the world. But when the maternal body is too visible, or contradicts ideas about maternal virtue, or is not quite the right kind of body, it signifies a disruption of social order and a source of shame or fear. Just as in the past, women today are beset with images and admonitions of how they should look, feel, and act as mothers.

Periodic controversies over breastfeeding illustrate one aspect of the maternal body that has consistently raised tensions in late twentieth- and early twenty-first-century America. The social media website Facebook has made controversial decisions to remove photos of breastfeeding mothers in accordance with its policy that forbids users to post obscene or sexually explicit material. As one reporter noted in 2009, "Facebook has said that it has no problem with breastfeeding, but that photos showing nipples are deemed to be a violation and can be removed."[14] Breastfeeding mothers have consistently encountered problems because the female breast has been sexualized to such a degree that the maternal function of breastfeeding cannot be enacted without raising the specter of inappropriate sexuality.[15] When the breast is seen as predominantly sexual, mothers cannot publicly make use of it for infant nourishment without being exposed to accusations of indecency. The medical profession recommends breastfeeding as the healthiest choice for both mothers and babies, and forty-nine states have laws that allow women to breastfeed in any public or private location, yet mothers are often made to feel uncomfortable or unwelcome when they breastfeed in public spaces.[16] In Cindy Stearns's sociological study of breastfeeding mothers in 1999, she discovered that "women were keenly aware that the activity of breastfeeding in public might result in negative feedback, or worse yet, legal action."[17] Indeed, responses to the removal of breastfeeding photos from Facebook indicate that few Americans object to the practice of breastfeeding, but they do not want to see it. The visibility of the maternal body is frequently perceived as disgusting or immodest. As one commenter responded online, "I classify breastfeeding as a personal and PRIVATE matter and do not wish to be exposed to such material."[18] In American society today the act of breastfeeding signifies good mothering, just as it did in the past, but we no longer embrace the varied pleasures linked to the act of nursing, fearing instead the confusion of sexuality and maternity. In the end, women are expected to be good mothers by breastfeeding their children while simultaneously keeping the physical aspects of motherhood invisible.

Equally problematic are present-day assumptions about what kinds of bodies are suitable for motherhood. We have seen how the prejudices of eighteenth- and nineteenth-century Americans led them to view nonwhite women and lower-class women as useful bodies at best, disruptive bodies at worst. In either case, these women were rarely valued for their social role as mothers. In contemporary America there continues to be an ongoing perception that lower-class women and women of color are less valuable as mothers and should be subject to reproductive control. African American women in particular have been devalued as mothers and perceived as hypersexual, too fertile, and in need of government regulation. Dorothy Roberts has explored the history of efforts to control black women's reproduction, from exploitative pronatalist practices during slavery, to eugenic sterilization measures in the first half of the twentieth century, to late twentieth-century government programs that paid for poor women to receive Norplant, a contraceptive implanted under the skin that was shown to have severe side effects.[19] Such measures have allowed race and class to define which women will be valued as mothers and which will be viewed as disorderly reproductive bodies.

In American society today there seem to be two conflicting strains of thought about the maternal body. First is the view that the figure of the mother is virtuous and culturally palatable only when her physical functions are subordinated to her moral and emotional role. This perception predominates in mainstream American culture and, as we have seen, has its roots in the late eighteenth and nineteenth centuries. Today's ideal mother does not exactly resemble the disembodied sentimental mother that emerged in early America (though there are strong similarities), but she does represent a continuing drive to refine the raw physicality of the body. The ideal mother of today is healthy, youthful, beautiful, usually white and well educated, and has many talents and interests, but ultimately derives her joy and sense of self-worth from the emotional bonds of motherhood. A 2011 article in an online parenting magazine summed up the ideal mother by juxtaposing the feelings of mothers and fathers. The expectant father thinks, "I'm afraid of what having a baby is going to do to our relationship," while the mother-to-be thinks, "It's going to be the best thing in the world!"[20] In many ways, expectations for mothers have changed little since the nineteenth century, for American society still often demands that women be child-centered and that they find their greatest fulfillment as mothers.

While this vision of motherhood privileges its affective bonds, feminist scholars and writers in the aftermath of the second-wave feminist movement of the 1970s have offered an alternative way of regarding motherhood by rigorously contesting the tendency to evade the fullness of maternal corporeality. More women have begun to explore the physicality of experiences such as pregnancy, childbirth, and lactation, both in private and in public texts and images. The feminist poet Alicia Ostriker, for instance, has pointed out the possibilities of pleasure while breastfeeding: "I don't believe I have ever seen a discussion of this experience; or indeed, any mention of the idea that we can be sexually aroused by being suckled. . . . Why do we not say this? Why are mothers always represented sentimentally, as having some sort of altruistically self-sacrificing 'maternal' feelings, as if they did not enjoy themselves? Is it so horrible if we enjoy ourselves: another love that dare not tell its name?"[21] Asserting the validity of physical experience over and against sentimental constructions of motherhood, Ostriker's work dwells on those aspects of maternity that tend to cause shame and discomfort. Similarly, the works of the poet Sharon Olds have explored the very facets of childbearing that American society most seeks to avoid, describing pregnancy with heavy physical imagery:

> my belly big with cowardice and safety,
> my stool black with iron pills,
> my huge breasts oozing mucus,
> my legs swelling, my hands swelling,
> my face swelling and darkening.

From the grotesqueness of corporeality Olds moves to celebrate the maternal body, exulting,

> I and the other women this exceptional
> act with the exceptional heroic body,
> this giving birth, this glistening verb.[22]

In a more scholarly vein, Della Pollock's analysis of childbirth narratives has offered a glimpse into the most intimate bodily experiences of childbearing. Pollock describes one mother's tortured memories of her body during pregnancy: "Furious with the instruments and procedures that had repeatedly, painfully penetrated her body to no avail, she also seemed now to want to claw open her belly herself, to break through the uterine wall, to see once and for all this baby and its fate, to *know* what to do."[23] These feminist texts, among many others, have asserted the need to view the maternal body without shame and without artifice, proclaiming its centrality to women's experience and insisting on the validity of that experience.

This feminist approach to representations of childbearing constitutes a radical departure from a long history of efforts to valorize the emotional aspects of motherhood while suppressing the physical. Following in this vein, this book seeks to restore the body to its rightful place in the history of motherhood by showing that prescriptions for how the maternal body was supposed to look, act, and feel have structured visions of ideal motherhood, while the physical labor of women's bodies has shaped their attitudes toward childbearing and childrearing. Looking for the maternal body in the distant past also helps shed light on many of the forces that shape women's experiences today. Many elements of the past are present in contemporary America, if in altered forms: the privileging of certain kinds of bodies and certain kinds of mothers; the constraint of women's choice and bodily autonomy in the service of motherhood; and uneasiness in the face of female corporeality. Putting the body at the center of the history of motherhood reveals the important ways in which corporeality has structured and continues to shape both women's lived experiences as mothers and cultural visions of motherhood.

# Notes

## Introduction

1. Gertrude Gouverneur Ogden Meredith to William Meredith, June 28, 1798, folder 1, box 51, Meredith Family Papers, Historical Society of Pennsylvania (hereafter HSP).

2. "The Advantages of Maternal Nurture," *Ladies' Monthly Museum*, 184. See also "The Advantage of Maternal Nurture," *Lady's Magazine and Musical Repository*, 290.

3. Sarah Preston (Everett) Hale to Alexander and Lucretia Everett, September 14, 1822, folder 6, box 9, Hale Family Papers, 1787–1988, Sophia Smith Collection, Smith College (hereafter SSC).

4. D'Emilio and Freedman, *Intimate Matters*, 58. See also Klepp, *Revolutionary Conceptions*, esp. chap. 1.

5. For an analysis of women's many roles in colonial America, see Ulrich, *Good Wives*. See also Boydston, *Home and Work*. For an analysis of women's shifting image from "help-meet" to mother, see Bloch, "Revaluing Motherhood."

6. See Klepp's discussion of colonial Americans' emphasis on fertility in *Revolutionary Conceptions*, esp. chap. 2. See also Spruill's analysis of the importance placed on fertility in the southern colonies in *Women's Life and Work*, chap. 3.

7. For a history of American fatherhood, see, for instance, S. Frank, *Life with Father*.

8. For more on this transitional period, see Cott, *The Bonds of Womanhood*; Degler, *At Odds*; Kerber, *Women of the Republic*.

9. Ruth Bloch describes the transitional process toward defining motherhood as a "longer-term, transnational, and essentially cultural rather than political process." Bloch, "Revaluing Motherhood," 57.

10. For a discussion of Enlightenment ideas about women's role in society, see Zagarri, *Revolutionary Backlash*, esp. 3–4. For an analysis and comparison of the respective roles of the Enlightenment and evangelical Christianity in the rise of the "moral mother," see Bloch, "Revaluing Motherhood."

11. As Nancy Schrom Dye and Daniel Blake Smith have argued, in the late eighteenth century and the early nineteenth century, "reliance on God gradually gave way to a more secular belief that a child's welfare lay primarily in the hands of loving, watchful mothers." Dye and Smith, "Mother Love and Infant Death," 330.

12. Kerber, "The Republican Mother." See also Zagarri, "Morals, Manners, and the Republican Mother"; and Norton, *Liberty's Daughters*.

13. For a full explanation of this ideology, see Theriot, *Mothers and Daughters*, 18. For further analysis of maternal ideology in the nineteenth century, see also Ryan, *The Empire of the Mother*, esp. chap. 2.

14. Ann M. Taylor, *Practical Hints to Young Females*, 2–3.

15. Bordo, *Unbearable Weight*, 3.

16. For an analysis of Plato's soul/body dichotomy, see Spelman, "Woman as Body." For more on perceptions of gender and embodiment, see also Shaw, "Performing Breastfeeding"; Schwarz, "Missing the Breast."

17. Theriot, *Mothers and Daughters*, 10.

18. A few scholars have considered the significance of continuity, particularly in the lives of women. Jeanne Boydston, for instance, has shown that cultural attitudes toward women's work in the early republic changed more swiftly and dramatically than did the actual nature of women's work, which was marked by long-term continuity. More broadly, Judith Bennett has challenged feminist scholars not to fixate on change, but to acknowledge the existence of a "patriarchal equilibrium" that has caused aspects of women's lives to be defined by continuity. More recently, Katy Simpson Smith has identified the significance of continuity in the history of motherhood. She notes that a focus on change over time results in a tendency to privilege the more dramatic upheavals of political and economic history, areas in which women in the eighteenth and nineteenth centuries were denied a significant role. The history of everyday lives, however, which is more able to encompass the experience of women, tends to reveal significant continuities. See Boydston, *Home and Work*; J. Bennett, *History Matters*; K. Smith, *We Have Raised All of You*, 6.

19. Leavitt, *Brought to Bed*, 107.

20. Maria Flagg to Lydia Nightingale, August 17, 1793, Maria Magdalen Flagg Letters, Schlesinger Library (hereafter SL).

21. Boydston, *Home and Work*, 145.

22. Several historians have explored the role that corporeality played in defining the middle class. Karen Halttunen, for instance, examines the fears of hypocrisy and the quest for authenticity that characterized antebellum America and reveals the ways in which women and men sought to stylize their bodies and shape their expressions so as to convey sincerity. John Kasson's work on etiquette in nineteenth-century America likewise demonstrates how the restraint of the body, the styling of gestures and expressions, and the meaning attributed to one's appearance and comportment helped Americans negotiate the urban milieu and identify themselves as part of the genteel middle class. Kathleen Brown's more recent history of hygiene in early America explores the importance of cleanliness and bodily management in the definition of civilization and the hardening of race- and class-based social divisions. Halttunen, *Confidence Men and Painted Women*; J. F. Kasson, *Rudeness and Civility*; Brown, *Foul Bodies*. For more on the importance of etiquette and bodily restraint, see also Bushman, *The Refinement of America*, esp. chap. 3.

23. On the question of regionalism, V. Lynn Kennedy has shown in her study of motherhood that southerners were exposed to the same gender ideology and prescriptive literature as readers in the North and articulated the same kinds of values with respect to motherhood, but southerners identified regional differences in the fulfillment of these values. See Kennedy, *Born Southern*.

24. Generally speaking, the discipline of history has come relatively late to the study of the body. For an analysis of the body as methodology in history, see Canning, "The Body as Method?"

25. See, for example, Carroll Smith-Rosenberg and Charles Rosenberg's argument that in the nineteenth century medical knowledge about women's bodies was deployed to reinforce socially constructed norms of femininity. Smith-Rosenberg and Rosenberg, "The Female Animal."

26. Historians have especially focused on the role of the body in defining race. Jennifer Morgan, for instance, examines European perceptions of African and Native American women's bodies and how their perceived failure to embody European notions of femininity helped to create and sustain racial ideology. Lars Schroeder applies an explicitly Foucauldian framework to the antebellum South and shows that nineteenth-century white middle-class and elite women and men were ideologically and textually constructed as disembodied, or "no-bodies," while enslaved women and men were exclusively associated with the body rather than the soul or the intellect. Dorothy Roberts's history of nineteenth- and twentieth-century efforts to control black women's reproduction highlights the ways in which black bodies have been historically more visible and more subject to control than white bodies. Morgan, "'Some Could Suckle over Their Shoulder'"; Schroeder, *Slave to the Body*; Roberts, *Killing the Black Body*.

27. See, for instance, Foucault, *Discipline and Punish*.

28. Butler, *Bodies That Matter*, 10.

29. Grosz, *Volatile Bodies*, vii.

30. C. Henderson, "Introduction: Bordering on the Black Body," 14.

## Chapter One

1. Porter, *Greatest Benefit*, 55–62, 65, 73–77, 130. For more on Galen, see also Keller, *Generating Bodies*, 32–33.

2. Keller, *Generating Bodies*, 9–10. For further analysis of the ways in which women came to be defined as radically different from men based on their reproductive bodies, see H. King, *Midwifery, Obstetrics and the Rise of Gynaecology*.

3. For more on Raynalde's text, see Porter, *Greatest Benefit*, 200; Keller, *Generating Bodies*, 76–80.

4. For more on Culpeper's text, see Porter, *Greatest Benefit*, 210; Keller, *Generating Bodies*, 85–89.

5. For more on Sharp, see Keller, *Generating Bodies*, 160–164.

6. Stone, *Complete Practice of Midwifery*, xiv.

7. For more on this transition in Britain, see Cody, "The Politics of Reproduction"; McGrath, *Seeing Her Sex*, 32–34; Moscucci, *Science of Woman*, 42–50; Wilson, *The Making of Man-Midwifery*; Wilson, "William Hunter."

8. For more on Smellie's influential texts, see McGrath, *Seeing Her Sex*, 64–72.

9. Leavitt, *Brought to Bed*, 38–39. For more on the transition to male practitioners in America, see also Speert, *Obstetrics and Gynecology in America*; Wertz and Wertz, *Lying-In*.

10. For more on Seaman, Bard, and Dewees, see Speert, *Obstetrics and Gynecology in America*, 126–127.

11. Porter, "A Touch of Danger."

12. Stone, *Complete Practice of Midwifery*, x.

13. Nihell, *Art of Midwifery*, xii, 223. See Clare Hanson's discussion of Nihell's text as a response to William Smellie's advocacy of man-midwifery in *A Cultural History of Pregnancy*, 16–17.

14. The development of obstetrics and gynecology in the nineteenth century demonstrates how important it is for historians to explore the practice of medicine as an example of what Evelyn Brooks Higginbotham has called technologies of race, discourses and systems meant to create and sustain racial (and, in this case, class) hierarchy. See Higginbotham, "African-American Women's History," 252.

15. Sharp, *Compleat Midwife's Companion*, 21. Unless otherwise noted, all citations are from the 1725 edition of this book.

16. Wagner, *Eros Revived*, 295.

17. Keller, *Generating Bodies*, 76.

18. Raynalde, *Birth of Mankind*, 40.

19. Ibid., 40.

20. Ibid., 8.

21. Keller, *Generating Bodies*, 85. For a detailed analysis of Culpeper's work, see Fissell, *Vernacular Bodies*, chap. 5.

22. Fissell, *Vernacular Bodies*, 143–144.

23. Culpeper, *Directory for Midwives*, 28. Unless otherwise noted, all citations are from the 1651 edition of this book.

24. Ibid., 81.

25. *The Compleat Midwifes Practice* was first issued in 1656 and went through multiple versions. It borrowed heavily from other texts, such as translations of works by the French midwife Louise Bourgeois. For more on this text, see Fissell, *Vernacular Bodies*, 183–189. Here I am quoting from a later version published by John Pechey. See *The Compleat Midwifes Practice Enlarged*, 30, 36–37.

26. Mary Fissell notes that Sharp's work borrowed heavily from a manual by Peter Chamberlen, which in turn borrowed from *The Compleat Midwifes Practice*. See Fissell, *Vernacular Bodies*, 197–199.

27. For an analysis of gender and anatomy in Jane Sharp's text, see Bricks, "Stones Like Women's Paps." See also Hobby, "'Secrets of the Female Sex.'"

28. Sharp, *Compleat Midwife's Companion*, 32.

29. Ibid., 30.

30. Ibid., 36.

31. *Aristotle's Masterpiece* went through three principal versions that were each reprinted numerous times, one originating in 1684, one in 1697, and one in the 1710s. The third iteration became the basis for the first known American edition (Boston, 1766). See Fissell, "Hairy Women and Naked Truths."

32. *Aristotle's Compleat Masterpiece*, 12.

33. Ibid., 17.

34. Ibid., 29.

35. Horowitz, *Rereading Sex*, 22.

36. Smellie, *Theory and Practice of Midwifery*, 441.

37. Ibid., 92.

38. Ibid., 103.

39. Ibid., 115.

40. Denman, *Practice of Midwifery*, 25, 32.

41. A. Hamilton, *Treatise of Midwifery*, 31.

42. Seaman, *Midwives Monitor*, 62.

43. Bard, *Compendium*, 25.

44. Ibid., 39.

45. Burns, *Principles of Midwifery*, 69–70.

46. Dewees, *Compendious System*, 46.

47. C. White, *Treatise on the Management*, 84.

48. Sawday, *The Body Emblazoned*, ix.

49. For a concise history of dissection, see Porter, *Greatest Benefit*, 132–133.

50. For more on the challenges of obtaining bodies to anatomize, see Sawday, *The Body Emblazoned*, chap. 4.

51. For more on Vesalius and his anatomical atlas, see Porter, *Greatest Benefit*, 178–181.

52. Vesalius, *Fabrica*, 378.

53. For further discussion of classical ideals of female beauty in medical texts, see Nichols, "The Man-Midwife's Tale," esp. chap. 4.

54. Estienne, *De dissectione*, esp. 275, 276, 287.

55. Rueff, *De conceptu*, n.p.

56. Sharp, *Compleat Midwife's Companion* (1724 ed.), 97. For other examples of the lifelike female figure in anatomy texts, see, for example, Van de Spiegel and Casseri, *De formato foetu*, tables 1–4. These images can be seen at Historical Anatomies on the Web, https://www.nlm.nih.gov/exhibition/historicalanatomies/spiegel_home.html.

57. Vesalius, *Fabrica*, 378. Raynalde, *Birth of Mankind*, 81.

58. Culpeper, *Directory for Midwives* (1671), n.p. Mauriceau, *Traité des maladies*, 3, 14.

59. Rueff, *De conceptu*, n.p.

60. Mauriceau, *Traité des maladies*, 3, 6, 14, 16, 33, 35.

61. For a discussion of some of the aesthetic and representational choices made by these authors and the artists and engravers involved, see McGrath, *Seeing Her Sex*, chap. 3.

62. See Smellie, *Set of Anatomical Tables*. This later edition also includes a fortieth table illustrating obstetrical instruments.

63. See Jenty, *Demonstrations of a Pregnant Uterus*. For more on van Rymsdyk's work for Charles Jenty, see McGrath, *Seeing Her Sex*, 73–76.

64. Hunter, *Gravid Uterus*, plate iv.

65. J. Hamilton, *Collection of Engravings*, 10.

66. Sharp, *Compleat Midwife's Companion*, 13. Smellie, *Theory and Practice of Midwifery*, 73–91. Denman, *Practice of Midwifery*, 1–24. Burton, *New System of Midwifery*, 3–6.

67. For a summary of Hippocrates's theory, see Smellie, *Theory and Practice of Midwifery*, xv.

68. For an outline of these key transitions in ideas about female reproduction, see Fissell, *Vernacular Bodies*, introduction.

69. For more on the association of "Woman" and "Nature" in the late eighteenth century, see Jordanova, *Sexual Visions*, esp. chap. 4. For a discussion of Enlightenment ideas of sexual difference, see Cavazza, "Women's Dialectics"; Moscucci, *Science of Woman*; Steinbrügge, *Moral Sex*.

70. Smellie, *Theory and Practice of Midwifery*, 99.

71. Burton, *New System of Midwifery*, 11.

72. C. White, *Treatise on the Management*, 106.

73. Denman, *Practice of Midwifery*, 39.

74. For more on Matthew Baillie, see Porter, *Greatest Benefit*, 264. See Bell, *Anatomy of the Brain*.

75. Burns, *Anatomy of the Gravid Uterus*, 3.

76. Mears, *Pupil of Nature*, 10.

77. Bichat, *General Anatomy*, 35.

78. Dewees, *Means of Lessening Pain*, 15–16. For more on Dewees, see Dunn, "William Potts Dewees."

79. Seaman, *Midwives Monitor*, 78, 87.

80. Bard, *Compendium*, 180.

81. Ramsbotham, *Obstetric Medicine*, 89.

82. Dewees, *Compendious System*, 51.

83. Merriman, *Difficult Parturition*, 89.

84. Ibid., 90.

85. Meigs, *Obstetrics*, 191.

86. Ibid., 235.

87. Aitken, *Principles of Midwifery*, 60.

88. Benjamin Rush, Medical Notes, 1804–1809, HSP.

89. Howard, *Treatise on Midwifery*, 8.

90. Nichols, "The Man-Midwife's Tale," 5.

91. Bedford, *Clinical Lectures*, 312.

92. For more on the perceived differences of African and Native American women with respect to sexuality and reproduction, see, for example, Morgan, "'Some Could Suckle over Their Shoulder.'"

93. Mackenzie, *Voyages from Montreal*, cxvi.

94. Plane, "Childbirth Practices among Native American Women."

95. See, for example, the Cherokee myth of Selu, the woman who brought forth corn and beans from her body, thus signifying the fertility and life-giving capacity of the female body; Perdue, *Cherokee Women*, 13–15.

96. Buchan, *Domestic Medicine*, 577, 600.

97. C. White, *Treatise on the Management*, 94.

98. Dewees, *Means of Lessening Pain*, 9.

99. Dewees, *Compendious System*, 105.

100. Ibid., 222.

101. For a discussion of ideas about pain in childbirth, see Wertz and Wertz, *Lying-In*, chap. 4.

102. S. Gregory, *Man-Midwifery Exposed*, 26. For more on Gregory's concerns about the use of man-midwives, see also S. Gregory, *Letters to Ladies*.

103. Schwartz, *Birthing a Slave*; Cooper Owens, "'Courageous Negro Servitors' and Laboring Irish Bodies." See also Bankole, *Slavery and Medicine*; Fisher, "Physicians and Slavery in the Antebellum Southern Medical Journal"; Savitt, *Medicine and Slavery*; Schroeder, *Slave to the Body*; Stowe, *Doctoring the South*.

104. Sims, *Story of My Life*, 236.

105. For more on Sims and the development of gynecological surgery, see Barker-Benfield, *The Horrors of the Half-Known Life*; McGregor, *Sexual Surgery*. For an analysis of the politics of race in Sims's work and in the development of gynecology, see Kapsalis, "Mastering the Female Pelvis."

106. Sims, *Story of My Life*, 233.

107. See, for example, William Smellie, whose treatise contained an entire section on the practice of "touching." Smellie, *Theory and Practice of Midwifery*, 184–189.

108. Sims, *Story of My Life*, 234.

109. Nihell, *Art of Midwifery*, 85.

110. Stevens, *Man-Midwifery Exposed*, 5.

111. Ewell, *Letters to Ladies*, 24.

112. G. Gregory, *Medical Morals*, 29–30.

113. Beach, *Improved System of Midwifery*, 13–14.

114. Quoted in Stowe, "Obstetrics and the Work of Doctoring," 325.

115. Raynalde, *Birth of Mankind*, 97.

116. Ibid.

117. Sharp, *Compleat Midwife's Companion*, 115.

118. Smellie, *Theory and Practice of Midwifery*, 119–120.

119. Ibid., 120.

120. A. Hamilton, *Treatise of Midwifery*, 165.

121. Aitken, *Principles of Midwifery*, 58.

122. C. White, *Treatise on the Management*, 94.

123. Denman, *Practice of Midwifery*, 161.

124. Dewees, *Compendious System*, 187–188.

125. Ibid., 190.

126. Warrington, *Obstetric Catechism*, 113–114.

127. Seaman, *Midwives Monitor*, 85.

128. Ulrich, "Women's Travail, Men's Labor," 176.

129. Burns, *Principles of Midwifery*, 372.

130. Seaman, *Midwives Monitor*, 92.

131. Dewees, *Means of Lessening Pain*, 54.

132. Dewees, *Compendious System*, 260.

133. Walter Channing, September 13, 1821, Midwifery Case Notebook, 1811–1822, folder 1, box 7, Walter Channing Papers, 1800–1872, permission of Massachusetts Historical Society (hereafter MHS).

## Chapter Two

1. February 26, 1797, in Drinker, *The Diary of Elizabeth Drinker*, 2:893.

2. February 27, 1800, ibid., 1279.

3. October 23, 1799, ibid., 1227.

4. Theriot, *Mothers and Daughters*, chap. 4.

5. March 25, 1790, vol. 18, p. 22, Sarah Logan Fisher Diaries, HSP.

6. Penelope Skinner Warren to Dr. Thomas Warren, August 8, 1840, folder 22, box 1, Skinner Family Papers, Southern Historical Collection (hereafter SHC).

7. Klepp, *Revolutionary Conceptions*, 5.

8. For birthrate statistics, see D'Emilio and Freedman, *Intimate Matters*, 58. Klepp shows that birthrates among white Americans differed somewhat by region. Birthrates declined most rapidly in New England, followed by the Mid-Atlantic, the South, and finally the frontier. She also notes that the poor tended to marry later and have smaller families. See Klepp, *Revolutionary Conceptions*, 15.

9. Klepp, *Revolutionary Conceptions*, 7.

10. Klepp uses the diaries of Elizabeth Sandwith Drinker to demonstrate a shift to numeracy in the late 1770s. Ibid., 115–117.

11. [Date unmarked], 1779, vol. 8, Sarah Logan Fisher Diaries, HSP.

12. January 1, 1782, in Drinker, *The Diary of Elizabeth Drinker*, 1:395.

13. Sarah Preston (Everett) Hale Common-Place Book, September 5, 1841, folder 3, box 9, Hale Family Papers, 1787–1988, SSC.

14. April 6, 1843, June 6, 1848, May 6, 1868, folder 1, box 1, Elizabeth Frances Perry Diary, SHC.

15. February 28–March 2, 1839, Kemble, *Journal of a Residence*, 229–230. It should be noted that such high fertility rates were not necessarily universal among enslaved women. Richard Follett's analysis of birthrates on Louisiana sugar planta-

tions, for instance, demonstrates that different cycles of labor over the course of a year, as well as other factors such as nutrition, climate, and disease, could have a significant impact on enslaved women's ability to conceive and/or carry a child to term. See Follett, "Heat, Sex, and Sugar."

16. For a discussion of the techniques that slave owners used to increase and enforce childbearing, see Schwartz, *Birthing a Slave*, esp. chaps. 1 and 3.

17. Rogers, *North Carolina Narratives*, vol. 11, part 2, 229.

18. Howell, *Arkansas Narratives*, vol. 2, part 3, 339–340.

19. For an analysis of slave breeding as a controversial concept in American historical writings, see Smithers, *Slave Breeding*.

20. Keckley, *Behind the Scenes*, 39.

21. I. Hutchinson, *Arkansas Narratives*, vol. 2, part 3, 374.

22. Slave owners often noted gynecological problems, such as "falling of the womb" (uterine prolapse). See, for example, Slave Records 1844–1864 and Slave Records 1844–1865, Glover Family Papers, South Caroliniana Library (hereafter SCL).

23. Letter to Mary Cranch, January 5, 1790, in Adams, *New Letters of Abigail Adams*, 36.

24. Letter to Charles Stier, February 24, 1813, in Calvert, *Mistress of Riversdale*, 255.

25. This was a common phrase used to evoke the suffering of childbirth. See, for example, September 1777, vol. 3, Sarah Logan Fisher Diaries, HSP; Mary Hubbard to Sally Townsend, September 11, 1799, Townsend Family Papers, 1676–1877, permission of MHS.

26. November 11, 1852, and January 22, 1860, in Neblett, *A Rebel Wife in Texas*, 62, 75.

27. January 1839, in Kemble, *Journal of a Residence*, 67.

28. Letter to Mary Cranch, June 27, 1790, in Adams, *New Letters of Abigail Adams*, 52.

29. June 15, 1797, in Drinker, *The Diary of Elizabeth Drinker*, 2:929–930.

30. Mary Hubbard to Sarah Townsend, September 11, 1799, box 1, Townsend Family Papers, permission of MHS.

31. Laura Randall to Louisa Elizabeth Cabell Carrington, May 23, 1831, Laura Henrietta Wirt Randall Papers, 1819–1857, Virginia Historical Society (hereafter VHS).

32. Mary Jackson Lee to Mary Cabot Lee Higginson, October 2, 1833, folder 7, box 1, Higginson-Lee Family Correspondence, 1825–1840, American Antiquarian Society (hereafter AAS).

33. Catherine M. Scholten notes the widespread understanding in colonial America that savin could serve as an abortifacient. See Scholten, *Childbearing in American Society*, 14. For slave owners' suspicion of women who used plants such as cotton root, see Fett, *Working Cures*, 65. For more on enslaved women's use of abortifacients, see Perrin, "Resisting Reproduction."

34. Perrin, "Resisting Reproduction," 262–263.

35. See Helen Lefkowitz Horowitz's discussion of the rise of reform physiology and newly invigorated debates about sexuality and family limitation in the 1830s. Lefkowitz, *Rereading Sex.*

36. See, for example, Jan Lewis and Kenneth A. Lockridge's analysis of efforts on the part of elite women in Virginia to limit their fertility. In calculating the intervals between children, they identify breastfeeding as a successful method that most likely allowed women to exert some control over their childbearing. J. Lewis and Lockridge, " 'Sally Has Been Sick,' "10.

37. October 23, 1799, in Drinker, *The Diary of Elizabeth Drinker,* 2:1227.

38. October 10, 1843, in Dall, *Daughter of Boston,* 76.

39. Margaret Izard Manigault to Elizabeth Manigault Morris, December 16, 1809, Louis Manigault Papers, Duke University (hereafter DU).

40. Womble, *Georgia Narratives,* vol. 4, part 4, 183.

41. Letter to Isabelle van Havre, July 15, 1811, in Calvert, *Mistress of Riversdale,* 240.

42. Daniel Scott Smith suggests that withdrawal or coitus interruptus was one of the most common contraceptive measures in nineteenth-century America. See D. S. Smith, "Family Limitation," 44, 50.

43. Kammen, "The Letters of Calista Hall," 232.

44. January 19, 1847, in Dall, *Daughter of Boston,* 90.

45. K. Smith, *We Have Raised All of You,* 2.

46. For more on childbearing, motherhood, and family life among enslaved mothers, see, for example, Fett, *Working Cures*; Jones, *Labor of Love, Labor of Sorrow*; Schwartz, *Birthing a Slave*; Stevenson, *Life in Black and White*; and D. White, *Ar'n't I a Woman?*

47. Howell, *Arkansas Narratives,* vol. 2, pt. 3, 340.

48. Schwartz, *Birthing a Slave,* 11.

49. John Campbell calculated a 35 percent infant mortality rate for a large plantation in South Carolina between the 1830s and 1861. See Campbell, "Work, Pregnancy, and Infant Mortality among Southern Slaves," 795. Jacqueline Jones estimates that overall infant mortality for slaves was roughly twice that of whites in 1850. See Jones, *Labor of Love, Labor of Sorrow,* 35.

50. Grayson, *Oklahoma Narratives,* 13:115–116.

51. Quoted in Perrin, "Resisting Reproduction," 262.

52. Letter to Isabelle van Havre, January 11, 1819, in Calvert, *Mistress of Riversdale,* 341.

53. December 10, 1844, in Dall, *Daughter of Boston,* 83.

54. December 13, 1805, in Drinker, *The Diary of Elizabeth Drinker,* 3:1885.

55. Esther Bowes Cox to Mary Cox Chesnut, June 11, 1797, folder 3, box 1, Cox-Chesnut Family Papers, 1792–1858, SCL.

56. Letter to Elizabeth Gibson, August 3, 1826, in E. Lewis, *George Washington's Beautiful Nelly,* 182.

57. Margaret Gregg to Susan [?], May 2, 1857, vol. 1 (typescript), Cox Family Papers, SCL.

58. Mary Jackson Lee to Mary Cabot Lee Higginson, June 30, 1833, folder 6, box 1, Higginson-Lee Family Correspondence, 1825–1840, AAS.

59. Elite Virginian Eleanor Lewis used the word "pregnant" in one letter, but she generally referred to approaching motherhood rather than to pregnancy as such. See letter to Elizabeth Bordley Gibson, April 13, 1828, in E. Lewis, *George Washington's Beautiful Nelly*, 193. See also the diary of Martha Heywood, a Mormon transplant to Utah, who consistently used the words "pregnant" and "pregnancy" during her childbearing years in the 1850s. Heywood, *Not by Bread Alone*, 59, 62, 86.

60. Letter to Mary Chesnut, September 4, 1797, folder 3, box 1, Cox-Chesnut Family Papers, 1792–1858, SCL; Ann Warder Diary, September 24, 1786, vol. 5, Ann Head Warder Papers, HSP; Matilda Henry to Sarah French, July 27, 1837, Sarah Scarborough Butler Henry French Papers, 1824–1914, VHS. For a discussion of an earlier colonial vocabulary for pregnancy, see Klepp, *Revolutionary Conceptions*, 3. See also Klepp, "Revolutionary Bodies."

61. For commonly used vocabulary, see, for example, May 24, 1797, in Drinker, *The Diary of Elizabeth Drinker*, 2:921; January 1, 1781, vol. 10, p. 25, and July 24, 1786, vol. 15, p. 49, Sarah Logan Fisher Diaries, HSP; Madaline Selima Edwards Diary, May 8, 1844, folder 16, Charles William Bradbury Papers, SHC; Matilda Henry to Sarah French, July 27, 1837, Sarah Scarborough Butler Henry French Papers, 1824–1914, VHS; July [?] 1848, p. 32, Juliana Paisley Gilmer Diary, 1840–1850, DU.

62. Ebenezer Pettigrew to Nancy (Ann) Pettigrew, March 6, 1818, folder 19, box 1, and January 5, 1830, folder 34, box 2, Pettigrew Family Papers, 1776–1926, SHC.

63. January 20, 1781, and January 25, 1781, vol. 10, p. 31, Sarah Logan Fisher Diaries, HSP.

64. Esther Bowes Cox to Mary Cox Chesnut, May 31, 1805, folder 11, box 1, Cox-Chesnut Family Papers, 1792–1858, SCL.

65. Letter to Marie-Louise Stier, May 12, 1804, in Calvert, *Mistress of Riversdale*, 82.

66. Letter to Isabelle van Havre, April 20, 1806, in ibid., 141–142.

67. May 23, 1787, vol. 16, p. 50, Sarah Logan Fisher Diaries, HSP.

68. August 9, 1787, vol. 16, p. 70, Sarah Logan Fisher Diaries, HSP.

69. Matilda Henry to Sarah French, July 27, 1837, Sarah Scarborough Butler Henry French Papers, 1824–1914, VHS.

70. August 12, 1781, vol. 10, p. 64, Sarah Logan Fisher Diaries, HSP.

71. September 21, 1783, vol. 12, p. 71, Sarah Logan Fisher Diaries, HSP.

72. Translation: "mine is a dog of an occupation."

73. Ellen Coolidge to Martha Jefferson Randolph, June 6, 1830, box 2, Correspondence of Ellen Wayles Randolph Coolidge, University of Virginia (hereafter UVA).

74. Eliza Robertson, July 5, 1855, p. 101, folder 2 (typescript), Eliza Ann Marsh Robertson Papers, 1843–1872, SHC.

75. Scholten, *Childbearing in American Society*, 16.

76. For more on the emergence of a culture of restraint and refinement in Revolutionary-era America, see Klepp, "Revolutionary Bodies."

77. January 15, 1807, in Drinker, *The Diary of Elizabeth Drinker*, 3:2002.

78. Caroline Gilman to Harriet Fay, December 17, 1827, folder 11/154/1, Caroline Howard Gilman Papers, 1810–1880, South Carolina Historical Society (hereafter SCHS).

79. Penelope Skinner Warren to Dr. Thomas Warren, August 16, 1840, box 1, folder 22, Skinner Family Papers, SHC.

80. Letter to Anna Rose Holder, June 8, 1857, Fox, *A Northern Woman in the Plantation South*, 53.

81. Esther Bowes Cox to Mary Cox Chesnut, October 10, 1809, folder 17, box 2, Cox-Chesnut Family Papers, 1792–1858, SCL.

82. Matilda Henry to Sarah French, July 27, 1837, Sarah Scarborough Butler Henry French Papers, 1824–1914, VHS.

83. See, for example, June 15, 1855, p. 96, folder 2 (typescript), Eliza Ann Marsh Robertson Papers, 1843–1872, SHC.

84. August 16, 1845, in Dall, *Daughter of Boston*, 84.

85. Wertz and Wertz, *Lying-In*, 44. See also Bogdan, "Care or Cure?," 92–99; and Leavitt, *Brought to Bed*, esp. chaps. 2 and 3.

86. Leavitt, *Brought to Bed*, 12.

87. See Leavitt's discussion of poor women being delivered by physicians in hospitals or charity institutions. Ibid., 74–77. Physicians' records also show that they occasionally treated poor women in their homes. See, for example, the obstetric records of the New Jersey physician Samuel Worcester Butler, in Samuel Worcester Butler Record Book, 1849–1858, HSP.

88. Most enslaved women were tended by midwives, but physicians might be called in for a complicated delivery. Marie Jenkins Schwartz argues that it became more common over the course of the antebellum period for slave owners to call in physicians. See Schwartz, *Birthing a Slave*, chap. 5.

89. Agnes Gamble Cabell to Louisa Cabell Carrington, November 2, 1825, Cabell-Carrington Papers, UVA.

90. Ellen Coolidge to Mrs. Nicholas Trist, May 9, 1826, box 2, Correspondence of Ellen Wayles Randolph Coolidge, UVA.

91. Letter to Isabelle van Havre, April 2, 1807, in Calvert, *Mistress of Riversdale*, 162.

92. Matilda Henry to Sarah French, March 24, 1835, Sarah Scarborough Butler Henry French Papers, 1824–1914, VHS.

93. See, for example, the diary of Mary Holyoke, who kept a record of friends and kinswomen who were "brought to bed." See Dow, *The Holyoke Diaries*.

94. October 16, 1812, vol. 1, case vol. 41–47, Mehitable Sullivan Cutler Amory Diaries, permission of MHS.

95. See, for example, a letter to Mary Cranch, November 24, 1788, in Adams, *New Letters of Abigail Adams*, 3; February 2, 1794, Elizabeth Cranch Norton Diaries (1781–1811), permission of MHS; letter to Elizabeth Gibson, February 7, 1796, in E. Lewis, *George Washington's Beautiful Nelly*, 24; Friday, June 28, 1850, box 131, Diary of Lucy Cocke, Papers of John Hartwell Cocke / Papers of the Cocke Family, UVA.

96. Letter to Mary Cranch, November 24, 1788, in Adams, *New Letters of Abigail Adams*, 3. Mary Hering to Mary Hering Middleton, September [?], 1800, folder/box 24/63/01, Hering Family Papers, 1674–1960, SCHS; Sarah Lindley Fisher to Elizabeth Rodman, February 9, 1839, folder 2, box 11, series 6, Logan-Fisher-Fox Family Papers, HSP; July 6, 1856, Persis Sibley Andrews Black diaries, 1842–1864, permission of MHS. For further examples, see also S. Dulles to Joseph Dulles, April 10, 1829, folder/box 12/58/14, Ann Heatly Reid Lovell, Estate and Family Papers, 1780–1854, SCHS; Thomas Kennedy to Nancy Kennedy, March 12, 1833, folder 5, box 1, Kennedy, Moore, and Southgate Family Papers, SHC.

97. September 1779, vol. 8, p. 74, Sarah Logan Fisher Diaries, HSP.

98. October 9, 1824, Diary of Martha Tabb Watkins Dyer, UVA.

99. Translation: "I must tell you that our cousin Catharine Codman gave birth last Saturday at four in the morning to a little girl. She suffered but little: she was only sick for four hours, and the baby came into the world without anyone in the family except her nurse Mrs. Stevens knowing what was happening. She is doing very well: the little miss is very small, but is doing marvelously." Georgina Margaret Amory Lowell to Anna C. Lowell, August 15, 1826, folder 2.3, box 2, John Lowell Papers, 1808–1851, permission of MHS.

100. Rachel Lazarus to Maria Edgeworth, November 3, 1828, in MacDonald, *The Education of the Heart*, 176.

101. Mary Rodman Fisher Fox Diary, April 23, 1850, vol. 19, p. 53, series 9, Logan-Fisher-Fox Family Papers, HSP.

102. For additional examples, see, for instance, October 13, 1851, Penelope Eliza Howard Alderman Diary, 1851–1856, SHC; March 26, 1756, in Burr, *The Journal of Esther Edwards Burr*, 188–189; Ann Cameron to Paul Cameron, March 8, 1834, folder 727, box 34, Cameron Family Papers, 1757–1978, SHC; Sarah Lindley Fisher to Elizabeth Rodman, February 9, 1839, folder 2, box 11, series 6, Logan-Fisher-Fox Family Papers, HSP; Sarah Evelina Ker, January 17, 1841, folder 73, box 7, Ker Family Papers, 1776–1996, SHC; Georgina Margaret Amory Lowell to Ann Tracy, September 9, 1827, folder 2.7, box 2, John Lowell Papers, 1808–1851, permission of MHS; February 2, 1794, Elizabeth Cranch Norton Diaries (1781–1811), permission of MHS.

103. J. Lewis and Lockridge, " 'Sally Has Been Sick,' " 6–8.

104. Mary Richardson Walker, December 7, 1838, in Drury, *First White Women over the Rockies*, 2:136.

105. Ibid.

106. Translation: "The child is very big, and the mother very little, it was her opinion that the child is dead."

107. Translation: "and with his instruments and much difficulty, he delivered her of a dead child."

108. Translation: "I was not in the chamber at the critical moment."

109. September 17, 1794, in Drinker, *The Diary of Elizabeth Drinker*, 1:594–595.

110. October 23, 1799, ibid., 2:1227.

111. June 15, 1797, ibid., 930.

112. June 16, 1797, ibid.

113. April 21, 1848, in Dall, *Daughter of Boston*, 102.

114. October 16, 1849, ibid., 119–120.

115. Jacobs, *Incidents*, 53.

116. Ibid., 15–16.

117. Heaton, *The World of Hannah Heaton*, 74.

118. September 1777, vol. 3, Sarah Logan Fisher Diaries, HSP.

119. Jane Williams to Eliza Haywood, January 30, 1804, folder 41, box 4, series 1, Ernest Haywood Collection, SHC.

120. November 2, 1805, James Anderson Casebook, 1804–1806, HSP.

121. Ellen Coolidge to Mrs. Nicholas Trist, May 9, 1826, box 2, Correspondence of Ellen Wayles Randolph Coolidge, UVA.

122. Sidney Carr to Jane Randolph, quoted in J. Lewis and Lockridge, " 'Sally Has Been Sick,' " 7.

123. April 4, 1853, in Neblett, *A Rebel Wife in Texas*, 67.

124. Matilda Henry to Sarah French, August 23, 1837, Sarah Scarborough Butler Henry French Papers, 1824–1914, VHS.

125. Mary Scott to Hannah Fox, January 6, 1826, vol. 1, series 1, Fox Family Papers, HSP.

126. Mary Middleton to Eliza Fisher, May 31, 1840, in Harrison, *Best Companions*, 140.

127. For more on the discovery and use of anesthesia, see Caton, *What a Blessing She Had Chloroform*; Pernick, *A Calculus of Suffering*; Wolf, *Deliver Me from Pain*.

128. Letter to Anne Longfellow Pierce, [date unknown],1847, Longfellow, *Mrs. Longfellow*, 129–130.

129. Case 28, June 28, 1857, Samuel Worcester Butler Record Book, 1849–1858, HSP.

130. Theriot, *Mothers and Daughters*, chap. 4.

131. Elizabeth Byles Ball to Anna Potts, July 18, 1760, Letterbook, 1757–1783, Ball Family Papers, HSP.

132. Rebecca Shoemaker, July 31, 1785, p. 366, Rebecca Shoemaker Papers, 1780–1786, HSP.

133. July 29, 1785, in Sansom, *The Diary of Hannah Callender Sansom*, 300.

134. Letter to Elizabeth Gibson, March 19, 1826, in E. Lewis, *George Washington's Beautiful Nelly*, 175.

135. Letter to Elizabeth Gibson April 5, 1825, ibid., 165.

136. Maria Flagg to Lydia Nightingale, August 17, 1793, Maria Magdalen Flagg Letters, SL.

137. See, for example, Susan Klepp's analysis of women's portraits in the eighteenth century, showing a transition from a visual emphasis on women's fertility to images that highlighted their moral and intellectual capacity. Klepp, *Revolutionary Conceptions*, chap. 4.

## Chapter Three

1. Ruth Perry notes that this prescriptive literature, as well as fiction and other print sources, contributed to the "invention of motherhood" in the eighteenth century—a new vision that celebrated the devotion of mothers and saw their moral influence as essential to the nation. Perry, "Colonizing the Breast," 206.

2. Mary Hunt Palmer Tyler, for instance, is generally credited with publishing the first medical advice manual by a woman in the United States. See Tyler, *The Maternal Physician*. For other popular texts by women, see, for example, Child, *The Mother's Book*; and Sigourney, *Letters to Mothers*.

3. For a discussion of the breast as a sacred symbol in the West from pre-Christian goddesses forward, see Yalom, *History of the Breast*, esp. chap. 1.

4. William Buchan, *Advice to Mothers*, 3.

5. For a useful summary of the growing emphasis on domestic ideology and motherhood in the Enlightenment, see Pollak, "Introduction," esp. 9–12.

6. See, for example, Kathleen Brown's discussion of female sensibility and the emphasis on female emotion as an essential part of good mothering. Brown, "The Life Cycle," esp. 37–39.

7. On the relationship among sentiment, sensibility, and moral virtue in the politics and culture of the Enlightenment, see, for example, Barker-Benfield, *The Culture of Sensibility*; Burnstein, *Sentimental Democracy*; Csengei, *Sympathy, Sensibility and the Literature of Feeling*; Goring, *The Rhetoric of Sensibility*; Himmelfarb, *The Roads to Modernity*; Knott, *Sensibility and the American Revolution*; Reddy, *The Navigation of Feeling*.

8. See, for example, Bloch's discussion of *Pamela* in her *Feminist Studies* article, "American Feminine Ideals in Transition," 108–109. For a discussion of the tension between maternal virtue and patriarchal authority in the novel, see Bowers, " 'A Point of Conscience.' " For a discussion of the convergence of female virtue, motherhood, and sexuality in *Pamela*, see Peters, "The Pregnant Pamela"; and Perry, "Colonizing the Breast," esp. 225–230. For a discussion of the tensions surrounding the female body in *Pamela*, see Gwilliam, "Pamela and the Duplicitous Body of Femininity."

9. Henry May asserts that Rousseau was widely read in America in the 1780s and 1790s and that his work *Emile* was particularly influential on new ideas of motherhood. See May, *The Enlightenment in America*. For more on Rousseau's vision of women's role in society, see, for example, Fermon, "Domesticating Women, Civilizing Men"; Weiss, "Sex, Freedom and Equality"; Wexler, " 'Made for Man's Delight.' "

10. Rousseau, *Emile*, 13.

11. Cox, *Claims of the Country*, 2:6.

12. For an analysis of gendered understandings of virtue, see Bloch, "Gendered Meanings of Virtue."

13. For a discussion of the concept of female influence in the context of religious revivalism, see Ryan, *Cradle of the Middle Class*, 73–74.

14. Bloch, "Revaluing Motherhood," 118–120.

15. Abbott, *The Mother at Home*, 167.

16. Cadogan, *Essay upon Nursing*, 3.

17. Moss, *Essay on the Management and Nursing of Children*, 65.

18. Cadogan, *Essay upon Nursing*, 7, 13.

19. Ibid., 28.

20. Ibid., 17.

21. H. Smith, *Letters to Married Women*, 66, 72, 73. This text was printed in numerous editions into the nineteenth century, including under the alternate title *The Female Monitor*.

22. A. Hamilton, *A Treatise of Midwifery*, 381.

23. Rousseau, *Emile*, 11.

24. H. Smith, *Letters to Married Women*, 59, 62, 65.

25. *The Nurse's Guide*, 23.

26. Ibid., 21.

27. Ibid., 23.

28. A. Hamilton, *A Treatise of Midwifery*, 381.

29. Hume, *An Exhortation*, 116.

30. Rates of wet nursing are difficult to measure, but the practice of hiring a wet nurse appears to have been less common among American elites than among British ones, although Janet Golden has shown that, at least early in the eighteenth century, it was relatively common for elite Bostonians to send their children to the surrounding countryside to be nursed. In addition, slaveholding Americans had the option of employing enslaved women as wet nurses, though the extent to which this occurred is difficult to measure with accuracy. Golden shows that women either chose not to breastfeed or were prevented from breastfeeding for a number of reasons, including disease, breast infections, fatigue, and death. For a history of infant feeding practices in America, see Golden, *A Social History of Wet Nursing*, esp. chap. 1. See also Fildes, "The English Wet-Nurse"; and Fildes, *Wet Nursing*.

31. H. Smith, *Letters to Married Women*, 66.

32. *The London Practice of Midwifery*, 257.

33. Cadogan, *Essay upon Nursing*, 7.

34. Hume, *An Exhortation*, 116.

35. Rousseau, *Emile*, 13.

36. *The Nurse's Guide*, 24–25.

37. Ibid., 25.

38. Cadogan, *Essay upon Nursing*, 27.

39. H. Smith, *Letters to Married Women*, 73–74.

40. Mears, *Pupil of Nature*, 139.

41. Buchan, *Advice to Mothers*, 30. Watkins, *Maternal Solicitude*, 8.

42. Dawbarn, *The Rights of Infants*, iv.

43. Barwell, *Advice to Mothers*, 25.

44. Tyler, *The Maternal Physician*, 8.

45. Searle, *Season of Maternal Solicitude*, 202–203.

46. Alcott, *The Young Mother*, 115.

47. Dewees, *Physical and Medical Treatment of Children*, 49.

48. Butler, *The American Lady*, 243.

49. Dewees, *Physical and Medical Treatment of Children*, 48.

50. Watkins, *Maternal Solicitude*, 9.

51. Buchan, *Advice to Mothers*, 61.

52. Ewell, *Letters to Ladies*, 219.

53. Sigourney, *Letters to Mothers*, 29.

54. Abbott, *The Mother at Home*, 161.

55. Bakewell, *The Mother's Practical Guide*, 31.

56. Buchan, *Advice to Mothers*, 64.

57. Dewees, *Physical and Medical Treatment of Children*, 40.

58. Dawbarn, *The Rights of Infants*, 11.

59. Mrs. S. Smith, "Anxious Mothers," 265–266.

60. Bull, *Hints to Mothers*, 193.

61. Allen, *The Young Mother*, 62.

62. Dewees, *Physical and Medical Treatment of Children*, xiii.

63. Beecher, *A Treatise on Domestic Economy*, 19.

64. Buchan, *Advice to Mothers*, 32.

65. Sigourney, "The Mother's Sacrifice," 222.

66. Sigourney, *Letters to Mothers*, vii.

67. Cadogan, *Essay upon Nursing*, 18.

68. See especially Perry, "Colonizing the Breast"; Treckel, "Breastfeeding and Maternal Sexuality"; Yalom, *History of the Breast*.

69. Perry, "Colonizing the Breast," 209.

70. Treckel, "Breastfeeding and Maternal Sexuality," 31.

71. Few scholars have noted this strain of eroticism in prescriptive literature. Ruth Perry briefly notes the "erotic symbiosis between infant and mother" in texts such as William Buchan's *Advice to Mothers*. But she sees this as further evidence of the "mutually exclusive nature of motherhood and sexual desire." In contrast, I emphasize the ways in which depictions of breastfeeding explored the mutual pleasures of infant, mother, and father and the ways in which these discussions played into notions of romantic love, thus uniting motherhood and sexuality. See Perry, "Colonizing the Breast," 228. In addition, Barbara Charlesworth Gelpi briefly mentions the eroticization of breastfeeding in her work on Percy Bysshe Shelley. See

Gelpi, "The Nursery Cave," 51–52. Ellen Pollak offers a similarly brief reference in her introduction to women in the Enlightenment. See Pollak, "Introduction," 10.

72. Karen Harvey offers a helpful synthesis of scholarship on women's sexuality and the body. See Harvey, "Sexuality and the Body," 78–99.

73. Cott, "Passionlessness," 221. Thomas Laqueur has also built on the notion of passionlessness, exploring the ways in which ideas about sexual anatomy and sexual pleasure functioned to delineate the difference between women and men, particularly beginning in the eighteenth century. See Laqueur, *Making Sex*, esp. chap. 5. More recently, April Haynes has explored the history of sexual reform and fears of masturbation to suggest that both women and men were in fact keenly aware of women's capacity for sexual passion and were openly addressing it in lectures and texts. See Haynes, *Riotous Flesh*.

74. See, for example Godbeer, *Sexual Revolution*; and Lyons, *Sex among the Rabble*.

75. Foucault, *The History of Sexuality: Volume 1: An Introduction*, 37.

76. D'Emilio and Freedman, *Intimate Matters*, 56.

77. Lystra, *Searching the Heart*, 59.

78. Schwarz, "Missing the Breast," 155.

79. Harvey, *Reading Sex in the Eighteenth Century*, 20.

80. Stretzer, *A New Description of Merryland*, 37–38.

81. Quoted in Yalom, *History of the Breast*, 71.

82. Recent scholarship in disciplines including sociology, anthropology, and medicine has identified a physiological correlation between sexual arousal and the physical stimulation of breastfeeding. In *Bearing Meaning: The Language of Birth*, Robbie Pfeufer Kahn explains that the hormone oxytocin stimulates labor, is released by nursing, and "also triggers orgasm, which results in rhythmic contractions of the uterus for as long as twenty minutes after lovemaking and during breastfeeding," (233–234).

83. Burton, *New System of Midwifery*, 10–11.

84. Mears, *Pupil of Nature*, 140.

85. See Buchan, *Advice to Mothers*, 31.

86. Ibid., 31, 61.

87. For the second reference to "thrilling sensations," see Buchan, ibid., 61.

88. For more on the connection between nerves and emotions in Enlightenment thought, see Burnstein, *Sentimental Democracy*, esp. chap. 1.

89. Dewees, *Physical and Medical Treatment of Children*, 50–51.

90. Hollick, *The Matron's Manual of Midwifery*, 79.

91. Darwin, *The Botanic Garden*, 90.

92. Freud, *On Sexuality*, 98.

93. "Woman," *Ladies' Literary Cabinet*, 5. The introduction to the excerpt reads: "The following idea of the formation of Woman, is extracted from a Treatise, entitled *Philosophia de l'Univers*, written by Dupont De Nemours.—Perhaps a more eloquent and delightful description never came from the pen of man."

94. H. Smith, *Letters to Married Women*, 78.

95. Ibid., 78–79.

96. Richardson, *Pamela*, 4:13.

97. Fowler, *Maternity*, 128.

98. Dawbarn, *The Rights of Infants*, 11.

99. Fowler, *Love and Parentage*, 58.

100. H. Smith, *Letters to Married Women*, 72–73.

101. Buchan, *Advice to Mothers*, 61.

102. Carroll Smith-Rosenberg has aptly noted that "sexual repression has most fascinated scholars of the 19th century." See Smith-Rosenberg, "Sex as Symbol in Victorian Purity." While Smith-Rosenberg's work (see, for example, "The Female World of Love and Ritual") as well as more recent work by scholars such as Karen Lystra has expanded to consider other attitudes toward sex, the concept of sexual repression still looms large in our understanding of the nineteenth century.

103. Lystra, *Searching the Heart*, 59, 77.

104. Buchan, *Advice to Mothers*, 61.

105. Ostriker, *The Mother/Child Papers*, 18.

106. Rich, *Of Woman Born*, 36.

107. See Yalom, *History of the Breast*, 254–255. Cindy Stearns also discusses the tension in today's society between the maternal and the sexual breast and cites the case of Karen Carter, who similarly lost custody of her child for more than a year for voicing her concerns about feelings of sexual arousal when breastfeeding. See Stearns, "Breastfeeding and the Good Maternal Body," 309.

108. Sigourney, *Letters*, 46.

109. Robins, "On a Mother and Her Infant," 107.


## Chapter Four

1. Mary Peabody to Maria Chase, August 19, 1831, folder 45, box 1, Peabody Family Papers, 1820–1853, SSC.

2. See, for instance, Fildes, *Breasts, Bottles and Babies*; Fildes, *Wet Nursing*; Golden, *A Social History of Wet Nursing*; Hoffert, *Private Matters*; Salmon, "The Cultural Significance of Breastfeeding"; Treckel, "Breastfeeding and Maternal Sexuality"; Wolf, *Don't Kill Your Baby*. One exception to the focus on practice and ideology is Sally McMillen's work on motherhood in the antebellum South, which includes an analysis of elite women's attitudes toward breastfeeding. See McMillen, *Motherhood in the Old South*, chap. 5.

3. March 31, 1763, in Drinker, *The Diary of Elizabeth Drinker*, 1:99.

4. Eliza Haywood to John Haywood, May 19, 1800, folder 30, box 3, series 1, Ernest Haywood Collection, SHC.

5. December 30, 1825, Caroline Olivia Laurens Diary, 1823–1827, SHC.

6. Narcissa Prentiss Whitman, March 30, 1837, in Drury, *First White Women over the Rockies*, 1:126.

7. Mary Holyoke, November 15, 22, and 30, 1771, in Dow, *The Holyoke Diaries*, 77.

8. John Campbell to Edward Campbell, August 9, 1804, box 1, Campbell Family Papers, DU.

9. Catherine Read to Betsy Ludlow, December 11, 1821, folder 15, box 1, Read Family, 1766–1843, SCL. References to "gathered breasts" were common. See also Sarah Lindley Fisher to Mary Miller, April 2, 1805, folder 1, box 11, series 6, Logan-Fisher-Fox Family Papers, HSP; Esther Cox to Mary Chesnut, September 27, 1800, folder 5, box 1, Cox-Chesnut, Family Papers, 1792–1858, SCL.

10. Mary Richardson Walker, Tuesday, December 11, 1838; Wednesday, December 12, 1838; Friday, December 14, 1838, in Drury, *First White Women over the Rockies*, 2:136.

11. Eliza Haywood to Jane Williams, December 20, 1803, folder 40, box 4, series 1, Ernest Haywood Collection, SHC.

12. Laura Randall to Louisa Elizabeth Cabell Carrington, November 20, 1822, p. 118, Laura Henrietta Wirt Randall Papers, 1819–1857, VHS.

13. August 1, 1788, in Ballard, *The Diary of Martha Ballard*, 101.

14. Esther Bowes Cox to Mary Cox Chesnut, March 25, 1800, folder 5, box 1, Cox-Chesnut Family Papers, 1792–1858, SCL.

15. Esther Bowes Cox to Mary Cox Chesnut, March 7, 1801, folder 6, box 1, Cox-Chesnut Family Papers, 1792–1858, SCL.

16. Letter to Mary Cranch, April 21, 1790, in Adams, *New Letters of Abigail Adams*, 45.

17. July 13, 1771, and July 22, 1771, in Drinker, *The Diary of Elizabeth Drinker*, 1:162, 163.

18. Esther Bowes Cox to Mary Cox Chesnut, November 9, 1797, folder 4, box 1, Cox-Chesnut Family Papers, 1792–1858, SCL.

19. Mary Richardson Walker, December 29, 1838; December 30, 1838, in Drury, *First White Women over the Rockies*, 2:139.

20. Agnes Cabell to Louisa Cabell Carrington, May 25, 1824, Cabell-Carrington Papers, UVA.

21. Letter to Elizabeth Bordley, April 27, 1827, in E. Lewis, *George Washington's Beautiful Nelly*, 188.

22. Sarah (Bennett) Hopkins to Erastus Hopkins, June 8, 1836, box/folder 28/664/02, Erastus Hopkins Correspondence, 1834–1838, SCHS.

23. Margaret Brooke to Robert Brooke, January 28, 1843, Papers of Robert S. Brooke, UVA.

24. Eliza Fisher to Mary Middleton, September 12, 1844, in Harrison, *Best Companions*, 401.

25. April 1, 1839, in Kemble, *Journal of a Residence*, 296.

26. December 7, 1802, in Drinker, *The Diary of Elizabeth Drinker*, 2:1597.

27. Jane Gay (Robertson) Bernard to John H. Bernard, February 25, 1819, Robertson Family Papers, 1818–1820, VHS.

28. Georgina Margaret Amory Lowell to Ann Tracy, September 9, 1827, folder 2.7, box 2, John Lowell Papers, 1808–1851, permission of MHS.

29. Rebecca Allen Turner, "Little Jesse's Diary," August 29, 1857, vol. M:6888, Turner Family Papers 1778–1929, DU.

30. Esther Bowes Cox to Mary Cox Chesnut, April 21, 1805, folder 11, box 1, Cox-Chesnut Family Papers, 1792–1858, SCL.

31. Mary Peabody to Maria Chase, August 19, 1831, folder 45, Peabody Family Papers, 1820–1853, SSC.

32. Gertrude Gouverneur Ogden Meredith to William Meredith, June 28, 1798, folder 1, box 51, Meredith Family Papers, HSP.

33. Sarah Cary to Polly Gray, March 29, 1785, in Curtis, *The Cary Letters*, 67.

34. Bard, *Compendium*, 108. Bard furthermore recommended rubbing the breasts and nipples during pregnancy and breastfeeding with olive oil, fresh lard, or butter, and, in cases of flattened nipples, placing a wax ring around the nipple to prevent clothing from pressing upon it.

35. Letter to Elizabeth Bordley, June 24, 1827, in E. Lewis, *George Washington's Beautiful Nelly*, 191.

36. *Portrait of Unidentified Woman Breastfeeding a Baby*, daguerreotype, ca. 1848, PC136-1z, SL; and *Portrait of Unidentified Woman Breastfeeding a Baby*, daguerreotype, ca. 1850, PC140-1z, SL. Based on the appearance of the women's clothing and accessories and the fact that most mothers would not have wanted to celebrate the fact that they were employing a wet nurse, I am working from the assumption that these woman were not wet nurses but were in fact the mothers of the infants they nursed. For similar images, see *Woman Breast-Feeding Her Infant*, daguerreotype, ca. 1845, Visual Collections—Slides and Digital Images, PAA82 1843A 70(a), Harvard Fine Arts Library; *Unidentified Woman Breastfeeding a Baby*, daguerreotype, ca. 1860, PC140-2z, SL; *Portrait of an Unidentified Woman Breastfeeding a Baby*, daguerreotype, ca. 1860s, PC140-4z, SL.

37. Caulfield, "Infant Feeding in Colonial America," 677.

38. Classified advertisement, *Boston News-Letter*, November 15–22, 1714, no. 553:2.

39. Classified advertisement, *New York Daily Advertiser*, January 30, 1795, no. 3108:4.

40. See, for example, classified advertisement, *Southern Patriot*, January 23, 1846, 55, no. 8264:3; and classified advertisement, *New York Gazette, and Weekly Mercury*, February 12, 1770, no. 955:4.

41. For more on the causes of failed maternal breastfeeding, see Golden, *A Social History of Wet Nursing*, 17–20.

42. Wertz and Wertz, *Lying-In*, 20; Ulrich, "'The Living Mother of a Living Child,'" 28, 31. See also Ulrich, *A Midwife's Tale*, 373n7.

43. Golden, *A Social History of Wet Nursing*, 18–19.

44. McMillen, *Motherhood in the Old South*, appendix I, table III. These statistics may not fully reflect maternal mortality rates, as they may not account for women who died after childbirth of related complications. For further estimates of nineteenth-century mortality rates, see also Berman, "The Practice of Obstetrics in

Rural America"; Vinovskis, "Mortality Rates and Trends in Massachusetts before 1860," esp. 201. Judith Walzer Leavitt argues that improvements in obstetrics have been quite recent: by 1930 there was still roughly 1 maternal death per 150 births. See Leavitt, *Brought to Bed*, 23–26.

45. *Trends in Maternal Mortality: 1990 to 2013*, 8.

46. D. B. Smith, *Inside the Great House*, 35.

47. McMillen, *Motherhood in the Old South*, 118.

48. Hoffert, *Private Matters*.

49. For information on the variations in wet nurse wages, see Golden, *A Social History of Wet Nursing*, 28–31.

50. Classified advertisement, *Independent Ledger*, August 14, 1780, 3, no. 114:3.

51. For a discussion of infant mortality related to wet nursing, see Golden, *A Social History of Wet Nursing*, 14.

52. Emily West and R. J. Knight have argued that wet nursing should be located "along a spectrum of gendered exploitation," ranging from the voluntary and informal wet nursing that occurred between friends and kinswomen, to the paid wet nursing performed by women who had few economic options, to the wet nursing performed by enslaved women who lacked the ability to choose how to use their bodies. West and Knight, "Mothers' Milk," 37.

53. For further analysis of the commodification of enslaved women's bodies, see, for instance, Morgan, *Laboring Women*; Schroeder, *Slave to the Body*; Schwartz, *Birthing a Slave*.

54. For further analysis of mothering in slavery, see Jones, *Labor of Love, Labor of Sorrow*, chapter 1; W. King, " 'Suffer with Them til Death' "; Roberts, *Killing the Black Body*, chap. 1; D. White, *Ar'n't I a Woman?*, esp. chap. 3.

55. February 28–March 2, 1839, in Kemble, *Journal of a Residence*, 215, 229–230.

56. Campbell, "Work, Pregnancy, and Infant Mortality," 795. McMillen, *Motherhood in the Old South*, appendix I, table VII.

57. West and Knight, "Mothers' Milk," 41.

58. Wallace, *Arkansas Narratives*, vol. 2, pt. 7, 42.

59. Robinson, *North Carolina Narratives*, vol. 11, pt. 2, 218–219.

60. Calhoun, "Ex-Slave Stories (Texas)," in *Texas Narratives*, vol. 16, pt. 1, 188.

61. West and Knight, "Mothers' Milk," 50.

62. Greeley, "Stories of Ex-Slaves," in *South Carolina Narratives*, vol. 14, pt. 2, 190.

63. Diary of Lucy Cocke, July 3, 1850, box 138, Papers of John Hartwell Cocke / Papers of the Cocke Family, UVA.

64. Book 2: Autobiography and Diary of Mrs. Eliza Clitherall, 1751–1860, [date?], vol. 7, p. 35, folder 19, box 2, Caroline Elizabeth Burgwin Clitherall Diaries, SHC.

65. Caroline Gilman to Harriet Fay, January 6, 1821, folder 11/154/2, Caroline Howard Gilman Papers, 1810–1880, SCHS.

66. July 15, 1765, in Drinker, *The Diary of Elizabeth Drinker*, 1:118.

67. Golden, *A Social History of Wet Nursing*, 33.

68. *Nurse's Guide*, 28–29.

69. Sharp, *Compleat Midwife's Companion*, 218.

70. Ibid., 219.

71. Dewees, *Physical and Medical Treatment of Children*, 174.

72. For an interesting analysis of the intrusive examination of the body of the wet nurse in both fiction and prescriptive texts in Victorian England, see Klimaszewski, "Examining the Wet Nurse," 232–346.

73. Alcott, *The Young Mother*, 136.

74. Golden, *A Social History of Wet Nursing*, 38–39.

75. "Wanted—A *Dry* Nurse" (cartoon), *Turner's 1839 Comick Almanack*.

76. Peggy Craig to Miss Montgomery, November 16, 1813, folder 13, box 1, Biddle and Craig Family Papers, HSP.

77. October 27, 1818, Lydia Smith Russell Diary, 1818, permission of MHS.

78. Eliza Middleton Fisher to Mary Hering Middleton, September 12, 1844, in Harrison, *Best Companions*, 401.

79. Eliza Fisher to Mary Middleton, December 19, 1844, ibid., 416.

80. March 26, 1845, Eliza Nevins Townsend Bellows Diary, 1843–1846, permission of MHS.

81. July 3, 1845, Eliza Nevins Townsend Bellows Diary, 1843–1846, permission of MHS.

82. Mary Jackson Lee to Mary Cabot Lee Higginson, August 19, 1834, folder 10, box 1, Higginson-Lee Family Correspondence, 1825–1840, AAS.

83. Mary Jackson Lee to Mary Cabot Lee Higginson, August 22, 1834, folder 10, box 1, Higginson-Lee Family Correspondence, 1825–1840, AAS.

84. Mary Jackson Lee to Mary Cabot Lee Higginson, August 25, 1834, folder 10, box 1, Higginson-Lee Family Correspondence, 1825–1840, AAS.

85. Mary Jackson Lee to Mary Cabot Lee Higginson, August 27, 1834, folder 10, box 1, Higginson-Lee Family Correspondence, 1825–1840, AAS.

86. Letter to Isabelle van Havre, February 18, 1805, in Calvert, *Mistress of Riversdale*, 111.

87. Mary Richardson Walker, January 6, 1839, in Drury, *First White Women over the Rockies*, 2:141.

88. Emily Chubbuck Judson to Jane A. Kelly, February 7, 1848, in Kendrick, *Life and Letters*, 288.

89. Ellen Coolidge to Mrs. Nicholas P. Trist, October 15, 1830, box 2, Correspondence of Ellen Wayles Randolph Coolidge, UVA.

## Chapter Five

1. Lehuu, *Carnival on the Page*, 7–8, 94, 115. For further discussion of the rise of sentimental culture in the nineteenth century and the role that women played as readers and writers, see Douglas, *Feminization of American Culture*.

2. The cultural emphasis on ideal motherhood began to decline, however, after the 1860s as the idealization of domesticity came under suspicion by those who sought greater freedom and opportunity for women in American society. For more on the shift in feminine literature in the second half of the nineteenth century, see P. Bennett, "'The Descent of the Angel,'" 593; P. Bennett, *Poets in the Public Sphere*; Mitchell, "A Wonderful Duty," 175.

3. For a discussion of sentimentalism as a literary mode, see Kete, *Sentimental Collaborations*, xiv. For more on the use of emotion and sentimentalism, see, for example, Blauvelt, *The Work of the Heart*; J. S. Kasson, *Marble Queens and Captives*; Noble, *Masochistic Pleasures*; Samuels, *The Culture of Sentiment*; Tompkins, *Sensational Designs*; Wearn, *Negotiating Motherhood*.

4. For more on the culture of the middle class in America, see, for example, Halttunen, *Confidence Men and Painted Women*; J. F. Kasson, *Rudeness and Civility*; Rubin, *Middlebrow Culture*, chap. 1; Ryan, *Cradle of the Middle Class*.

5. By referring to the self-invention and self-regulation of the middle class, I borrow specifically from Michel Foucault's argument that the middle class turned its technologies of discipline and regulation on itself in order to create and reaffirm its own image before attempting to reform society at large. Sentimental culture played a significant role in these processes. See Foucault, *The History of Sexuality: Volume 1: An Introduction*, esp. 121–124.

6. As Jeanne Boydston has written, "For all of its exuberance and apparent self-confidence as the new arbiters of America's morals . . . the emerging middle class expressed a constant anxiety over its economic vulnerability." Domestic culture provided a reassuring antidote to that anxiety. Boydston, *Home and Work*, 72. Ann Douglas has also addressed the convergence of the market economy and sentimentalism, explaining that "many nineteenth-century Americans in the Northeast acted every day as if they believed that economic expansion, urbanization, and industrialization represented the greatest good." In Douglas's analysis, sentimental culture then became a means of contesting these processes—"a form of dragging one's heels." Douglas, *Feminization of American Culture*, 12.

7. Rubin, *Middlebrow Culture*, 3–5.

8. Lehuu, *Carnival on the Page*, 96–98.

9. Kete, *Sentimental Collaborations*, 54.

10. Mary P. Ryan notes that the American middle class is a somewhat nebulous concept, but that the Second Great Awakening was driven primarily by those who fell somewhere between the wealthy and the working poor. Ryan, *Cradle of the Middle Class*, 13–14.

11. For more on the culture of millennialism, see Johnson, *Shopkeeper's Millennium*; Moorhead, "Between Progress and Apocalypse."

12. As Barbara Welter has argued, piety was the first trait attached to the concept of "true womanhood." Thus women's influence, particularly as mothers, was placed at the heart of evangelical religion. See Welter, "Cult of True Womanhood."

For more on the role of women in evangelical religion, see Ryan, *Cradle of the Middle Class*, esp. chap. 2.

13. For more on the evangelical understanding of motherhood and the role of maternal associations, see Meckel, "Educating a Ministry of Mothers."

14. For a discussion of the concept of female influence, particularly as it was described and enacted in sentimental culture, see Douglas, *Feminization of American Culture*, 9.

15. Sigourney, *Letters to Mothers*, 9.

16. "Autumn Thoughts," *Boston Literary Magazine*, 307.

17. For the very early history of American women's magazines, see Zuckerman, *Popular Women's Magazines*.

18. K. Smith, *We Have Raised All of You*, chap. 9.

19. MacDonald, *The Education of the Heart*.

20. Darton, *A Present for a Little Girl*, title page.

21. Upton, *My Childhood*, n.p.

22. Ann Taylor, *My Mother*.

23. Sproat, *Ditties for Children*; see, for example, 12, 14, 19–21.

24. See, for example, an image of mother and daughter walking out in Woodworth, *Holiday Book*, 66. See also an image of a mother bending over three children and their toys in Goodrich, *Peter Parley's Winter Evening Tales*, engraved title page.

25. Because of their use of graphics, publications such as magazines and giftbooks were relatively expensive compared to novels, which might be purchased for as little as seventy-five cents or a dollar. See Aronson, *Taking Liberties*, 14; Lehuu, *Carnival on the Page*, 77.

26. For more on the importance of fashion plates in *Godey's*, see Lehuu, "Sentimental Figures."

27. Patterson, *Art for the Middle Classes*, 9–11.

28. Ibid., 15.

29. Lehuu, *Carnival on the Page*, 78.

30. Ibid., 103.

31. Ibid., 115–117.

32. See, for example, *The Gipsy Mother*, an image based on a painting by David Wilkie, which was paired with a poem in which a "Gipsy" woman melded maternal sentiment with terrible curses, signaling disorderly and twisted motherhood. See Lamb, "The Gipsy's Malison," in *The Gem of the Season*, 122. See also an image of an old mother and her young daughter, accompanied by a poem titled "Help My Mother." The woman's wrinkled face and humble garb signaled her poverty and distress, eliciting pity rather than reverence from the viewer. See Hesse, *Help My Mother* (graphic), and Dix, "Help My Mother" (poem), *Godey's Magazine and Lady's Book*, 38.

33. Tucker, *The Empty Cradle* (graphic), and "The Empty Cradle" (poem), *Godey's Magazine and Lady's Book*, 12.

34. Wright, *The Dying Babe*, in *Casket; or Youth's Pocket Library*, n.p. For similar images of bereaved mothers, see, for instance, Agate, *The Dead Boy*, in *Christian Keepsake and Missionary Annual*, n.p.; Corbould, *The Mother and Babe*, in *The Iris: An Illuminated Souvenir for 1851*, n.p.

35. Weir, *Maternal Affection*, in *The American Juvenile Keepsake*, n.p.

36. *Mother and Infant*, in *Mother's Assistant, and Young Lady's Friend*, n.p.

37. Robins, "On a Mother and Her Infant," *Mother's Assistant and Young Lady's Friend*, 107.

38. Murillo, *The Christian Mother*, in *Godey's Lady's Book*, n.p.

39. Neal, "The Christian Mother," *Godey's Lady's Book*, 67.

40. Lehuu, *Carnival on the Page*, 117.

41. Timbrell, *Maternal Instruction*, in *Godey's Magazine and Lady's Book*, n.p.

42. Andrews and Smith, *Infant Devotion*, in *Rose of Sharon, a Religious Souvenir*, n.p.

43. Leslie, *The Mother*, in *The Gem of the Season*, n.p.

44. Hesse, *Help My Mother*.

45. Witherington, *A Summer Scene for a Winter Month*, in *Godey's Lady's Book*, n.p.

46. Gainsborough, *The Cottage Door*, in *The Lady's Book*, n.p. Variations of this image also appear in numerous giftbooks. See, for instance, *Gift of Friendship* (Lowell, MA, 1848) and *The Amaranth, or Token of Remembrance* (Boston, 1849).

47. Versions of this image appeared in both magazines and giftbooks. See, for example, Sharpe, *The Unlooked for Return*, in *The Lady's Book*, n.p.; Sharpe, *The Unlooked-for Return*, in *The Keepsake*, 27.

48. For more on the popularity of sentimental poetry, see, for example Mary Louise Kete's discussion of *Harriet Gould's Book*, an album of verse written by friends and family for a New England woman in the antebellum period. The album contains original verse as well as copies and adaptations of published poems. Kete, *Sentimental Collaborations*, chap. 1. See also Cavitch, *American Elegy*.

49. P. Bennett, "Not Just Filler and Not Just Sentimental," 202.

50. Okker, *Our Sister Editors*, 140–142. For more on Sarah Josepha Hale's agenda as editor of *Godey's*, see also Sommers, "*Godey's Lady's Book*."

51. Searle, *Season of Maternal Solicitude*, 8.

52. Richardson, *Pamela*, 3:168.

53. Ibid., 300.

54. For a more in-depth discussion of the convergence of female virtue, sexuality, and motherhood in *Pamela*, see Peters, "The Pregnant Pamela."

55. Richardson, *Clarissa*, 706.

56. [Darwin], "Elegant Extracts," *New-Hampshire Sentinel*, 4. See also [Darwin], "Maternal Fondness," *Columbian Phoenix and Boston Review*, 445.

57. "Verses to My First-Born," *Cincinnati Literary Gazette*, 96. See also "Verses to My First Born," *Ladies' Literary Cabinet*, 88.

58. "The Good Mother," *Lady's Weekly Miscellany*, 320. For almost identical imagery, see also "Sonnet, on Divine Providence," *New-York Daily Gazette*, 2.

59. "The Mother to Her Child," *Lady's Weekly Miscellany*, 64.

60. "A Mother's Prayer, on the Birth of Her Child," *Lady's Monthly Museum*, 111.

61. Cist, "A Mother's Love," *Godey's Lady's Book*, 109.

62. M'Cabe, "The Stepmother," *Godey's Lady's Book*, 339.

63. See, for example, Cavitch, *American Elegy*; Frank, *Representations of Death*; D. Henderson, *Grief and Genre*; Kete, *Sentimental Collaborations*.

64. Alcott, "The Morality of Beauty," *Mother's Assistant, and Young Lady's Friend*, 68.

65. Norton, "The English Mother," *The Lady's Book [Godey's]*, 182.

66. Noble, *Masochistic Pleasures*, 32.

67. Carpenter, "A Mother's Smile," in *The Young Ladies' Oasis*, 77.

68. Kilbourn, "To My Mother," *Godey's Lady's Book*, 93.

69. Willis, "Mother's Voice," *Mother's Assistant, and Young Lady's Friend*, 86.

70. Waterman, "My Mother," *Godey's Magazine and Lady's Book*, 45.

71. [Sigourney], "Child at a Mother's Grave," *The Farmers' Cabinet*, 4.

72. Montgomery, "A Mother's Love," *The Christian Journal, and Literary Register*, 379.

73. Sompayrac, "To My Mother in Heaven," *Mother's Assistant, and Young Lady's Friend*, 156.

74. Dyer, "Maternal Love," *Mother's Assistant, and Young Lady's Friend*, 6.

75. Cist, "A Mother's Love," 109.

76. "Autumn Thoughts," 307.

77. "A Mother," *Mother's Assistant, and Young Lady's Friend*, 38.

78. Robins, "On a Mother and Her Infant," 107.

79. "A Mother's Prayer, on the Birth of Her Child," 110–111.

80. Cooley, "My Mother's Good-By," *Godey's Magazine and Lady's Book*, 108.

81. Wolfe, "The Memory of My Mother," *Mother's Magazine and Family Monitor*, 254.

82. This estimate comes from examining the holdings of the Library Company of Philadelphia, which possesses a nearly complete run of the magazine during this time span, for a total of roughly forty volumes (excepting a few missing volumes, each representing six issues).

83. "My Mother's Grave," *Mrs. Whittelsey's Magazine for Mothers and Daughters*, 94.

84. Sigourney, "The Mother's Parting Gift," *Mother's Assistant, and Young Lady's Friend*, 80.

85. Lander, "Baptism of the Dying Mother's Child," *Mother's Magazine and Family Monitor*, 60.

86. "The Women of Philadelphia," in Stanton, Anthony, and Gage, *History of Woman Suffrage*, 1:804.

87. Kirkland, "General Introduction," in Reid, *Woman, Her Education and Influence*, 12.

88. Knill, "A Mother's Prayers," *Mother's Assistant, and Young Lady's Friend*, 6.

89. See, for instance, "Maternal Influence," *The Lady's Book* [*Godey's*], 73.

90. Wise, "The Bereaved Mother," *Mother's Assistant, and Young Lady's Friend*, 7.

91. Noble, *Masochistic Pleasures*, 36.

92. Lehuu, *Carnival on the Page*, 105.

## Chapter Six

1. For more on antislavery giftbooks and their role in fund-raising, see Fritz and Fee, "To Give the Gift of Freedom."

2. Laura Ferguson, introductory material in Basker, *Early American Abolitionists*, 277–278. See also Basker, *Amazing Grace*, xl, 641.

3. "Address to the Heart, on the Subject of American Slavery," *American Museum*, 538.

4. Husband, *Antislavery Discourse*, 1–2.

5. Chaney, *Fugitive Vision*, 23.

6. Bernier, "'Iron Arguments,'" 69.

7. Berlant, "The Female Woman," 269.

8. Husband, *Antislavery Discourse*, 5.

9. Ibid., 16.

10. Wood, *The Poetry of Slavery*, xxiv.

11. The *Liberator*, for instance, which disseminated poetry and prose, was published from 1831 through 1865 and had a circulation of about 2,300 by 1834, with a majority of African American subscribers. See Ripley, *Black Abolitionist Papers*, 3:9. In contrast, mainstream publications such as *Godey's Lady's Book* reached tens of thousands of subscribers. Subscriptions to *Godey's*, for instance, reached around 150,000. See Zuckerman, *Popular Women's Magazines*, 3.

12. Two extensive anthologies testify to the importance of antislavery poetry but have yet to be joined by equally extensive analyses of the poetry and its role in the antislavery movement. See Basker, *Amazing Grace*, and Wood, *The Poetry of Slavery*.

13. Salerno, *Sister Societies*, 17.

14. For more on women's involvement in the antislavery movement, see also Cima, *Performing Anti-slavery*; Jeffrey, *The Great Silent Army of Abolitionism*; Yellin, *Women and Sisters*; Zaeske, *Signatures of Citizenship*.

15. "The Slave Mother," *Liberator* 5, no. 2, January 10, 1835, 8.

16. Russell, "The Slave Mother," in *The Harp of Freedom*, 253.

17. [N.], "The Slave Mother's Appeal," *Zion's Herald*, 1.

18. "The Slave Mother," *Religious Intelligencer*, 375.

19. For a detailed analysis of the mind/body hierarchy and its relation to racial ideology, particularly in the antebellum South, see, for example, Etter, *The Good Body*; Schroeder, *Slave to the Body*.

20. "O, Pity the Slave Mother," in *The Anti-slavery Harp*, 6.

21. Norton, "The English Mother," *The Lady's Book* [*Godey's*], 182.

22. [W. G. K.], "The Slave Mother's Lament for Her Children," *National Era*, 157.

23. Lowell, "The Slave Mother," *Christian Secretary*, 4.

24. "The Slave Mother," *Liberator* 5, no. 2, January 10, 1835, 8.

25. Sigourney, "The Mother," in *Poems*, 85.

26. "O, Pity the Slave Mother," in *The Anti-slavery Harp*, 6.

27. Lowell, "The Slave Mother," *Christian Secretary*, 4.

28. Paulina, "The Slave Mother to Her Child," *National Era*, 121.

29. Goulu, "The Slave Mother's Prayer," *Ladies' Literary Portfolio*, 389.

30. [W. H.], "The Slave-Mother," *Philanthropist*, o_4.

31. Ibid.

32. "The Slave Mother," *Liberator* 5, no. 2, January 10, 1835, 8.

33. "The Slave Mother," *Boston Recorder*, 80.

34. Hutchinson, "The Bereaved Mother," in *The Anti-slavery Harp*, 19.

35. "The Slave Mother," *Liberator* 3, no. 48, November 30, 1833, 192.

36. Burleigh, "The Dying Slave Mother," *Liberty Bell*, 31–36.

37. Eames, "The Slave Mother," *National Era*, 149.

38. Charlotte Elizabeth, "The Slave Mother and Her Babe," *Liberator*, 104.

39. Clark, " 'The Sacred Rights of the Weak,' " 465.

40. Halttunen, "Humanitarianism and the Pornography of Pain," 304.

41. Charlotte Elizabeth, "The Slave Mother and Her Babe," *Liberator*, 104.

42. [W. H.], "The Slave-Mother," *Philanthropist*, o_4.

43. Sorisio, *Fleshing Out America*, 48.

44. Goddu, "Anti-slavery's Panoramic Perspective," 12.

45. Teresa A. Goddu estimates as many as 40,000 depictions of slavery each year during the 1830s. Ibid.

46. Wood, *Black Milk*, 27–28. See also Wood, *Blind Memory*.

47. Goddu, "The Antislavery Almanac," 132.

48. Chaney, *Fugitive Vision*, 6.

49. Goddu, "Anti-slavery's Panoramic Perspective," 12–13.

50. Maurie D. McInnis has shown that depictions of auctions and the separation of families were at the heart of antislavery art and visual culture. See McInnis, *Slaves Waiting for Sale*.

51. "[African American female slave being separated from her children by slave dealers]," in *American Anti-slavery Almanac for 1838*.

52. *Views of Slavery* (broadside) (New York, ca. 1836).

53. "Selling a Mother from Her Child," in *American Anti-slavery Almanac for 1840*, 15.

54. Hutchinson, "The Bereaved Mother," in *The Anti-slavery Harp*, 19.

55. [Cover with illustration], *American Anti-slavery Almanac for 1843*.

56. Lasser, "Voyeuristic Abolitionism."

57. See, for example, "Flogging American Women," in Bourne, *Picture of Slavery*, 100.

58. Bourne, *Picture of Slavery*, 88.

59. Etter, *The Good Body*, 87.

60. Sorisio, *Fleshing Out America*. For more on race, gender, and the body, see, for example, Gould, *The Mismeasure of Man*; Schroeder, *Slave to the Body*.

## Conclusion

1. April 13, 1756, in Burr, *The Journal of Esther Edwards Burr*, 192.

2. Hannah Heath to Ann White, January 23, 1796, Letterbook, Hannah Williams Heath Diaries, 1805–1832, permission of MHS.

3. Sarah Preston (Everett) Hale to Alexander and Lucretia Everett, September 14, 1822, folder 6, box 9, Hale Family Papers, 1787–1988, SSC.

4. Gertrude Gouverneur Ogden Meredith to William Meredith, February 26, 1797, folder 1, box 51, Meredith Family Papers, HSP, and April 16, 1854, folder 1, Jane Evans Elliot Diaries, 1837–1882, SHC.

5. January 27, 1784, vol. 13, p. 5, Sarah Logan Fisher Diaries, HSP.

6. For birthrate statistics, see D'Emilio and Freedman, *Intimate Matters*, 58. See also Leavitt, *Brought to Bed*, 19.

7. Theriot, *Mothers and Daughters*, 81–82.

8. Saur, *Maternity*, 195.

9. Duffey, *What Women Should Know*, 117.

10. For more on the philosophy of voluntary motherhood, see Gordon, *Woman's Body, Woman's Right*.

11. For more on contraceptive technology and availability, see D'Emilio and Freedman, *Intimate Matters*, esp. pt. 2.

12. Quoted in Leavitt, *Brought to Bed*, 33.

13. Quoted in Wertz and Wertz, *Lying-In*, 118.

14. Wortham, "Facebook Won't Budge on Breastfeeding Photos."

15. See, for example, Cindy Stearns's discussion of sexuality and motherhood in "Breastfeeding and the Good Maternal Body," 309.

16. "Breastfeeding Laws," National Conference of State Legislatures.

17. Stearns, "Breastfeeding and the Good Maternal Body," 311.

18. Marty, online comment, January 2, 2009.

19. Roberts, *Killing the Black Body*.

20. "Modern Family."

21. Ostriker, *The Mother/Child Papers*, 33.

22. Olds, "The Language of the Brag," in *Satan Says*, 44–45.

23. Pollock, *Telling Bodies Performing Birth*, 29.

# Bibliography

Unpublished Archival Sources

American Antiquarian Society, Worcester, Massachusetts
  Higginson-Lee Family Correspondence, 1825–1840
Harvard Fine Arts Library, Harvard University, Cambridge, Massachusetts
  *Woman Breast-Feeding Her Infant*. Visual Collections-Slides and Digital Images,
    PAA82 1843A 70(a)
Historical Society of Pennsylvania, Philadelphia, Pennsylvania
  James Anderson Casebook, 1804–1806
  Ball Family Papers
  Biddle and Craig Family Papers
  Samuel Worcester Butler Record Book, 1849–1858
  Sarah Logan Fisher Diaries
  Fox Family Papers
  Logan-Fisher-Fox Family Papers
  Meredith Family Papers
  Benjamin Rush, Medical Notes, 1804–1809
  Rebecca Shoemaker Papers, 1780–1786
  Ann Head Warder Papers
Massachusetts Historical Society, Boston, Massachusetts
  Mehitable Sullivan Cutler Amory Diaries
  Eliza Nevins Townsend Bellows Diary, 1843–1846
  Persis Sibley Andrews Black Diaries, 1842–1864
  Walter Channing Papers, 1800–1872
  Hannah Williams Heath Diaries, 1805–1832
  John Lowell Papers, 1808–1851
  Elizabeth Cranch Norton Diaries, 1781–1811
  Diary of Experience (Wight) Richardson, Sudbury, Massachusetts, 1728–1782
    Transcribed and compiled by Ellen (Richardson) Glueck and Thelma
    (Smith) Ernst, 1978
  Lydia Smith Russell Diary, 1818
  Townsend Family Papers, 1676–1877
Rubenstein Rare Book and Manuscript Library, Duke University, Durham,
    North Carolina
  Campbell Family Papers
  Juliana Paisley Gilmer Diary, 1840–1850

Louis Manigault Papers

Turner Family Papers, 1778–1929

Schlesinger Library, Radcliffe Institute, Harvard University, Cambridge, Massachusetts

Maria Magdalen Flagg Letters

*Portrait of Unidentified Woman Breastfeeding a Baby*, ca. 1848, PC136-1z

*Portrait of Unidentified Woman Breastfeeding a Baby*, ca. 1850, PC140-1z

*Portrait of an Unidentified Woman Breastfeeding a Baby*, ca. 1860s, PC140-4z

*Unidentified Woman Breastfeeding a Baby*, ca. 1860, PC140-2z

Small Special Collections Library, University of Virginia, Charlottesville, Virginia

Papers of Robert S. Brooke

Cabell-Carrington Papers

Papers of John Hartwell Cocke / Papers of the Cocke Family

Correspondence of Ellen Wayles Randolph Coolidge

Diary of Martha Tabb Watkins Dyer

Sophia Smith Collection, Smith College, Northampton, Massachusetts

Hale Family Papers, 1787–1988

Peabody Family Papers, 1820–1853

South Carolina Historical Society, Charleston, South Carolina

Caroline Howard Gilman Papers, 1810–1880

Hering Family Papers, 1674–1960

Erastus Hopkins Correspondence, 1834–1838

Ann Heatly Reid Lovell, Estate and Family Papers, 1780–1854

South Caroliniana Library, University of South Carolina, Columbia, South Carolina

Cox-Chesnut Family Papers, 1792–1858

Cox Family Papers

Glover Family Papers.

Read Family, 1766–1843

Southern Historical Collection, University of North Carolina, Chapel Hill, North Carolina

Penelope Eliza Howard Alderman Diary, 1851–1856

Charles William Bradbury Papers

Cameron Family Papers, 1757–1978

Caroline Elizabeth Burgwin Clitherall Diaries

Jane Evans Elliot Diaries, 1837–1882

Ernest Haywood Collection

Kennedy, Moore, and Southgate Family Papers

Ker Family Papers, 1776–1996

Caroline Olivia Laurens Diary, 1823–1827

Elizabeth Frances Perry Diary

Pettigrew Family Papers, 1776–1926

Eliza Ann Marsh Robertson Papers, 1843–1872

Skinner Family Papers

Virginia Historical Society, Richmond, Virginia

Sarah Scarborough Butler Henry French Papers, 1824–1914

Laura Henrietta Wirt Randall Papers, 1819–1857

Robertson Family Papers, 1818–1820

## Published Primary Sources

Abbott, John S. C. *The Mother at Home; or, the Principles of Maternal Duty Familiarly Illustrated.* Reprinted in *Family in America*, edited by David J. Rothman and Sheila M. Rothman. New York: Arno Press and the New York Times, 1972.

Adams, Abigail. *New Letters of Abigail Adams, 1788–1801.* Edited by Steward Mitchell. Boston: Houghton Mifflin, 1947.

"Address to the Heart, on the Subject of American Slavery." *The American Museum; or, Repository of Ancient and Modern Fugitive Pieces* 1, no. 6, June 1787, 538. ProQuest: American Periodicals Series.

"The Advantage of Maternal Nurture." *Lady's Magazine and Musical Repository* 2, November 1801, 290–291.

"The Advantages of Maternal Nurture." *Ladies' Monthly Museum*, 1799, 183–185.

"[African American female slave being separated from her children by slave dealers]." In *American Anti-slavery Almanac for 1838.* Boston: Webster and Southard, 1838. Schomburg Center for Research in Black Culture, Manuscripts, Archives and Rare Books Division, New York Public Library. New York Public Library Digital Collections. Accessed October 16, 2015. http://digitalcollections.nypl.org/items/510d47da-7590-a3d9-e040-e00a18064a99.

Agate, Frederick Styles, artist. *The Dead Boy.* In *Christian Keepsake and Missionary Annual*, edited by John A. Clark, n.p. Philadelphia; New York: William Marshall and Co.; Sherman and Trevett, at the Protestant Episcopal Press, 1838.

Aitken, John. *Principles of Midwifery, or Puerperal Medicine.* 2nd ed. Edinburgh, 1785.

Alcott, William A. "The Morality of Beauty." *Mother's Assistant, and Young Lady's Friend, and Family Journal*, no. 3, March 1841, 68–70.

———. *The Young Mother, or Management of Children in Regard to Health.* 2nd ed. Boston: Light and Stearns, 1836.

Allen, Ann H. *The Young Mother and Nurse's Oracle: For the Benefit of the Uninitiated.* Cincinnati: E. Mendenhall, 1858.

[Cover with illustration]. *American Anti-slavery Almanac for 1843.* New York: American Anti-slavery Society, 1843. Schomburg Center for Research in Black Culture, Manuscripts, Archives and Rare Books Division, New York Public Library. New York Public Library Digital Collections. Accessed October 16, 2015. http://digitalcollections.nypl.org/items/510d47da-753a-a3d9-e040-e00a18064a99.

Andrews, J., and H. W. Smith. *Infant Devotion.* In *Rose of Sharon, a Religious Souvenir,* edited by Mrs. C. M. Sawyer, n.p. Boston: A. Tompkins and B. B. Mussey and Co., 1850.

*Aristotle's Compleat Masterpiece. In Three Parts; Displaying the Secrets of Nature in the Generation of Man.* 23rd ed. London: Booksellers, 1749.

"Autumn Thoughts." *The Boston Literary Magazine* 1, no. 7, November 1832, 307–308.

Bakewell, Mrs. J. *The Mother's Practical Guide in the Early Training of Her Children Containing Directions for Their Physical, Intellectual, and Moral Education.* New York: G. Lane and P. P. Sandford, 1843.

Ballard, Martha. *The Diary of Martha Ballard, 1785–1812.* Edited by Robert R. McCausland and Cynthia MacAlman McCausland. Rockport, ME: Picton Press, 1992.

Bard, Samuel. *A Compendium of the Theory and Practice of Midwifery.* 5th ed. New York: Collins and Co., 1819.

Barwell, Louisa Mary Bacon. *Advice to Mothers on the Treatment of Infants: With Directions for Self-Management before, during, and after Pregnancy.* Philadelphia: Leary and Getz, 1853.

Basker, James G., ed. *Amazing Grace: An Anthology of Poems about Slavery, 1660–1810.* New Haven, CT: Yale University Press, 2002.

———. *Early American Abolitionists: A Collection of Anti-slavery Writings, 1760–1820.* New York: Gilder Lehrman Institute of American History, 2005.

Beach, Wooster. *An Improved System of Midwifery.* New York, 1851.

Bedford, Gunning S. *Clinical Lectures on the Diseases of Women and Children.* New York: Samual S. and W. Wood, 1855.

Beecher, Catharine E. *A Treatise on Domestic Economy, for the Use of Young Ladies at Home and at School.* Boston: Marsh, Capen, Lyon, and Webb, 1841.

Bell, Charles. *The Anatomy of the Brain, Explained in a Series of Engravings.* London: C. Whittingham, 1802.

Bichat, Xavier. *General Anatomy, Applied to Physiology and Medicine.* Translated by George Hayward. Boston: Richardson and Lord, 1822.

Bourne, George. *Picture of Slavery in the United States of America.* Middletown, CT: Edwin Hunt, 1834. Reprint. Detroit: Negro History Press, 1972.

"Breastfeeding Laws." National Conference of State Legislatures. Accessed August 1, 2016, http://www.ncsl.org/issues-research/health/breastfeeding-state-laws.aspx.

Buchan, William. *Advice to Mothers; on the Subject of Their Own Health; and of the Means of Promoting the Health, Strength, and Beauty of Their Offspring.* 1803. Boston: Joseph Bumstead, 1809.

———. *Domestic Medicine: or a Treatise on the Prevention and Cure of Diseases.* 8th ed. London: W. Strahan, 1784.

Bull, Thomas. *Hints to Mothers, for the Management of Health during the Period of Pregnancy, and in the Lying-in Room; with an Exposure of Popular Errors in Connexion with Those Subjects.* From the 3rd London ed. New York: Wiley and Putnam, 1842.

Burleigh, G. S. "The Dying Slave Mother." *The Liberty Bell*, January 1, 1842, 31–36.

Burns, John. *The Anatomy of the Gravid Uterus, with Practical Inferences Relative to Pregnancy and Labour.* Glasgow: University Press, 1799.

———. *The Principles of Midwifery; Including the Diseases of Women and Children.* 9th ed. London: Longman, Orme, Brown, Green, and Longmans, 1837.

Burr, Esther Edwards. *The Journal of Esther Edwards Burr, 1754–1757.* Edited by Laurie Crumpacker and Carol F. Karlsen. New Haven, CT: Yale University Press, 1984.

Burton, John. *An Essay towards a Complete New System of Midwifery, Theoretical and Practical.* London, 1751.

Butler, Charles. *The American Lady.* Philadelphia: Hogan and Thompson, 1849.

Cadogan, William. *An Essay upon Nursing and the Management of Children, from Their Birth to Three Years of Age.* Reprinted in *Three Treatises on Child Rearing.* New York: Garland, 1985.

Calhoun, Jeff. "Ex-Slave Stories (Texas)." *Texas Narratives*, vol. 16, pt. 1, 188–190. Born in Slavery: Slave Narratives from the Federal Writers' Project, 1936–1938. Library of Congress. http://memory.loc.gov/ammem/snhtml/snhome.html.

Calvert, Rosalie Stier. *Mistress of Riversdale: The Plantation Letters of Rosalie Stier Calvert, 1795–1821.* Edited and translated by Margaret Law Callcott. Baltimore: Johns Hopkins University Press, 1991.

Carpenter. "A Mother's Smile." In *The Young Ladies' Oasis: or, Gems of Prose and Poetry*, edited by N. L. Ferguson, 77. Lowell, MA: Nathaniel L. Dayton, 1852.

Charlotte Elizabeth. "The Slave Mother and Her Babe." *Liberator* 14, no. 26, June 28, 1844, 104. ProQuest: American Periodicals Series.

Child, Lydia Maria. *The Mother's Book.* Boston: Carter, Hendee and Babcock, 1831.

Cist, Lewis J. "A Mother's Love." *Godey's Lady's Book* 20, March 1840, 109.

Classified advertisement. *Boston News-Letter*, November 15–22, 1714, no. 553:2. Readex: America's Historical Newspapers.

Classified advertisement. *Independent Ledger*, August 14, 1780, 3, no. 114:3. Readex: America's Historical Newspapers.

Classified advertisement. *New York Daily Advertiser*, January 30, 1795, no. 3108:4. Readex: America's Historical Newspapers.

Classified advertisement. *New York Gazette, and Weekly Mercury*, February 12, 1770, no. 955:4. Readex: America's Historical Newspapers.

Classified advertisement. *Southern Patriot* [Charleston, SC], January 23, 1846, 55, no. 8264:3. . Readex: America's Historical Newspapers.

*The Compleat Midwifes Practice Enlarged.* London: H. Rhodes, J. Philips, J. Taylor, and K. Bentley, 1698. Early English Books Online: Text Creation Partnership. Accessed March 18, 2016. http://name.umdl.umich.edu/A53913.0001.001.

Cooley, Thomas M. "My Mother's Good-By." *Godey's Magazine and Lady's Book* 29, September 1844, 108.

Corbould, Edward Henry, painter, and Alfred Heath, engraver. *The Mother and Babe.* In *The Iris: An Illuminated Souvenir for 1851*, edited by John S. Hart, n.p. Philadelphia: Lippincott, Grambo, and Co., 1850.

Cox, Margaret. *Claims of the Country on American Females*. Vol. 2. Columbus: I. N. Whiting, 1842.

Culpeper, Nicholas. *A Directory for Midwives or, a Guide for Women, in their Conception, Bearing, and Suckling their Children*. London: Peter Cole, 1651.

——. *A Directory for Midwives, or a Guide for Women, in Their Conception, Bearing, and Suckling Their Children*. London: John Streater, 1671. Wellcome Library, London. Accessed March 28, 2016. http://wellcomeimages.org /indexplus/image/L0046155.html.

Curtis, Caroline G., ed. *The Cary Letters*. Cambridge: Riverside Press, 1891.

Dall, Caroline Healey. *Daughter of Boston: The Extraordinary Diary of a Nineteenth-Century Woman*. Edited by Helen R. Deese. Boston: Beacon Press, 2005.

Darton, William. *A Present for a Little Girl*. Philadelphia: Jacob Johnson, 1804. Readex: Early American Imprints, Series 2: Shaw-Shoemaker.

Darwin, Erasmus. *The Botanic Garden*. 2nd American ed. New York: T. and J. Swords, 1807.

——. "Elegant Extracts: From Darwin." *New-Hampshire Sentinel* 4, no. 176, July 31, 1802, 4. Readex. America's Historical Newspapers.

——. "Maternal Fondness." *The Columbian Phenix and Boston Review* 1, July 1800, 445. ProQuest: American Periodicals Series.

Dawbarn, Mrs. *The Rights of Infants, or, a Letter from a Mother to a Daughter Relative to the Nursing of Infants*. Wisbech, UK: John White, 1805.

Denman, Thomas. *An Introduction to the Practice of Midwifery*. Brattleborough, VT: William Fessenden, 1807.

Dewees, William Potts. *A Compendious System of Midwifery, Chiefly Designed to Facilitate the Inquiries of Those Who May Be Pursuing This Branch of Study*. Philadelphia: Carey and Lea, 1832.

——. *An Essay on the Means of Lessening Pain and Facilitating Certain Cases of Difficult Parturition*. Philadelphia: Thomas Dobson and Son, 1819.

——. *A Treatise on the Diseases of Females*. Philadelphia: H. C. Carey and I. Lea, 1826.

——. *A Treatise on the Physical and Medical Treatment of Children*, 3rd ed. Philadelphia: Carey, Lea and Carey, 1829.

Dix, J. Ross. "Help My Mother." *Godey's Magazine and Lady's Book* 30, January 1845, 38.

Dow, George Francis, ed. *The Holyoke Diaries, 1709–1856*. Salem, MA: Essex Institute, 1911.

Drinker, Elizabeth Sandwith. *The Diary of Elizabeth Drinker: The Life Cycle of an Eighteenth-Century Woman*. 3 vols. Edited by Elaine Forman Crane. Boston: Northeastern University Press, 1994.

Drury, Clifford Merrill, ed. *First White Women over the Rockies: Diaries, Letters, and Biographical Sketches of the Six Women of the Oregon Mission Who Made the Overland Journey in 1836 and 1838*. Vol. 1, *Mrs. Marcus Whitman,*

*Mrs. Henry H. Spalding, Mrs. William H. Gray, and Mrs. Asa B. Smith.* Glendale, CA: Arthur H. Clark Co., 1963.

——. *First White Women over the Rockies: Diaries, Letters, and Biographical Sketches of the Six Women of the Oregon Mission Who Made the Overland Journey in 1836 and 1838.* Vol. 2, *Mrs. Elkanah Walker and Mrs. Cushing Eells.* Glendale, CA: Arthur H. Clark Co., 1963.

Duffey, Mrs. E. B. *What Women Should Know: A Woman's Book about Women.* Reprinted in *Sex, Marriage and Society,* edited by Charles Rosenberg and Carroll Smith-Rosenberg. New York: Arno Press, 1974.

Dyer, Rev. E. P. "Maternal Love." *The Mother's Assistant, and Young Lady's Friend,* January 1850, 6.

Eames, E. Jessup. "The Slave Mother." *National Era* 9, no. 455, September 20, 1855, 149. ProQuest: American Periodicals Series.

"The Empty Cradle." *Godey's Magazine and Lady's Book* 34, January 1847, 12.

Estienne, Charles. *De dissectione partium corporis humani libri tres.* Parisiis [Paris]: Apud Simonem Colinaeum, 1545.

Ewell, Thomas. *Letters to Ladies, Detailing Important Information, concerning Themselves and Infants.* Philadelphia: Printed for the Author, 1817.

Fowler, Orson Squire. *Love and Parentage, Applied to the Improvement of Offspring.* 13th ed. New York: Fowlers and Wells, 1850.

——. *Maternity, or the Bearing and Nursing of Children.* New York: Fowler and Wells, 1848.

Fox, Tryphena. *A Northern Woman in the Plantation South: Letters of Tryphena Blanche Holder Fox, 1856–1876.* Edited by Wilma King. Columbia: University of South Carolina Press, 1993.

Gainsborough, Thomas, artist, and Thomas Kelly, engraver. *The Cottage Door.* In *The Lady's Book* 4, March 1832, n.p.

"The Good Mother." *Lady's Weekly Miscellany* 7, no. 20, September 10, 1808, 320. ProQuest: American Periodicals Series.

Goodrich, Samuel Griswold. *Peter Parley's Winter Evening Tales.* Boston: S. G. Goodrich and Co., 1830.

Goulu, Hannah F. "The Slave Mother's Prayer." *The Ladies' Literary Portfolio: A General Miscellany Devoted to the Fine Arts and Sciences* 1, no. 49, November 18, 1829, 389. ProQuest: American Periodicals Series.

Grayson, Mary. *Oklahoma Narratives.* Vol. 13, 115–123. Born in Slavery: Slave Narratives from the Federal Writers' Project, 1936–1938. Library of Congress. http://memory.loc.gov/ammem/snhtml/snhome.html.

Greeley, Sim. "Stories of Ex-Slaves." *South Carolina Narratives.* Vol. 14, pt. 2, 190–194. Born in Slavery: Slave Narratives from the Federal Writers' Project, 1936–1938. Library of Congress. http://memory.loc.gov/ammem/snhtml/snhome.html.

Gregory, George. *Medical Morals.* New York, 1853. Reprinted in *The Male Mid-wife and the Female Doctor: The Gynecology Controversy in Nineteenth-Century America.* New York: Arno Press, 1974.

Gregory, Samuel. *Letters to Ladies, in Favor of Female Physicians.* Boston, 1850. Reprinted in *The Male Mid-wife and the Female Doctor: The Gynecology Controversy in Nineteenth-Century America.* New York: Arno Press, 1974.

———. *Man-Midwifery Exposed and Corrected.* Boston, 1848. Reprinted in *The Male Mid-wife and the Female Doctor: The Gynecology Controversy in Nineteenth-Century America.* New York: Arno Press, 1974.

Hamilton, Alexander. *A Treatise of Midwifery, Comprehending the Management of Female Complaints, and the Treatment of Children in Early Infancy.* London: J. Murray, 1781.

Hamilton, James. *A Collection of Engravings, Designed to Facilitate the Study of Midwifery, Explained and Illustrated.* London: G. G. and J. Robinson, 1796.

Harrison, Eliza Cope, ed. *Best Companions: Letters of Eliza Middleton Fisher and Her Mother, Mary Hering Middleton, from Charleston, Philadelphia, and Newport, 1839–1846.* Columbia: University of South Carolina Press, 2001.

Heaton, Hannah. *The World of Hannah Heaton: The Diary of an Eighteenth-Century New England Farm Woman.* Edited by Barbara E. Lacey. DeKalb: Northern Illinois University Press, 2003.

Hesse, A., artist, and H. S. Sadd, engraver. *Help My Mother.* In *Godey's Magazine and Lady's Book* 30, January 1845, n.p.

Heywood, Martha Spence. *Not by Bread Alone: The Journal of Martha Spence Heywood, 1850–1856.* Edited by Juanita Brooks. Salt Lake City: Utah State Historical Society, 1978.

Hollick, Frederick. *The Matron's Manual of Midwifery, and the Diseases of Women during Pregnancy and in Child Bed.* New York: T. S. Strong, 1848.

Howard, Horton. *A Treatise on Midwifery and the Diseases of Women and Children; Adapted to the Use of Heads of Families, and Females Particularly.* Cincinnati: J. Kost, 1852.

Howell, Josephine. *Arkansas Narratives.* Vol. 2, pt. 3, 339–340. Born in Slavery: Slave Narratives from the Federal Writers' Project, 1936–1938. Library of Congress. http://memory.loc.gov/ammem/snhtml/snhome.html.

Hume, Sophia. *An Exhortation to the Inhabitants of the Province of South-Carolina, to Bring Their Deeds to the Light of Christ in Their Own Consciences.* London: Luke Hinde, 1752.

Hunter, William. *The Anatomy of the Human Gravid Uterus.* Birmingham, UK, 1774.

Hutchinson, Ida Blackshear. *Arkansas Narratives.* Vol. 2, pt. 3, 369–378. Born in Slavery: Slave Narratives from the Federal Writers' Project, 1936–1938. Library of Congress. http://memory.loc.gov/ammem/snhtml/snhome.html.

Hutchinson, J. "The Bereaved Mother." In *The Anti-slavery Harp; a Collection of Songs for Anti-slavery Meetings*, edited by William Wells Brown, 19. Boston: Bela March, 1848.

Jacobs, Harriet. *Incidents in the Life of a Slave Girl.* Mineola, NY: Dover Publications, 2001. First published 1861.

Jenty, Charles. *The Demonstrations of a Pregnant Uterus of a Woman at Her Full Term*. London: Fetter Lane, 1757.

Kammen, Carol, ed. "The Letters of Calista Hall." *New York History* 63, no. 9, April 1982, 209–234.

Keckley, Elizabeth. *Behind the Scenes, or, Thirty Years a Slave, and Four Years in the White House*. New York: G. W. Carleton and Co., 1868.

Kemble, Frances Anne. *Journal of a Residence on a Georgian Plantation in 1838–1839*. Edited by John A. Scott. Athens: University of Georgia Press, 1984.

Kendrick, Asahel C., ed. *The Life and Letters of Mrs. Emily C. Judson*. New York: Sheldon and Co., 1860.

Kilbourn, P. Kenyon. "To My Mother." *Godey's Lady's Book* 26, February 1843, 93.

Kirkland, Mrs. C. M. "General Introduction." In *Woman, Her Education and Influence*, by Mrs. Hugo Reid, 9–29. New York: Fowlers and Wells, 1848.

Knill, Richard. "A Mother's Prayers." *The Mother's Assistant, and Young Lady's Friend* 1, no. 1, January 1841, 6.

Lamb, Charles. "The Gipsy's Malison." In *The Gem of the Season*, 122. New York: Leavitt, Trow and Co., 1848.

Lander, Meta. "Baptism of the Dying Mother's Child." *Mother's Magazine and Family Monitor* 19, 1851, 60.

Leslie, C. R., artist, and John Sartain, engraver. *The Mother*. In *The Gem of the Season*, n.p. New York: Leavitt, Trow, and Co., 1848.

Lewis, Eleanor Parke Custis. *George Washington's Beautiful Nelly: The Letters of Eleanor Parke Custis Lewis to Elizabeth Bordley Gibson, 1794–1851*. Edited by Patricia Brady. Columbia: University of South Carolina Press, 2006.

*The London Practice of Midwifery, or, a Manual for Students*. London: James Wallis, 1803.

Longfellow, Fanny Appleton. *Mrs. Longfellow: Selected Letters and Journals of Fanny Appleton Longfellow*. Edited by Edward Wagenknecht. New York: Longmans, Green, 1956.

Lowell, Maria. "The Slave Mother." *Christian Secretary* 24, no. 45, January 16, 1846, 4. ProQuest: American Periodicals Series, 1846.

MacDonald, Edgar E., ed. *The Education of the Heart: The Correspondence of Rachel Mordecai Lazarus and Maria Edgeworth*. Chapel Hill: University of North Carolina Press, 1977.

Mackenzie, Sir Alexander. *Voyages from Montreal, on the River St. Lawrence, through the Continent of North America, to the Frozen and Pacific Oceans in the Years 1789 and 1793*. Philadelphia: John Morgan, 1802. Readex: Early American Imprints, Series 2: Shaw-Shoemaker.

Marty. Online comment. January 2, 2009. Response to Jenna Wortham, "Facebook Won't Budge on Breastfeeding Photos," *New York Times*, January 2, 2009. Accessed August 1, 2016. http://bits.blogs.nytimes.com/2009/01/02 /breastfeeding-facebook-photos/#.

"Maternal Influence." *The Lady's Book* [*Godey's*] 11, July 1835, 73.

Mauriceau, François. *Traité des maladies des femmes grosses*. 2nd ed. Paris, 1675.

M'Cabe, Jonathan C. "The Stepmother." *Godey's Lady's Book* 24, June 1842, 339.

Mears, Martha. *The Pupil of Nature; or Candid Advice to the Fair Sex*. London, 1797.

Meigs, Charles D. *Obstetrics: The Science and the Art*. 2nd ed. Philadelphia: Blanchard and Lea, 1852.

Merriman, Samuel. *A Synopsis of the Various Kinds of Difficult Parturition, with Practical Remarks on the Management of Labours*. 2nd ed. London: J. Callow, 1814.

"Modern Family." *Fit Pregnancy*. Weider Publications, 2011. Accessed August 1, 2016. http://www.fitpregnancy.com/motherhood/motherhood/modern-family.

Montgomery. "A Mother's Love." *The Christian Journal, and Literary Register* 3, no. 12, December 1, 1819, 379. ProQuest: American Periodicals Series.

Moss, William. *An Essay on the Management and Nursing of Children in the Earlier Periods of Infancy, and on the Treatment and Rule of Conduct Requisite for the Mother during Pregnancy, and Lying-In*. London: J. Johnson, 1781.

"A Mother." *The Mother's Assistant, and Young Lady's Friend* 1, no. 2, February 1841, 38.

*Mother and Infant* (engraving). In *The Mother's Assistant, and Young Lady's Friend* 8, no. 5, May 1846, n.p.

"A Mother's Prayer, on the Birth of Her Child." *The Lady's Monthly Museum or Polite Repository of Amusement and Instruction* 8, February 1810, 110–111.

"The Mother to Her Child." *Lady's Weekly Miscellany* 7, no. 4, May 21, 1808, 64. ProQuest: American Periodicals Series.

Murillo, Bartolomé Esteban, artist, and Rice and Butter, engravers. *The Christian Mother*. In *Godey's Lady's Book* 41, August 1850, n.p.

"My Mother's Grave." *Mrs. Whittelsey's Magazine for Mothers and Daughters* 2, 1851, 94.

[N.]. "The Slave Mother's Appeal." *Zion's Herald* 8, no. 15, April 12, 1837, 1. ProQuest: American Periodicals Series.

Neal, Alice B. "The Christian Mother." *Godey's Lady's Book* 41, August 1850, 67.

Neblett, Elizabeth Scott. *A Rebel Wife in Texas: The Diary and Letters of Elizabeth Scott Neblett, 1852–1864*. Edited by Erika L. Murr. Baton Rouge: Louisiana State University Press, 2001.

Nihell, Elizabeth. *Treatise on the Art of Midwifery*. New York: Classics of Obstetrics and Gynecology Library, 1994.

Norton, Mrs. "The English Mother." *The Lady's Book* [*Godey's*] 3, September 1831, 182.

*The Nurse's Guide: or, the Right Method of Bringing Up Young Children*. London, 1729. Reprinted in *Three Treatises on Child Rearing*. New York: Garland, 1985.

Olds, Sharon. "The Language of the Brag." In *Satan Says*, 44–45. Pittsburgh: University of Pittsburgh Press, 1980.

"O, Pity the Slave Mother." In *The Anti-slavery Harp; a Collection of Songs for Anti-slavery Meetings*, edited by William Wells Brown, 6. Boston: Bela March, 1848.

Ostriker, Alicia Suskin. *The Mother/Child Papers.* Boston: Beacon Press, 1980.

Paulina. "The Slave Mother to Her Child." *National Era* 4, no. 31, August 1, 1850, 121. ProQuest: American Periodicals Series.

Ramsbotham, Francis Henry. *The Principles and Practice of Obstetric Medicine and Surgery.* Philadelphia: Lea and Blanchard, 1843.

Raynalde, Thomas, trans. *The Birth of Mankind, Otherwise Called, the Woman's Book.* 4th ed. London, 1654.

Rich, Adrienne. *Of Woman Born: Motherhood as Experience and Institution.* New York: W. W. Norton, 1986.

Richardson, Samuel. *Clarissa; or, The History of a Young Lady.* Edited by Angus Ross. Harmondsworth, Middlesex: Penguin Books, 1985.

———. *Pamela: or, Virtue Rewarded.* Vol. 3. London: C. Rivington and J. Osborn, 1742.

———. *Pamela: or, Virtue Rewarded.* Vol. 4. London: W. Strahan, 1785.

Ripley, C. Peter, ed. *The Black Abolitionist Papers.* 5 vols. Chapel Hill: University of North Carolina Press, 1985.

Robins, Mr. E. W. "On a Mother and Her Infant." *The Mother's Assistant and Young Lady's Friend* 6, no. 6, 1845, 107.

Robinson, Celia. *North Carolina Narratives.* Vol. 11, pt. 2, 216–219. Born in Slavery: Slave Narratives from the Federal Writers' Project, 1936–1938. Library of Congress. http://memory.loc.gov/ammem/snhtml/snhome.html.

Rogers, Hattie. *North Carolina Narratives.* Vol. 11, pt. 2, 226–231. Born in Slavery: Slave Narratives from the Federal Writers' Project, 1936–1938. Library of Congress. http://memory.loc.gov/ammem/snhtml/snhome.html.

Rousseau, Jean-Jacques. *Emile.* 1762. Translated by Barbara Foxley. London, 1966.

Rueff, Jacob. *De conceptu et generatione hominis.* Frankfurt, 1580.

Russell, George. "The Slave Mother." In *The Harp of Freedom*, edited by George W. Clark, 252–253. New York: Miller, Orton, and Mulligan, 1856.

Sansom, Hannah Callender. *The Diary of Hannah Callender Sansom: Sense and Sensibility in the Age of the American Revolution.* Edited by Susan E. Klepp and Karin Wulf. Ithaca, NY: Cornell University Press, 2010.

Saur, Mrs. P. B. *Maternity: A Book for Every Wife and Mother.* Chicago: L. P. Miller and Co., 1891. First published 1888.

Seaman, Valentine. *The Midwives Monitor and Mothers Mirror: Being Three Concluding Lectures of a Course of Instruction on Midwifery.* New York: Isaac Collins, 1800. Readex: Early American Imprints, Series 1: Evans.

Searle, Thomas. *A Companion for the Season of Maternal Solicitude.* New York: Moore and Payne, Collins and Hannay, 1834.

*Selling a Mother from Her Child.* In *American Anti-slavery Almanac for 1840*, 15. Boston: Webster and Southard, 1840. Schomburg Center for Research in Black Culture, Manuscripts, Archives and Rare Books Division, New York Public Library. New York Public Library Digital Collections. Accessed October 16, 2015. http://digitalcollections.nypl.org/items/510d47da-7532-a3d9-e040 -e00a18064a99.

Sharp, Jane. *The Compleat Midwife's Companion: Or, the Art of Midwifry Improv'd* (London: J. Marshall, 1724), 97. Wellcome Images. Accessed April 4, 2017. https://wellcomeimages.org/.

——. *The Compleat Midwife's Companion: Or, the Art of Midwifry Improv'd.* 4th ed. London: John Marshall, 1725.

Sharpe, Louisa, artist. *The Unlooked for Return.* In *The Lady's Book* 7, November 1833, n.p.

Sharpe, Louisa, artist, and Joseph Goodyear, engraver. *The Unlooked-for Return.* In *The Keepsake*, 27. London: Longman, 1833.

Sigourney, Lydia H. "Child at a Mother's Grave." *The Farmers' Cabinet* 34, no. 22, January 29, 1836, 4.

——. *Letters to Mothers.* 2nd ed. New York: Harper and Brothers, 1839.

——. "The Mother." In *Poems*, 85. Philadelphia: Key and Biddle, 1834.

——. "The Mother's Parting Gift." *The Mother's Assistant, and Young Lady's Friend* 9, no. 4, October 1846, 80.

——. "The Mother's Sacrifice." *The Mother's Assistant and Young Lady's Friend* 1, no. 10, October 1841, 222.

Sims, J. Marion. *The Story of My Life.* New York: D. Appleton and Co., 1885.

"The Slave Mother." *Boston Recorder* 19, no. 20, May 17, 1834, 80. ProQuest: American Periodicals Series.

"The Slave Mother." *Liberator* 3, no. 48, November 30, 1833, 192. ProQuest: American Periodicals Series.

"The Slave Mother." *Liberator* 5, no. 2, January 10, 1835, 8. ProQuest: American Periodicals Series.

"The Slave Mother." *The Religious Intelligencer* 2, November 12, 1836, 375. ProQuest: American Periodicals Series.

Smellie, William. *A Set of Anatomical Tables, and an Abridgment of the Practice of Midwifery.* Edinburgh: Charles Elliot; London: C. Elliot and T. Kay, 1790.

——. *A Treatise on the Theory and Practice of Midwifery.* 4th ed. London: D. Wilson and T. Durham, 1762.

Smith, Hugh. *Letters to Married Women on Nursing and the Management of Children.* 6th ed. London: C. and G. Kearsley, 1792.

Smith, Mrs. Seba. "Anxious Mothers." *The Mother's Assistant and Young Lady's Friend* 2, no. 12, 1842, 265–266.

Sompayrac, Mrs. P. P. "To My Mother in Heaven." *The Mother's Assistant, and Young Lady's Friend*, June 1851, 156.

"Sonnet, on Divine Providence." *New-York Daily Gazette*, no. 390, March 27, 1790, 2. Readex: America's Historical Newspapers.

Sproat, Nancy. *Ditties for Children. By a Lady of Boston.* Philadelphia: Johnson and Warner, 1813. Readex: Early American Imprints, Series 2: Shaw-Shoemaker.

Stevens, John. *Man-Midwifery Exposed, or The Danger and Immorality of Employing Men in Midwifery Proved, and the Remedy for the Evil Found.* London: William Horsell, 1849.

Stone, Sarah. *A Complete Practice of Midwifery.* London: T. Cooper, 1737.

Stretzer, Thomas. *A New Description of Merryland: Containing, a Topographical, Geographical, and Natural History of That Country.* 10th ed. London: E. Curll, 1742.

Taylor, Ann. *My Mother: A Poem by a Lady.* Philadelphia: William Charles, 1816. Readex: Early American Imprints, Series 2: Shaw-Shoemaker.

Taylor, Ann Martin. *Practical Hints to Young Females.* Boston: Wells and Lilly, 1816.

Timbrell, J. C., artist, and J. Bannister, engraver. *Maternal Instruction.* In *Godey's Magazine and Lady's Book* 30, March 1845, n.p.

Tucker, W. E., engraver. *The Empty Cradle.* In *Godey's Magazine and Lady's Book* 34, January 1847, n.p.

Tyler, Mary Hunt Palmer. *The Maternal Physician; A Treatise on the Nurture and Management of Infants, from the Birth until Two Years Old.* New York: Isaac Riley, 1811.

Upton, William. *My Childhood: A Poem.* Philadelphia: William Charles, 1816. Readex: Early American Imprints, Series 2: Shaw-Shoemaker.

Van de Spiegel, Adriaan, and Giulio Cesare Casseri. *De formato foetu liber singularis.* Padua: Io. Bap. de Martinis and Livius Pasquatus, 1626.

"Verses to My First-Born." *The Cincinnati Literary Gazette* 2, no. 12, September 18, 1824, 96.

"Verses to My First Born." *Ladies' Literary Cabinet* 4, July 21, 1821, 88.

Vesalius, Andreas. *De humani corporis fabrica libri septem.* Basileae [Basel]: Ex officina Joannis Oporini, 1543.

*Views of Slavery* (broadside). New York, 1836. Graphics—Print Department— Political Cartoons—1836 Vie P.2003.10, Library Company of Philadelphia.

Wallace, Willie. *Arkansas Narratives.* Vol. 2, pt. 7, 42–43. Born in Slavery: Slave Narratives from the Federal Writers' Project, 1936–1938. Library of Congress. http://memory.loc.gov/ammem/snhtml/snhome.html.

"Wanted—A *Dry* Nurse" (cartoon). *Turner's 1839 Comick Almanack.* New York, 1838.

Warrington, Joseph. *Obstetric Catechism; Containing Two Thousand Three Hundred and Forty-Seven Questions and Answers on Obstetrics Proper.* Philadelphia, 1854.

Waterman, George. "My Mother." *Godey's Magazine and Lady's Book* 28, January 1844, 45.

Watkins, Mary. *Maternal Solicitude, or, Lady's Manual: Comprising a Brief View of the Happy Advantages Resulting from an Early Attention to Secure a Good Constitution in Their Infants.* New York, 1809.

Weir, Robert Walter, artist, and T. Illman, engraver. *Maternal Affection.* In *The American Juvenile Keepsake*, edited by Mrs. Hoffland, n.p. New York: C. Wells, 1834.

[W. H.]. "The Slave-Mother." *Philanthropist* 6, no. 18, November 3, 1841, 0_4. ProQuest: American Periodicals Series.

White, Charles. *Treatise on the Management of Pregnant and Lying-In Women.* London: Edward and Charles Dilly, 1773.

Willis. "Mother's Voice." *The Mother's Assistant, and Young Lady's Friend,* June 1851, 86.

Wise, Daniel. "The Bereaved Mother." *The Mother's Assistant, and Young Lady's Friend,* no. 1, January 1850, 7–9.

Witherington, W. F., artist, and A. L. Dick, engraver. *A Summer Scene for a Winter Month.* In *Godey's Lady's Book* 30, January 1845, n.p.

[W. K. G.] "The Slave Mother's Lament for Her Children." *National Era* 2, no. 92, October 5, 1848, 157. ProQuest: American Periodicals Series.

Wolfe, A. R. "The Memory of My Mother." *The Mother's Magazine and Family Monitor* 19, 1851, 254.

"Woman." *Ladies' Literary Cabinet, Being a Repository of Miscellaneous Literary Productions, Both Original and Selected, in Prose and Verse* 7, no. 1, December 21, 1822, 5.

"The Women of Philadelphia." *Public Ledger and Daily Transcript.* Reprinted in *History of Woman Suffrage,* vol. 1, edited by Elizabeth Cady Stanton, Susan B. Anthony, and Matilda Joslyn Gage, 804. New York: Fowler and Wells, 1881.

Womble, George. *Georgia Narratives.* Vol. 4, pt. 4, 179–193. Born in Slavery: Slave Narratives from the Federal Writers' Project, 1936–1938. Library of Congress. http://memory.loc.gov/ammem/snhtml/snhome.html.

Wood, Marcus, ed. *The Poetry of Slavery: An Anglo American Anthology.* Oxford: Oxford University Press, 2003.

Woodworth, Francis Chandler. *Holiday Book.* New York: Clark, Austin, and Smith, 1853.

Wortham, Jenna. "Facebook Won't Budge on Breastfeeding Photos." *New York Times,* January 2, 2009. Accessed August 1, 2016. http://bits.blogs.nytimes.com /2009/01/02/breastfeeding-facebook-photos/#.

Wright, John Massey, artist, and E. Gallaudet, engraver. *The Dying Babe.* In *Casket; or Youth's Pocket Library,* n.p. Boston: George Davidson, 1830.

## Secondary Sources

Aronson, Amy Beth. *Taking Liberties: Early American Women's Magazines and Their Readers.* Westport, CT: Praeger, 2002.

Bankole, Katherine Kemi. *Slavery and Medicine: Enslavement and Medical Practices in Antebellum Louisiana.* New York: Garland, 1998.

Barker-Benfield, G. J. *The Culture of Sensibility: Sex and Society in Eighteenth-Century Britain.* Chicago: University of Chicago Press, 1992.

———. *The Horrors of the Half-Known Life: Male Attitudes toward Women and Sexuality in Nineteenth-Century America.* New York: Harper and Row, 1976.

Bennett, Judith M. *History Matters: Patriarchy and the Challenge of Feminism.* Philadelphia: University of Pennsylvania Press, 2006.

Bennett, Paula Bernat. " 'The Descent of the Angel': Interrogating Domestic Ideology in American Women's Poetry, 1858–1890." *American Literary History* 7, no. 4 (Winter 1995): 591–610.

———. "Not Just Filler and Not Just Sentimental: Women's Poetry in American Victorian Periodicals, 1860–1900." In *Periodical Literature in Nineteenth-Century America*, edited by Kenneth M. Price and Susan Balasco Smith, 201–219. Charlottesville: University Press of Virginia, 1995.

———. *Poets in the Public Sphere: The Emancipatory Project of American Women's Poetry, 1800–1900.* Princeton, NJ: Princeton University Press, 2003.

Berlant, Lauren. "The Female Woman: Fanny Fern and the Form of Sentiment." In *The Culture of Sentiment: Race, Gender, and Sentimentality in Nineteenth-Century America*, edited by Shirley Samuels, 265–281. New York: Oxford University Press, 1992.

Berman, Paul. "The Practice of Obstetrics in Rural America, 1800–1860." *Journal of the History of Medicine and Allied Sciences* 50, no. 2 (April 1995): 175–193.

Bernier, Celeste-Marie. " 'Iron Arguments': Spectacle, Rhetoric and the Slave Body in New England and British Antislavery Oratory." *European Journal of American Culture* 26 (2007): 57–78.

Blauvelt, Martha Tomhave. *The Work of the Heart: Young Women and Emotion, 1780–1830.* Charlottesville: University Press of Virginia, 2007.

Bloch, Ruth H. "American Feminine Ideals in Transition: The Rise of the Moral Mother, 1785–1815." *Feminist Studies* 4, no. 2 (June 1978): 100–126.

———. "The Gendered Meanings of Virtue in Revolutionary America." *Signs* 13, no. 1 (Autumn 1987): 37–58.

———. "Revaluing Motherhood: American Feminine Ideals in Transition; The Rise of the Moral Mother, 1785–1815." In *Gender and Morality in Anglo-American Culture, 1650–1800*, 57–77. Berkeley: University of California Press, 2003.

Bogdan, Janet. "Care or Cure? Childbirth Practices in Nineteenth-Century America." *Feminist Studies* 4 (1978): 92–99.

Bordo, Susan. *Unbearable Weight: Feminism, Western Culture, and the Body.* Berkeley: University of California Press, 1993.

Bowers, Toni. " 'A Point of Conscience': Breastfeeding and Maternal Authority in *Pamela*, Part 2." In *Inventing Maternity: Politics, Science, and Literature, 1650–1865*, edited by Susan C. Greenfield and Carol Barash, 138–158. Lexington: University Press of Kentucky, 1999.

Boydston, Jeanne. *Home and Work: Housework, Wages, and the Ideology of Labor in the Early Republic.* New York: Oxford University Press, 1990.

Bricks, Caroline. "Stones Like Women's Paps: Revising Gender in Jane Sharp's Midwives Book." *Journal for Early Modern Cultural Studies* 7, no. 2 (Fall/Winter 2007): 1–27.

Brown, Kathleen M. *Foul Bodies: Cleanliness in Early America*. New Haven, CT: Yale University Press, 2009.

———. "The Life Cycle: Motherhood during the Enlightenment." In *A Cultural History of Women in the Age of Enlightenment*, edited by Ellen Pollak, 29–43. London: Bloomsbury, 2013.

Burnstein, Andrew. *Sentimental Democracy: The Evolution of America's Romantic Self-Image*. New York: Hill and Wang, 1999.

Bushman, Richard L. *The Refinement of America: Persons, Houses, Cities*. New York: Vintage Books, 1993.

Butler, Judith. *Bodies That Matter: On the Discursive Limits of "Sex."* New York: Routledge, 1993.

Campbell, John. "Work, Pregnancy, and Infant Mortality among Southern Slaves." *Journal of Interdisciplinary History* 14, no. 4 (Spring 1984): 793–812.

Canning, Kathleen. "The Body as Method? Reflections on the Place of the Body in Gender History." *Gender and History* 11, no. 3 (November 1999): 499–513.

Caton, Donald. *What a Blessing She Had Chloroform: The Medical and Social Response to the Pain of Childbirth from 1800 to the Present*. New Haven, CT: Yale University Press, 1999.

Caulfield, Ernest. "Infant Feeding in Colonial America." *Journal of Pediatrics* 41 (1952): 673–687.

Cavazza, Marta. "Women's Dialectics, or The Thinking Uterus: An Eighteenth-Century Controversy on Gender and Education." In *The Faces of Nature in Enlightenment Europe*, edited by Lorraine Daston and Gianna Pomata, 237–257. Berlin: BWV-Berliner Wissenschafts-Verlag, 2003.

Cavitch, Max. *American Elegy: The Poetry of Mourning from the Puritans to Whitman*. Minneapolis: University of Minnesota Press, 2007.

Chaney, Michael A. *Fugitive Vision: Slave Image and Black Identity in Antebellum Narrative*. Bloomington: Indiana University Press, 2008.

Cima, Gay Gibson. *Performing Anti-slavery: Activist Women on Antebellum Stages*. Cambridge: Cambridge University Press, 2014.

Clark, Elizabeth B. "'The Sacred Rights of the Weak': Pain, Sympathy, and the Culture of Individual Rights in Antebellum America." *Journal of American History* 82, no. 2 (September 1995): 463–493.

Cody, Lisa Forman. "The Politics of Reproduction: From Midwives' Alternative Public Sphere to the Public Spectacle of Man-Midwifery." *Eighteenth-Century Studies* 32, no. 4 (Summer 1999): 477–495.

Cooper Owens, Deirdre Benia. "'Courageous Negro Servitors' and Laboring Irish Bodies: An Examination of Antebellum-Era Modern American Gynecology." Ph.D. diss., University of California–Los Angeles, 2008.

Cott, Nancy F. *The Bonds of Womanhood: "Woman's Sphere" in New England, 1780–1835*. New Haven, CT: Yale University Press, 1977.

———. "Passionlessness: An Interpretation of Victorian Sexual Ideology, 1790–1850." *Signs* 4, no. 2 (Winter 1978): 219–236.

Csengei, Ildiko. *Sympathy, Sensibility and the Literature of Feeling in the Eighteenth Century*. New York: Palgrave Macmillan, 2012.

Degler, Carl N. *At Odds: Women and the Family in America from the Revolution to the Present*. New York: Oxford University Press, 1980.

D'Emilio, John, and Estelle B. Freedman. *Intimate Matters: A History of Sexuality in America*. 2nd ed. Chicago: University of Chicago Press, 1997.

Douglas, Ann. *The Feminization of American Culture*. New York: Knopf, 1977.

Dunn, Peter M. "William Potts Dewees (1768–1841) of Pennsylvania: Pioneer of Perinatal Medicine in America." *Archives of Disease in Childhood* 75 (1996): F69–F70.

Dye, Nancy Schrom, and Daniel Blake Smith. "Mother Love and Infant Death, 1750–1920." *Journal of American History* 73, no. 2 (September 1973): 329–353.

Etter, William M. *The Good Body: Normalizing Visions in Nineteenth-Century American Literature and Culture, 1836–1867*. Newcastle upon Tyne: Cambridge Scholars, 2010.

Fermon, Nicole. "Domesticating Women, Civilizing Men: Rousseau's Political Program." *Sociological Quarterly* 35, no. 3 (August 1994): 431–442.

Fett, Sharla M. *Working Cures: Healing, Health, and Power on Southern Slave Plantations*. Chapel Hill: University of North Carolina Press, 2002.

Fildes, Valerie A. *Breasts, Bottles and Babies: A History of Infant Feeding*. Edinburgh: Edinburgh University Press, 1986.

——. "The English Wet-Nurse and Her Role in Infant Care, 1538–1800." *Medical History* 32 (1988): 142–173.

——. *Wet Nursing: A History from Antiquity to the Present*. Oxford: Basil Blackwell, 1988.

Fisher, Walter. "Physicians and Slavery in the Antebellum Medical Journal." *Journal of the History of Medicine and Allied Sciences* 23 (January 1968): 36–49.

Fissell, Mary. "Hairy Women and Naked Truths: Gender and the Politics of Knowledge in 'Aristotle's Masterpiece.'" *William and Mary Quarterly* 60, no. 1 (January 2003): 43–74.

——. *Vernacular Bodies: The Politics of Reproduction in Early Modern England*. Oxford: Oxford University Press, 2004.

Follett, Richard. "Heat, Sex, and Sugar: Pregnancy and Childbearing in the Slave Quarters." *Journal of Family History* 28, no. 4 (October 2003): 510–539.

Foucault, Michel. *Discipline and Punish: The Birth of the Prison*. 2nd ed. Translated by Alan Sheridan. New York: Vintage Books, 1995.

——. *The History of Sexuality: Volume 1: An Introduction*. Translated by Robert Hurley. New York: Vintage Books, 1990.

Frank, Lucy E., ed. *Representations of Death in Nineteenth-Century U.S. Writing and Culture*. Aldershot, Hants, UK: Ashgate, 2007.

Frank, Stephen M. *Life with Father: Parenthood and Masculinity in the Nineteenth-Century American North*. Baltimore: Johns Hopkins University Press, 1998.

Freud, Sigmund. *On Sexuality: Three Essays on the Theory of Sexuality*. Translated by James Strachey. Edited by Angela Richards. New York: Penguin Books, 1977.

Fritz, Meaghan M., and Frank E. Fee Jr. "To Give the Gift of Freedom: Gift Books and the War on Slavery." *American Periodicals* 23, no. 1 (2013): 60–82.

Gay, Peter. *Education of the Senses*. Vol. 1 of *The Bourgeois Experience: Victoria to Freud*. New York: Norton, 1984.

——. *The Tender Passion*. Vol. 2 of *The Bourgeois Experience: Victoria to Freud*. New York: W. W. Norton, 1986.

Gelpi, Barbara Charlesworth. "The Nursery Cave: Shelley and the Maternal." In *The New Shelley: Later Twentieth-Century Views*, edited by G. Kim Bank, 42–63. New York: St. Martin's Press.

Godbeer, Richard. *Sexual Revolution in Early America*. Baltimore: Johns Hopkins University Press, 2002.

Goddu, Teresa A. "The Antislavery Almanac and the Discourse of Numeracy." *Book History* 12 (2009): 129–155.

——. "Anti-slavery's Panoramic Perspective." *MELUS: Multi-ethnic Literature of the U.S.* 39, no. 2 (Summer 2014): 12–41.

Golden, Janet Lynne. *A Social History of Wet Nursing in America: From Breast to Bottle*. Columbus: Ohio State University Press, 2001.

Gordon, Linda. *Woman's Body, Woman's Right: Birth Control in America*. New York: Penguin Books, 1990.

Goring, Paul. *The Rhetoric of Sensibility in Eighteenth-Century Culture*. Cambridge: Cambridge University Press, 2005.

Gould, Stephen Jay. *The Mismeasure of Man*. Rev. ed. New York: W. W. Norton, 1996.

Grosz, Elizabeth. *Volatile Bodies: Toward a Corporeal Feminism*. Bloomington: Indiana University Press, 1994.

Gwilliam, Tassie. "Pamela and the Duplicitous Body of Femininity." *Representations*, no. 34 (Spring 1991): 104–133.

Halttunen, Karen. *Confidence Men and Painted Women: A Study of Middle-Class Culture in America, 1830–1870*. New Haven, CT: Yale University Press, 1982.

——. "Humanitarianism and the Pornography of Pain in Anglo-American Culture." *American Historical Review* 100, no. 2 (April 1995): 303–334.

Hanson, Clare. *A Cultural History of Pregnancy: Pregnancy, Medicine and Culture, 1750–2000*. New York: Palgrave Macmillan, 2004.

Harvey, Karen. *Reading Sex in the Eighteenth Century: Bodies and Gender in English Erotic Culture*. Cambridge: Cambridge University Press, 2004.

———. "Sexuality and the Body." In *Women's History: Britain, 1700–1850*, edited by Hannah Barker and Elain Chalus, 78–99. London: Routledge, 2005.

Haynes, April R. *Riotous Flesh: Women, Physiology, and the Solitary Vice in Nineteenth-Century America*. Chicago: University of Chicago Press, 2015.

Henderson, Carole E. "Introduction: Bordering on the Black Body; Text and Subtext in America's Literature and Culture." In *America and the Black Body: Identity Politics in Print and Visual Culture*, edited by Carole E. Henderson, 13–24. Madison, NJ: Fairleigh Dickinson University Press, 2009.

Henderson, Desirée. *Grief and Genre in American Literature, 1790–1870*. Farnham, Surrey, UK: Ashgate, 2011.

Higginbotham, Evelyn Brooks. "African-American Women's History and the Metalanguage of Race." *Signs* 17, no. 2 (Winter 1992): 251–274.

Himmelfarb, Gertrude. *The Roads to Modernity: The British, French, and American Enlightenments*. New York: Knopf, 2004.

Hobby, E. " 'Secrets of the Female Sex': Jane Sharp, the Reproductive Female Body, and Early Modern Midwifery Manuals." *Women's Writing: The Elizabethan Period* 8, no. 2 (2001): 201–212.

Hoffert, Sylvia D. *Private Matters: American Attitudes toward Childbearing and Infant Nurture in the Urban North, 1800–1860*. Urbana: University of Illinois Press, 1989.

Horowitz, Helen Lefkowitz. *Rereading Sex: Battles over Sexual Knowledge and Suppression in Nineteenth-Century America*. New York: Vintage Books, 2003.

Husband, Julie. *Antislavery Discourse and Nineteenth-Century American Literature: Incendiary Pictures*. New York: Palgrave Macmillan, 2010.

Jeffrey, Julie Roy. *The Great Silent Army of Abolitionism: Ordinary Women and the Antislavery Movement*. Chapel Hill: University of North Carolina Press, 1998.

Johnson, Paul E. *A Shopkeeper's Millennium: Society and Revivals in Rochester, New York, 1815–1837*. New York: Hill and Wang, 2004.

Jones, Jacqueline. *Labor of Love, Labor of Sorrow: Black Women, Work and the Family, from Slavery to the Present*. New York: Basic Books, 1985.

Jordanova, Ludmilla. *Sexual Visions: Images of Gender in Science and Medicine between the Eighteenth and Twentieth Centuries*. Madison: University of Wisconsin Press, 1989.

Kahn, Robbie Pfeufer. *Bearing Meaning: The Language of Birth*. Urbana: University of Illinois Press, 1995.

Kapsalis, Terri. "Mastering the Female Pelvis: Race and the Tools of Reproduction." In *Skin Deep, Spirit Strong: The Black Female Body in American Culture*, edited by Kimberly Wallace-Sanders, 263–300. Ann Arbor: University of Michigan Press, 2002.

Kasson, John F. *Rudeness and Civility: Manners in Nineteenth-Century Urban America*. New York: Hill and Wang, 1990.

Kasson, Joy S. *Marble Queens and Captives: Women in Nineteenth-Century American Sculpture.* New Haven, CT: Yale University Press, 1990.

Keller, Eve. *Generating Bodies and Gendered Selves: The Rhetoric of Reproduction in Early Modern England.* Seattle: University of Washington Press, 2007.

Kennedy, V. Lynn. *Born Southern: Childbirth, Motherhood, and Social Networks in the Old South.* Baltimore: Johns Hopkins University Press, 2010.

Kerber, Linda K. "The Republican Mother: Women and the Enlightenment—An American Perspective." *American Quarterly* 28, no. 2 (Summer 1976): 187–205.

———. *Women of the Republic: Intellect and Ideology in Revolutionary America.* Chapel Hill: University of North Carolina Press, 1980.

Kete, Mary Louise. *Sentimental Collaborations: Mourning and Middle-Class Identity in Nineteenth-Century America.* Durham, NC: Duke University Press, 2000.

King, Helen. *Midwifery, Obstetrics and the Rise of Gynaecology: The Uses of a Sixteenth-Century Compendium.* Burlington, VT: Ashgate, 2007.

King, Wilma. "'Suffer with Them til Death': Slave Women and Their Children in Nineteenth-Century America." In *More Than Chattel: Black Women and Slavery in the Americas,* edited by David Barry Gaspar and Darlene Clark Hine, 147–168. Bloomington: Indiana University Press, 1996.

Klepp, Susan E. "Revolutionary Bodies: Women and the Fertility Transition in the Mid-Atlantic Region, 1760–1820." *Journal of American History* 85, no. 3 (December 1998): 910–945.

———. *Revolutionary Conceptions: Women, Fertility, and Family Limitation in America, 1760–1820.* Chapel Hill: University of North Carolina Press, 2009.

Klimaszewski, Melisa. "Examining the Wet Nurse: Breasts, Power, and Penetration in Victorian England." *Women's Studies* 35, no. 4 (2006): 232–346.

Knott, Sarah. *Sensibility and the American Revolution.* Chapel Hill: University of North Carolina Press, 2009.

Laqueur, Thomas. *Making Sex: Body and Gender from the Greeks to Freud.* Cambridge, MA: Harvard University Press, 1990.

Lasser, Carol. "Voyeuristic Abolitionism: Sex, Gender, and the Transformation of Antislavery Rhetoric." *Journal of the Early Republic* 28, no. 1 (Spring 2008): 83–114.

Leavitt, Judith Walzer. *Brought to Bed: Childbearing in America, 1750–1950.* New York: Oxford University Press, 1986.

Lehuu, Isabelle. *Carnival on the Page: Popular Print Media in Antebellum America.* Chapel Hill: University of North Carolina Press, 2000.

———. "Sentimental Figures: Reading *Godey's Lady's Book* in Antebellum America." In *The Culture of Sentiment: Race, Gender, and Sentimentality in Nineteenth-Century America,* edited by Shirley Samuels, 73–91. New York: Oxford University Press, 1992.

Lewis, Jan, and Kenneth A. Lockridge, "'Sally Has Been Sick': Pregnancy and Family Limitation among Virginia Gentry Women, 1780–1830." *Journal of Social History* 22, no. 1 (Autumn 1988): 5–19.

Lyons, Clare A. *Sex among the Rabble: An Intimate History of Gender and Power in the Age of Revolution, Philadelphia, 1730–1830.* Chapel Hill: University of North Carolina Press, 2006.

Lystra, Karen. *Searching the Heart: Women, Men, and Romantic Love in Nineteenth-century America.* New York: Oxford University Press, 1989.

Maines, Rachel P. *The Technology of Orgasm: "Hysteria," the Vibrator, and Women's Sexual Satisfaction.* Baltimore: Johns Hopkins University Press, 1999.

Marcus, Steven. *The Other Victorians: A Study of Sexuality and Pornography in Mid-Nineteenth-Century England.* New York: Basic Books, 1966.

May, Henry F. *The Enlightenment in America.* New York: Oxford University Press, 1976.

McGrath, Roberta. *Seeing Her Sex: Medical Archives and the Female Body.* Manchester, UK: Manchester University Press, 2002.

McGregor, Deborah Kuhn. *Sexual Surgery and the Origins of Gynecology: J. Marion Sims, His Hospital, and His Patients.* New York: Garland, 1989.

McInnis, Maurie D. *Slaves Waiting for Sale: Abolitionist Art and the American Slave Trade.* Chicago: University of Chicago Press, 2011.

McMillen, Sally G. *Motherhood in the Old South: Pregnancy, Childbirth, and Infant Rearing.* Baton Rouge: Louisiana State University Press, 1990.

Meckel, Richard A. "Educating a Ministry of Mothers: Evangelical Maternal Associations, 1815–1860." *Journal of the Early Republic* 2, no. 4 (Winter 1982): 403–423.

Mitchell, Sarah. "A Wonderful Duty: A Study of Motherhood in *Godey's* Magazine." In *Seeking a Voice: Images of Gender and Race in the Nineteenth-Century Press,* edited by David B. Sachsman, S. Kittrell Rusing, and Roy Morris Jr., 171–178. West Lafayette, IN: Purdue University Press, 2009.

Moorhead, James H. "Between Progress and Apocalypse: A Reassessment of Millennialism in American Religious Thought, 1800–1880." *Journal of American History* 71, no. 3 (December 1984): 524–542.

Morgan, Jennifer L. *Laboring Women: Reproduction and Gender in New World Slavery.* Philadelphia: University of Pennsylvania Press, 2004.

———. "'Some Could Suckle over Their Shoulder': Male Travelers, Female Bodies, and the Gendering of Racial Ideology, 1500–1770." *William and Mary Quarterly* 54, no. 1 (January 1997): 167–192.

Moscucci, Ornella. *The Science of Woman: Gynaecology and Gender in England, 1800–1929.* Cambridge: Cambridge University Press, 1990.

Nichols, Marcia. "The Man-Midwife's Tale: Re-reading Male-Authored Midwifery Guides in Britain and America, 1750–1820." Ph.D. diss., University of South Carolina, 2010.

Noble, Marianne. *The Masochistic Pleasures of Sentimental Literature*. Princeton, NJ: Princeton University Press, 2000.

Norton, Mary Beth. *Liberty's Daughters: The Revolutionary Experience of American Women, 1750–1800*. Boston: Little, Brown, 1980.

Okker, Patricia. *Our Sister Editors: Sarah J. Hale and the Tradition of Nineteenth-Century American Women Editors*. Athens: University of Georgia Press, 1995.

Patterson, Cynthia Lee. *Art for the Middle Classes: America's Illustrated Magazines of the 1840s*. Jackson: University Press of Mississippi, 2010.

Perdue, Theda. *Cherokee Women: Gender and Culture Change, 1700–1835*. Lincoln: University of Nebraska Press, 1999.

Pernick, Martin S. *A Calculus of Suffering: Pain, Professionalism, and Anesthesia in Nineteenth-Century America*. New York: Columbia University Press, 1985.

Perrin, Liese M. "Resisting Reproduction: Reconsidering Slave Contraception in the Old South." *Journal of American Studies* 35, no. 2 (August 2001): 255–274.

Perry, Ruth. "Colonizing the Breast: Sexuality and Maternity in Eighteenth-Century England." *Journal of the History of Sexuality* 2, no. 2 (October 1991): 204–234.

Peters, Dolores. "The Pregnant Pamela: Characterization and Popular Medical Attitudes in the Eighteenth Century." *Eighteenth-Century Studies* 14, no. 4 (Summer 1981): 432–451.

Plane, Ann Marie. "Childbirth Practices among Native American Women of New England and Canada, 1600–1800." In *Women and Health in America*, edited by Judith Walzer Leavitt, 38–47. 2nd ed. Madison: University of Wisconsin Press, 1999.

Pollak, Ellen. "Introduction: Women Daring to Know in the Age of Enlightenment." In *A Cultural History of Women in the Age of Enlightenment*, edited by Ellen Pollak, 1–27. London: Bloomsbury, 2013.

Pollock, Della. *Telling Bodies Performing Birth*. New York: Columbia University Press, 1999.

Porter, Roy. *The Greatest Benefit to Mankind: A Medical History of Humanity*. New York: W. W. Norton, 1997.

———. "A Touch of Danger: The Man-Midwife as Sexual Predator." In *Sexual Underworlds of the Enlightenment*, edited by G. S. Rousseau and Roy Porter, 207–232. Chapel Hill: University of North Carolina Press, 1988.

Reddy, William M. *The Navigation of Feeling: A Framework for the History of Emotions*. Cambridge: Cambridge University Press, 2001.

Roberts, Dorothy E. *Killing the Black Body: Race, Reproduction, and the Meaning of Liberty*. New York: Pantheon Books, 1997.

Rubin, Joan Shelley. *The Making of Middlebrow Culture*. Chapel Hill: University of North Carolina Press, 1992.

Ryan, Mary P. *Cradle of the Middle Class: The Family in Oneida County, New York, 1790–1865.* Cambridge: Cambridge University Press, 1981.

———. *The Empire of the Mother: American Writing about Domesticity, 1830–1860.* New York: Institute for Research in History and Haworth Press, 1982.

Salerno, Beth A. *Sister Societies: Women's Antislavery Organizations in Antebellum America.* DeKalb: Northern Illinois University Press, 2005.

Salmon, Marylynn. "The Cultural Significance of Breastfeeding and Infant Care in Early Modern England and America." *Journal of Social History* 28, no. 2 (1994): 247–269.

Samuels, Shirley, ed. *The Culture of Sentiment: Race, Gender, and Sentimentality in Nineteenth-Century America.* New York: Oxford University Press, 1992.

Savitt, Todd. *Medicine and Slavery: The Diseases and Health Care of Blacks in Antebellum Virginia.* Urbana: University of Illinois Press, 2002.

Sawday, Jonathan. *The Body Emblazoned: Dissection and the Human Body in Renaissance Culture.* London: Routledge, 1995.

Scholten, Catherine M. *Childbearing in American Society, 1650–1850.* New York: New York University Press, 1985.

Schroeder, Lars. *Slave to the Body: Black Bodies, White No-Bodies and the Regulative Dualism of Body-Politics in the Old South.* Frankfurt: Peter Lang, 2003.

Schwartz, Marie Jenkins. *Birthing a Slave: Motherhood and Medicine in the Antebellum South.* Cambridge, MA: Harvard University Press, 2009.

Schwarz, Kathryn. "Missing the Breast: Desire, Disease, and the Singular Effect of Amazons." In *The Body in Parts: Fantasies of Corporeality in Early Modern Europe,* edited by David Hillman and Carla Mazzio, 147–169. New York: Routledge, 1997.

Seidman, Steven. "The Power of Desire and the Danger of Pleasure: Victorian Sexuality Reconsidered." *Journal of Social History* 24 (1990): 47–67.

Shaw, Rhonda. "Performing Breastfeeding: Embodiment, Ethics and the Maternal Subject." *Feminist Review* 78 (2004): 99–116.

Smith, Daniel Blake. *Inside the Great House: Planter Family Life in Eighteenth-Century Chesapeake Society.* Ithaca, NY: Cornell University Press, 1980.

Smith, Daniel Scott. "Family Limitation, Sexual Control, and Domestic Feminism in Victorian America." *Feminist Studies* 1, no. 3/4 (Winter-Spring 1973): 40–57.

Smith, Katy Simpson. *We Have Raised All of You: Motherhood in the South, 1750–1835.* Baton Rouge: Louisiana State University Press, 2013.

Smithers, Gregory D. *Slave Breeding: Sex, Violence, and Memory in African American History.* Gainesville: University Press of Florida, 2012.

Smith-Rosenberg, Carroll. "The Female World of Love and Ritual: Relationships between Women in Nineteenth-Century America." *Signs* 1, no. 1 (Autumn 1975): 1–29.

———. "Sex as Symbol in Victorian Purity: An Ethnohistorical Analysis of Jacksonian America." *American Journal of Sociology*, 84 (1978): S212–S247.

Smith-Rosenberg, Carroll, and Charles Rosenberg. "The Female Animal: Medical and Biological Views of Woman and Her Role in Nineteenth-Century America." *Journal of American History* 60, no. 2 (September 1973): 332–356.

Sommers, Joseph Michael. "*Godey's Lady's Book*: Sarah Hale and the Construction of Sentimental Nationalism." *College Literature* 37, no. 3 (Summer 2010): 43–61.

Sorisio, Carolyn. *Fleshing Out America: Race, Gender, and the Politics of the Body in American Literature, 1833–1879.* Athens: University of Georgia Press, 2002.

Speert, Harold. *Obstetrics and Gynecology in America: A History.* Chicago: American College of Obstetricians and Gynecologists, 1980.

Spelman, Elizabeth V. "Woman as Body: Ancient and Contemporary Views." *Feminist Studies* 8, no. 1 (Spring 1982): 109–131.

Spruill, Julia Cherry. *Women's Life and Work in the Southern Colonies.* New York: W. W. Norton, 1972.

Stearns, Cindy A. "Breastfeeding and the Good Maternal Body." *Gender and Society* 13, no. 3 (June 1999): 308–325.

Steinbrügge, Lieselotte. *The Moral Sex: Woman's Nature in the French Enlightenment.* Translated by Pamela E. Selwyn. New York: Oxford University Press, 1995.

Stevenson, Brenda E. *Life in Black and White: Family and Community in the Slave South.* New York: Oxford University Press, 1996.

Stowe, Steven M. *Doctoring the South: Southern Physicians and Everyday Medicine in the Mid-Nineteenth Century.* Chapel Hill: University of North Carolina Press, 2004.

———. "Obstetrics and the Work of Doctoring in the Mid-Nineteenth-Century American South." In *Midwifery Theory and Practice*, vol. 1 of *Childbirth: Changing Ideas and Practices in Britain and America, 1600 to the Present*, edited by Philip K. Wilson, 306–333. New York: Garland, 1996.

Theriot, Nancy M. *Mothers and Daughters in Nineteenth-century America: The Biosocial Construction of Femininity.* Lexington: University Press of Kentucky, 1996.

———. "Women's Voices in Nineteenth-Century Medical Discourse: A Step toward Deconstructing Science." *Signs* 19, no. 1 (Autumn 1993): 1–31.

Tompkins, Jane. *Sensational Designs: The Cultural Work of American Fiction, 1790–1860.* New York: Oxford University Press, 1986.

Treckel, Paula A. "Breastfeeding and Maternal Sexuality in Colonial America." *Journal of Interdisciplinary History* 20, no. 1 (1989): 25–51.

*Trends in Maternal Mortality: 1990 to 2013.* Estimates by WHO, UNICEF, UNFPA, the World Bank and the United Nations Population Division. Executive Summary. Geneva: World Health Organization, 2014. Accessed July 4, 2016. http://www.who.int/reproductivehealth/publications/monitoring/maternal -mortality-2013/en/.

Ulrich, Laurel Thatcher. *Good Wives: Image and Reality in the Lives of Women in Northern New England, 1650–1750*. New York: Vintage Books, 1991.

———. " 'The Living Mother of a Living Child': Midwifery and Mortality in Post-Revolutionary New England." *William and Mary Quarterly* 46, no. 1 (January 1989): 27–48.

———. *A Midwife's Tale: The Life of Martha Ballard, Based on Her Diary, 1785–1812*. New York: Vintage Books, 1990.

———. "Women's Travail, Men's Labor: Birth Stories from Eighteenth-Century New England Diaries." In *Women's Work in New England, 1620–1920*, edited by Peter Benes and Jane Montague Benes, 170–183. Dublin Seminar for New England Folklife. Boston: Boston University, 2003.

Vinovskis, Maris A. "Mortality Rates and Trends in Massachusetts before 1860." *Journal of Economic History* 32, no. 1 (March 1972): 184–213.

Wagner, Peter. *Eros Revived: Erotica of the Enlightenment in England and America*. London: Secker and Warburg, 1988.

Wearn, Mary McCartin. *Negotiating Motherhood in Nineteenth-Century American Literature*. New York: Routledge, 2008.

Weiss, Penny A. "Sex, Freedom and Equality in Rousseau's 'Emile.' " *Polity* 22, no. 4 (Summer 1990): 603–625.

Welter, Barbara. "The Cult of True Womanhood: 1820–1860." *American Quarterly* 18, no. 2 (Summer 1966): 151–174.

Wertz, Richard W., and Dorothy C. Wertz. *Lying-In: A History of Childbirth in America*. New Haven, CT: Yale University Press, 1989.

West, Emily, and R. J. Knight. "Mothers' Milk: Slavery, Wet-Nursing, and Black and White Women in the Antebellum South." *Journal of Southern History* 83, no. 1 (February 2017): 37–68.

Wexler, Victor G. " 'Made for Man's Delight': Rousseau as Antifeminist." *American Historical Review* 81, no. 2 (April 1976): 266–291.

White, Deborah Gray. *Ar'n't I a Woman? Female Slaves in the Plantation South*. Rev. ed. New York: W. W. Norton, 1999.

Wilson, Adrian. *The Making of Man-Midwifery: Childbirth in England, 1660–1770*. Cambridge, MA: Harvard University Press, 1995.

———. "William Hunter and the Varieties of Man-Midwifery." In *William Hunter and the Eighteenth-Century Medical World*, edited by W. F. Bynum and Roy Porter, 343–370. Cambridge: Cambridge University Press, 1985.

Wolf, Jacqueline H. *Deliver Me from Pain: Anesthesia and Birth in America*. Baltimore: Johns Hopkins University Press, 2009.

———. *Don't Kill Your Baby: Public Health and the Decline of Breastfeeding in the Nineteenth and Twentieth Centuries*. Columbus: Ohio State University Press, 2001.

Wood, Marcus. *Black Milk: Imagining Slavery in the Visual Cultures of Brazil and America*. Oxford: Oxford University Press, 2013.

———. *Blind Memory: Visual Representations of Slavery in England and America, 1780–1865*. New York: Routledge, 2000.

Yalom, Marilynn. *A History of the Breast*. New York: Knopf, 1997.

Yellin, Jean Fagan. *Women and Sisters: The Antislavery Feminists in American Culture*. New Haven, CT: Yale University Press, 1992.

Zaeske, Susan. *Signatures of Citizenship: Petitioning, Antislavery, and Women's Political Identity*. Chapel Hill: University of North Carolina Press, 2003.

Zagarri, Rosemarie. "Morals, Manners, and the Republican Mother." *American Quarterly* 44, no. 2 (June 1992): 192–215.

———. *Revolutionary Backlash: Women and Politics in the Early American Republic*. Philadelphia: University of Pennsylvania Press, 2007.

Zuckerman, Mary Ellen. *A History of Popular Women's Magazines in the United States, 1792–1995*. Westport, CT: Greenwood Press, 1998.

# Index

Abbott, John, 90, 98

Abortifacients, 61, 219n33. *See also* Birth control

Adams, Abigail, 59, 61, 74, 120

Aitken, John, 38, 47

Alcott, William A., 96, 137, 165

Allen, Ann, 99

Ambivalence: to breastfeeding, 115, 117, 125; to motherhood, 5, 9–10, 52, 55, 58, 65, 72, 85, 203

*American Anti-slavery Almanac*, 192, 194, 196–197

American Anti-slavery Society, 191–192

American Revolution, 3, 56, 89, 138

Amory, Mehitable, 74

Anarcha, 42

Anatomical atlases, 15, 25, 29

Anderson, James, 81

Antislavery: movement, 175, 179, 188, 191, 198, 238n12; poetry, 10–11, 177–191; print culture, 175–178, 190–191, 198, 200–201, 204; visual culture, 191–199

*The Anti-slavery Harp*, 181

Aristotle, 14

*Aristotle's Masterpiece*, 20–22, 215n21

*Autographs for Freedom*, 175

Baillie, Matthew, 34

Ball, Elizabeth Byles, 84

Ballard, Martha, 119, 129

Bard, Samuel, 15, 23, 31, 36, 38, 48, 125

Barwell, Louisa Mary Bacon, 96

Beach, Wooster, 45

Beecher, Catharine E., 99

Bell, Charles, 34

Bellows, Eliza Nevins Townsend, 141, 143

Bernard, Jane Gay (Robertson), 122

Bichat, Marie François Xavier, 35

Biological essentialism, 12, 201

Birth control, 61, 63, 103, 205–206, 220n42. *See also* Abortifacients; Fertility: limitation of; Norplant

Black, Persis Sibley Andrews, 74–75

*Boston Medical and Surgical Journal*, 206

*Boston Recorder*, 186

Bourne, George, 198–199; *Picture of Slavery in the United States of America*, 198

Breastfeeding: complications with, 62, 87–88, 99–100, 115, 118–121; controversies over, 207–208; early medical arguments for, 91–96; and enslaved women, 62, 131–135; and erotic pleasure, 101–112, 227n71, 228n82, 229n107; for fertility limitation, 62, 220n36; as a pleasure, 87, 97–100, 113–114, 123–124; and poor health, 121–123. *See also* Daguerreotypes; Wet nurses

Brooke, Margaret, 121

Brown, William Wells, 181

Buchan, William, 40, 88, 95, 97–99, 105–106, 110–112, 227n71

Bull, Thomas, 99

Burns, John, 23, 35, 49

Burr, Esther Edwards, 203

Burton, John, 32, 34, 105
Butler, Samuel Worcester, 83, 222n87

Cabell, Agnes, 73, 121
Cadogan, William, 91–92, 94–95, 100
Calhoun, Jeff, 133
Calvert, Rosalie Stier, 59–60, 63, 65, 68, 74, 142–143
Campbell, John, 118
Carr, Sidney, 82
Cary, Sarah, 125
Channing, Walter, 50, 83
Chesnut, Mary Cox, 66, 119–120, 123
Childbirth: anesthetized, 2, 82–83, 205; birth positions, 49; enslaved women's narratives of, 79–81; fear of death during, 83–84; fear of pain during, 81–83; medical descriptions of, 44–47, 49–50; pathologization of, 17, 38–41, 43; personal narratives of, 75–81; vocabulary for, 74–75, 83–84
Children's books, images of mothers in, 149–151, 157
Clitherall, Caroline Elizabeth Burgwin, 134
Cocke, Lucy, 133–134
The Compleat Midwifes Practice, 214nn25–26
Continuity, 2, 6, 9, 52–53, 203, 212n18
Contraceptives. See Birth control
Coolidge, Ellen Wayles Randolph, 69–70, 73, 81–82, 143–144
Corporeality: female, 5, 210; and breastfeeding, 87, 110, 141; and childbearing, 54, 67, 70, 85, 209; and enslaved women, 11, 43, 131, 177–178, 187–188, 190, 192, 195, 198, 200–201; and medical literature, 18; and motherhood, 5, 8, 144, 161–162, 209; and race and class, 39, 116, 141, 204, 212n22; and sentimental motherhood, 171, 199. See also Disembodiment; Embodiment

Cox, Esther Bowes, 66–68, 71, 120, 123
Cox, Margaret, 90
Craig, Peggy, 138
Culpeper, Nicholas, 14, 19–20, 22, 26, 32; A Directory for Midwives, 14, 19

Daguerreotypes, breastfeeding, 125–128, 231n36
Dall, Caroline Healey, 62, 65, 71, 79
Darwin, Erasmus, 107, 163, 165; The Botanic Garden, 163
Dawbarn, Mrs., 95, 109
Denman, Thomas, 22–23, 32, 34, 47
Dewees, William Potts, 15, 23, 36, 40–41, 48, 50, 96–99, 106, 137
Disembodiment: and race, 201; in sentimental culture, 161, 204. See also Corporeality; Embodiment
Dissection, 24–25, 28–30
Drinker, Elizabeth Sandwith: breastfeeding, 62, 117, 122; numeracy, 218n10; pregnancy and childbirth, 52–53, 56, 61–62, 66–67, 70, 77–79; wet nurses, 120, 135–136
Du Pont de Nemours, Pierre Samuel, 107, 228n93; Philosophia de l'univers, 107, 228n93
Dyer, E. P., Reverend, 167
Dyer, Martha Tabb Watkins, 75–76

Edwards, Jonathan, 21
Embodiment, 11, 201; and breastfeeding, 148; and enslaved women, 178, 199; in medical literature, 51; women's expressions of, 13, 55; women's perceptions of, 8. See also Corporeality; Disembodiment
Enlightenment, 3, 33, 88–90, 106, 169
Enslaved women: in antislavery poetry, 10–11, 177–191; and breastfeeding, 62, 131–135; and childbirth narratives, 79–81; and fertility, 57–58, 64, 218n15; meaning of motherhood for,

9, 54–55, 60, 63–64, 84–85; medical views and treatment of, 41–43, 73, 222n88; sexual vulnerability and coercion, 58–59, 176, 178, 199; visual depictions of, 10–11, 192–199; as wet nurses, 116, 130, 133–134, 143, 226n30, 232n52. *See also* Antislavery; Slave narratives
Estienne, Charles, 25–26, 28
Ewell, Thomas, 44, 97

Facebook, 207–208
Fertility: fertility revolution, 2; limitation of, 53, 61–63, 67, 220n36; meaning for enslaved women, 57–58, 64; meaning for women, 56–59, 63–65; numeracy, 56, 218n10; rates of, 6, 55–56, 205, 218n8, 218n15. *See also* Breastfeeding
Fisher, Eliza Middleton, 122, 140–141, 143
Fisher, Sarah Lindley, 74, 230n9
Fisher, Sarah Logan, 55–56, 68–69, 74–76, 81
Flagg, Maria Magdalen, 6, 84
Foucault, Michel, 11–12, 102, 234n5
Fowler, Orson Squire, 109
Fox, Mary Rodman Fisher, 76
Fox, Tryphena, 70–71
Freud, Sigmund, 107

Gaffney, Mary, 64
Gainsborough, Thomas, 157
Galen, 14, 25
Giftbooks, 146–147, 149–153, 156–157, 159–160, 192, 235n25; antislavery giftbooks, 175
Gilman, Caroline Howard, 70, 134
*Godey's Lady's Book*, 151, 157, 160, 170, 179, 238n11
*Graham's Lady's and Gentleman's Magazine*, 151
Grayson, Mary, 64

Greeley, Sim, 133
Gregg, Margaret, 66
Gregory, George, 45
Gregory, Samuel, 41
Gynecology, 14, 214n14; enslaved women and the development of, 41–43

Hale, Sarah Josepha, 160
Hale, Sarah Preston (Everett), 2, 56–57, 203
Hall, Calista, 63
Hamilton, Alexander, 23, 47, 92–93
Hamilton, James, 28, 31
Haywood, Eliza, 117, 119
Heath, Hannah Williams, 203
Henry, Matilda, 69, 71, 74, 82
Hering, Mary, 74
Hippocrates, 14, 33
Hollick, Frederick, 106–107
Holyoke, Mary, 118, 222n93
Hopkins, Sarah (Bennett), 121
Howard, Horton, 38
Howell, Josephine, 58, 64
Hubbard, Mary, 61
Hume, Sophia, 93
Hunter, William, 28–31; *The Anatomy of the Human Gravid Uterus*, 29
Hutchinson, Ida Blackshear, 58

Imperial motherhood, 4
Infant mortality. *See* Mortality: infant

Jacobs, Harriet, 79–80
Jenty, Charles, 28–29
Judson, Emily Chubbuck, 143

Kemble, Frances Anne, 57, 60, 122, 132

*Ladies' Literary Portfolio*, 184
*The Lady's Magazine and Repository of Entertaining Knowledge*, 149
Laurens, Caroline Olivia, 117

Lazarus, Rachel Mordecai, 75–76, 149
Lee, Mary Jackson, 61, 67, 142
Lewis, Eleanor Parke Custis, 66, 84, 121, 125, 221n59
*Liberator*, 175, 179, 182, 185, 187, 189, 238n11
*Liberty Bell*, 175, 187
Longfellow, Fanny Appleton, 83
Lowell, Georgina Margaret Amory, 75–76, 123

Mackenzie, Sir Alexander, 39–40
Manigault, Margaret Izard, 62
Man-midwives. *See* Midwifery: professionalization of
Maternal mortality. *See* Mortality: maternal
Mauriceau, François, 27–28
Mears, Martha, 35, 95, 105–106
Meigs, Charles, 37, 83
Meredith, Gertrude Gouverneur Ogden, 1, 124–125
Merriman, Samuel, 37
Middle class(es), 4, 7, 56, 138, 146–147, 212n22, 234nn5–6, 234n10
Middle-class culture, 7, 11, 173. *See also* Sentimental culture
Middleton, Mary Hering, 82
Midwifery: female midwives, 14–16, 22, 29, 72–73, 87; professionalization of, 6, 15, 21–23, 28, 35, 45–46, 72–73
*Miss Leslie's Magazine*, 151
Moral mother, 3–4, 90. *See also* Moral motherhood
Moral motherhood, 89. *See also* Moral mother
Mortality: infant, 64, 91–92, 131–132, 152, 220n49; maternal, 129–130, 171, 231n44
Moss, William, 91
*Mother's Assistant, and Young Lady's Friend*, 167
Murillo, Bartolomé Esteban, 156

*National Anti-slavery Standard*, 175
*National Era*, 188
Neblett, Elizabeth Scott, 53, 60, 82
Nihell, Elizabeth, 16, 44
Norplant, 208
*North Star*, 175
*The Nurse's Guide*, 92–93, 95

Obstetrics. *See* Midwifery
Olds, Sharon, 209–210
Ostriker, Alicia, 112, 209

Paré, Ambroise, 105
Passionlessness. *See* Sexuality: passionlessness
Peabody, Mary, 123
Perry, Elizabeth Frances, 57
Pettigrew, Ebenezer, 67
*Philanthropist*, 185
Photographs. *See* Daguerreotypes
Plato, 4
Portraits. *See* Daguerreotypes
Pregnancy: medical depictions of, 20, 23, 29, 36; pathologization of, 17, 38; in public, 70–72; vocabulary of, 67–68, 72, 221n59; women's descriptions of, 54–60, 68–70, 77, 85. *See also* Fertility

Randall, Laura Henrietta Wirt, 61, 119
Raynalde, Thomas, 14, 19, 21–22, 26, 45, 49
Read, Catherine, 118
Religion: evangelical, 3, 90, 147, 166, 234n12; Protestantism, 33, 156. *See also* Second Great Awakening
Republican mother, 3. *See also* Republican motherhood
Republican motherhood, 4. *See also* Republican mother
Rich, Adrienne, 112–113
Richardson, Experience (Wight), 53

Richardson, Samuel, 89, 108, 161–162; *Clarissa*, 162; *Pamela*, 89, 108, 161–162
Robertson, Eliza Ann Marsh, 70–71
Robinson, Celia, 132
Rogers, Hattie, 58
Romantic love, 99, 101, 103, 109, 111, 160–161, 227n71
Rösslin, Eucharius, 19
Rousseau, Jean-Jacques, 89, 92, 94, 225n9; *Emile*, 89, 225n9
Rueff, Jacob, 26, 28
Russell, Lydia Smith, 138–139

Sansom, Hannah Callender, 84
Scott, Mary, 82
Seaman, Valentine, 23, 36, 49
Searle, Thomas, 96
Second Great Awakening, 147, 234n10
Second-wave feminist movement, 209
Sensibility, 3, 89–90, 146–147, 156, 160, 176, 188; and breastfeeding, 87, 91, 96, 98, 100, 106, 113, 125; in men, 108; and wet nurses, 135, 137
Sentimental culture, 146–147, 156, 176–178, 182–183, 185, 201–202, 234nn5–6. *See also* Sentimentalism
Sentimentalism, 88–89, 91, 97, 146, 151, 234n6; in antislavery print culture, 175–178, 183, 196, 199–200. *See also* Sentimental culture
Sentimental maternal ideal, 5, 7, 111–112, 114. *See also* Sentimental mother; Sentimental motherhood
Sentimental mother, 4, 6–10, 86, 113–114, 209; and breastfeeding, 86, 88, 90–91, 98, 101, 125, 204; and enslaved mothers, 181, 191, 198, 199–200; in popular print culture, 146–148, 151–152, 156, 160; and race and class, 7; and sexuality, 111, 113–114; and wet nurses, 143. *See also* Sentimental maternal ideal; Sentimental motherhood

Sentimental motherhood, 4–6, 97, 123; and enslaved women, 178, 183–184, 189; in popular print culture, 146–148, 166–167; and race and class, 7, 116, 205; and sexuality, 102, 111; and wet nurses, 140, 144–145. *See also* Sentimental maternal ideal; Sentimental mother
Sexuality: fears of sexual impropriety, 15–16, 18, 21–23, 29, 32, 44–45, 50; medical discussions of, 18–23; and motherhood, 101–103, 108, 111–112, 162, 207–208, 227n71; passionlessness, 102, 228n73; sexual ideology, 18, 102. *See also* Breastfeeding: and erotic pleasure
Sharp, Jane, 14, 18, 20, 22, 26–27, 32, 46, 136–137, 214n26; *Midwives Book* (later *The Compleat Midwife's Companion*), 14
Sharpe, Louisa, 158
Shippen, William, 15
Shoemaker, Rebecca, 84
Sigourney, Lydia H., 97–98, 100, 113, 171, 183; *Letters to Mothers*, 100
Simpson, James Young, 82
Sims, James Marion, 42–43
Slave narratives, 8, 54, 175, 179
Smellie, William, 15, 21–23, 28–29, 31–34, 46; *Treatise on the Theory and Practice of Midwifery*, 15
Smith, Hugh, 92–93, 95, 108–110
Steven, John, 44
Stone, Sarah, 15–16
Stretzer, Thomas, 104; *A New Description of Merryland*, 104
Surville, Madame de (Marguerite-Eléonore Clotilde de Vallon-Chalys de Surville), 163

Taylor, Ann, 150
Transcendent mother, 11, 148–149, 161, 166–168, 172–175, 177, 183, 186–187, 190, 199, 201, 204

Turner, Rebecca Allen, 123
Tyler, Mary Hunt Palmer, 225n2

Uterus: agency of, 9, 16–18, 32, 35–38, 51; medical descriptions of, 22–23, 32–38, 41, 44, 46, 49; medical illustrations of, 24–31; operations on, 42–43; physicians fear of, 36–38

Van Rymsdyk, Jan, 29
Vesalius, Andreas, 25–26, 28; *De humani corporis fabrica*, 25
*Views of Slavery* (broadside), 194, 197–198
Voluntary motherhood, 206

Walker, Mary Richardson, 76–77, 118, 121, 143
Wallace, Willie, 132
Warren, Penelope Skinner, 55, 70

Warrington, Joseph, 48; *Obstetric Catechism*, 48
Watkins, Mary, 95, 97
Wet nurses: in advertisements, 128–129; enslaved, 116, 130, 133–135, 143, 226n30, 232n52; informal, 129–130, 134–136, 232n52; in prescriptive literature, 87, 93–94, 128, 135–138, 144; rates of use, 129–130, 226n30; visual depictions of, 138–139; women's attitudes toward, 10, 115–116, 120, 135–136, 138–144, 204
White, Charles, 24, 34, 40, 47
Whitman, Narcissa Prentiss, 117
Williams, Jane, 81
Womb. *See* Uterus
Womble, George, 62

*Zion's Herald*, 180

CPSIA information can be obtained
at www.ICGtesting.com
Printed in the USA
LVOW12s0832060418
572529LV00005B/244/P